HEGEL AND THE FOUNDATIONS OF LITERARY THEORY

Do the various forms of literary theory – deconstruction, Marxism, new historicism, feminism, postcolonialism, and cultural/digital studies – have anything in common? If so, what are the fundamental principles of theory? What is its ideological orientation? Can it still be of use to us in understanding basic intellectual and ethical dilemmas of our time? These questions continue to perplex both students and teachers of literary theory. Habib finds the answers in theory's largely unacknowledged roots in the thought of German philosopher Hegel. Hegel's insights continue to frame the very terms of theory to this day. Habib explains Hegel's complex ideas and how they have percolated through the intellectual history of the last century. This book will interest teachers and students of literature, literary theory and the history of ideas, illuminating how our modern world came into being, and how we can better understand the salient issues of our own time.

M.A.R. HABIB is Professor of English at Rutgers University, and is currently Visiting Professor at the Gulf University for Science and Technology in Kuwait. He is the author of nine books, including *The Early T. S. Eliot and Western Philosophy* (1999), and the editor of *The Cambridge History of Literary Criticism: Vol. VI: The Nineteenth Century* (2013), both published by Cambridge University Press.

T0364309

HEGEL AND THE FOUNDATIONS OF LITERARY THEORY

M. A. R. HABIB

CAMBRIDGE
UNIVERSITY PRESS

Shaftesbury Road, Cambridge CB2 8EA, United Kingdom

One Liberty Plaza, 20th Floor, New York, NY 10006, USA

477 Williamstown Road, Port Melbourne, VIC 3207, Australia

314–321, 3rd Floor, Plot 3, Splendor Forum, Jasola District Centre, New Delhi – 110025, India

103 Penang Road, #05–06/07, Visioncrest Commercial, Singapore 238467

Cambridge University Press is part of Cambridge University Press & Assessment, a department of the University of Cambridge.

We share the University's mission to contribute to society through the pursuit of education, learning and research at the highest international levels of excellence.

www.cambridge.org
Information on this title: www.cambridge.org/9781108457859

DOI: 10.1017/9781108602952

First published 2019
First paperback edition 2022

A catalogue record for this publication is available from the British Library

ISBN   978-1-108-47138-1   Hardback
ISBN   978-1-108-45785-9   Paperback

This book is gratefully dedicated to:
Angela Miller
Advait Ubhayakar
Jessica White
Jim McGauley
Alyson Howe

Contents

vii

Preface

Is literary theory dead? Has it really given way to a resurgence of more conventional modes of reading texts? Do the various forms of theory – including deconstruction, Marxism, new historicism, feminism, postcolonialism, and cultural/digital studies – have anything in common? If so, what are the fundamental principles of theory? What are its ideological orientations? Can it still be of use to us in understanding basic intellectual and ethical dilemmas of our time? These questions continue to perplex both students and teachers of literary theory.

The proposed book aims to answer these questions with reference to theory's largely unacknowledged background in Hegel. Many of the often-cited accomplishments of theory were prefigured by Hegel. It was Hegel who first offered a comprehensive critique of the notions of identity and essence; it was Hegel who showed that both subjectivity and objectivity are constructions; that we achieve humanity only through mutual recognition; and it was Hegel who pioneered the insights that the linguistic sign is "arbitrary," and that "reason" is historical and social in its very nature.

Hegel's insights continue to frame the very terms of theory, including posthumanism in all its inflections, as well as media/digital studies. This pervasive impact of Hegel has generally gone unrecognized, though as Jean Michel Rabaté points out, "a grounding in the patient reading of Hegel ... is ... an essential step on the way to an understanding of Theory."[1] There are indeed several specialized studies that astutely analyze the influence of Hegel, whether direct or indirect, positive or negative, on specific fields and thinkers. For example, there are studies that relate Hegel to Marx, feminist philosophy, Deleuze, and language (which are

---

[1] Jean Michel Rabaté, *The Future of Theory* (Oxford: Blackwell, 2002), pp. 21–3. This book contains an excellent concise overview of some of the ways in which Hegel's insights pervade theory, pp. 21–45.

referenced in this book). But most of these, though excellent, are very technical and are written for specialists. What is urgently needed, I believe, is an accessible overview of Hegel's relation to the foundations or fundamental principles and assumptions of literary theory as a whole. Hence the proposed book is the first comprehensive study of its kind.[2]

Understanding what modern literary theory owes to Hegel will help us – especially in what is now being dubbed a "post-theoretical" age – to situate the achievements and limitations of theory in a more accurate historical context. It will also help us to assess more comprehensively the connections of literary theory to the past, to the traditions of Western thought, and hence to see more clearly what future intellectual possibilities lie open to the various fields that comprise theory.

This book makes no pretense to contribute to Hegel scholarship. It does, however, strive to make Hegel speak accessible English, to make his basic modes of thought intelligible to a relatively wide readership, to show that his thinking underlies our world on many levels. Hegel helps us understand how our identities are often created for us; how we inhabit the terrifyingly ubiquitous economic and ideological edifice of capitalism; how we engage with the worlds of religion, art, and politics; how we negotiate the frameworks of gender; how we confront the persisting legacies of colonialism and regionalism; and the ways in which we contribute or are unable to contribute to the shaping of our world and of language. Another task of this book is to show – without burying it under a mass of jargon – how literary theory is profoundly relevant to all these issues. What Hegel has to say and what theory has to say are simply too important to be imprisoned within any kind of linguistic or technical obscurity. They concern most of the important dimensions of our world.

As such, this book is intended not only for teachers and students of literature and literary theory but also for more general readers interested in the history of ideas, in how our modern world came into being, and how we can better understand the salient issues of our own time. I aim to furnish a clear, detailed, accurate, and readable exposition of both the basic principles of literary theory and of Hegel's difficult ideas on many subjects – logic, the history of philosophy, language, gender, and the political state – for an audience which is presumed to be interested in, but

---

[2] I should also mention Andrew Cole's recent book, *The Birth of Theory* (Chicago: University of Chicago Press, 2014). This work deals with Hegel's relation to theory and has caused much controversy, but does not overlap with the present work, which is somewhat broader in its scope. I have written two detailed reviews of this book, both published in well-known philosophical journals.

unfamiliar with, those ideas. While there is a coherent argument running through the book, each chapter should be fairly self-sufficient, enabling students to explore subjects or themes of particular concern to them. I hope that this book is clearly enough written to serve as an introduction not only to Hegel but also to the various branches of literary theory, its basic principles, and its foundations.

In writing this book, I have consulted with some of the foremost scholars of Hegel and Marx, including Frederick Beiser, Jere Surber, Terrell Carver, Allen Wood, Thomas Kemple, John O'Neill, and Michael Baur. I have also sought help from the German historian Andrew Lees and the German language specialist Lori Lantz, as well as the sociologists Thomas Kemple and Keith Hall, and the African historian Teshale Tibebu. I received much insightful assistance from a number of eminent literary theorists, including Terry Eagleton, Fredric Jameson, and from Stuart Barnett who edited a splendid series of essays on Hegel and Derrida. Zhao Ng and Alicia Broggi of Oxford University gave me valuable feedback for the sections on Antigone. I also owe much to Chris Fitter, Joe Barbarese, the late Frank Kermode, and my dear departed friend, Michael Payne. Any errors or oversights are of course entirely my responsibility.

I should like to thank, finally, a group of my graduate and undergraduate students who gave me persistent and insightful feedback over a period of two years to ensure that what I said was clear and intelligible. I will always be grateful for their help, and I dedicate this book to them: Angela Miller, Jessica White, Jim McGauley, Advait Ubhayakar, and Alyson Howe.

Introduction

Hegel in Our World

In a recent best-seller entitled *The Grand Design*, the authors Stephen Hawking and Leonard Mlodinow confidently proclaim on the first page that philosophy is "dead." Why? They say it has not kept up with the latest scientific developments. In the next few pages, they offer what they take to be a number of "radical" ideas: that the universe does not have "an independent existence," that knowledge of the world is not just derived from "direct observation" through our senses, that we can construct various "models" of reality, that there is no single theory but only a collection of overlapping theories that can explain "everything," and that our presence "selects" which universes are compatible with our existence.[1]

Ironically, every single one of these "radical" ideas is over 200 years old and was expressed in the work of various philosophers, most notably in that of Hegel. What prevents us from seeing this – and what tempts us into viewing old ideas as "radical" – is a tendency to remain unfamiliar with his thought, or to view it as defunct and superseded. Perhaps we have fallen too complacently into the habit of affirming that certain kinds of thinking or certain figures are "dead." Over a decade ago, both conservatives and liberals were confidently proclaiming that Marx was dead, though many phenomena in recent history – such as the global spread of capitalism and the widening gap between the world's rich and poor – have belied this claim. And over a century ago, thinkers were proudly proclaiming that "God is dead" – a statement usually attributed to Nietzsche but which can be traced to Hegel's *Phenomenology*. Indeed, it has long been fashionable in our postmodern and poststructuralist world to view Hegel as dead. But, in our century, it has become clearer than ever that each of these "deaths" – of Hegel, Marx, and God – is

---

[1] Stephen Hawking and Leonard Mlodinow, *The Grand Design* (New York: Bantam, 2012), pp. 5–9.

fraught with problems. If, as Sylvia Plath said, dying is an art, then these three have done it exceptionally well. Their ghosts, if you will, continue to speak and to shape both our thought and our world. This book will be concerned primarily not with Marx, but with the thinker who made him possible; not with God, but with the thinker who first proclaimed both his death and his reincarnated possibility: Hegel.

Our world is deeply pervaded by Hegelian thinking, but most people – having avoided Hegel's works – are simply unaware of what we owe to him. When we say, for example, that we need to look at the whole picture, or that we can't divorce something from its context, or that everything is related, or when we talk of the movement of history, or say that science moves through higher stages, or that religion and philosophy take different paths toward the same truths, or that our identity is shaped by our world and vice versa, or that we create ourselves through our work, or that our rights and our very subjectivity are born in mutual recognition, or that reality lies deeper than appearances, or that the concept of God is somehow a projection of human subjectivity, or even when we make ethnocentric pronouncements about the superiority of our culture – in all these cases we are somehow repeating and reaffirming Hegelian insights.

A number of literary theorists have expressed this unacknowledged influence very well. The American critic Paul de Man states, "Whether we know it, or like it, or not, most of us are Hegelians ... Few thinkers have so many disciples who never read a word of their master's writings."[2] Stuart Barnett also talks of an "invisible yet rampant Hegelianism."[3] Jacques Derrida called Hegel the "last philosopher of the book and the first philosopher of writing." For Derrida, logocentrism, the reliance of language and thought upon reference to a stabilizing transcendent reality, begins with the Bible and reaches its climax in Hegel. Derrida's statement implies that the structure of Hegel's dialectic is the enabling condition of its own supersession. It is a dialectic that can lead to Sartre or collapse into Nietzsche. From a Marxist viewpoint, Hegel is among other things the philosopher of the French Revolution, his system being the supreme articulation of bourgeois political ascendancy in Europe.

The difficulty of escaping Hegel's influence has been aptly registered by Michel Foucault's comment that "our age, whether through logic or

---

epistemology, whether through Marx or through Nietzsche, is attempting to flee Hegel ... But truly to escape Hegel involves an exact appreciation of the price we have to pay to detach ourselves from him ... We have to determine the extent to which our anti-Hegelianism is possibly one of his tricks directed against us, at the end of which he stands, motionless, waiting for us."[4] And, according to Alexandre Kojève (who himself exerted a profound influence on Hegel's reception by literary theorists in France), "Hegel's discourse exhausts *all* the *possibilities* of thought. One cannot bring up any discourse in opposition to him which would not already be a part of his own discourse."[5] In a similar vein, William Desmond states that "Hegel strangely is both a Hegelian and a post-Hegelian philosopher," viewed as both panlogist and irrationalist, religious and atheist, foundationalist and deconstructionist, a thinker of identity and also of difference.[6] In short, whatever our own niche in the humanities, we continue to mirror Hegel's blinding centrality to our world. We are compelled to acknowledge the historical summarizing power of Hegel as well as the seemingly limitless shadow cast by his thought over our own endeavors.

Hegel's Significance in Modern Thought

Why is it that Hegel occupies such a central position in modern Western thought? Why do his ideas continue to exert such a profound influence across a broad array of disciplines? Why do some people swear by him while many others swear *at* him?[7] To answer these questions, we need to understand the historical context in which Hegel's thinking was forged. Conceived in the wake of the French Revolution of 1789, Hegel's vast philosophical system represents the most articulate expression of a bourgeois worldview. In the early nineteenth century the bourgeoisie was a revolutionary class, attempting to wrest political power from the feudal aristocracy. Its success transformed the entire structure of European (and American) society, laying the political, economic, and cultural groundwork of the entire modern Western world. The old

---

[4] Michel Foucault, *The Archaeology of Knowledge and the Discourse on Language*, trans. A. M. Sheridan Smith (New York: Pantheon, 1972), p. 235.

[5] Alexandre Kojève, *Introduction to the Reading of Hegel: Lectures on the Phenomenology of Spirit*, trans. James H. Nichols, Jr. (New York: Cornell University Press, 1980), p. 194.

[6] William Desmond, "Introd.," *Hegel and his Critics: Philosophy in the Aftermath of Hegel*, ed. William Desmond (New York: State University of New York Press, 1989), pp. viii–x.

[7] Hegel's philosophy has been called a "totalitarianism of reason," Ernst Behler, "Introduction," in G. W. F. Hegel, *Encyclopedia of the Philosophical Sciences in Outline and Critical Writings* (New York: Continuum, 1990), p. xi. Karl Popper also sees Hegel as the prelude to modern totalitarianism.

Christian-feudal state, a hierarchy based on divine authority, monarchy, and a hereditary aristocracy, was sustained by an ethic of obedience, loyalty, and honor. Bourgeois hegemony displaced this feudal structure with its own political framework and values. The new political ideals were democracy, equality, individualism (as expressed primarily in property rights), freedom of trade and of profit-making (which had been severely restricted under feudalism).

Hegel brings together the two broad movements that express this transition from a feudal world to a bourgeois society. The first is the Enlightenment, whose main streams were materialism, rationalism, and empiricism, all of which found institutionalized expression in the growth of science, technology, and industry. The other movement, Romanticism, reacted against the divisive, atomistic, and disintegrative tendencies of Enlightenment reason. Romanticism aimed to see the world as a totality and to restore a vision of unity between the individual and nature, individual and society, individual and God. In synthesizing these two tendencies, Hegel made considerable use of Kant's philosophy, which itself proved an agent of historical mediation between Enlightenment thought and the growth of movements such as Romanticism in the nineteenth century. Hence Hegel's system encapsulates the entire movement of modern Western philosophy, from the Enlightenment through Romanticism, stressing the supreme value of reason as well as the need for a totalizing vision of the world and human history.

In turn, Hegel's system exerted a profound and seminal influence on many major streams of subsequent Western thought. These include the Anglo-American idealism of the later nineteenth century, Marxism, and historicism, as well as the thought of many twentieth-century theorists ranging from feminists such as Simone de Beauvoir and Julia Kristeva to so-called poststructuralist thinkers such as Jacques Lacan and Jacques Derrida. Moreover, many systems of thought arose in direct reaction against Hegel. These included major figures in the existentialist tradition such as Kierkegaard and Sartre; the tradition of heterological thinkers from Schopenhauer through Nietzsche to Bataille; the sociological positivism of Comte, Durkheim, and Herbert Spencer; the realism advanced in the earlier works of Bertrand Russell and G. E. Moore; and the analytic philosophies and various brands of empiricism and logical positivism which survived through the twentieth century.

In their diverse ways, many of these modes of thought – including many branches of literary theory – rejected the notions of totality, of historical progress, the idea that things in the world were somehow essentially related, and the notion of reason itself. As noted earlier, a widespread reaction against Hegel's thought came in the form of positivism, a generally conservative philosophy which held that the world as it is given, the world that is immediately presented to us – by our own senses, by tradition, by the past, by the history of feudalism – is the only reality we can know. As Theodore Adorno characterized it, Hegel's philosophy was a "philosophy of the negative," which attempted to challenge the world as merely given and to refashion both the world and human subjectivity in the (then) revolutionary light of bourgeois rationality. While many literary theories have embraced this "negative" potential, they have sharply criticized the notion of rationality as well as Hegel's Eurocentrism and masculinism. But, as will be argued in this book, their central critical instrument is derived from Hegel himself – the dialectic as arrested in its second or "negative" phase. We can see, then, that most modern European systems of thought arose as modifications of, or reactions against, Hegel's dialectic. Hegel has enabled our worlds of thought on many levels, even those that are vehemently opposed to him.

Hegel and Liberal Humanism

In order to grasp Hegel's impact on literary theory, we need to situate this impact within the broader context of liberal humanism. Hegel is *the* philosopher of liberal humanism. This has been recognized by scholars of Hegel such as J. N. Findlay, as well as by Marxist commentators such as Lukács.[8] Ripalda sees Hegel's entire life as a "struggle to reach an understanding of capital."[9] Instructively, Teshale Tibebu, whose primary concern is with Hegel's connections to race and imperialism, sees Hegel's social philosophy as a "reflection of the capitalist world system."[10] And Adorno sees Hegel as a thinker who ascertained the "limits of bourgeois society" but who, as a "bourgeois idealist," was unable to resolve the contradictions of that society (TS, 80).[11] In his massively intricate study *The Young Hegel*, Georg Lukács states that Hegel aims "to grasp the true inner

---

[8] J. N. Findlay explicitly refers to Hegel as "The Philosopher of ... Liberal Humanism" in his *Hegel: A Re-examination* (New York: Macmillan, 1965), p. 354.
[9] José María Ripalda, *The Divided Nation: The Roots of a Bourgeois Thinker, G.W.F. Hegel* (Netherlands: Van Gorcum, 1977), p. 163.
[10] Teshale Tibebu, *Hegel and the Third World: The Making of Eurocentrism in World History* (New York: Syracuse University Press, 2011), p. 326. Hereafter cited as HTW.
[11] Theodor W. Adorno, *Hegel: Three Studies*, trans. S.W. Nicholson (Cambridge, MA and London: MIT Press, 1993), p. 80. Hereafter cited as *TS*.

structure, the real motive forces of the present and of capitalism and to define the dialectic of its movement ... His preoccupation with this theme in fact determines the structure of his system and the particular character of the dialectic as well as the greatness of his achievement."[12] Hegel, as we shall see in the next chapters, is the philosopher *par excellence* who expressed the contradictions of capitalist society. Marx acknowledged as much when he stated that Hegel's standpoint was that of "modern political economy."

Having said all this, we do perhaps need to ask: What is liberal humanism? Generally, liberal humanism might be described as the spectrum of philosophical and political orientations that emerge from, express, shape, and justify the capitalist economic system. What is the core of these orientations, of the liberal humanist worldview? The commonly held perception is that liberal humanism embraces a fixed and static view of identity, of the human subject, that it believes in an objective, independent world, and that language is an instrument that represents this independent reality.[13] This is what I have called the "myth" of liberal humanism.[14] This myth has a foundational importance for much literary theory, which has to a certain extent come to rely on this "straw person," attacking the notions of fixed identity, etc. However, it's simply not true that these notions are principles of bourgeois thought. Rather, they are Medieval notions that go back to Plato and Aristotle, and they were challenged even in Plato's later dialogues, in the Neoplatonic tradition, and in the writings of Aquinas.

The bourgeois thinkers of the Enlightenment were radical precisely because they *challenged* these notions. They undermined, for example, the idea of a stable human self or ego. Locke regarded the self as a *tabula*

---

[12] Georg Lukács, *The Young Hegel: Studies in the Relations between Dialectics and Economics*, trans. Rodney Livingstone (London: Merlin Press, 1975), p. xxvii. Hereafter cited as YH.

[13] In his discussion of liberal humanism, Peter Barry rehearses some of these characterizations in a book which otherwise, I think, is an excellent introduction to theory for undergraduate students. Peter Barry, *Beginning Theory: An Introduction to Literary and Cultural Theory* (1995; rpt. Manchester and New York: Manchester University Press, 2002), pp. 13–21. Barry states that liberal humanism became current in the 1970s, embodying "the kind of criticism which held sway before theory" (p. 3). He tends to over-identify liberal humanism with New Criticism and its focus on the "words on the page." But, of course, liberal humanism was far broader, and it would be more feasible to think of the New Criticism as merely one of its expressions. Barry does, however, valuably point to one significant feature of "literary" liberal humanism, viz., its characteristic refusal to articulate its positions, as with F. R. Leavis's refusal to spell out his critical principles (p. 16). One might also cite Arnold and his refusal to define great literature except by ostensive definition, by pointing to examples or "touchstones."

[14] See M. A. R. Habib *Modern Literary Theory and Criticism: A History* (Oxford: Blackwell, 2008), pp. 225–32.

rasa or blank slate, which acquires character only as experience writes upon it. Hume saw the self as a convention. Kant viewed it as a necessary presupposition for the coherence of our experience. Hegel conceived it as a product of historical forces and reciprocal interaction with other selves. The only stable subject in bourgeois thought is that presupposed by bourgeois economics, as an abstract unit of economic value, competition, production, and consumption. All these philosophers strongly impugn the Aristotelian notion of "substance" as the underlying reality of identity and the world (Kant even makes substance one of the subjective categories *through* which we view the world); they challenge the notion of essence, which Locke effectively relocates from reality to language. In fact, long before Saussure, Locke recognized the arbitrariness of the sign.[15] Equally, the major philosophers of the bourgeois Enlightenment wished to reject any transcendent basis for political sovereignty, morality, or for their formulations of identity, subjectivity, and the external world. They even rejected the notion of "reality" as grounded in any extra-human basis: they saw it as a projection of the human mind, of human categories of understanding, and of human language.[16]

We can certainly say that liberal humanism was a product of the mainstream philosophies of the bourgeois Enlightenment, such as rationalism, empiricism, and utilitarianism. The economic principles of bourgeois ideology, such as rationality, *laissez-faire* economics and free competition, were formulated by the classical economists Adam Smith, Jean-Baptiste Say, and David Ricardo. The political principles of democracy, individual rights, and constitutional government were expressed by figures such as Rousseau, John Locke, and Thomas Paine. The imperial ideology and mission not only to conquer other parts of the world for their economic resources but to submit them also to the civilizing effects of

---

[15] Indeed, in his groundbreaking study of Locke, William Walker presents this philosopher as much more complex than conventional accounts suggest, as a "proto-Nietzschean" thinker who enlists various forms of figural representation when dealing with the mind and its ideas, as well as in his treatment of history and the political state. In *Locke, Literary Criticism, and Philosophy* (Cambridge and New York: Cambridge University Press, 1994), pp. 156–88.

[16] In their now classic study of liberal humanism, Wilson H. Coates and Hayden V. White saw the secular humanism of the Renaissance as articulating "a new theory of civilization," based on an integrated program of educational reform. Along with Protestant Christianity and modern science, this eventually impelled the aim of modern liberal humanism as a "liberation from all transcendentalists aspiration." Hence Western intellectual history since the early modern period was viewed as the rise of liberal humanism which, impelled in particular by science and the Enlightenment, has sought religious, political, and economic freedom. In *The Emergence of Liberal Humanism: An Intellectual History of Western Europe: Volume I* (London and New York: McGraw-Hill, 1966), pp. 4–5.

Western literature and culture were expressed by figures such as Thomas Babington Macaulay, and many politicians, philosophers and scientists. All of these tendencies, as refracted partly through the philosophy of Kant, achieve a kind of synthesis in the philosophy of Hegel, the supreme expression of bourgeois thought, built on the philosophical principles of the Protestant Reformation and the French Revolution, uniting the divergent modes of Enlightenment thought such as rationalism and empiricism, and combining these with a Romantic emphasis on totality and the unity of subject and object, all integrated into a Eurocentric notion of historical progress.

However, the foregoing tendencies – toward rationalism, empiricism, scientism (an inordinate aspiration to scientific status) – yield an incomplete picture. For, when we turn to what has been viewed as liberal humanism in the registers of literature and literary criticism, we find another, almost *opposed*, set of values, as enshrined saliently in the work of Matthew Arnold, Irving Babbitt, and F. R. Leavis.[17] Most generally, we find an anti-theoretical and even anti-rationalist impulse, sometimes grounded on a mystical or theological basis. We find an insistence on a loosely empirical method, on "practical" criticism, which shies away from broad conceptual or historical schemes.[18] We often find a belief in "human nature" as something stable and permanent, as well as a belief in universal and timeless truth. We find a commitment to the past or to "tradition." This commitment often embodies a desire to return – as with Edmund Burke and other opponents of bourgeois reform – to an alleged pre-bourgeois harmony and stability, resting on permanent values. And we find an insistence on the moral and civilizing nature of literature, viewed as a broad education in sensibility and (a redefined) citizenship. "Literary" liberal humanism might be viewed as an afterthought of liberal bourgeois humanism, a concerted attempt of bourgeois humanism to correct itself, to counteract or at least to temper its own most mechanizing and spiritually debilitating tendencies and excesses.

Hence, what we call liberal humanism has included *both* formalism and historicism, both scientism and moralism, both rationalism and

---

[17] See also Terry Eagleton's comment that "The impotence of liberal humanism is a symptom of its essentially contradictory relationship to modern capitalism. For although it forms part of the 'official' ideology of such society, and the 'humanities' exist to reproduce it, the social order within which it exists has in one sense very little time for it at all." In *Literary Theory: An Introduction* (1983; rpt. London and Minneapolis: Blackwell/University of Minnesota Press, 1996), p. 174.

[18] For a fascinating discussion of these issues, see John Schad's "Epilogue" in *life. after. theory*, eds. Michael Payne and John Schad (London: Continuum, 2003), pp. 168–89.

empiricism, both objectivism and subjectivism. Again, the commonly held view of liberal humanism – as harboring fixed notions of identity, the human subject, an independent external world, and as affirming that language represents reality – is a myth. This myth of liberal humanism sets up a straw person, applicable, if at all, only to its reactive literary variant. It is important to realize, however, that the liberal humanist desire in literary and artistic spheres to reverse or react against or harmonize the foregoing "philistine" tendencies of bourgeois thought is not something haphazard but a process so consistent and continuous that it emerges as a structural phenomenon, this internal contradiction – between bourgeois thought and the humanistic modes of its subversion – being embodied in the Hegelian dialectic.

Indeed, two important features of liberal humanism are worth noting: first, that it has always been changing.[19] In fact, it could be argued that its very essence is change: not that of total transformation but of self-enlargement and sublation or continual expansion to include and assimilate what is currently external to it. The second feature is its capacity to contain contradictions; as Walt Whitman might say, it is large and contains multitudes. For example, the liberal humanism of each of the Enlightenment philosophers is different from that of the others as well as from that of Matthew Arnold or Irving Babbitt. In this sense, the very essence of liberal-humanist thought is nonidentity or an essential fluidity of identity, identity as a process, or even a refusal of identity. Hegel recognized that bourgeois ideals embrace many seemingly contradictory movements, and his thought both expresses these contradictions and situates or annuls or sublates them within a larger ethical scheme.

---

[19] Catherine Belsey usefully defines liberal humanism as "the ruling assumptions, values and meanings of the modern epoch. Liberal humanism, laying claim to be both natural and universal, was produced in the interests of the bourgeois class which came to power in the second half of the seventeenth century." She acknowledges that liberal humanism "is not an unchanging, homogeneous, unified essence," and that it has been sustained by "often contradictory ... discourses and institutions." She states that the common feature of liberal humanism is a commitment to the "unified subject" as "the free, unconstrained author of meaning and action, the origin of history." But this reading of the past as "the triumphant march of progress," she says, is now being challenged as it emerges more clearly that the liberal-humanist subject was "constructed in conflict and contradiction – with conflicting and contradictory consequences." *The Subject of Tragedy: Identity and Difference in Renaissance Drama* (1985; rpt. London and New York: Routledge, 2014), pp. 7–9. On the other hand, Richard Freadman and Seumas Miller shrewdly observe that much theory has a reductive conception of humanism as the "distinctive intellectual mode of capitalism," grounded on two features, an atomistic view of the self and a commitment to evaluative discourse on both moral and aesthetic planes. In *Re-Thinking Theory: A Critique of Contemporary Literary Theory and an Alternative Account* (Cambridge and New York: Cambridge University Press, 1992), pp. 1–9.

Hence, the commonly cited accomplishments of much literary theory – the critique of essentialism, the discrediting of correspondence theories of truth and meaning, the deconstruction of identity, the exhibition of the social and historical nature of subjectivity and objectivity, the emphasis on the constitutive role of language in that construction – had already been conducted *within* bourgeois thought, in the pages of Locke, Hume, Kant, and especially Hegel. They had also been conducted in the alternative or "heterological" streams of thought, from Schopenhauer through Kierkegaard, Nietzsche, Bergson, and Heidegger, which had explicitly challenged the principles of the bourgeois Enlightenment.[20] Again, there is a continuity and common ground between liberal bourgeois thought and the channels of its own subversion – one of which, significantly, has been the vastly rich tributary of literary theory.

Indeed, literary theory in nearly all its modes involves a "negative," rather Hegelian, endeavor to break down the Aristotelian notion of identity at various levels and in numerous contexts, ranging from gender and race through psychoanalytic notions to subjectivity, authorship, and textuality. The notion of identity is closely tied to the Aristotelian conception of substance or essence as the underlying reality of things. For example, we might want to question the idea that the term "man" or "woman" has an intrinsic identity. This questioning of identity opens up a number of other insights: First, the identity of the world as a series of objects is not separate from our own identity as subjects; we create the world just as it creates us. Second, subjectivity is inherently intersubjective; it can be created only in interaction with other subjects, just as objects themselves exist not in isolation but with a broad set of relations. Third, the identity of both subjects and objects, since it is necessarily

---

[20] The foregoing account is intended only as a sketch of the main tendencies of liberal humanism, which is a vast subject in itself, the details of whose manifold developments lie beyond the scope of this book. Needless to say, there are many political and sociological studies that document the various modulations and fragmentations of liberalism in particular circumstances. For example, in a British post-World War I context, liberalism was bifurcated into two streams, left and centrist, devoted in various degrees to individual liberty, private property, social justice, and welfare. Liberal theorists such as Leonard Hobhouse in his *The Metaphysical Theory of the State* (1918) and J. A. Hobson in his *Democracy After the War* (1917) attacked the neo-Hegelian idealists such as Bernard Bosanquet and, to a lesser extent, T.H. Green. In an atmosphere of anti-German sentiment, British liberals rejected the "false and wicked doctrine," deriving from Hegel, of the State as the neutral agent of a rational society. They stressed the rights – and independence – of the individual as against what they saw as the coercive power of the Hegelian State, which they saw as subsuming individual subjectivity and as identifying freedom with law. The general point here is that, in such a context, Hegel's influence was viewed as a pernicious threat to liberalism, not an expression of it. Michael Freeden, *Liberalism Divided: A Study in British Political Thought 1914–1939* (Oxford: Clarendon Press, 1986), pp. 4–37.

produced through social interaction, is also historical – it is a historically cumulative identity. Finally, if it is our collective subjectivity that creates the world we know, then language – the system of concepts that expresses our worldview – is instrumental in that creation. Where philosophers used to talk about the connection between thought and reality, we now view language as interposed within that connection. It is language that enables the construction of both thought and reality, of both our subjectivity and the objectivity of the world, language which mediates their relation. Derrida has beautifully expressed this in saying that our epoch must "determine as language the totality of its problematic horizon."[21] All of these insights are anticipated within the liberal humanist tradition, of which Hegel might be seen as the exemplar.[22]

Much literary theory, then, is internally structured by the heritage of liberal humanist philosophy, its pluralistic ability – as embodied in the Hegelian dialectic – to encompass several divergent perspectives under the umbrella of its own expansive and changing identity. It was Hegel who articulated the capacity of bourgeois thought to sublate (to both transcend and internalize, to both annul yet preserve at a higher level) opposition or variance from itself. His system inscribes and prefigures the internal structure of capitalism, its ability to absorb everything else – art, literature, religion, love, socialism, other cultures – into its own structures of economic value and significance, into its own expansive and ever-changing identity.

This movement is also the inner dialectic of imperialism; its drive not only to conquer but to assimilate and integrate the Other – a movement equally embodied in Hegel's dialectic. The Other is always necessary to capitalism, as something whose overcoming renews, reassures, reaffirms, redefines, and revitalizes its own sociopolitical identity and economic existence. Ultimately, the pivotal notions of literary theory – difference, otherness, the challenges to identity, the view of meaning and all objects as relational – are Hegelian insights and represent modifications *within* the parameters of bourgeois thought. Even the undermining of authorship is a refraction through a linguistic focus of the Hegelian notion that historical forces periodically achieve a point of concentration in, and act

[21] Jacques Derrida, *Of Grammatology*, trans. Gayatri Chakravorty Spivak (Baltimore and London: Johns Hopkins University Press, 1982), p. 6.
[22] In fact, James Seaton argues powerfully for the continuing existence and value of a humanistic tradition in literature, deriving from Aristotle, in his fascinating study *Literary Criticism from Plato to Postmodernism: The Humanistic Alternative* (Cambridge and New York: Cambridge University Press, 2014), pp. 73–109.

through, certain individuals. Marxism itself has sometimes been co-opted into these extensions, these self-subversions, these dialectically unresolved antitheses, of bourgeois humanism, with Marxist theory sometimes floating free of the historical conditions which have been traditionally necessary to its distinctive Marxist characteristic.

Before outlining the argument of this book, I want to clarify that what I mean by "literary theory" is simply the common understanding of this term that has pervaded literary and cultural studies for the last fifty or so years. It refers to the broad range of discursive practices that include Marxist and feminist criticism, cultural studies, deconstruction, postcolonial criticism, psychoanalytic theory, and now global studies. Of course, in addressing "literature," literary theory (a) has broadened the definition of literature to include a wide range of contemporary textualities such as television, media, social media, and popular culture in general; and (b) has extended its own scope in order to address fundamental issues such as gender, ethics, the dynamics of capitalism and imperialism, and more generally, the nature of subjectivity, objectivity, and their relation[23] (I apologize for sounding like Andrew Ramsay when he characterizes his father's work).[24]

Structure and Argument of This Book

How many times have we heard the criticism that theory is "political," that it drags politics into the literature classroom? There is a reason for this, which furnishes part of the basic thesis of this book: *In general, literary theory is an implicit critique of capitalism.* To begin with, it impugns what it takes to be the foundational notions of bourgeois ideology such as identity, subject–object dualism, language as a representational system, the idea that relations between entities are external to those entities, and the atomistic conception of political and economic reality. All the fundamental notions of bourgeois economics – capital, labor, value, exchange, commodity, property, and money – presuppose a world that is viewed as composed of discrete, mutually distinct objects as well as of independent subjects whose identities can be assessed in terms of economic assets as regards possession or buying power. Indeed, a longstanding motivation

---

[23] Stein Haugrom Olsen sees the central characteristic of literary theory as its propensity to generalize and systematize, *The End of Literary Theory* (Cambridge and New York: Cambridge University Press, 1987), pp. 116–20.

[24] There is a well-known scene in Virginia Woolf's *To the Lighthouse* where the artist Lily Briscoe asks Andrew Ramsay what his father's books are about. His answer is a popular characterization of philosophy: "Subject and object and the nature of reality." *To the Lighthouse* (1927; rpt. London and Glasgow: Collins/Granada, 1985), p. 26.

of theory – stretching back to the German Romantics and through the Victorian liberal humanists such as Arnold – has been to resist the reduction of the "human" to its exclusively economic characterization. Equally, theory challenges the binary thinking and scientism that sustains bourgeois thought, as for example the dualisms of mind and body, or woman and man. Theory rejects the classificatory thinking that separates the various disciplines and modes of inquiry, which has insisted, for example, on the autonomy of literature.

Bourgeois ideology fully emerged into the literary-critical domain with the New Criticism of the early twentieth century, which insisted on isolating literature from every other area of life. This is hardly to say that the New Critics themselves were bourgeois ideologues. Rather, whatever their professed religious and ideological allegiances, they were invoking positivist bourgeois philosophical presuppositions in the very *form* of their inquiry, in demarcating the object of their investigations as independent and in viewing their methodology as aspiring to scientific status in its autonomy – just as Durkheim and Herbert Spencer had done for their respective fields. As Marcuse has shown, this sociological positivism arose initially as a reaction against Hegel's "negative" philosophy, which rejected the world as given.

Nearly every mode of "literary" theory can be seen as a reaction against such scientism and positivism, and as a return to Hegelian negativity. In general, theory has sought to reestablish literature's connections with larger questions such as the construction of gender, the nature of power, the consequences of class, the exploration of psychology, the impact of race and ethnicity, the operations of ideology, the legacies of imperialism, and the functions of language. In so broadening its inquiries, theory has effectively engaged in a critique of the various components of the workings of capitalism, as well as its political, psychological, intellectual, and aesthetic ramifications. Theory, by its very nature, has been political. It has reinstated, in its own variety of ways, a Hegelian orientation toward negating – rejecting, superseding, and reconfiguring – the world as it is given, the world as broken into irreducibly individual elements. It has insisted on the relational character of these elements while rejecting any notion of totality.

The foregoing paragraphs describe the central argument of this book, which can be broken down as follows: (a) inasmuch as it is founded on the principles enumerated earlier – concerning the nature of identity, subjectivity, objectivity, and language – literary theory, in its various modes, is rehearsing insights that were articulated by Hegel; (b) many literary theories react against Hegel's notions of totality and progress as well as his Eurocentrism. But their central instrument is taken from Hegel himself – the dialectic as arrested in its second stage, the stage of "difference," refusing to admit progression from this to a third stage, which might effect any kind of metaphysical closure; (c) hence much literary theory retracts Hegelian content into the status of *form*, of method; what in Hegel is a necessary union of form and content is viewed in modern theory as mere form, method, strategy. Absolute Spirit becomes a metaphor for collective, historical, cumulative subjectivity; and subjectivity itself becomes a metaphor for a certain situatedness within language; and (d) the main lines of intersection of modern theory with Hegel – and perhaps the most fruitful way in which we might approach Hegel's influence – lies in the fact that Hegel's dialectic in its very structure expresses the alienations and internal contradictions of capitalism as an economic formation and of liberal humanism as its ideological expression.[25]

Hence, much modern literary theory – permeated everywhere by Hegelian thinking – is in many ways a continuation of, not a subversion of, liberal humanism, merely deepening bourgeois ideology's retreat into irreducible particularism. How can we advance beyond this freezing of the dialectic, this abrogation of the universal, beyond recalcitrant regionalism? How can we overcome the divisions and dualisms that Hegel perceived in modern bourgeois life: between self and world, self and other, between real and ideal, sense and intellect, idea and form, family and civil society, civil society and state, woman and man, ruler and ruled, colonizer and colonized, master and slave?

The foregoing represents the broad argument of this book and the questions motivating it. The book is divided into two broad sections. The first part aims to offer a clear exposition of Hegel's fundamental ideas. Chapter 1 attempts to furnish a lucid explanation of Hegel's dialectic, with an indication of its various contexts in Hegel's work, as well as some of its diverse foundations, ranging from Hegel's early comments on love and sex to Christian theology and skepticism. Chapter 2 sketches the broad historical context in which Hegel's ideas took shape, situating the Prussia of Hegel's time within larger European developments.

Chapter 3 attempts to show how Hegel's philosophy was structured by his engagement with emergent capitalism and his endeavor to reconcile

[25] Feuerbach in 1839 characterized Hegel's philosophy as a philosophy of "difference" which stresses the hierarchical differences between various systems of thought and peoples but not what they share. Ludwig Feuerbach, "Towards a Critique of Hegel's Philosophy," in *The Young Hegelians: An Anthology*, ed. Lawrence S. Stepelvich (Amherst: Humanity Books, 1999), pp. 95–6. Some theorists have attempted to distinguish their conception of difference from Hegel's, as we shall see in a later chapter.

the domains of family, civil society, and the state, within a broad histori-cal scheme. Hegel's reflections on bourgeois society yield the overarching context for the crucial themes that will be pursued in the course of this book: the structure of the dialectic, the nature of identity and differ-ence, subjectivity and the politics of recognition, as well as language, gender, and empire. These reflections, as expounded in the *Philosophy of Right,* represent the system into which Hegel's thought matured and his clearest contextualization of these pivotal themes. Chapter 4 offers an exposition of Hegel's highly influential views of identity and difference, which underlie the deconstruction of identity in much literary theory. Chapter 5 situates Hegel's views of identity within his attempt to inte-grate the insights of bourgeois political economy into a larger philosophi-cal vision of capitalism and the subjectivities it engenders.

The second part of the book looks at the ways in which various branches of literary theory have read the dialectic. In general, I argue that literary theorists have subjected Hegel's work to a broad range of what I call "creative misreadings," in an attempt to distinguish what is living from what is dead in Hegel, so as to bring the power of his thought to bear on important contemporary concerns.[26] Such a strategy, I would argue, characterizes Marx as much as anyone else. We might call this strategy "strategic Hegelianism." This part of the book is divided into three sections, the first of which concerns Hegel's metaphysics and his conceptions of language. Chapter 6 examines the connections between Hegel and deconstruction, showing in effect how deconstruction explic-itly situates itself at the second stage of the dialectic, and how its concep-tion of "difference" differs from that of Hegel.

Chapter 7 offers a detailed account of Hegel's views on language, drawing on his earlier and later works. This chapter demonstrates how the notions of language as a system of signs, of the sign as arbitrary, and of language as structuring the very process of thought – which are usu-ally attributed by literary theorists to Saussure – were in fact articulated much earlier by Hegel. Chapter 8 shows how Saussure's views of the sign and Barthes's views of semiology effectively reiterate Hegelian positions. It then analyzes in detail Derrida's commentary on Hegel's notions of language, while Chapter 9 examines Julia Kristeva's theory of language as

---

[26] George Armstrong Kelly suggests that contemporary interest in Hegel's philosophy is "due chiefly to the suggestive expansion of its insights rather than to any desire for systematic reconstruction," "Notes on Hegel's 'Lordship and Bondage'," in *Hegel's Dialectic of Desire and Recognition: Texts and Commentary,* ed. John O'Neill (New York: State University of New York Press, 1996), p. 253.

founded on Hegelian negativity. These two chapters show how Derrida's and Kristeva's views are integral to their respective outlooks in philosophy and psychoanalysis, and their self-situation in relation to capitalism.

The next section focuses on "The Politics of Recognition," so crucial to both Marxism and Gender Studies. Chapter 10 expounds Hegel's "master–slave dialectic" as formulated in the *Phenomenology*, showing how this dialectic is integral to Hegel's view of subjectivity as requiring reciprocal recognition, and discussing the importance of this view for later thinkers. The next chapter is devoted to readings of the master–slave dialectic in literary theory, examining the "allegorical" readings offered by Gilles Deleuze and Jacques Derrida. Chapter 13 analyzes Marx's detailed assessments of Hegel's dialectic in a number of texts, including the *Economic and Philosophic Manuscripts* (1844) and the *Grundrisse*. The two subsequent chapters examine the treatment of dialectic by other Marxist thinkers: Chapter 14 focuses on the dialectic of the culture industry as elaborated by Horkheimer and Adorno. The next chapter assesses Žižek's radical rereading of the dialectic as enabling "difference" and as engaging an "empty" subject in its expression of capitalist economics.

The final section moves to the consideration of Hegel and gender. Chapter 16 recounts Hegel's views of women in general, after which it examines his famous (or infamous) analysis of the ancient Greek drama *Antigone*. Chapter 17 assesses the responses to Hegel's critique of *Antigone* on the part of two major theorists of gender, Luce Irigaray and Judith Butler, as well as by Derrida, who reads that critique in terms of the master–slave dialectic. Chapter 18 concludes this entire section by offering an overview of feminism's various encounters with Hegel, an account of the historical context of Hegel's views on gender, and an attempt to address the question of his legacy for feminism.

The conclusion extends the overall argument of the book to address some of the more recent developments of theory, which have generally moved in the direction of posthumanism. It argues that Hegel enables us both to contextualize these recent currents and to overcome the impasses in which they are mired by pointing toward a conception of dialectical humanism which accords due place to the notions of reason and totality. Such a conception may help us understand and articulate some of the salient dilemmas of our own day. Each of the chapters will focus on certain prominent thinkers, so that instead of offering merely generalized overviews of the entire area in question, these chapters will provide close readings of selected texts to evince precisely the connections of each mode of thought to Hegel.

PART I

Hegel: The Historical and Philosophical Setting

CHAPTER I

The Hegelian Dialectic

Before we can address the crucial question of how Hegel's philosophy expresses fundamental characteristics of capitalism and liberal humanism, we need to understand some very basic features of his thought, namely its historicist and dialectical nature. We can say briefly that historicism in the metaphysical sense[1] is the belief that everything – people, institutions, events, cultures – are essentially determined by a given set of historical conditions, and that history has some purpose and direction through the operation of certain laws or motivating principles. Hegel himself saw history as evolving toward freedom, which he envisioned as a state where both human thinking (subjectivity) and human institutions (the objective world) had achieved rationality. When this harmony has been attained, people will freely obey laws because they recognize them to be rational. Hegel saw this movement toward freedom operating historically, from the Oriental World, where only one person – the Emperor – is free, to the Greek and Roman World, where some people are free, to the modern world where all are free.[2] Hegel viewed this historical movement as driven by Absolute spirit or God; Marx was later to replace this with class struggle as the moving force of history.

What this chapter will focus on is the second important feature of Hegel's thought, its dialectical character. It should be mentioned here that the usually cited triad of thesis, antithesis, and synthesis is not how

[1] Recently, there has been renewed debate about the meaning and various senses of historicism. Some define it in terms of a belief in the general laws and ends of history; but others see it simply as the belief that the human world is determined by its history, while rejecting all such laws and ends. Clearly, Hegel has a "metaphysical" view of history as conforming to purposes. For a superbly detailed account of historicism, see Frederick C. Beiser, *The German Historicist Tradition* (Oxford: Oxford University Press, 2011).

[2] *Hegel's Lectures on the History of Philosophy*, III, trans. E. S. Haldane and Frances H. Simson (London and New York: Routledge and Kegan Paul/Humanities Press, 1963), pp. 217–18, 295, 363–9, 427–8.

Hegel himself explains the dialectic.[3] According to Hegel, philosophical thought does not occur in a linear fashion, always moving on the same level. It does not simply apprehend an object in the world merely once and then move on to other objects. Rather, the dialectic is a progression through increasing levels of comprehensiveness, whereby we look at an object from a relatively narrow perspective and then broaden this vision, so that we effectively traverse through several views of a given object, each view "preserving" yet transcending the previous one through a strategy that Hegel calls "sublation," a strategy essential to the dialectical process. In this sense, our own exposition in this chapter will be dialectical since it will take us through increasingly broad perspectives as to what "dialectical" means.[4]

Hegel sees the dialectic as operating on three broad levels: logical, phenomenological (the forms taken by consciousness) and historical. We'll begin by trying to arrive at a fairly basic understanding of what is meant by "dialectic." We can then examine what Hegel himself says in his earlier and later works. We'll also indicate how a number of thinkers have

---

[3] Partly because of W. T. Stace's book *The Philosophy of Hegel* (1924), the reading of Hegel's dialectic in terms of this formula was widespread until 1958 when Gustav E. Mueller published his article "The Hegel Legend of 'Thesis-Antithesis-Synthesis'," *Journal of the History of Ideas*, 19.3 (1958), 411–14. Mueller called the triad of thesis-antithesis-synthesis the "most vexing and devastating Hegel legend" and attributed it not only to Stace but also to Marx. He notes that Hegel refers to this triad only twice, once in the *Phenomenology* as a "lifeless schema" and once in the student notes published as the *History of Philosophy* as a "spiritless scheme." He also observes that the new important Hegel literature of the twentieth century – by Theodor Haering, Hermann Glockner, and many others – has simply disregarded the legend, which he says is "a convenient method of embalming Hegel" (411–14). Likewise, some scholars such as Walter Kaufmann insist that Hegel spurns this formula, which was coined by Fichte, but he does acknowledge that Hegel has a "preference for triadic arrangements," Hegel: A Reinterpretation (1965; rpt. Notre Dame, IN: University of Notre Dame Press, 1978), pp. 154–5. But others, perhaps more circumspectly, have seen it as a vague, rather than false, characterization of Hegel's method. See, for example, Michael Forster, "Hegel's Dialectical Method," in *The Cambridge Companion to Hegel*, ed. Frederick C. Beiser (Cambridge and New York: Cambridge University Press, 1993), p. 131. Hereafter cited as *CCH*.

[4] In the *Science of Logic* Hegel remarks that sublation is "one of the most important notions in philosophy." He explains that *sublate* has a twofold meaning: "to preserve, to maintain, and equally … to cause to cease, to put an end to." So what is sublated has "lost its immediacy but is not on that account annihilated." Hegel finds it remarkable that a language has come to use the same word for two opposite meanings, and that it is "a delight to speculative thought to find in the language words which have in themselves a speculative meaning." We might add that our English word "sublate" derives from the past participle of the irregular Latin verb *tollo, tollere, sustuli, sublatum*. This also has the same dual meaning, but, in Hegel's eyes, "does not go so far." Hegel further explains that something is sublated "only insofar as it has entered into unity with its opposite … as something reflected, it may fittingly be called a *moment*." *Hegel's Science of Logic*, trans. A. V. Miller (London and New York: George Allen & Unwin/Humanities Press, 1976), pp. 106–7. Hereafter cited as *SL*.

interpreted the dialectic. By the end of this process, we should have a fairly clear idea of what dialectic means, or at least, of its range of meanings, which are not reducible to any fixed formula. Indeed, the Marxist thinker Adorno does not see the dialectic as falling under any single definition, but he suggests that "the central nerve of the dialectic as a method is determinate negation."[5]

The dialectic might be characterized as a way of *thinking* about things. But for Hegel, it is equally a movement of *reality itself*. Indeed, for Hegel, thinking must be dialectical in order to grasp reality in its true dialectical nature. But this does not mean that somehow there is an independent reality "out there" that is dialectical. As Alexandre Kojève influentially stated, thought is dialectical because being itself is dialectical. It is not pure being, but rather "Being revealed by Speech or Thought" that has a dialectical structure.[6] Jean Hyppolite, who also exerted a profound impact on literary theory, develops this line of thinking further. He suggests that being "speaks itself" in humankind, and that we "see in human language the very medium of the dialectic."[7] What is modern about Hegel is the idea that the dialectical nature of both thought and world can be ascertained only as reciprocal. In other words, by the time thought grasps reality as dialectical, it has also grasped it as, in its deepest core, an expression of its own movement. Thought finds at the foundation of reality its own operations. And it grasps its *own* character as dialectical, as not simply *given* but as having evolved through various stages of sophistication.[8]

---

[5] Theodor W. Adorno, *Hegel: Three Studies*, trans. S. W. Nicholson (Cambridge, MA and London: MIT Press, 1993), pp. 9, 80. Hereafter cited as *TS*. In his intricate study, Brady Bowman explains that dialectical thinking is driven by Hegel's notion of negativity, *Hegel and the Metaphysics of Absolute Negativity* (Cambridge and New York: Cambridge University Press, 2013), pp. 245–7.

[6] Kojève, *Introduction to the Reading of Hegel*, pp. 170–1.

[7] Jean Hyppolite, *Logic and Existence*, trans. Leonard Lawlor and Amit Sen (1953; rpt. Albany, NY: SUNY Press, 1997), pp. 6, 27.

[8] Other useful characterizations of the dialectic include Richard Norman's exposition of Hegel's dialectic as identifying conceptual and temporal dimensions. The conceptual dialectic breaks down oppositions, entails contradiction, a stress on flux whereby a complete sequence of concepts is progressively generated, and a stress of the systematic structure ordering concepts. The temporal dialectic comprehends the history of philosophy as a progressive elaboration of the complete philosophical system, and the history of social and political life as a progression through various stages of the conceptual dialectic, Richard Norman and Sean Sayers, *Hegel, Marx and Dialectic: A Debate* (Sussex and New Jersey: Harvester/Humanities Press, 1980), pp. 31–41. Charles Taylor also suggests that the "historical" and "ontological" aspects of the dialectic are required to explain each other, *Hegel and Modern Society* (Cambridge and New York: Cambridge University Press, 1979), pp. 58–9. Further characterizations by Frederick Beiser and others will be cited later.

1.1   The Death of the Object

As a mode of thought, dialectic exhibits a number of features. The foremost of these is *negation*, a refusal to take what is immediately given as real. This is related to the other features: we will view phenomena not as fixed entities but as moments in a *process*; and we will regard things not as independent but as integrally related. Both of these features mean that we need to view any given entity in its context, and that this context is intrinsic to its meaning and identity. Finally, we will see both human rationality and reality itself as having *degrees*; and we will see both as being intrinsically historical – in other words, there is no exercise of human reason nor is there any reality that somehow floats free of history.

At its simplest level, the dialectic might be characterized as moving through three stages. Initially an object is viewed in its given immediacy and particularity as self-identical. In the second stage the object's "identity" is viewed as externalized or dispersed through the totality of its social and historical relations (its "other," which might be defined in various ways): it is viewed in its universal aspect. In the third stage the object's identity is viewed as mediated (rather than immediately given) and as a combination of universal and particular. In this way, the object undergoes a kind of "death," a negation, as something merely given and particular and contingently related to its surroundings. Its true life resides in its universal and essential dimensions. This general movement could be comprehended on many levels, in various terms, and from diverse perspectives, depending on context. For example, it could be characterized as traversing the following movements:

	Universal (abstract)	>	Particular	>	Concrete universal
or	Unity	>	Diversity	>	Unity-in-diversity
or	Identity	>	Other	>	Identity-in-other
or	Immediate unity	>	Otherness	>	Mediated unity
or	Object	>	Subject	>	Subject-object unity

To illustrate this general process, we might initially think that a "bank" was something outside us, with an independent existence (an immediate identity or unity or independent object). But we then learn that what constitutes a bank are relations that extend beyond its immediate existence – into its connections with other banks, financial markets, currencies, law, and political developments. Finally, we understand the term "bank" to be an institution that reflects or integrates those relations. And we learn that in fact, not only the financial operations occurring in the bank but even its physical design and structure are products of a collective and historically accumulated human subjectivity. If the human race were to be wiped out tomorrow and if Martians were to arrive on our planet, they would not recognize the building: it has significance only in human terms, as a product of human thought and labor.

Here's another example of dialectical thinking. In a classroom, I don't merely perceive a piece of chalk and then a blackboard and then a row of desks. As stated earlier, dialectical thought perceives an object in increasingly broadened contexts. It may first confront the object as something that is apparently independent. Initially, the piece of chalk seems to exist on its own: I can hold it alone, and it is certainly not physically connected with anything else. This is my first engagement with the object, the first phase of dialectical thinking, which confronts the object in its given-ness and particularity. In the second phase, I see the object in two kinds of relations: (a) to the universal, in other words, to the essence of what constitutes "chalk" and how this particular piece of chalk belongs to a given class of objects; and (b) as related – in both its particularity and its universality – to everything around it, to everything that is *not* chalk: it is related to the blackboard, the eraser, the desks, and the chairs. In this phase, the "identity" of the chalk is seen as "externalized" into its relations with everything else.

In the third phase, I understand the principle underlying these connections and the essential relations underlying the identity of the chalk. For example, I may understand that the chalk, along with blackboard, chairs, and desks, are all the physical appurtenances of a specific system of education. Or, I may see a commercial principle underlying their connections and I may relate them in terms of the process or place of their manufacture and the modes of their marketing. Indeed, I may see these two registers – educational and economic – as themselves integrally related. The point is that what initially appeared to me as something self-subsistent now proves to be internally related to a large network of other entities, forces, or motivations, which have their ultimate grounding in (collective and historical) human subjectivity. Moreover, in using dialectical thinking, I am engaging in a progressive critique of my own modes of thought, and understanding with progressive intricacy how what we call "reality" is not simply somehow "there" but needs to be *understood* to merit such status.

1.2   Some Interpretations of Dialectic

It might be helpful to cite some characterizations of the dialectic by noted Hegelian scholars. Alexandre Kojève famously explained the dialectic in terms of a thesis which describes the real in its aspect of identity, taking something as given; an antithesis which describes the real in its aspect of negativity; and the synthesis that describes the being as a totality, as a result or product (*Werk*). He sees the fundamental categories of the dialectic as immediacy (*Unmittelbarkeit*) and mediation (*Vermittlung*). The immediate entity is a given static being, devoid of action and self-consciousness. The mediated entity is "action realized in a product, freedom, dialectical movement, and discursive understanding of itself and of its world" (Kojève, 207–8).

The Hegelian scholar Frederick C. Beiser usefully characterizes the three stages of the dialectic in Hegel's early logic as follows. We begin with a finite concept which presumes, like the absolute, to have an independent and self-sufficient meaning. In the second stage, such a claim comes into conflict with the fact that this concept actually depends for its meaning on another concept (which might stake an equal claim to independence). In the third stage, this contradiction is resolved by adopting a broader perspective, which comprehends the claims of both concepts. This process might be repeated through progressive dialectics "until we come to the complete *system* of all concepts, which is alone adequate to describe the absolute." Beiser reminds us of the important fact that Hegel's dialectic is not everywhere the same. In the *Phenomenology*, for example, this dialectic deals not with concepts but with the various standpoints of consciousness. Nevertheless, says Beiser, "the basic structure and purpose of the dialectic are the same." Most fundamentally, the dialectic was a response to the "problem of metaphysics" as laid down by Kant and his successors: how can we have conceptual knowledge of reality (or, in Hegel's terminology, the absolute)? (*CCH*, 18–19).

Similarly, Michael Forster suggests that the dialectic is "a method of exposition in which each category in turn is shown to be implicitly self-contradictory and to develop necessarily into the next (thus forming a continuously connected hierarchical series culminating in an all-embracing category that Hegel calls the Absolute Idea)" (*CCH*, 132). Like Beiser, Forster affirms the importance of this dialectic throughout all aspects of Hegel's philosophy, and he sees this method as designed to express the "underlying structure common to both our thought and the world of natural and spiritual phenomena," as well as serving important philosophical functions such as the teaching and justification of Hegel's system (*CCH*, 134–40).

1.3 The Dialectic in Literature

Those of us who are students of literature might be heartened to know that dialectical thinking in a broad sense isn't by any means confined to Hegel or even to the discipline of philosophy. Much great literature – being both original and critical – exhibits dialectical thinking. Shelley's "Ode to the West Wind" is a peculiarly fitting example. This famous poem is addressed to the powerful west wind which it characterizes as both "destroyer and preserver."

First, the poet shows the wind's effect upon the earth:

> O wild West Wind, thou breath of Autumn's being,
> Thou, from whose unseen presence the leaves dead
> Are driven, like ghosts from an enchanter fleeing,

and then upon the sky:

> Thou on whose stream, mid the steep sky's commotion,
> Loose clouds like earth's decaying leaves are shed,
> Shook from the tangled boughs of Heaven and Ocean,

and finally upon the seas:

> Thou who didst waken from his summer dreams
> The blue Mediterranean, where he lay,
> Lull'd by the coil of his crystalline streams,

Hence, the first three phases of the poem show the unifying effect of the wind on three dimensions of nature – the earth, the sky, and the sea – while the fourth stage identifies the poet with these three dimensions:

> If I were a dead leaf thou mightest bear;
> If I were a swift cloud to fly with thee;
> A wave to pant beneath thy power ...

This development leads to the climax, in the fifth phase, of the poet's complete identification with the wind:

> Make me thy lyre, even as the forest is:
> What if my leaves are falling like its own!
> The tumult of thy mighty harmonies
>
> Will take from both a deep, autumnal tone,
> Sweet though in sadness. Be thou, Spirit fierce,
> My spirit! Be thou me, impetuous one!

The first three sections together might be seen as comprising the first dialectical stage, whereby the elements of nature are confronted in their immediacy and also as potentially mediated by the action of the wind; but this potential is not realized until the wind is identified with the human spirit, revealing that the unity of nature as expressed by the action of the wind actually has its basis in human subjectivity. Hence, the second dialectical stage occurs in the fourth part of the poem when the poet's identity is dispersed through the various elements of nature. In this stage, all of the elements of the poem – leaves, clouds, waves, wind, and humanity – are reduced to merely relational status, subsisting in an unresolved complex. In the third stage, the elements of nature are identified with the poet's emerging self, which metaphorically bears falling leaves, a self which first becomes the "lyre" of the wind, expressing or miming its effects on nature, a self which realizes its full subjectivity when its identification with the wind, the very source of life and death, is complete. What initially was confronted as substance, as externality – "O wild West Wind" – is now seen as the deepest core of human subjectivity, in interrogative rather than categorical communion with itself (the poet brilliantly ends with a question rather than an assertion). In other words, subjectivity infuses its own integrity with the question that ends the poem: "If Winter comes, can Spring be far behind?" Being a great poet, Shelley avoids simplification. The dialectical process remains insecure; the sublation of the poet's precatory posture remains incomplete, uncertain of its own supersession.

Or, again, we could take an example from a nineteenth-century feminist. In a broad sense, Margaret Fuller's view of the relation between the sexes is dialectical, as in her statement: "Harmony exists no less in difference than in likeness, if only the same key-note govern both parts. Woman the poem, man the poet; woman the heart, man the head; such divisions are only important when they are never to be transcended."[9] Indeed, the woman could well sing the deeds and give "voice to the life of the man" (*WNC*, 80). As in Hegel, positive and negative are themselves only in relation, and each could occupy the other's perspective. Fuller suggests that "male and female represent the two sides of the great radical dualism. But, in fact, they are perpetually passing into one another. Fluid hardens to solid, solid rushes to fluid. There is no wholly masculine man, no purely feminine woman" (*WNC*, 115–16). The very language here is Hegelian, and we will hear these dialectical tones in Freud, Virginia Woolf, and many other writers.

---

[9] Margaret Fuller and Arthur Buckminster Fuller, *Woman in the Nineteenth Century, and Kindred Papers Relating to the Sphere, Condition, and Duties of Woman* (Boston: John P. Jewett, 1855), p. 79. Hereafter cited as *WNC*.

Nonetheless, there is a limit to the Hegelianism – whether explicit or implicit – of feminist thinkers. Fuller recognizes that so far, woman has existed *only* in relation: in relation to her father, her husband, her children. Woman has been reduced to daughter, wife, and mother. Once these relations are removed, there is no identity left. So Fuller states that if

> any individual live too much in relations, so that he becomes a stranger to the resources of his own nature, he falls after a while into distraction, or imbecility, from which he can only be cured by a time of isolation ... To be fit for relations in time, souls, whether of man or woman, must be able to do without them in spirit. (*WNC*, 119)

So woman should abandon any thought of "being taught and led by men" (for men "do not look at both sides," and she should instead dedicate herself to the "Sun of Truth" (*WNC*, 119). Women should "retire within themselves and explore the groundwork of being till they find their peculiar secret." Then they can "come forth again, renovated and baptized" (*WNC*, 121).

Again, this is a dialectical procedure; or more accurately, it refuses dialectic in order to achieve dialectic. A woman retires into her own being, to explore an identity beyond the relations in which she is immersed; she can then come back out into the world of relation with a subjectivity that will *integrate* those relations rather than being absorbed and exhausted by them. In an ultimately Hegelian vein, Fuller avers that "Truth and Love are sought in the light of freedom" (*WNC*, 130). Hence, like Hegel and like Mary Wollstonecraft, she equates the effective pursuit of truth, or rationality, with freedom. A being can achieve humanity and subjectivity only through the active endeavor of its own consciousness, through the free use of its own reason, not through mere obedience to an Other. So Fuller states that "Woman, self-centered, would never be absorbed by any relation" (*WNC*, 176). Woman's being must be centered on itself, not on another. It is this self-centering that allows its entrance into the fullness of relations as a genuine human subject. Woman must achieve what Hegel would call "being-in-and-for-self," an achieved or mediated identity.

1.4   Hegel's Expositions of Dialectic

Das Wahre ist das Ganze ... The true is the whole.
Phenomenology of Spirit, §20

We can now turn to Hegel's own formulations of the dialectical process, starting with the most renowned expositions and then engaging with some less well-known texts, which indicate the foundations and development of the dialectic. Our account will consider: (a) the *Phenomenology*; (b) the lesser *Logic* and *Science of Logic*, which are the most often cited; (c) Hegel's rather exquisite early fragment on "love" (1797–8), which anticipates his dialectical thinking; and (d) Hegel's dialectical vision of God in his earlier theological writings and his later lectures on the philosophy of religion. This chapter will end by briefly considering Hegel's highly instructive account of the connection between the dialectic and skepticism. This will be particularly germane to much literary theory whose treatment of Hegel is profoundly shaped by its general disposition toward skepticism.

1.4.1   *The* Phenomenology

In a famous passage in the *Phenomenology*, Hegel describes the dialectical process as a movement from "substance" to "subject," a movement that is necessary for us to grasp truth:

> everything turns on grasping and expressing the True, not only as *Substance*, but equally as *Subject* ... This (living) substance is, as Subject, pure, *simple negativity*, and is for this very reason the bifurcation of the simple; it is the doubling which sets up opposition, and then again the negation of this indifferent diversity and of its antithesis (the immediate simplicity). Only this *self-restoring* sameness, or this reflection in otherness within itself – not an *original* or *immediate* unity as such, is the True. It is the process of its own becoming, the circle that presupposes its end as its goal, having its end also as its beginning; and only by being worked out to its end, is it actual.[10]
>
> alles darauf an, das Wahre nicht als Substanz, sondern ebensosehr als Subjekt aufzufassen und auszudrücken ... Die lebendige Substanz ... ist als Subjekt die reine einfache Negativität, eben dadurch die Entzweiung des Einfachen, oder die entgegensetzende Verdopplung, welche wieder die Negation dieser gleichgültigen Verschiedenheit und ihres Gegensatzes ist; nur diese sich wiederherstellende Gleichheit oder die Reflexion im Anderssein in sich selbst – nicht eine ursprüngliche Einheit als solche, oder unmittelbare als solche, ist das Wahre. Es ist das Werden seiner selbst, der Kreis, der sein Ende als seinen Zweck voraussetzt und zum Anfange hat, und nur durch die Ausführung und sein Ende wirklich ist.[11]

---

[10] *Hegel's Phenomenology of Spirit*, trans A. V. Miller (Oxford: Oxford University Press, 1979), §17–18.

[11] G. W. F. Hegel, "Enzyklopädie der philosophischen Wissenschaften," in *Werkausgabe*, 20 vols, ed. Eva Moldenhauer and Karl Markus Michel, Vol. 8 (Frankfurt: Suhrkamp, 1969f), pp. 22-3. Hereafter cited as *Werke*. It might be noted that the presence of the word root *ein* also creates a much stronger echo between the words *einfach* and *Einheit* than that in the English translation,

Hence, we initially confront the world as substance, as something external and foreign to us; but as our thought progresses, we realize increasingly that the world is constituted by our own rational operations, our own historical and collective subjectivity. What we previously perceived as "substance" we now perceive as "subject." In this passage, "negativity" refers to the power of substance to bifurcate or divide itself: it has the power to alienate itself from itself by positing itself in something else, in an "other" (lit. "in otherness," *im Anderssein*).[12] It started off as substance, as a simple identity. But now, in the second dialectical stage, it posits its own identity as external to itself, in its relations with an "other" (the "indifferent diversity").

So the first two stages are the "immediate unity" (ursprüngliche *Einheit*) and the external "indifferent diversity" (*gleichgültigen Verschiedenheit*), which are in antithesis. This is the "opposition" or "antithesis," which is set up by the "doubling" of the initial identity through "simple negativity" or self-negation. The third stage is the negation of *both* sides of this antithesis, of the simple identity and its other. This stage is one of "*self-restoring* sameness (*wiederherstellende Gleichheit*), or ... reflection in otherness within itself." In other words, by negating (or, rather, sublating) both terms of the antithesis, the initial simple identity is now a *mediated* identity that integrates the other within itself. The general point here is that the movement from substance to subject is achieved by negating what is immediately given, by viewing it as ultimately comprised by and integrating its relations with what is outside it, its other. We'll see in a later chapter that, for Hegel, this movement encapsulates the movement of modern thought itself and corresponds to the actual historical development of various societies toward modern capitalism.

We can illustrate this process using an example given by Hegel himself. We might see the growth of a plant as having three stages: bud, blossom, and fruit. If we take the bud on its own (our first perspective), it appears

---

where the terms are "simple" and "unity." Similarly, the word "immediate" – *unmittelbar* – is also a common word, but arguably the connotation of "unmediated" is stronger in German than in English. I thank my colleague Lori Lantz, a professional translator, for her help here.

[12] Hyppolite famously called this passage of Hegel's the "basis of his entire philosophical system," and pointed out that part of Hegel's purpose here is to impugn Spinoza's concept of substance as a single, independent, infinite entity. Hegel saw Spinoza's monism as lacking any negativity whereby the finite underwent a dialectic of self-negation and therefore any movement toward subjectivity. Hegel's passage is also directed at Schelling's Absolute, which is similarly abstract. See Jean Hyppolite, *Genesis and Structure of Hegel's Phenomenology of Spirit*, trans. Samuel Cherniak and John Heckman (1946; rpt. Evanston, IL: Northwestern University Press, 1974), pp. 29, 81, 107–8, 153–4, 332. Hereafter cited as *PS*.

to be self-identical, having its essence within itself. But soon the bud disappears when the blossom shows forth, and the blossom in its turn gives way to the fruit. So, in actuality, the essence of the bud was not contained in its own immediate existence: it referred beyond itself to the blossom. And the essence of the blossom extends back to its bud and forward to its fruit. So each of these stages actually has its "essence" outside of itself, and its very identity seems to be constituted by a diversity that is external to it. But they all achieve their true identity as essential elements of the overall process which is "plant," the principle of totality that unites them in a necessary connection (*PS*, §2). Considered in isolation, merely as given, each aspect of the plant had the character of "substance." But considered together as aspects in a process that is formulated by thought, they become "subject," or conscious elements of the movement of thought itself.

Hence Hegel characterizes the entire process as a movement from substance to subject, from a perspective that initially views an entity as alien or "other," through an increasingly broadening perspective that recognizes that entity as constituted in its *essence* and universal significance by a subjective process, by consciousness itself. In other words, subjectivity for Hegel is a *process*, which apprehends what is rational, essential, and universal in the object as the product of the subject's own operations, as revealing the very form of subjectivity – not the personal and contingent subjectivity of any given individual but of a communal, historically accumulated subjectivity.

1.4.2   *The Encyclopaedia (Lesser* Logic) *and the* Science of Logic

In the first part of the *Encyclopaedia of the Philosophical Sciences*, known as the Lesser *Logic*, Hegel's expositions allow us to understand the dialectical process in terms of the kinds of thinking it requires. He distinguishes three basic modes of thought: Understanding, Dialectic, and Speculation or "Positive Reason," which apprehend respectively each of these three stages. The Understanding views the world as composed of distinct particular things; Dialectic (used in a narrower sense here) ascertains the contradictory and dynamic nature of things; and Speculation "apprehends the unity of terms ... in their opposition" (*Enc*, 113–19). We can illustrate this process using a well-known example. In his *Logic*, Hegel takes us through the well-known dialectic whereby "being" gives way before its opposite, "nothing," and the two are united in "becoming." Why is the notion of "being" taken by itself insufficient? Hegel sees "being" as a contentless abstraction: being in itself has no determinate qualities. Pure being, says Hegel, is "the absolute abstraction" because its purity consists in "an absolute absence of attributes." Hence this pure being *is* nothing (*Dieses reine Sein ... das Nichts ist*); there is no ground on which these two terms can be distinguished since both are without content (*Enc*, §86–7; *Werke*, 8: 182–6).[13] Since being both implies its opposite (nothing) and is also indistinguishable from it, the ground of their simultaneous opposition and identity must lie outside of them. They are perpetually passing into each other, and this indefinite transition between them needs to be expressed by a third term, namely "becoming."

So this is one example of the dialectical process. We began with "being" posited as simple self-identity, as seen by the Understanding; but when this was reflected upon by Dialectic, its identity appeared to subsist outside of itself, in "nothing" (its "other"); on further broadening our perspective to the standpoint of Speculation, we can see that the initial two terms are both aspects of "becoming," which is the unity in which they can be distinguished (*SL*, 82–3, 92–3). The dialectic, of course, does not end here; we have simply depicted a small and initial section of what will be a vast ongoing process. But, as Michael Forster states, this exposition of dialectic in the *Logic* is important since it serves as the archetype of the dialectic in other domains, such as nature, spirit, and consciousness (*CCH*, 131).

1.4.3   *The Dialectic of Love*

The foregoing represents some of Hegel's more mature formulations of dialectic in his philosophical texts. But the dialectic is nothing if not sexy. And we might get a more complete picture of it from Hegel's use of it in contexts that we can all relate to, namely those of love and religion (at my age, it's mostly the latter). Since his earliest writings Hegel had always been concerned with the various oppositions in life: between subject and object, between people (on the basis of rank, property, and power), between spirit and nature, between soul and body, between human beings and God, and not least between woman and man.

In a fragment entitled *Love*, which he wrote in late 1797 or early 1798, Hegel furnishes us with some fascinating early anticipations of the dialectical process. A fundamental dialectical principle is given in Hegel's statement that "nothing carries the root of its own being in itself ... the

---

[13] Most of this account is based on Hegel's "lesser" Logic, which is the first part of the *Encyclopedia*, since this contains his clearest exposition. But see also Hegel's *Science of Logic*, pp. 128–32, 479.

one exists only for the other" (*ETW*, 304). In one aspect, this is the principle of the intrinsically relational nature of all existence; nothing can be understood apart from the relations in which it subsists. In another aspect, it is the principle of reciprocity: existence is intrinsically *for* an "other" and enabled by another. According to Hegel, this principle is lacking in the lowest level of love, where there is

> no living union between the individual and his world; the object, severed from the subject, is dead; and the only love possible is a sort of relationship between the living subject and the dead objects by which he is surrounded ... the individual in his innermost nature is something opposed [to objectivity]; he is an independent unit for whom everything else is a world external to him. (*ETW*, 303)

The objects surrounding the individual are "dead" because they are independent, sustaining no reciprocity with him, and affording no reflection of himself. They are deprived of life, of any infusion of subjectivity. We can begin to see here that what Hegel will later call the "fear of death"[14] is essentially a fear that one will be reduced to a lifeless object rather than treated as a living subject. To cling on to one's material life is to fail "to be free of absolute objectivity," to fail to rise to the level of subjectivity, to be a subject. Hegel calls death a "complete negation of relations" (*ETW*, 315–6).

"True union, or love proper," says Hegel, "exists only between living beings who are alike in power and thus in one another's eyes living beings from every point of view; in no respect is either dead for the other. This genuine love excludes all oppositions" (*ETW*, 303). What Hegel now describes is a graphic anticipation of the dialectical process. It is in the physical dimension of love, in sexual union, that the lovers come together: "What in the first instance is most the individual's own is united into the whole in the lovers' touch and contact." The separate self of each of the two lovers, he says, "disappears," and gives way to new unity, "a living child." But now, this child, this seed

> breaks free from its original unity, turns ever more and more to opposition, and begins to develop. Each stage of its development is a separation, and its aim in each is to regain for itself the full riches of life [enjoyed by the parents]. Thus the process is: unity, separated opposites, reunion (*ETW*, 307–8).[15]

---

[14] This occurs in the famous master–slave dialectic, which as we will see is a struggle between two individuals for recognition.
[15] In all the quotations from Hegel's *Early Theological Writings* the interpolations in square brackets are those of the editor.

Here, we begin to see the germ of the dialectic, a dialectic which itself anticipates Freud, Lacan, and many others. One thinks of Lacan's "mirror stage" which marks the descent of the child into the worlds of subjectivity, objectivity, relation, and – embracing all of these – language. But for Lacan there is no return; merely an endless quest for the mother along an infinite chain of signifiers. Lacan's child wanders forlornly and forever through the second stage of the dialectic, unable to recapture the original comforting unity. But the "original unity" in Hegel's paragraph is not between mother and child. Rather, it is the undifferentiated unity of the child itself. Hegel states that after their union, the lovers separate again, but "in the child their union has become unseparated" (*ETW*, 308).

Much of the present book is concerned with the ways in which Hegel's philosophy archetypally expresses various fundamental features of, and tensions within, capitalism. This is certainly true of his dialectic of love, which is effectively seen as a means of transcending the individualism and atomism of bourgeois society. The very definition of love, for Hegel, is an endeavor to overcome the separation between oneself and the "dead" objects by which one is surrounded. The individual must overcome his status as "an independent unit for whom everything else is a world external to him." As we shall see in a later chapter, this is exactly how Hegel describes the individual in bourgeois civil society, which represents the second stage of a larger, historical dialectic. What enables one to overcome this sense of separateness for Hegel is not speculative Reason as in his mature works, but love (anticipating his description of the family in his *Philosophy of Right*).[16]

However, even love – notwithstanding its unifying disposition – is situated by Hegel stolidly within capitalist property relations. He states that the union of lovers is threatened by their "multiplex opposition" in terms of property rights. Each of the lovers is still in connection with much that is "dead," the external objects that belong individually to each of them. Seeing the other lover in possession of objects entails seeing the "individuality which has willed this possession." In other words, the very recognition of someone as individual involves recognizing her as an owner of property. Even if the use of property were common to both, says Hegel, the thought of who has the right to it "would never be

---

[16] For an interesting application of Hegel's logic to familial love, see Toula Nicolacopoulos and George Vassilacopoulos, *Hegel and the Logical Structure of Love: An Essay on Sexualities, Family and the Law* (Aldershot, Brookfield, WI, Singapore, and Sidney: Ashgate, 1999), esp. pp. 115–26. But this book does not draw upon Hegel's early fragment.

forgotten." Hegel tells us starkly that "no relation to an object is possible except mastery over it," and even lovers cannot help reflecting on this aspect of their relations (*ETW*, 308).

These comments appear to anticipate, if only obliquely, Hegel's master–slave dialectic. But perhaps more importantly, they illustrate that even what we call a union of "love" is indissolubly grounded in numerous other kinds of relationships – especially economic – which impinge from the *inside* upon that union. Such is love within capitalism. But ideally, according to Hegel, when we deal with other human beings, we must not view them as objects to be "mastered," to be subsumed as projections of our own subjective interests and desires. Rather, we must treat them as *subjects*. In the master–slave dialectic we will see this drama of subjects fighting to be recognized as subjects, as human beings, as something living, rather than as objects whose entire orientation is toward their own "death," their abrogation by subjectivity. Indeed, the master–slave dialectic could be read as an attempt to transcend the social relations imposed by capitalism.

1.4.4   God as Dialectic

1.4.4.1   Earlier Writings

If human sexuality and love furnish one avenue into understanding dialectic, another is furnished by Hegel's developing attempts to grapple with the Christian conception of the Trinity.[17] How can God be both one and three? This is a dilemma that had haunted much Christian theology for many centuries. Hegel's ingenious answer is that God is not a thing, an entity, but a *process*. For Hegel, the Trinity is a process that involves the division of an original Divine unity which is subsequently restored. In his early essay entitled *The Positivity of the Christian Religion*, Hegel criticizes the degeneration of Christianity from its earlier appropriate stress on moral perfection embodied in Jesus to its later immersion in pointless disputes about the nature of divinity, and the attempt to reduce God to an object.[18] Instead of being viewed as an ideal, God was

[17] For a very thorough account of Hegel's treatment of the Trinity, see Dale M. Schlitt, *Hegel's Trinitarian Claim: A Critical Reflection* (Leiden: E. J. Brill, 1984), which sees Hegel's "logically reformulated Trinitarian" claim as problematic, pp. 66–73.

[18] The first two parts of this essay were written in 1795–6, and the third part probably in 1800. This essay, together with *The Spirit of Christianity* (1798–9), the fragment on "Love" (1797/1798), and "Fragment of a System" (1800) are collected in Herman Nohl's *Hegels theologische Jugendschriften* (Tübingen: J. C. B. Mohr, 1907). They are translated as: G. W. F. Hegel, *Early Theological Writings*, trans. T. M. Knox and Richard Kroner (1948; rpt. Philadelphia: University of Pennsylvania Press, 1971). Hereafter cited as *ETW*.

demoted to the same plane as natural objects, and thinkers reaped much confusion from attempting to apply finite categories such as "number" and "difference" to something that was in its essence infinite (*ETW*, 161).

Indeed, Hegel insists that God undergoes a self-partitioning to return subsequently to unity (*ETW*, 256–7). Complementing this is his insistence that human beings find their essence outside of themselves, in God. Here is one of Hegel's characterizations of the relationship between God and Jesus: "Father and son are simply modifications of the same life, not opposite essences, not a plurality of absolute substantialities" (*ETW*, 260–1). For Hegel, then, God must be approached not as an object but as an infinite *subject* who enables our own subjectivity. It is because we partake in him that we can see ourselves as part of a living totality rather than as a "dead" multiplicity of unrelated individuals (*ETW*, 308). So religion, like love, is regarded in even Hegel's early writings as a means of transcending what he will later characterize as the dead objectivity and individualism of capitalism.

1.4.4.2   Later Writings

These reflections will be refined much later in Hegel's *Lectures on the Philosophy of Religion*.[19] In his lectures of 1827, he saw the Trinity as "the fundamental characteristic" of the Christian religion. In the lectures of 1831, this notion becomes the central focus. The triune God, according to Hegel, undergoes self-differentiation to become an object for himself; he knows himself in finite consciousness, which is a stage in the divine process (*LPR*, 23). These lectures, dating back to a manuscript of 1821, all employ a threefold division, but the content of this division changes (through the various series of lectures) from an initial triad of being, essence, and concept, through a triad based on the interplay of nature and spirit, to a triad that now moves through the stages of immediacy, separation, and reconciliation.

In his religious writings, Hegel persistently states that God has three moments, the first being the idea of God in and for itself, the second being God's self-differentiation (into God and Nature, which is his creation), while the third is the Idea as it appears in finite spirit or humanity,

---

[19] For a fuller exposition, see Peter C. Hodgson, *Hegel and Christian Theology: A Reading of the Lectures on the Philosophy of Religion* (Oxford: Oxford University Press, 2005), pp. 127–40, and 247–84, which address the contemporary theological significance of Hegel. There is an illuminating section on Hegel's "dialectic of religion" in *Hegel and the Philosophy of Religion: The Wofford Symposium*, ed. Darrel E. Christensen (Martinus Nijhoff: The Hague, 1970), pp. 217–42.

in the three-stage history of estrangement, redemption, and reconciliation (*LPR*, 18). We perhaps also need to remind ourselves here that
Hegel does not reserve this tripartite thinking especially for God. Rather,
this is how the world is in general, and this is how thought operates. So
Hegel does not see himself as attempting to resolve some remote mystery
(as the Trinity would be for sense or the mere Understanding); rather, he
is treating in dialectical fashion a phenomenon that, like everything else,
has a dialectical development.

1.5 Epilogue

We began this chapter by trying to define the Hegelian dialectic. By now
we can see that this dialectic is always a dynamic process and it can be
approached from many angles according to context. Moreover, it has
diverse foundations. We have considered the roots of Hegel's dialectic in
his conceptions of love and religion because these are particularly illuminating. But it also has roots in Hegel's thinking about the history of philosophy, where he traces dialectical thinking in its various modulations
to the Eleatics, Zeno, Heraclitus, Plato, Aristotle, and the Neoplatonic
philosophers (*LHP, II*, 67, 69–70, 73–6, 195). Hegel also interestingly
equates the unfolding structure of God and humanity's knowledge of
him with the structure of the syllogism (*LPR*, 415). These specialized
reflections would take us too far afield of our aim here, which is to attain
a general but accurate picture of what constitutes Hegelian dialectic.

In summary, we might say the dialectic is a mode of thinking which
recognizes that the self and world stand in necessary connection, that the
structure of reality as comprehended is itself dialectical, that thought is
not a static system of classification but a self-criticizing and progressive
process, and that the world as simply given to our senses is not worthy of
the name "reality." The dialectic embodies a moving perspective, always
in flux. Moreover, things in the world are defined by their relations; they
can't be grasped in isolation, abstracted from their connections with other
things, but must be understood within their historical contexts. As Hegel
states in his *Philosophy of Right*, "What is actual is rational, and what is
rational is actual."[20] Reality is not simply a vast and incoherent assemblage
of unrelated and unalterable things or facts (as crude empiricism would
have it); rather, in its core, it is rational, historically progressive, and

[20] *Hegel's Philosophy of Right*, trans. T. M. Knox (Oxford: Oxford University Press, 1967), p. 10.
Hereafter cited as *PR*.

potentially unified, answering to the deepest demands of our own rational selves. Hence the dialectic is a mode of thought that is not only rational but relational and historical (*SL*, 128–32, 479). We will see later that the dialectic as formulated by Hegel is a historically cumulative process.

We can also perhaps now understand that what we conventionally call the Hegelian dialectic does not designate a fixed operation or process that always rigidly invokes the same oppositions or the same categories. If we comb through Hegel's works trying to find such a formula, we'll be disappointed. And we'll probably end up imposing some formula upon what he actually says, whether this be thesis, antithesis, and synthesis, or a formula that always privileges certain terms such as identity and difference. It's important to remember, then, that the dialectic is itself dynamic, developing, perpetually open to whatever subject matter it engages, and cannot be reduced to some static formula. In such a reduced format, it could hardly be called dialectic. For example, even the unity of God is not somehow fixed; for Hegel, this unity always abides but "is continually becoming more determinate" (*LPR*, 127–8).

In concluding this chapter, I want to make a few anticipatory remarks about how Hegel's dialectic relates in general to the various branches of literary theory. Since the orientation of much literary theory has been broadly skeptical, it is especially interesting to see how Hegel treats this orientation. In his *Lectures on the History of Philosophy* Hegel accords considerable importance to skepticism as an element of dialectical thinking.[21] He notes that skepticism has the reputation of being "the most formidable adversary of philosophy" and of being "invincible." It is "the art of dissolving everything determinate and exhibiting it in its nullity" (*LHP, II*, 302–3). Hegel stresses that the Greek word σκέπτειν (*skeptein*) means "to investigate or seek." The proper orientation of skepticism is not a purely negative doubt but the ἐποχή (*epoche*), the withholding of assent and this is what gives rises to a state of intellectual and spiritual freedom (*LHP, II*, 307–8). But this skepticism, in Hegel's vision, prepares the path for properly dialectical or Speculative thinking (*LHP, II*, 314–15).

It is this final step, of course, which modern theory has refused to take. It has situated itself effectively at the second stage of Hegel's

---

[21] Important studies on Hegel's history of philosophy include *Hegel and the History of Philosophy*, ed. Joseph J. O'Malley, K. W. Algozin, and Frederick G. Weiss (The Hague: Martinus Nijhoff, 1974), and *Hegel's History of Philosophy: New Interpretations*, ed. David A. Duquette (Albany, NY: SUNY Press, 2003), which contains essays on the role of skepticism for Hegel and his connection with Derrida.

dialectic – the stage where identity is dispersed through difference and relation, the stage of openness, of particularity that is not subsumed into any overarching totality or teleology. It is also a stage that cannot resolve the contradictions of the reflective Understanding, the faculty that sees things atomistically as independent and unrelated. It is a stage of negation of the world, where the individual is unable find truth in the world or to see herself reflected in it. We will see in the next few chapters that this is the kind of thinking that Hegel views as inhering in capitalism. It is also the kind of skeptical thinking that he sees as characterizing the ancient Roman world, his description of which has often been compared to modern capitalist society. Skeptical consciousness is a "*lost* self-consciousness," and internally divided, affirming the nullity of sense-experience, ethical principles, and intellection, yet relying on all these (*PS*, §205).

In both of these societies, ancient Roman and modern capitalist, Hegel sees private citizens as "atoms" related only by an "external bond." The Roman world in particular experiences a decline of community life and withdrawal into private life. This "atomistic ethos" is characterized by abstract universality, whereby an individual's existence was abstract, identified merely with property rights. The Roman world is for Hegel, as in the *Phenomenology*, the world of the "unhappy consciousness," which effectively unites into one consciousness aware of its own divided nature the unconsciously contradictory elements of skepticism. This is a world where consciousness is internally conflicted, a world where a person is unable to find the absolute truth or the divine expressed in the rhythms of ordinary life, either in the natural world or in the political state (*PS*, §206–20; *LHP, II*, 322). If capitalism, as expressed in civil society, were left to its own devices, it also would result in an unhappy disjunction between the individual and her world. Skepticism is the philosophy that characterizes this abstract individuality and its relation to the larger world (*LHP, II*, 317).

As we shall see over the next two chapters, Hegel's dialectic – far from being an abstract philosophical method – was conceived partly as an expression of the overcoming of such alienation. Wherever we turn in Hegel's thought – to his logic, his metaphysics, to his political theory or philosophy of history or his analyses of religion – we will find an impulse to posit Otherness and alienation and to overcome it. Much modern theory, both being shaped by the very forces Hegel saw as characterizing capitalism and also reacting against them, situates itself within an impasse of "invincible" skepticism.

CHAPTER 2

Historical Backgrounds

Now that we've grasped some of Hegel's basic ideas – as expressed in his dialectical thinking – we can, in this chapter and the next, sketch the overarching context for the thesis detailed in the introduction, namely that capitalism and liberal humanism as expounded by Hegel – that is, as understood in all their contradictions – yield the scene on which modern literary theory supervenes. This context includes the nature of Hegel's relation to both the Enlightenment and Romanticism which, in a sense comprise the "thesis" and "antithesis" within liberal humanism. In order to determine where Hegel stands in respect of these, we can't afford to ignore how his thought relates to the actual historical conditions in the Prussia of his time. Only then will we be in a position to assess Hegel's views on the various dimensions of capitalism – the nature of subjectivity, property, gender, class, family, civil society, and state – and the often Hegelian forms in which literary theorists have formulated their profound concern with these themes. We can begin with a brief account of Hegel's antipathy to feudalism and his engagement with Enlightenment thought and the values of the French Revolution. Finally, we can consider the historical conditions in Hegel's Prussia, which in turn will help us to situate his thought in relation to Romanticism.

2.1 Hegel and Feudalism

Perhaps the overarching feature of Hegel's engagement with his own historical context is the strength and consistency of his reaction against the architectonic of feudalism. As Hegel was to observe, this system was hardly based upon individual merit, and its legal and political structure was irrational and largely hereditary. Moreover, in the feudal system, commerce was not only strictly regulated and somewhat insulated from the broader world, but was grounded to some extent on Christian doctrine, which stressed the social welfare of the community, opposing excessive profit-making, and condemning usury. Undoubtedly, these beneficent ideals were not always realized. The medieval Church, of course, fostered a disposition toward life that might be called "other-worldly," viewing *this* (worldly) life as transient, worthless, and merely a preparation for the life hereafter. Pervasive poverty, instability, and illiteracy tended to intensify such religious sentiment and exerted an orientation toward withdrawal from the world, from the pursuit of wealth and power, and a focusing on the means to salvation. In his *Phenomenology*, Hegel describes the mentality engendered by this phase of history – the Roman Empire passing into the early medieval world – as the "unhappy consciousness."

In his political essays Hegel criticized feudal institutions and any attempts to retain them. In 1798, for example, he argued that the magistrates of Württemberg should be elected by the people.[1] In various other essays he upbraided the Estates Assembly for its attachment to feudal laws governing property. Hegel was a keen observer of political and economic reform in England, and in 1831 he wrote a long essay on the proposed English Reform Bill. In it, he is sympathetic to the alleged aims of the Bill, namely "to bring justice and fairness into the way in which the various classes [*Klassen*] and sections of the populace are allowed to participate in the election of Members of Parliament" (*PW*, 234). But he is extremely skeptical that this aim will be realized, pointing out the many corruptions in the English electoral system, the Church, and especially the backwardness of English property laws as compared with the more rational developments in European nations. "England," he says, "has lagged so conspicuously behind the other civilized states of Europe in institutions based on genuine right, for the simple reason that the power of government lies in the hands of those who possess so many privileges which contradict a rational constitutional law and a genuine legislation" (*PW*, 239). In all these cases, Hegel's emphasis is on replacing feudal structures of irrational privilege and "positive" law with institutions and laws grounded upon reason.

However, the feudal system itself existed within broader currents of economic transformation. The fourteenth through the seventeenth centuries had witnessed tendencies that would later foster the growth of capitalism: the accumulation of wealth which was invested for profit, the growth of banking and credit facilities, regulated associations of

[1] Hegel, *Political Writings*, ed. Laurence Dickey and H. B. Nisbet, trans. H. B. Nisbet (Cambridge: Cambridge University Press, 1999), pp. 1–5. Hereafter cited as *PW*.

companies and joint-stock companies, the decline of the feudal manufacturing guilds, and the growth of new industries such as mining and
wool, and the revolutionizing of agricultural methods. These trends were
accompanied by economic nationalism, an ethic of competition, and
intensifying imperialism. By the seventeenth century, England, France,
Italy, Spain, Portugal, and Holland had become imperial powers; and
trade had become a worldwide, rather than a national or local phenomenon. By the end of the seventeenth century the bourgeoisie had achieved
economic hegemony.

2.2 The French Revolution and Enlightenment

This hegemony was one of the causes of the French Revolution of 1789:
though the middle classes had risen to a dominant economic position,
they were without correlative political privileges. These classes were
opposed to the age-old policies of mercantilism, which established government control over monopolies, wages, and prices. The feudal system
of privileges ensured that the higher clergy and certain classes of nobles
monopolized government. Peasants resented the fees and land taxes they
were obliged to pay to their lords; and the urban masses suffered greatly
from high prices.

All this, however, was about to change rapidly in Hegel's time. He
and his friends – like many of the Romantic poets – were excited by
the prospects promised by the French Revolution, which essentially displaced feudal power (of the king, nobility, and clergy) with the hegemony
and values of the bourgeoisie. Intellectual influences on the Revolution
stemmed largely from the Enlightenment, whose major tendencies, as
we have seen, were toward rationalism, empiricism, pragmatism, and
utilitarianism. These tendencies, inspired by thinkers such as John Locke
(1632–1704) and David Hume (1711–76) in Britain, Voltaire (1694–
1778), Diderot (1713–1784); and d'Alembert (1717–1783) in France,
as well as Gotthold Lessing (1729–81) in Germany, formed the core of
liberal-bourgeois thought.

The more specific influences on the French Revolution included
Locke's *Second Treatise of Civil Government* (1690), which justified
the new political system in England that prevailed after the English
Revolution of 1688. Locke condemned despotic monarchy and the
absolute sovereignty of parliaments, even suggesting that the people had
a right to resist tyranny. Voltaire advocated an enlightened monarchy
or republic governed by the bourgeois classes. Baron de Montesquieu

(1689–1755) also influenced the first stage of the French Revolution, advancing a liberal theory based on a separation of executive, legislative, and judicial powers. Jean Jacques Rousseau (1712–78) exerted a powerful impact on the second stage of the Revolution through his theories of democracy, egalitarianism, and the evils of private property, as advocated in his *Social Contract* and *Discourse on the Origin of Inequality*. A final intellectual factor in the background of the revolution was the growth of bourgeois economics in the hands of political economists such as Adam Smith, who vehemently crusaded against mercantilism and advocated (with varying qualifications) the doctrine of economic *laissez-faire* and labor theories of value.

Of course, Hegel's enthusiasm for the French Revolution waned in the wake of the so-called Terror of 1793–4, which saw the execution of thousands. Moreover, he saw the French Revolutionaries as devoted to a "negative" or "abstract" freedom, a mere absence of constraints. Nonetheless, the achievements of the Revolution were impressive and included the drafting of the first genuinely democratic constitution produced by a modern state (though this was not put into effect), the abolition of all remaining feudal rights, the fixing of maximum prices on grain, the division of large estates to be sold to poorer citizens, the separation of Church and State, the abolition of slavery in the French colonies, the expulsion of the invading armies of Prussia and Britain from France, and the relative stabilizing of the French economy.[2]

When Napoleon became emperor of France in 1804, his autocratic rule tempered some of the liberal ideals of the French Revolution. However, he confirmed and developed certain accomplishments of the Revolution, centralizing the government, continuing tax reforms, maintaining the redistribution of vast estates and the abolition of serfdom, and perpetuating reforms begun by the Revolution in the spheres of education, criminal and civil law (known in their revised form as the Code Napoleon, which promulgated equal rights – except for women). Some of the revolutionary fervor spread to Hegel's Prussia, where it met with some resistance, and these developments were transported into the legal structures of other countries such as Italy and Switzerland.

2.3   The Rise of Bourgeois Thought

When we talk of Hegel as a bourgeois philosopher, we need to recall that in his day the bourgeoisie was a revolutionary class, struggling to overturn the edifice of feudalism. For centuries, the traditions of classical and

---

[2] Eric Hobsbawm, *The Age of Revolution* (1962; rpt. Vintage Books, 1996), pp. 90–91.

Christian thought had denigrated commerce and the pursuit of profit. These traditions had included Plato, Aristotle, the Christian Gospels (think of Jesus' reaction to the use of the temple for commerce), and the Church Fathers such as St. Jerome and St. Augustine. But as the market expanded during the late medieval period through trade and agricultural surplus, the Scholastic theologians, notably St. Thomas Aquinas and John Duns Scotus, recognized to some extent the need and function of labor, commerce, and property. They still, however, linked the pursuit of profit in itself with the sin of avarice, and especially excoriated usury.[3]

Max Weber's thesis linking Protestantism with the rise of capitalism is well-known. But the reformers themselves were hardly possessed of a capitalistic spirit. Luther was hostile to commerce and usury; and while Calvin permitted money-lending, he banished professional money-lenders from Geneva (*MM*, 12). There did exist, however, a more individualistic and secular strain in Western thinking, a tradition of civil jurisprudence that was eventually developed into "natural jurisprudence" in the early modern era. While the classical republican and Christian traditions had denigrated commerce as detrimental to civic and spiritual virtue, civil law, as developed in the later Middle Ages and founded on Roman Code of Civil Law compiled in the sixth century, was focused not on virtue but on freedom of trade, property, and individual rights. These values were expressed powerfully in the seventeenth century by Hugo Grotius, Thomas Hobbes, Locke, Hume, and Spinoza, who called for a reorientation of people's concerns toward the present life rather than the afterlife, toward the "this-worldliness" that Weber saw as eventually fostered by Protestantism, especially in its Calvinist guise. In the eighteenth century, the benefits of commerce were extolled by Voltaire, as well as by Adam Smith and the other bourgeois economists (*MM*, 16–19). The one economic principle on which many of them agreed was what Smith referred to as the "invisible hand," or the idea that each person, working toward his particular interests, was led by larger forces to contribute to the benefit of the whole.

This principle will be central to Hegel's analysis of bourgeois society in the *Philosophy of Right*. Like the aforementioned thinkers, he is reacting against a long tradition which demotes private commerce, profit, private property, and individualism. But, unlike those other thinkers, Hegel

---

[3] My account here is indebted to Jerry Z. Muller, *The Mind and the Market: Capitalism in Western Thought* (New York: Random House, 2002), pp. 6–9. Hereafter cited as *MM*. I have also benefited from extended consultations with the German historian Andrew Lees.

resuscitates these elements in the name of Protestant Christianity, which he sees as a crucial vehicle for the fulfillment of Reason. Where the classical and Christian traditions had argued that attention to commerce and profit and self-interest detracts from civic duty and virtue, Hegel endeavors to show that the capitalist market represents not only an advance over feudal economics in terms of the progress of freedom, but that it also offers a venue in which virtue can be exercised in a free and rational manner.

2.4   Hegel's State and Historical Conditions in Prussia

The State described in *Philosophy of Right* is an ideal State, which was never realized in Hegel's lifetime, least of all in Hegel's Prussia. In Hegel's day (until 1803), Germany comprised more than three hundred kingdoms, principalities, and provinces, including Prussia and Austria, each with its own laws and customs. This loose confederation of German-speaking states had been united since 800 by the Holy Roman Empire, which was now rapidly crumbling and soon to be dissolved by Napoleon.[4] This was the situation bequeathed by the Treaty of Westphalia, which marked the end of the Thirty Years' War (1618–48), fought largely between the Catholic Holy Roman Emperor and a number of Protestant principalities and states. The ravaging by feudal warfare, the fragmentation of states, and the nature of absolutism in Prussia caused her to lag behind England and France in terms of capitalist development and political liberalism. Marx and other commentators have noted that the German bourgeoisie was weak compared to its English and French counterparts, and Germany has been characterized, even after its reforms, as an "industrial feudal society" still dominated by a feudal aristocracy.[5]

Recently, this picture has been challenged in favor of more complex and nuanced explanations of the connections between capitalism, liberalism, and the bourgeois class.[6] Joyce Appleby stresses that capitalism is internally structured by the specific political and cultural circumstances

---

[4] See Joyce Appleby, *The Relentless Revolution: A History of Capitalism* (London and New York: W. W. Norton, 2010), pp. 168–9. Hereafter cited as *RR*.

[5] See, for example, Ralf Dahrendorf, *Society and Democracy in Germany* (New York: Anchor, 1969), p. 58.

[6] For an astute account of these explanations, see Colin Mooers, *The Making of Bourgeois Europe: Absolutism, Revolution, and the Rise of Capitalism in England, France, and Germany* (London and New York: Verso, 1991), pp. 103–5. Hereafter cited as *MBE*.

in which it occurs and that England, for example, cannot be considered as a template for capitalist development (*RR*, 21). She further notes that many other countries in Europe – including England, France, Belgium, the Netherlands, and Russia – had by this time acquired strong national identities. As such, modernization in Germany was strongly linked to the impetus toward nationalism, which itself was fueled by the French Revolution and its Napoleonic aftermath (*RR*, 164–8). Without entering into the details of these debates, we can at least highlight the features of developments in Germany, and particularly Prussia, that are pertinent to an understanding of Hegel.

In the provinces subjugated by Napoleon and under his protectorate, the Code Napoléon brought equality before the law, freedom of religion, and removal of many of the privileges of feudalism. After its defeat by Napoleon at Jena and Auerstädt in 1806, Prussia was in a dire situation, in economic and political ruin, having been obliged to cede much of its territory and population and to pay indemnity for the French army of occupation. But Hegel saw this victory as an index of much-needed political and economic reform in Prussia. His comments on witnessing Napoleon riding through Jena after his victory are well-known and have been much derided ("I saw the Emperor – this world-soul ... an individual, who, concentrated here at a single point, astride a horse, reaches out over the world and masters it").[7]

Indeed, from 1807, Prussia was rebuilt through a series of radical reforms, embodied in the so-called Edict of Emancipation. The civil service class, into which Hegel was born, was the driving force toward modernization and economic reform. The masterminds behind these reforms, in King Fredrick William III's bureaucracy, were Karl Freiherr vom Stein (an admirer of Adam Smith)[8] and Karl August von Hardenberg. The Edict included articles on the universal right to property and to engage in any lawful business, abrogation of the nobility's privileges, and the abolition of serfdom.[9] Agriculture was made more economically viable and efficient, and occupations were opened up to all classes. The political structure was impelled toward a constitutional monarchy by the

---

[7] Letter to Immanuel Niethammer, October 13, 1806, in *Hegel: The Letters*, trans. Clark Butler and Christiane Seiler (Bloomington: Indiana University Press, 1984), p. 114. Hereafter cited as *HL*.

[8] The (complex) influence of Adam Smith and economic liberalism on these architects of Prussian reform is well documented in Carl William Hasek, *The Introduction of Adam Smith's Doctrines into Germany* (New York: Columbia University, 1925), pp. 89–106.

[9] See Liah Greenfeld, *The Spirit of Capitalism: Nationalism and Economic Growth* (Cambridge, MA and London: Harvard University Press, 2001), p. 193. Hereafter cited as *SC*.

summoning of various assemblies with consultative powers. The power of the feudal barons was constrained, and freedom of trade was encouraged, not least by curtailing the monopolies of the feudal guilds. As Muller states, "Prussia thus became a pioneer in the dissolution of the feudal agrarian order and its replacement by a society in which property was divorced from political domination [*Herrschaft*]." Moreover, the reformers brought together a cohort of progressive administrators and intellectuals, and founded a new university in the Prussian capital, Berlin. In 1818, they recruited Hegel as Chair of Philosophy (*MM*, 145–7).

These were all reforms – the so-called revolution from above – that were included in Hegel's vision of the State. This vision also called for a professionalization of the State bureaucracy that Frederick William I had undertaken much earlier, whereby careers in the state administration were available on the strength of merit rather than social rank or inherited privilege (*MBE*, 117–18). Hegel has often been accused of being a servant or lackey of the State. But the foregoing context shows that the State he served was progressive and liberal in its intentions. Ironically, the reformers wanted, like Hegel, to increase the power of the State to break the power of the Prussian nobility and the guilds. Hegel's "glorification" of the Prussian State as an embodiment of Reason was in fact an extolling of this program of liberal reform. But these liberal intentions of the Prussian administration were thwarted after the defeat of Napoleon at Waterloo in 1815, which acted as an impetus to the aristocratic and conservative forces of reaction, resulting in a harsh reactionary backlash in Prussia. An edict of 1816 rendered more stringent the requirements for emancipation from serfdom. The repressive Karlsbad Decrees of 1819 directed against the revolutionary potential of German nationalism, brought the period of Prussian reform to an end. The Decrees were, proximately, a response to revolutionary violence and also to demands for reform from "below" by, for example, Jakob Fries, Chair of Philosophy at the University of Jena, who was dismissed from his post. These measures suppressed much freedom of speech and instituted governmental monitoring at schools and universities.

In fact, the state as Hegel describes it in his *Philosophy of Right* is clearly *not* the Prussian State after these various forms of regression had set in. In his inaugural address at the University of Berlin in 1818, Hegel saw Germany as having recently undergone a "rebirth" whereby it was recognized that everything, including the political process, must be measured according to the standards of Reason. But the "spiritual supremacy" he here ascribes to the Prussian State is based precisely on its embodiment of the rational reforms that led to that rebirth (*PW*, 182–3). His later writing, including the *Philosophy of Right*, gives no indication that he endorsed the reactionary tendencies that pushed back against these reforms.[10]

Viewed from a longer-term perspective, political and economic reform in Prussia was sluggish. The police and the military retained a precapitalist organization, and landowners retained certain police powers. The number of landless peasants increased considerably from the middle of the eighteenth century until the mid-nineteenth century. As Appleby observes, conditions for agricultural workers, even after the transition from serfdom to free labor, remained poor; and the feudal guilds continued to suppress competition and innovations until well beyond 1850 (*RR*, 170–1). Ironically, the protection of property served not only economic mobilization but also the counterrevolutionary interests of the *Junkers* or landed nobility (*MBE*, 129–33). As Colin Mooers says,

> Although the state was increasingly forced to introduce measures which had the effect of undermining the old order, it strove at the same time to preserve those aspects of the old society which were vital to its own independent sources of economic surplus ... agrarian reform, for example, was intended to create an independent peasantry which would provide a constant source of taxation revenue. Its overall effect, however, was to hasten the dispossession of the peasantry. (*MBE*, 134)

All these forms of conservative reaction were characteristic of the Prussia of Hegel's time but not of his vision of the State. Moreover, the freeing of the serfs has been interpreted not as some Hegelian rationality realizing itself but as a means for the monarchy to increase its power over the nobility, as "the last great triumph of royal absolutism over nobility."[11] Hegel had viewed the class of civil servants in the employ of the State as a disinterested and "universal" class, committed wholly to the interest of the State. In other words, the State, for Hegel, was a purely political entity, far above any economic interest. But, in reality, this was hardly the case since the State bureaucracy had its own social and economic agenda, often competing, for example, with the nobility over agricultural surplus produced by the peasants (*MBE*, 118, 130–2). Hegel never lived

---

[10] T. M. Knox and Charles Taylor have convincingly refuted such claims of Hegel's "Prussianism" and the misconception of him as a "proto-Fascist apologist for totalitarianism." See T. M. Knox, "Hegel and Prussianism," *Philosophy*, 15 (1940), 51–63; and Taylor, *Hegel and Modern Society*, pp. vii, 83–92.

[11] Jerome Blum, *The End of the Old Order in Rural Europe* (Princeton: Princeton University Press, 1978), p. 373.

to see the new German empire of 1871 engineered by Bismarck, as the new industrial giant of Europe, with the King of Prussia as its Emperor (*RR*, 173). The overall point here is that, no matter how Hegel may have accommodated himself to the actualities of the Prussian State, that State is not the one described in the *Philosophy of Right*.

2.5   Hegel, Prussia, and Romanticism

Hegel was well aware of the contradictions and dilemmas of bourgeois society as expressed by many of the Romantics, including Friedrich Schiller and his own friend, the poet Friedrich Holderlin. Much like the English Romantic poet Shelley, Schiller saw in art and letters the remedy for the ills of a bourgeois world corrupted by the principles of mechanism and utility: "*Utility* is the great idol of the time, for which all powers slave and all talents should pay homage."[12] It was only art that could transcend the various forms of disintegration created by the capitalist market: this must be an art which "vanishes from the noisy mart of the century" (*AEM*, 226). And, like Shelley, Schiller was a fierce advocate of freedom, staunchly opposed to authoritarianism of any kind. He also propounded a model of history as essentially divided between an ideal, harmonious past and a fragmented present.

It is in the famous sixth letter that Schiller draws a contrast between the ancient Greek world and modern civilization, a contrast that is echoed in much of Hegel's own work, including the *Phenomenology* and the *Philosophy of History*. In the Greek world, says Schiller, the powers of the mind, sense, and intellect worked in harmony, and they had not yet engaged in hostile partition and mutual separation of their frontiers (*AEM*, 232). In the modern world, these faculties are fragmented, with not only individuals but entire classes developing only one part of their potential while the rest remains stunted. Greek society, says Schiller, received its form from "all-uniting Nature," whereas modern culture is based on "all-dividing understanding" (*AEM*, 232). Again, this comes very close to Hegel's terminology, which sees Greek culture as embodying an "immediate" unity and modern capitalist culture as essentially embodying division and disintegration.

---

[12] Friedrich Schiller, "Over the Aesthetical Education of Man," in *Friedrich Schiller: Poet of Freedom*, trans. William F. Wertz, Jr. (New York: New Benjamin Franklin House, 1985), p. 225. Hereafter cited as *AEM*.

For both Schiller and Hegel, the Greek world enshrines a harmony between individual and state, an organic wholeness, whereas the modern state (until it becomes rational) is atomistic. Schiller depicts powerfully the various dualisms that afflict modern bourgeois institutions: "the state and church, the laws and the customs, were now torn asunder; enjoyment was separated from work, the means from the end, the effort from the reward. Eternally chained to only a single fragment of the Whole, man only develops himself as a fragment." The "concrete life" of the individual is destroyed so that "the abstract of the Whole may devour his scanty existence, and eternally the state remains foreign to its citizens" (*AEM*, 234). Foreshadowing the ideas of both Hegel and Marx on alienation, Schiller effectively describes here how human individuality is reduced to an abstract unity, much like the individual of Hegel's Roman Empire. Where the mature Hegel will diverge from Schiller, and indeed from all Romantics, is in his view that these dualisms must be transcended not by art but by Reason, by more rational social configurations existing in harmony with rational human beings. In his earlier writings, as we have seen, Hegel granted such unifying and harmonizing functions to both love and religion. But the picture isn't quite so simple: even in his later writings on aesthetics, he conceded a certain autonomy and unifying power to art.

To understand where exactly Hegel did stand in relation to the realities of the Prussian State, it will be useful to have recourse also to Liah Greenfeld's analysis of the overall German historical and intellectual context. According to Greenfeld, the new nationalistic consciousness was effectively a creation of German intellectuals, an educated middle class, which found itself marginalized in the last quarter of the eighteenth century. This "status-inconsistency" reflected the contradiction between the rigid social structure of German societies which admitted of no social mobility and the new spirit of the German Enlightenment or *Aufklärung*, which viewed educated reason as the supreme social value. According to Greenfeld, this class developed a specifically anti-Enlightenment worldview, which began as Romanticism and then became the framework of German national consciousness.

Against Enlightenment reason, this class posited the notions of "totality" and "individuality." But it defined individuality – and here we suspect that Greenfeld is thinking of Hegel (where Hegel himself was thinking of Aristotle) – not as traits that are unique to a particular person but rather those characteristics that all held in common. The Romantics condemned reason – which they saw as destroying the totality and individuality of human nature – as the weapon of mutilation and alienation. Equally, they condemned modern society as the institutionalization of this divisive reason, believing that it constricted human nature, for example, by the principle of division of labor which contravened the principle of totality.

In effect, the Romantics envisioned, according to Greenfeld, a society that was totalitarian in that there would be no private sphere free from the "joys of participation." The portentous political implications of such "totalitarianism" were formulated by Adam Müller, the political philosopher of Romanticism (*SC*, 155–9). Significantly, Müller was a vehement opponent of Adam Smith, excoriating him for his individualism, antisocial spirit, which deprived people of freedom and subjected them to the vagaries of the market, and for isolating the process of material production from social and cultural forces, as well as from the moral dimensions of human nature (*SC*, 197–9).[13] In Müller's conception, being true to one's human nature, becoming truly an individual, meant abrogating one's self within the higher individuality of the State (and again, we hear the voice of Hegel here).

In the Romantics' eyes, according to Greenfeld, the State should be "intolerant" of the independence of its members. Moreover, in this conception, "liberty" was defined as the ability to realize one's individuality by giving up one's freedom and submitting to the authority of the state (again, this begins to approach Hegel's definition of freedom). Greenfeld does proceed to mention Hegel explicitly, as the thinker who "performed the magic trick" of reconciling "patently irreconcilable propositions," namely that one could achieve individuality only by becoming a member of a particular social class (*SC*, 159–60). It was, suggests Greenfeld, an "external event," the victory of the French Revolutionary armies, that "transformed the Romantic mentality into German nationalism, eventually making it the German mentality" (*SC*, 161).

Finally, Greenfeld describes the academic debate concerning economics which went on in German universities during the last quarter of the eighteenth century. Smith's *Wealth of Nations* was translated into German in the same year that it was published (1776), and provoked a healthy debate. While it initially evoked much opposition, it eventually garnered much uncritical support. One German academic even compared it to the

---

[13] For an excellent account of the important contrasts between the views of Müller and Hegel, see Domenico Losurdo, *Hegel and the Freedom of the Moderns* (Durham, NC: Duke University Press, 2004) pp. 172–4.

Word of God (*SC,* 180, 184). However, the resemblance of German economic thinking – and we shall discuss later whether or not this applies to
Hegel – to Smith's ideas was often superficial, and those who identified
with Smith often subscribed to ideas that were diametrically opposed to
his (*SC,* 185). On a pragmatic level, Greenfeld observes, "Professors in
Germany were civil servants; they knew which hand fed them, and to a
degree their preoccupation with economics ... could be attributed to a
vested interest in making themselves useful and keeping that hand boun-
tiful" (*SC,* 162).

While Greenfeld ostensibly describes the general reaction of the
Romantics, what she is actually describing is the reaction of *Müller* and
Hegel. In other words, she is not describing the Romantic reaction *against*
the State but rather Hegel's *accommodation* to the State. While Greenfeld's
contextualization of Hegel's thought is extremely useful, I would argue
that it is implausible to characterize this accommodation – or Hegel's
general outlook – as Romantic. Hegel was in the most profound sense
a rationalist and saw human history as the progressive unfurling of the
operations of reason in both the world and the human mind. Though he
was influenced to some extent by Goethe, Schelling, and Solger, in general he responded negatively to the ideas of the Romantics. Nonetheless,
his own philosophical system shares some fundamental affinities with
Romanticism, such as the view that subjectivity and objectivity are mutually dependent processes. But Hegel's account of these processes took
non-Romantic directions.

Hence, Hegel's account of capitalism and his reaction to bourgeois
society is not the reaction that characterized the Romantics.[14] While he
shares some of *Müller's* views, he does not share his antipathy to Adam
Smith. Having said this, his implementation of Adam Smith's principles is heavily circumscribed by the need to situate civil society within
a framework where it is intrinsically related to both family and state,
which are both forms of unity, as opposed to its own status as intrinsically atomistic and fragmented. Hegel sees a number of contradictions
in bourgeois society: freedom vs government control; public vs private
treatment of social problems; a conflict within the individual, who

---

[14] Even in his earlier writings Hegel derides most aspects of Romanticism. In the Preface to the
Phenomenology, he states that "nowadays, philosophizing by the light of nature, which regards itself
as too good for the Notion, and as being an intuitive and poetic thinking in virtue of this defi-
ciency, brings to the market the arbitrary combinations of an imagination that has only been disor-
ganized by its thoughts, an imagery that is neither fish nor flesh, neither poetry nor philosophy"
(*Phen,* § 68).

belongs to both family and State, as well as civil society; the polarization of wealth and poverty; and an imperialism which is necessarily generated by these contradictions. In this desire to contextualize capitalism, Hegel displays an affinity with the Romantic propensity toward totalization. But the higher totality he posits is a rational one, and the result of historical evolution. As for being a paid servant of the State, it is worth recalling that the civil servants who recruited him were among the architects of liberal reform in Prussia. Those reforms found expression in Hegel's vision of the State but, sadly, were not fully realized in actuality.

CHAPTER 3

Hegel, Philosopher of Capitalism

[T]he whole sphere of civil society is the territory of mediation where there is free play for every idiosyncrasy, every talent, every accident of birth and fortune, and where waves of passion gush forth, regulated only by reason glinting through them.
Hegel, Philosophy of Right, §182, Add

Sell when you can: you are not for all markets.
Rosalind to Phebe in Shakespeare, As You Like It (5.3)

We exist in the age of global capital. No matter where we live in the world today, capitalism – in one or other of its many forms – is integral to our lives at every level. It affects everything we do, ranging from shopping through enrolling in a college, karate school, or gym to attending a church, synagogue, or mosque. It even conditions the way we love and many aspects of our emotional lives. Capitalism, having emerged over the last few centuries as a radical break from feudalism, is one of the larger shaping forces behind modernity and our world. Hegel was the first major philosopher to offer a direct and sustained treatment of capitalism – which he called "bourgeois" or "civil" society; and in this, he anticipated and influenced many analyses of capitalism on the part of Marx, Weber, Nietzsche, Bergson, and several literary and cultural theorists.

In economic terms, capitalism might be defined as a system characterized by a number of features: the owning of the means of economic production by private individuals or companies; a free market economy, where prices and the flow of money are not regulated by the state; property rights, which protect innovation and private ownership; the enforcement of contracts to guard against contingency; the predominance of large financial institutions and corporations; a view of society as comprising an aggregate of individuals; a tendency to promote individual initiative and to frown on government control; the regarding of work as a means of individual self-realization; and an emphasis on rationality, efficiency, and self-discipline. Hegel recognized and wrote extensively about the importance of all of these. But, of course, capitalism is not simply an economic system. It has engendered specific ways of thinking about ourselves and the world, specific modes of being and relating to others. In fact, in her magisterial history, Joyce Appleby defines capitalism as a "cultural system rooted in economic practices."[1]

In the last century or so, numerous literary and cultural theorists as well as philosophers, sociologists, and economists, have explored these various dimensions of capitalism. They comprise quite a long tradition, which includes Voltaire, Edmund Burke, Marx, Weber, Durkheim, Matthew Arnold, Nietzsche, Bergson, Freud, Sartre, Simone de Beauvoir, Lukács, Adorno, Horkheimer, Michèle Barrett, Frantz Fanon, and, more recently, Roland Barthes, Derrida, Baudrillard, Julia Kristeva, Judith Butler, Gayatri Spivak, Terry Eagleton, Fredric Jameson, James Galbraith, Thomas Piketty, Alain Badiou, and Slavoj Žižek. Several novelists, notably Dickens, Balzac, Zola, and Conrad, also dealt with the effects of capitalism on human relationships. As will be evident from this highly selective list, capitalism has been examined from numerous perspectives, including those of Marxism, positivism, political conservatism, liberal humanism, feminism, postmodernism, structuralism, psychoanalysis, and postcolonialism.

In fact, the assessment of capitalism in its multiple facets is integral to modern European intellectual history.[2] And how could it not be? We live in a world that has been shaped by developments of capitalism over the last three centuries. The issues that have concerned the above thinkers naturally include economic dilemmas such as the crippling disparity

---

[1] Appleby, *The Relentless Revolution*, p. 25. See also Terrell Carver, *Postmodern Marx* (1998), which illuminates the psychological orientation of individuals within capitalism. Interestingly, Thomas Piketty's best-selling book, *Capital in the Twenty-First Century*, trans. Arthur Goldhammer (2013; rpt. Cambridge, MA: Harvard University Press, 2014) focuses valuably on the economic dimensions of capitalism and concludes that the central contradiction of capitalism – which continues to generate a global disparity of wealth, is that the private rate of return on capital will continue to exceed the rate of growth of income and output. In other words, capital "reproduces itself faster than output decreases" (p. 571). The solution, according to Piketty, is a progressive annual tax on capital (p. 572). But, as Piketty himself acknowledges, this hardly addresses the numerous other problems created by capitalism, which require economists and social scientists to participate in the public discourse to continue classical political economy's search for how economics might play its part in an ideal society (p. 574). It's all the more surprising, then, that Piketty's otherwise excellent account does not mention Hegel, whose thought embodies the first attempt to integrate bourgeois economics into a philosophical system. Piketty's goal is in some ways the same as Hegel's, viz., to "ensure that the general interest takes precedence over private interest" (pp. 1–3).

[2] For a detailed account of these developments, to which mine is indebted, see Muller, *The Mind and the Market*, pp. x–xi.

between rich and poor, the necessity for imperial expansion, and the division of labor. But of course the ramifications of capitalism extend far beyond economics to issues of central interest to literary theory such as the ideological construction of subjectivity, the status of language, the discourse of gender, the nature of culture, the foundations of ethics and morality, the role of education and technology, the multiplication of needs, the conflict between self-interest and the state, the relations between nations, and the various levels of devastation wrought by vicissitudes of the market as well as by colonialism and global warming. As Appleby rightly emphasizes, capitalism represented such an "astounding break from precedent," such a "startling departure from the norms that had prevailed for four thousand years," that it engendered not just new ways of thinking but a "reconceived human nature" (*RR*, 4, 12, 15). As such, theorists have probed into all of the above-named issues; and we will find nearly all of them treated systematically in the work of Hegel.

Hegel was *the* philosopher of capitalism. By this, I mean that it was Hegel who furnished capitalism with its profoundest and most articulate expression. He did not merely advocate the central philosophy of capitalism – liberalism – as did John Locke and Thomas Paine; nor merely its economics, as did the bourgeois economists Adam Smith, Jean-Baptiste Say, and David Ricardo; nor merely its discontents, as did Blake, Schiller, and many Romantics. Rather, he attempted to understand capitalism *in* its very essence of internal contradiction and division, in its neuroses and pathologies, in its historical situation as a revolutionary light kindled within feudalism by the torch of trade and Protestant reform, in its differential relation to the development of Reason and religion, and in its conflicting ethical implications for human worth and purpose. In other words, he brought to the analysis of capitalism a dialectical understanding. And, even more strikingly, his dialectic is internally structured by the need to resolve the contradiction that was capitalism. Hegel's philosophy arose out of that historical moment when the capitalist world was struggling to be born, within the womb of a feudal world mired in superstition, caprice, and decay. This historical moment conditions both the form and content of Hegel's thinking.[3]

---

[3] This chapter was written prior to the publication of a recent book *Hegel and Capitalism*, ed. Andrew Buchwalter (New York: SUNY Press, 2015), hereafter cited as *HC*. I am gratified to see that this excellent volume confirms my claims in this paragraph. In his superb introduction entitled "Hegel and Capitalism," Buchwalter states that Hegel's "general conceptual framework, expressed above all in its notion of dialectics, can itself be construed as a response to the phenomenon of modern capitalism" (p. 2).

Hegel's encounter with capitalism was, of course, itself a rather extended process, beginning in the early 1800s when he first came across the writings of the bourgeois economists Adam Smith, Adam Ferguson, and James Steuart. His analyses of various aspects of capitalism, such as social labor, the mechanization of labor, and alienation, occur in a number of earlier texts, ranging from his doctoral dissertation *The Difference between Fichte's and Schelling's System of Philosophy* through the first and second *Philosophies of Spirit* (*Realphilosophie* I and II) to the *Phenomenology*. While the current chapter acknowledges the import of these texts, it will focus on Hegel's *Philosophy of Right*, which presents his fullest and most mature account of bourgeois society.[4]

3.1   Hegel's *Philosophy of Right*: The Principle of Right

Central to Hegel's description of modern society is his description of *bürgerliche Gesellschaft*, which is usually translated as "civil society" but can also be rendered as "bourgeois society."[5] Hegel sees civil society as a development of the modern Western world since the Renaissance. In the *Philosophy of Right*, he situates civil society within a larger social, political, and ethical scheme. The word *Recht* can be translated as "right" or "law," but in this text it has a broader meaning, encompassing the spheres of civil law, morality, and ethical life.

Crucially, *Recht* is integral to the radically new conception of the human self that Hegel sees as emerging with capitalism, a conception that is still with us today. Instead of viewing their identities as merely given by God or tradition, people view themselves as free rational agents, who are able to create themselves, to shape their own subjectivity (Wood, *CCH*, 417). Hegel states that the origin of *Recht* is the human will because it is in our will that we find our individuality and know ourselves as self-determined and free. Hegel defines the principle of "right" as the "self-consciousness which apprehends itself through thinking as

---

[4] For an account of Hegel's evolving understanding of capitalism, I would refer the reader to Michalis Skomvoulis's excellent essay "Hegel Discovers Capitalism: Critique of Individualism, Social Labor, and Reification during the Jena period (1801–1807)," in *Hegel and Capitalism*, ed. Buchwalter, pp. 19–34. See also Ardis Collins's essay "Anonymity, Responsibility, and the Many Faces of Capitalism: Hegel and the Crisis of the Modern Self," which deals with Hegel's treatment of capitalism in the *Phenomenology* (*HC*, 53–69). Nicholas Mowad argues that in the *Phenomenology*, Hegel offers a more damning critique of capitalism (*HC*, 72–4, 79–81).

[5] Cf. Allen Wood: "Civil society for Hegel is 'bourgeois' society in the sense that its dominant ethical principles are those arising from the urban middle class" but is actually broader than this since it includes the professional class, landed nobility, rural peasantry, and civil service. Allen Wood, "Hegel's Ethics," in *Cambridge Companion to Hegel*, ed. Beiser, p. 421. Hereafter cited as *CCH*.

essentially human" and free from all contingency. Hence the various "moments" of *Recht* are the progressive objects of the will: individual right, property, morality, family, and the state.[6]

Hegel states that the will progresses through three basic phases. In its immediate embodiment, in the first phase, the will exists as "personality" in the form of "abstract right." In the second phase, the will is divided between subjective individuality, on the one hand, and implicit universality, on the other. In other words, the individual will is inwardly informed by the idea of what is good, or the implicit idea of a universal will, but it exists apart from, or in opposition to, it. Finally, these two sides, the subjective apprehension of what is good, and the realization of this in the actual world, are united, in the sphere of "ethical life." This ethical order in turn develops through the three stages of family, civil society, and the state. The family represents the natural or immediate embodiment of the ethical order; civil society represents the ethical order "in its division" and in the "phase of relation," while the state enshrines the free uniting of the individual will with the universal will. States in their interrelation embody the "universal world spirit" which manifests itself through the process of world history (*EPR*, §33; *PR*, §33, 157).

It's important to realize that Hegel's analysis of capitalism or "bourgeois society" places it within this larger scheme. Civil or bourgeois society is the second phase of a dialectic that moves from the family to the state. The family is the ethical moment in its immediacy and unity (*EPR*, §157–8). Hegel sees the family as the sphere of intuition, and we shall examine in a later chapter his notorious view that woman's "destiny" is effectively to remain in this sphere, while man moves from the sphere of family to that of civil society and self-definition through work. For now, we need to note merely that the individual acquires right *as* an individual only when the family begins to dissolve.

The family, then, is the result of a dialectic that moves from individual will as conceived in abstract isolation ("personality") to this will as grasped in its relations to the universal will or more general and objective ideas of "right." According to Hegel, the will is first embodied in property. Like his progressive contemporaries who were aiming to modernize Prussia, Hegel understood the importance of both the market and of private property. It is well-known that Marx saw private property as one of

---

[6] *Hegel's Philosophy of Right*, §4–7, 19. A more recent edition of this text is *Hegel's Elements of the Philosophy of Right*, ed. Allen W. Wood, trans. H. B. Nisbet (Cambridge: Cambridge University Press, 1991), hereafter cited as *EPR*. I refer to both of these splendid editions in order to make certain points clear to students unfamiliar with Hegel.

the foundational defects of capitalism, and he astutely saw, as we shall discuss in a later chapter, that the sanctioning of private property was integral to Hegel's dialectic. But if we look at things from Hegel's historical horizon, we can understand the central role he ascribes to property rights.

3.2   Hegel on Property

Under feudalism, property was largely hereditary and was inexorably tied to political power, as with the landed nobility. In other words, property was not an index of individual merit or industriousness or freedom. This is why, for example, the rising agrarian capitalist landowners in England struggled so hard against centralized state power in the seventeenth century to procure and protect their property rights against the forces of privilege and customary rights; ownership of property was clearly integral to the exercise of political power. Hegel and his fellow reformers wished to extricate property rights from feudal political privilege, and to view the ownership of property as a universal right.

The seeds of Hegel's conception of property might be traced back to John Locke. In the famous chapter on "property" in his *Two Treatises of Government*, Locke had argued that "every man has 'property' in his own 'person.' This nobody has any right to but himself. The 'labour' of his body and the 'work' of his hands, we may say, are properly his."[7] Locke goes on to say that if a person exerts his labor on something in nature, he thereby makes it his property. While God gave the world to "men in common," he also gave it "to the use of the industrious and rational" who could appropriate it through their labor (*TT*, 132). Moreover, inasmuch as man is "master of himself, and proprietor of his own person, and the actions or labour of it," he contains within himself "the great foundation of property" (*TT*, 138). While Locke says that a man has a right to possess as much as he needs without letting it "spoil," he acknowledges that the invention of money – which is relatively durable – enables and can justify vaster accumulation (*TT*, 134, 138–9). On this account, some critics, such as C. B. Macpherson, have viewed Locke as a proponent of capitalist accumulation and possessive individualism.[8]

---

[7] John Locke, *Two Treatises of Government* (London, Melbourne, and Toronto: Dent, 1982), p. 130. Hereafter cited as *TT*.

[8] C. B. Macpherson, *The Political Theory of Possessive Individualism: Hobbes to Locke* (Oxford: Clarendon Press, 1962).

Without engaging in this debate, we can simply observe here the similarities between certain views of Locke – the "father" of classical liberalism – and those of Hegel. What is remarkable is that both philosophers, in their different ways, view the category of property as integral to the very definition of the human self. In other words, the self in its very essence is a "bourgeois" self. In its self-possession – its ability to master and discipline its own impulses – the self is defined as the very capacity to possess, as a potential bearer of property, as a potential unit of bourgeois society.

Where Locke says that we can appropriate something by putting our labor into it (or, as he says, by "mixing" our labor with it), Hegel states that we have the right to put our will into anything and thereby possess it. This is the "absolute *right of appropriation* which human beings have over all things [*Sachen*]" (*EPR*, §44). Locke views property as beginning in one's own "person." Hegel states: "that I, as free will, am an object to myself in what I possess and only become an actual will by this means constitutes the genuine and rightful element in possession, the determination of *property* ... property is the first embodiment of freedom" (*EPR*, §45; *PR*, §45). In other words, my very sense of myself as an individual, with free choice, finds its external expression in property. Locke, like Adam Smith later, sees the function of government as merely protecting man's natural right to property and liberty. Hegel further states that the very essence of property is to be *possessed*, to have the character of being "this" or "mine" – which he calls "the important doctrine of the necessity of private property" (*PR*, §46, *Add*). Moreover, Hegel further advances over Locke in understanding that what property rights essentially regulate is the relation between various people, various property owners. Property is the medium through which individuals *recognize* one another. Property, as "the *embodiment* of personality ... involves its recognizability by others" (*PR*, §51).

As will be seen later, the master–slave dialectic – a phase of consciousness in Hegel's *Phenomenology* – was an abstract struggle for recognition in a state of nature, long prior to the advent of civil society. In civil society, recognition occurs through property because this is the index of individual freedom. Interestingly, both struggles involve a renunciation of, and mastery over, the immediate demands of existence. For Hegel (as for Locke) possession of oneself entails overcoming one's *"immediate existence"* and becoming one's own property (*EPR*, §57). My body as a purely immediate or natural existence with its disorderly appetites, says Hegel, is not in conformity with my mind. I possess my life and body only insofar as my will is in them (*EPR*, §47). Once we are literally thus in possession of ourselves, we have, according to Hegel, attained a selfhood characterized by a freedom whose external form is property. Hegel even goes so far as to say that "in his property a person exists for the first time as reason" because it is in property that she supersedes her immediate existence or "pure subjectivity" (*PR*, §41, *Add*). A contract enshrines mutual recognition as persons and property owners; it expresses a relation between one will and another (*EPR*, §71).

For Hegel, then, property is an expression and recognition of a person's individuality and subjective freedom, a freedom that characterizes the modern era. Freedom of personality, says Hegel, began to blossom through the spread of Christianity about 1,500 years ago; but it was only very recently that the "*freedom of property* has been recognized here and there as a principle" (*EPR*, §62). Hegel characterizes civil society as composed of *Burghers* or bourgeois (literally, free inhabitants of a *Burgh* or town), who are "private persons" focused on their own (civil) interests rather than political life (*PR*, §187, 190). Bourgeois society, as Hegel describes it, comprises an aggregate of such free individuals exercising their rights to property. Civil society, he says, is

> an association of members as *self-sufficient individuals* in what is therefore a *formal universality*, occasioned by their *needs* and by the legal constitution as a means of security for persons and property, and by an external organization [the State] for attaining their particular and common interests. (*EPR*, §157; *PR*, §157)

In other words, each of these individuals, while following his self-interest, is also pursuing the "universal" aims of the good of the community as a whole. But this pursuit of the universal is "abstract" because (a) it is at this stage merely unconscious and implicit, and (b) it is not directed by the higher authority of the State. A little later, Hegel explains that in civil society, universality exists only abstractly, as the right to property (*EPR*, §208). Implicit in Hegel's comments is that the sphere of business presupposes the right to property inasmuch as this is a requisite of economic efficiency and the promotion of trade.

3.3   The Characteristics of Bourgeois Society

What are the features of capitalist society, according to Hegel? To begin with, it is a realm that fosters the free exercise of individuality: "to *particularity* it gives the right to develop and express itself in all directions"

(*EPR*, §184). Each individual feels the need to assert himself by "some distinctive quality," and man is concerned with "*his own opinion*" (*EPR*, §193–4). We need to recall that the sphere of bourgeois society for Hegel represents the second dialectical phase of ethical life, the phase of "difference" and of externalization.[9] In this phase, the level of thought attained by members of a society is that of the Understanding, which has the ability to universalize and to perceive differences. However, since the Understanding perceives the world atomistically, as a series of intrinsically unconnected finite objects, it does not have the capacity to resolve differences, to see these objects – including the self and other selves – as part of a larger totality. Education in bourgeois society, says Hegel, "is the education of the understanding in general," requiring not merely the possession of a "multiplicity of ideas and facts, but also a flexibility and rapidity of mind." Moreover, what Hegel calls "practical" education is acquired through what he effectively describes as the bourgeois work ethic, through the discipline of work, the "*habit of being occupied* in one way or another," and of adapting one's activity to the material worked on and the interests of other workers even as one realizes one's own aptitudes (*EPR*, §197).

Indeed, for Hegel, civil society *is* the State "as the Understanding envisages it" (*PR*, §183, 187). In other words, the State as conceived by the Understanding is the capitalist market, comprising an atomistic mass of individuals, each seeking his private interests with only an abstract or implicit apprehension of any universal aim or interest. Hegel even goes so far as to say that civil society estranges the individual from family ties, and that each individual is a "*son of civil society*" which is a "*universal family*" (*EPR*, §238–9). Moreover, imbued with this level of understanding (if you will pardon the pun), the individual is divided, torn between universality and his own particularity, between an abstractly apprehended universal good and his own bodily appetites, struggling against his own "pure subjectivity of demeanor, against the immediacy of desire, against the empty subjectivity of feeling and the caprice of inclination." Hegel states that the final purpose of education in the civil sphere is precisely to facilitate this struggle (*EPR*, §107; *PR*, §107). Anyone who has raised children will be well acquainted with this struggle, which is perhaps endemic to humanity but is liable to be intensified in a culture grounded upon a free market and what Hegel calls free subjectivity.

---

[9] Buchwalter usefully argues that Hegel's appreciation of the "modalities of modern economic life" led him to integrate principles of "negativity" and "finitude" into his account of absolute philosophy (*HC*, 6).

The movements of "reciprocal production and exchange" in civil society, says Hegel, become crystallized in the division into three basic classes, which again crucially exhibit a dialectical movement. The "substantial" or immediate class is the agricultural class, whose mode of subsistence is tied to nature and traditional ties of family, owing little to "reflection" (thought) or independence of will (*EPR*, §203). The next class is the "reflecting" or business class. Whenever Hegel talks of "reflection," he is referring to the level of thought characteristic of Understanding. For its means of livelihood, this class adapts raw materials and it "relies for its livelihood on its *work*, on *reflection* and the understanding, and essentially on its mediation of the needs and work of others." The work of this class is divided into craftsmanship, mass production or manufacture, and the business of exchange, principally "through the universal means of exchange, namely money, in which the abstract value of all goods is actualized – trade" (*EPR*, §204). The third class is the "universal class" of civil servants, which addresses the "*universal interests* of society" (*EPR*, §205). Hegel does emphasize that our belonging to a given class, while dependent to some extent on birth and other accidental circumstances, is finally determined by our individual will (*EPR*, §206).

For Hegel, then, the business class is the driving force of civil society, existing as the middle term between a relatively immobile agricultural class and a civil service that is employed by the State. It is the business class that is characterized by a focus on the particular, on private ends (*EPR*, §250). Hegel does not speak of a working class, though, as we shall see in a moment, he does anticipate some of Marx's insights into how capitalism engenders a divide between rich and poor. Hegel was astutely aware of the dangers of an unbridled market, and had he been alive today he might be shocked to see his worst nightmares realized, for example, in the effects of deregulation on Wall Street.

At the root of these nightmares was the prospect of unrestrained individuality, which is bound, ultimately, to prove destructive. Hegel issues a warning which rings familiar to us in the age of global capitalism:

> Particularity [*für sich*] in itself, on the one hand indulging itself in all directions as it satisfies its needs, contingent arbitrariness, and subjective caprice, destroys itself and its substantive concept in the act of enjoyment; on the other hand, the satisfaction of need, necessary and accidental alike, is accidental because it breeds new desires without end, is in thoroughgoing dependence on caprice and external accident, and is held in check by the power of universality. In these contrasts and their complexity, civil society affords a spectacle of extravagance and want as well as of the physical and ethical degeneration common to them both. (*EPR*, §185; *PR*, §185)

Here we have a clear statement of the ills of a society based on unrestrained individualism and what Hegel calls "negative" or unrestrained freedom. The multiplication of needs becomes arbitrary and endless, and the distinction between necessary and accidental need becomes confused. In such an endlessly self-propelling market, there arises not only a gulf between luxury and penury, but also "ethical degeneration." Interestingly, Hegel also notes the physical "degeneration" that accompanies both extravagance and want.

It should be mentioned that Hegel was not in favor of popular elections because he thought this would give a voice to individuals who would vote on the basis of mere caprice and subjective whims. Popular suffrage, he thought, would lead to electoral indifference, with the election in danger of falling into the "control of a few people, of a faction," which would not represent the general interest (*EPR*, §311, *Rem*). He characterized public opinion as a "hotch-potch of truth and endless error" (PR, §317, *Rem*). He did believe, however, that "[a]ll ... branches of society ... have equal rights of representation" but that these rights should be exercised through the Estates Assembly in the legislature (*PR*, §311, *Rem*). Hegel also believed that a person can enter any class "on the strength of his skill," and that every citizen should have the right to join the "universal" class of civil servants (*PR*, §291, 308).

3.4 Anticipating Marx

Hegel crucially anticipates Marx in respect of his insights into both poverty and alienation through division of labor. To begin with the latter, Hegel observes that the distribution of economic needs and means brings about an "abstracting process" that results in division of labor. While the "abstraction of one man's skill and means of production from another's" completes the dependence of people upon one another in the satisfaction of their needs, it also "makes work increasingly *mechanical*, so that the human being is eventually able to step aside and let a *machine* take his place" (*EPR*, §198). Clearly, this anticipates Marx's views of alienation inasmuch as Hegel sees work as the essential medium for the realization of one's subjectivity and individuality. When work becomes mechanized and specialized, it is no longer an expression of oneself.[10]

---

[10] In the second *Philosophy of Spirit* (*Realphilosophie II*), Hegel also talks about the "abstract" and mechanized labor that is one of the consequences of division of labor. Human labor becomes abstract labor because it no longer supplies natural needs but the multiplicity of social needs. A vast number of people "are condemned to a labour that is totally stupefying." *Hegel and the*

As regards poverty, Hegel acknowledges that economic disparity is inherent in capitalism, in the complex of accidents that drive the market, together with unequal access to resources and skills.[11] Civil society's restless promotion of individualism, and the urge to maximize profits through redistribution of labor and the means of production, in fact, aggravates such inequality (*EPR*, §185, 243). There arises a penurious class, a "rabble of paupers," from whom society has "withdrawn ... the natural means of acquisition ... their poverty leaves them more or less deprived of all the advantages of society, of the opportunity of acquiring skill or education of any kind, as well as of the administration of justice, the public health services, and often even of the consolations of religion." In this "rabble" is created a "loss of the sense of right and wrong, of honesty and ... self-respect" (*PR*, §241, 244).

Hegel anticipates Marx not only in viewing poverty as a structural concomitant to capitalism but equally in seeing it as one side of an extreme polarization. At the same time that mass poverty is engendered, there arises "the concentration of disproportionate wealth in a few hands" (*PR*, §244). At one point, Hegel comes very close to the formulations of Marx in saying that the multiplication of needs and their satisfaction beget luxury on the one hand, but at the same time "dependence and want increase *ad infinitum*, and the material to meet these is permanently barred to the needy man because it consists of external objects with the special character of being property, the embodiment of the free will of others" (*PR*, §195). Here Hegel, like Marx, characterizes poverty in terms of differential relations to property; in Hegel's definition, the poor person is effectively deprived of freedom since property does not enshrine her free will.

Unable to offer a solution for poverty, Hegel concludes by observing this major contradiction of capitalism: that "despite an excess of wealth civil society is not rich enough, i.e. its own resources are insufficient to check excessive poverty and the creation of a penurious rabble" (*PR*, §245). In fairness to Hegel, the situation he describes here is one where the individualistic tendencies of civil society are given free reign (though there were a number of peasant uprisings in Hegel's Prussia at the end of the eighteenth century, which must have inspired his distaste), and the

---

Human Spirit: A Translation of the Jena Lectures on the Philosophy of Spirit (1805–6), trans. Leo Rauch (Detroit: Wayne State University Press, 1983), pp. 121, 139–40.

[11] See Thomas Piketty's interesting analysis of this discrepancy between rich and poor as a global phenomenon in *Capital in the Twenty-First Century*, pp. 430–70.

final goal of human community as Hegel conceives it is not civil society but the State. In long retrospect, however, we can see that the tendencies he describes have become exacerbated on a global scale, beyond anything that he might have imagined.

3.5 Capitalism and Colonialism

Again, before Marx, Hegel saw that capitalism was intrinsically imperialistic: "This inner dialectic of civil society thus drives it – or at any rate drives a specific civil society – to push beyond its own limits and seek markets, and so its necessary means of subsistence, in other lands" (*PR*, §246). What is the "inner dialectic"? The "this" refers to the previous paragraph, which described the dialectic of wealth and poverty, and civil society's inability to transcend it. Hence, imperial expansion of its markets is one way in which civil society can increase its wealth and means of subsistence. But for Hegel, such expansion is an integral element of a market driven by industry. Family life, Hegel observes (and by implication the life of the agricultural classes), is rooted to the soil. In contrast, the "natural element for industry, animating its outward movement, is the sea." The bourgeois work ethic, like the capitalist market and the pursuit of profit, involves risk and adventure. Since the "passion for gain involves risk," says Hegel, "industry though bent on gain yet lifts itself above it; instead of remaining rooted to the soil and the limited circle of civil life with its pleasures and desires, it embraces the element of flux, danger, and destruction" (*PR*, §247).

We are reminded here of the master–slave dialectic, but now the players are different: the "master," the one who is willing to risk all and conquer the world, is the bourgeoisie; while the "slave" is he who is content (like the agricultural class) to remain in the "circle of civil life," repeating endlessly the lifestyle and cycles of the past. Another contrast is also pertinent here: in his philosophy of history, Hegel had drawn a stark contrast between an outward-looking Europe, orientated toward the sea beyond its own borders, and a stagnant Asia, sunk in tradition and superstition. He draws exactly the same contrast in this paragraph between Europe on the one hand, and Egypt and India on the other, which have remained stagnant in "miserable superstition" because they "eschewed sea-faring" (*EPR*, §247; *PR*, §247). So, for Hegel, imperial conquest is driven not only by necessities of the market but by the qualities integral to that market such as the desire to expand one's horizon, to encounter and overcome otherness, and to establish communication between distant countries. The sea becomes a symbol of all these qualities, a symbol of the expansive nature of capitalism itself – which is embodied, as we shall soon see, in the expansive movement of the Hegelian dialectic. Hegel appears to support colonizing activity both when it is "sporadic," as in individual ventures and when it is "systematic." Indeed, he explicitly states that the public authority should undertake a "directive function" in imperial exploits (*PR*, §249).

3.6   Hegel and Economics

The foregoing furnishes an incomplete picture of Hegel's vision of civil society; it represents that part of civil society comprised by an aggregation of individual interests and economic competition. To get a fuller picture, we need to recall that Hegel sees civil society as composed of three elements: a system of needs, the protection of property through the justice system, and the molding of particular interests into common interests by what Hegel calls "corporations" (*EPR*, §188). The "system of needs" is an idea that Hegel adapts from Adam Smith, the idea that one person's need and satisfaction of this is mediated "through his work and ... satisfaction of the needs of *all the others*" (*EPR*, §188). Smith, of course, had famously declared in his *Wealth of Nations* (1776) that individuals, if left (*laissez-faire*) to work in their own rational self-interest, would unwittingly contribute to the economic betterment of a society. When a person directs his labor, says Smith, "in such a manner as its produce may be of the greatest value, he intends only his own gain, and he is in this, as in many other cases, led by an invisible hand to promote an end which was no part of his intention."[12] Hegel cites the bourgeois economists Smith, J. B. Say, and David Ricardo as the proponents of political economy, which is a science that has "arisen out of the conditions of the modern world" and which starts "from this view of needs and labour" (*EPR*, §189, *Rem*; *PR*, §189, *Rem*).

So, beneath the appearance of self-interest lie the universal laws of economics. These laws form the framework of the sphere of civil society, whose actual content is the pursuit of selfish ends. Hegel even paraphrases Smith's principle of the invisible hand: "this medley of arbitrariness [in civil society] generates universal characteristics by its own working ... To discover this necessary element here is the object of political economy"

---

[12] Adam Smith, *The Wealth of Nations* (1776; rpt. New York: Alfred A. Knopf, 1910), bk. IV, chap. 2, §9, p. 400.

(*PR*, §189, Add). The main principle that Hegel derives from political economy is that needs and the means of satisfying them necessitate a "reciprocal relation of individuals to one another" (*PR*, §192). In other words, human beings come to realize that in order to attain their own ends, they must work with others so that, as Hegel says, in the "attainment of selfish ends ... there is formed a system of complete interdependence, wherein the livelihood, happiness, and legal status of one man is interwoven with the livelihood, happiness, and rights of all" (*PR*, §183).

While this "system of needs" creates a framework of interdependence within which unbridled individualism might be curtailed or at least directed by an invisible dialectic toward more universal ends, Hegel does not quite share Smith's benign vision of self-interest. Marx, as we shall see, viewed Hegel as occupying the standpoint of political economy. But this was not entirely accurate because Hegel characterizes political economy itself as working at the level of the Understanding, drawing general rules from a mass of details. In fact, Hegel calls this operation merely the "show [*Schneinen*] of rationality" (*PR*, §189, *Rem*). While the Understanding might regard civil society based on this "system of interdependence" as the "State," this is hardly Hegel's vision of the State. For Hegel, that system of interdependence contains an unresolved contradiction between the universal and particular, with no conscious harmony between self-interest and aims that might be acknowledged as universal. As we have seen, Hegel calls this the "external state, the state based on need, the state as the Understanding envisages it" (*PR*, §183).

Hence, in capitalism, the ethical order is split and "lost in its extremes," and the Idea exists "only as the *relative totality*" (*EPR*, §184). Hegel also rejects the view of classical liberalism and classical political economy that the function of the State consists in merely "protecting and securing everyone's life, property, and caprice," for this treats the State as an organization to satisfy material necessities and deprives the State of any "ethical character" (*PR*, §270). We have already seen that, even with the mutual dependence of needs among people, civil society according to Hegel cannot curb its riot of individualism and leads to an endless multiplication of needs, as well as an inexorable rift between luxury and destitution, and the need for perpetual expansion of markets through colonization.[13]

---

[13] As Michalis Skomvoulis argues, in Hegel's earlier writings also, such as the two *Philosophies of Spirit*, the "image of the market that emerges ... is not that of a harmonious order, but of a complex mechanism that is inherently unstable" (*HC*, 29).

3.7   Corporations

The instrument for restraining inordinate individualism, for Hegel, is the corporation. By *Korporation*, Hegel means neither what we mean by corporation nor a trade union but rather an organization that has been variously rendered as "trade guild" or "guild corporation" or "incorporated trade."[14] A member of civil society belongs voluntarily to a corporation on the basis of some "particular skill" or occupational pursuit. The corporation's responsibility is to oversee the interests of its specific area of business, to co-opt and educate its members, and to protect its members against contingencies of the market or personal misfortune. The corporation is like "a *second* family" to its members (*EPR*, §251–2). Hegel further explains that as the "*family* is the first *ethical* root of the state," so "the *corporation* is the second, and it is based in civil society" (*EPR*, §255).

Most importantly, membership of a corporation transforms the nature of work, making it rational instead of natural, freeing it from personal caprice and contingency, and elevating it to "conscious activity for a common end" (*EPR*, §254). The business class, says Hegel, is "essentially concentrated on the particular," and it is the corporation that reorientates it toward the "comparatively disinterested end" of the whole, though this "whole" is not the entire State but the group whose interest is represented by the corporation. Without the corporation, the "luxury and love of extravagance of the professional [*gewerbetreibenden*] classes" will lead to the ills and economic disparities already spoken of (*EPR*, §253). From a larger perspective, if the family comprises a type of unity, civil society represents a mass of "unorganized atoms," which return to a broader unity in the corporation. The family and the corporation are thus "the two moments" around which the atoms of civil society "revolve." According to this dialectic, the two moments of particularity and universality are united in an immediate fashion in the family; they are sundered in civil society; and united at a higher level in the corporation – but only in an "inward" or implicit fashion (*EPR*, §255; *PR*, §255). They will achieve true and explicit unity only in the State.

3.8   The State

It is the State, then, which embodies both the conscious unity of particular interests and genuinely universal interests. The State is a political

---

[14] See T. M. Knox's note on this, pointing out that *Korporationen* are societies that include both employers and employed, and comprise not only economic organizations but also religious bodies, learned societies, and town councils (*PR*, 360).

entity comprising the legislature, executive, and a judiciary concentrated into a constitutional monarchy (*EPR*, §260). As the third moment of ethical life, the State represents the culmination of the dialectic that moves from the family through civil society: from an immediate unity of universal and particular in the family, through their disjunction and division in civil society, to a conscious and rational unity in the State (the unity achieved by the corporation, we remember, is relative and incomplete). These three moments correlate to Hegel's distinction of the classes in terms of their occupation, namely agriculture, business or industry, and civil service. In the family (the sphere of the agricultural class), individuals are united with one another in an intuitive manner through love, which is reason in its immediacy.

In civil society (the sphere of business), individuals break free of family ties and pursue their own private ends, rising in this endeavor from the plane of intuition to that of Understanding. In the State (the sphere of civil service), the mentality of citizens rises to that of Reason whereby they see their own wills, their own interests, embodied in the universal will of the State, in its rational laws and institutions. There is a coincidence here of subjective and objective, of right and duty, of universal with particular will, which Hegel calls freedom. Only in the State, says Hegel, does an individual have ethical life, and he finds his satisfaction and his right realized in his duty. Hence, while the universal interests of the state are pursued, individual freedom, right, and fulfillment are also recognized. Rationality is precisely this unity of subjective and objective freedom (*EPR*, §258–60). There is a dialectical progression here on several levels:

family	>	civil society	>	State
agriculture (landowners)	>	industry (bourgeoisie)	>	civil service
immediate unity	>	difference	>	mediated unity
intuition	>	Understanding	>	Reason
subjectivity	>	objectivity	>	unity of subjective-objective

Moreover, we need to recall that this is part of a larger historical dialectic which moves from:

Ancient Greek world	>	Roman world	>	Modern (German) world

Hegel sees the Greek world as characterized by an immediate or unreflecting unity between individual will and the State. The Roman world, he sees as a realm of division and differentiation, of atomistic individuals, where private self-consciousness is alienated from the abstract universality of State power. In the German world, he sees the principle of subjective freedom (which existed only implicitly in the Greek world) as realized through the Protestant Reformation, first in the form of religious faith and then as matured into reflection and Reason. In this modern world, subjectivity, which itself has become rational, is reconciled with the objective and rational institutions and laws of the State. Hence, in the larger scheme of things, Hegel assimilates civil society or capitalism with the state of affairs in the Roman world, where individuals were defined in terms of their formal rights, a realm characterized by insatiable self-will.[15]

While Hegel famously proclaims that the Owl of Minerva flies only with the falling of dusk, that philosophy expresses the world as it is, after the fact, not as it might or will be (*EPR*, 13), his own vision of the State is largely idealistic. The State, as Hegel envisages it, never *arrives*, is never *realized*; we are left with capitalism or what he would call civil society with all of its defects and contradictions. Hegel's State – as the march of God, as the Absolute Idea realized on earth, as the coincidence of subjective with objective in Reason, as the historical supersession of superstition and despotism, as the sublation of the contradictions of capitalism – is predominantly speculation, an idealist dream. In this sense, Marx as we shall see, was right to say that Hegel's dialectic sublates capitalism merely to reinstate it in its alienated condition, though his understanding of Hegel's account of religion in this context is hardly accurate.

All in all, Hegel characterizes capitalist society (a) as an assemblage of individuals each pursuing his own interests, both economically and culturally; (b) as a realm which fosters individuality of outlook and expression, as well as relative equality of opportunity; (c) as a market where individuals essentially realize themselves through work and achieve recognition through their possession of property; (d) as a culture where the

---

[15] According to Richard Norman, Hegel regards the history of social and political life as a progression through various stages of the conceptual dialectic, from the ancient world where the individual is absorbed in the life of the community, through the feudal world, which is a "self-estranged" world where individuals exist only as isolated particulars in relations between vassal, lord, and monarch, and individuals experience as something alien the power of the state and the power of economic wealth to, finally, the modern world where the individual once again finds himself at home in the universal life of society by rationally and freely accepting it. Thus, the three epochs represent the principles of the universal, the particular, and their synthesis. See Norman and Sayers, *Hegel, Marx and Dialectic*, p. 41.

individual is internally riven, between an implicit recognition of universal interests and the vestigial demands of his own nature; and (e) as correlative with a mode of thought – the Understanding – which is analytic and able to perceive differences but not unity, since it is focused on particulars. In the next chapters, we can examine Hegel's notions of identity and how these issued at least in part through his engagement with the bourgeois political economists. This will set the stage for a deeper grasp of how his fundamental notions widely influenced literary theory.

CHAPTER 4

Hegel on Identity and Difference

It would probably not be an exaggeration to say that, for the last fifty or sixty years, literary theory has been insistently, even obsessively, concerned with the nature of identity. Indeed, in some sense, this has been true of much of Western thought in general. The systematic treatment of identity goes all the way back to Aristotle. The more recent phenomenon of "identity politics," centered on issues of gender, race, and ethnicity, has been growing since the 1970s and is still alive and well in our own era, though it continues to attract its fair share of critics in both political and academic realms. The number of books, articles, student papers, and media discussions devoted to the notion of identity is simply staggering.

What is it about "identity" that has generated so much recent interest and heated debate? Here is a statement from the Caribbean-American writer and activist Audre Lourde (1934–92), which succinctly encapsulates the various intersections and ramifications of identity:

> As a Black lesbian feminist comfortable with the many different ingredients of my identity, and a woman committed to racial and sexual freedom from oppression, I find I am constantly being encouraged to pluck out some one aspect of myself and present this as the meaningful whole, eclipsing or denying the other parts of myself. But this is a destructive and fragmenting way to live. My fullest concentration of energy is available to me only when I integrate all the parts of who I am, openly, allowing power from particular sources of my living to flow back and forth freely through all my different selves, without the restrictions of externally imposed definition.

Like many Critical Race theorists and Critical Race feminists, Lourde sees identity as "intersectional" and "multiplicative." Like David Hume, she sees the "self" as a convention, a fiction. Like Hegel and Marx, she posits an ideal of integrated identity. And like Judith Butler, she sees the self as a *performance* that actually brings many selves into play.

To understand the force of these modern conceptions of identity, we need to recall that since Aristotle until around the time of the Enlightenment, identity was typically conceived as something relatively stable and given. For Aristotle, identity is underlain by a notion that is central to his entire philosophy: the notion of "substance," which he regarded as the essence or fundamental reality underlying anything in the world. For Aristotle, the question "What is being?" (τί τὸ ὂν) is the same as "What is substance?" (τίς ἡ οὐσία).[1] The substance of a given entity is its essential identity.

The notion of identity and substance underlie the laws of logic as for-mulated by Aristotle and developed by numerous subsequent thinkers into our own day. These are the laws of identity, noncontradiction and the excluded middle. The law of identity states that "A is A."[2] This may seem obvious or trivial until we substitute any important concept for the term *A*. For example, if we say that "a Greek is a Greek," we are suggesting that a Greek has a certain identity, a fixed set of qualities. Continuing this example, the law of noncontradiction states that something cannot be both *A* and *not-A* (*Met, I-IX*, 1011b–13); so we would have to say that a person cannot be both a Greek and not a Greek. The law of the excluded middle tells us that something must be either *A* or *not-A* (*Met, I-IX*, 1011b–23); hence we must say that someone is *either* a Greek *or* not a Greek.

What these laws – which are the same law viewed from differing per-spectives – tell us, then, is that a Greek has a definable essence, a certain set of qualities, which non-Greeks do not have. And that there can be no mixture or blending of Greek and non-Greek qualities. Hence Greek might be associated with qualities such as rational, political, lawful – all equated with "civilization" – while non-Greek might be viewed as irra-tional, chaotically individual, and lawless – qualities associated with barbarianism. The Greeks (including Aristotle) did in fact think in this way, dividing the world into Greeks and barbarians. The rulers of other empires, including Persians, Romans, Arabs, Ottomans, and Europeans, similarly persuaded themselves of their own superiority and their own unique attributes.

---

[1] Aristotle, *The Metaphysics I-IX*, Loeb Classical Library, trans. Hugh Tredennick (London and Massachusetts: Heinemann/Harvard University Press, 1947), *I–IX*, Book ζ, pp. 312–3. Hereafter cited as *Met.I-IX*.

[2] Aristotle, *The Categories: On Interpretation; Prior Analytics*, Loeb Classical Library, trans. Harold P. Cooke and Hugh Tredennick (London and Massachusetts: Heinemann/Harvard University Press, 1973), 3a10–13; 3b34; 8a19. Hereafter cited as *Cat*.

Hence the laws of logic can be seen as highly coercive, suggesting a fixed essence of identity, establishing a hierarchy between terms, and refusing to allow for any middle ground. These features will be equally apparent if, instead of "Greek," we use the terms "man" and "woman," or "master" and "slave." These "laws" still govern the ways in which we think today, promoting a view of the world as classified into sharply distinct identities according to class, nation, race, religion, and gender.

In brief, we might say that "identity" is central to our conceptions of subjectivity and objectivity. As such, it underlies explorations into a wide number of issues, including the nature of the self, gender, family, authorship, textuality, history, human rights, law, and what we call reality. How we understand the notion of identity will shape seminally our conceptions of all of these issues. For example, in this era of globalism, we are often faced with a conflict between the idea of universal human rights and local customs, between international law and national legislation, between general goals of feminism and feminism as shaped by indigenous contexts. Underlying these debates are assumptions about identity: can we speak, even provisionally and strategically, of the "human"? Or of "woman"? I will argue that, in large part, Hegel gave us a vocabulary pertaining to identity and difference that enables us at least to formulate these questions in a manner that might address the demands of both universalism and regionalism.

4.1   Hegel on Identity and Difference

As expounded in Hegel's *Logic*, it is clear that dialectical thinking constitutes an attack upon traditional logic, which is based upon the notion of identity. Without understanding this, much of the import of modern literary and cultural theory – which reenacts this onslaught in altered contexts – will be lost. Hegel's own logic, enlisting the notion of "identity in difference," is in part an attempt to overcome the separations between thought and reality, subject and object, which were implied in the empiricist philosophies of Locke and Hume and made explicit in Kant's distinction of phenomena and noumena.

4.2   The Modes of Thought: Understanding, Dialectic, Speculation

Before we can understand Hegel's ideas about identity and difference, we need to recall that Hegel sees thought as operating on a number of levels, which are intrinsic to dialectical thinking. As we have seen, in his Lesser

Logic, Hegel distinguishes three basic modes of thought: Understanding (*Verstand*), which views the world as static and as composed of distinct or particular entities (*Enc,* §80); Dialectic (*Dialektik*), which ascertains the contradictory and dynamic nature of things, but is unable to reconcile these contradictions (*Enc,* §81); and Speculation, or "Positive Reason" (*Positiv-Vernünftige*) which "apprehends the unity of terms ... in their opposition" (*Enc,* §82).

The first of these, Understanding, is higher than reliance on our mere senses or immediate perception. It invests its objects with the form of universality. For example, we see a given object not simply as a mass of sense-impressions but as a "table." In other words, we recognize that its features, such as rectangularity or flatness, allow it to be placed under this particular category of objects. But the identity of a table, as given by the Understanding, is abstract, and isolated from that of other objects. Understanding tells us that the table is distinct from, say, the chair, or the iPhone. Hence, this is a separative and analytic type of thought which treats each object as distinct and independent, and which informs our everyday thinking about things. As we have seen, Hegel sees this mode of thought as characteristic of capitalism.

The principle of Understanding, then, is *identity* since it apprehends "existing objects in their specific differences" (*Enc,* §80, *Zus*). According to Hegel, this is the principle that informs mathematics and the empirical sciences. In one branch of mathematics, for example, magnitude is the feature highlighted; in geometry, we focus on figure. Similarly, each branch of knowledge identifies one or two features as the object of its sustained investigation. Hegel acknowledges that there is an indispensable place for the Understanding: without it, there would be no focus, no fixity or accuracy either in theory or practice. A political state, for example, needs a "clear differentiation of orders and callings"; and in a dramatic poem, the various characters need to be faithfully maintained, with their different aims and interests clearly exhibited. Indeed, the Understanding is crucial in philosophy, since every thought must be grasped in its full precision (*Enc,* §80, *Zus*).

The strength of Understanding, however, is also its limitation, according to Hegel: it cannot pass beyond a view of the world as comprising particular objects, all with their distinct identities, and all separate from one another, with no essential relation. This is where thought must move on to the "Dialectical" stage, where our "finite characterizations ... supersede themselves, and pass into their opposites." It should be said that Hegel is here using "Dialectic" in a specialized sense, which does not refer to the entire procedure that we usually call the Hegelian dialectic. Nor is he using it in its ordinary sense of an argumentative to and fro, a passing from one viewpoint to its opposite. Nor does he mean what he calls "Sophistry," which highlights a partial principle; for example, I could argue that my need to survive is the foremost consideration, and therefore that I am justified in stealing, lying, or doing whatever answers to this need (*Enc*, §81, *Zus*). Rather, Dialectic is "the indwelling tendency outwards by which the one-sidedness and limitation of the predicates of understanding is seen in its true light, and shown to be the negation of them" (*Enc*, §81).

What does Hegel mean by this? Fortunately, he gives an example. Using the mere Understanding, we see "life" and "death" as two separate phenomena. We will define them as having opposite characteristics, and the relation between them will be one of simple, abstract, difference or opposition. "Life" has one identity and "death" has another; these two identities are mutually distinct and different. In Hegelian terminology, we might say that "life" is identical with itself, and "death" is identical with itself, and that each is different from the other. When, however, we rise to a higher way of thinking – that of Dialectic – we will no longer view life and death as separate; we will see that the one flows into the other, and that each presupposes the other. In other words, life and death are no longer "self-identical": death is a very part of the identity of life and vice-versa. The two terms do not stand in some merely accidental relation or opposition but are essentially and *internally* related. The relation is not somehow external to the terms themselves but structures those very terms. In the same way, the terms "mother" and "daughter" structure each other: "daughter" cannot have meaning on its own, without relation to "mother." It is in this way that Dialectic demonstrates the "finitude of the partial categories of understanding" (*Enc*, §81, *Zus*).

Historically, Hegel traces Dialectic back to Plato, who gave it an objective form. With Socrates, who used the "dialectical" method of question and answer to advance a given philosophical inquiry, Hegel says that the dialectical element had a predominantly subjective form, namely irony. By this, Hegel appears to mean that "dialectic" characterized the intersubjective pursuit of knowledge. It was Plato, he says, who used the dialectical method to "show the finitude of all hard and fast terms of understanding" (*Enc*, §81, *Zus*). This could refer, firstly, to Plato's theory of Forms, whereby all things in the material or natural world are seen as finite and merely imperfect copies of their true essences, which exist in a higher world of pure ideas or essences. This is what Hegel himself calls the "Dialectic of the finite" (*die Dialektik des Endlichen*) whereby each finite thing is incomplete and contradictory as taken in isolation, and has its true being or essence elsewhere, in what is beyond it; Hegel often refers to this "beyond" as God, who is the Absolute, the only true and self-subsistent reality, on which all else is dependent (*Enc*, §81, *Zus*).[3]

More specifically, Hegel is referring to Plato's rather enigmatic dialogue *Parmenides*, which attempts both to justify the theory of Forms against various objections and – as part of the same process – to demonstrate that the absolute or all-encompassing *One* (for example, an essence or pure idea in the world of Forms) is also the *Many* or the multitude of particular things that exist in the physical world. The "one" and the "many" are merely different dimensions or aspects of the same reality: their identities are mutually defined. Hegel also sees Kant as a precursor of Dialectic. Kant had demonstrated the "antinomies" of pure reason: if we rely just on reason, without grounding our claims in sense-experience, we can argue with equal justification for two opposed things. For example, we can "prove" that there is a God and that there isn't; we can "prove" that the world has a beginning in time and that it doesn't. Hegel says that in modern times Kant "resuscitated the name of Dialectic, and restored it to its post of honour." His antinomies showed that "every abstract proposition of understanding, taken precisely as it is given, naturally veers round into its opposite" (*Enc*, §81, *Zus*).

A final, fascinating aspect of Dialectic relates to modern notions of deconstruction. We have seen Hegel's comments on skepticism in the *Phenomenology*. Here, he also stresses that skepticism is a belief in "the nothingness of all finite existence," a kind of "hopelessness" about everything that the Understanding views as stable and fixed. Hegel traces modern skepticism to an era just before Kant, and also to Kant's philosophy itself, which denies the truth of the "supersensible" and insists that we restrict our inquiries to the "facts of sense" (*Enc*, §81, *Zus*). Anticipating deconstruction, Hegel states that "when the Dialectical principle is employed by the understanding separately and independently ... Dialectic becomes scepticism; in which the result that ensues from its action is presented as a mere negation" (*Enc*, §81). Indeed, Hegel's term for Dialectic is "negative reason" (*negativ-vernünftige*) (*Enc*, §79; *Werke*, 8: 168).

As will be seen later in this book, this negative reason embodies the beginnings of what we would today call a deconstructive perspective,

---

[3] *Enzyklopädie der philosophischen Wissenschaften, Werke*, 8:174.

where we might see every entity as indiscriminately related to every other entity, with no hierarchy, no identifiable point of origin, no foundation, and no purpose. To go back to Hegel's example, we might see that "life" and "death" are related to each other and have their identity in the other. We might see, then, that the self-identity of each is undermined or destroyed, but we are frozen at this insight; we do not know how we might conceive any positive identity of these terms or how the connection between life and death might be viewed from a broader perspective. Or again, we might show that conventional morality is founded upon a concept such as "God," which is not a self-subsisting entity but merely subsists through *relation* to a collective humanity. But once we have "destroyed" that concept, we have nothing with which we can replace it. A further example might be gleaned from feminism and gender studies, which have deconstructed the concept of "woman" as defined by centuries of male thinking and control. However, as of now, it might be argued that these disciplines are still, historically, at the stage of "Dialectic" since they have not yet somehow replaced those discredited understandings of "woman" with a positive notion that commands general consensus.

Having arrived at this impasse of pure negation, we must, according to Hegel, move on to a higher stage of thinking called Speculation or "Positive Reason," which "apprehends the unity of terms (propositions) in their opposition" (*die Einheit der Bestimmungen in ihrer Entgegensetzung*) (*Enc*, §82; *Werke*, 8: 176). What does Hegel mean by this? To begin with, he points out that, while Dialectic is "Negative Reason," which dismantles or undermines the one-sided propositions of Understanding, the result of Dialectic is actually positive: It is not merely empty nothingness, but a product, a negation of specific propositions. Hence, Dialectic has shown us that "life" or "death" each has its identity beyond itself; applied to things as a whole, it shows us, negatively, that the identity of every phenomenon lies beyond its own immediacy, dispersed in relations that lie beyond it. In other words, its identity is "externalized" in mediation.

This is all we can discern from the vantage point of Dialectic. It is a negative vision which tells us merely what identity is *not*, that identity is not comprised by what lies immediately before us. Its positive potential lies in the fact that it is part of a process: the negation that has led to it anticipates a further negation – of itself – into the broader perspective of Speculation. It preserves the truth of what it has negated, and its own truth is preserved in its own negation by Speculation. In the stage of Speculation, we will once more view "life" as self-identical, but its identity here is not immediate but mediated: Our concept of "life" will include within itself both its identity with, and difference from, death.

4.3   Hegel on Identity

We can now see how Hegel's notions of identity and difference diverge from the traditional treatment of these notions. Hegel's *Logic* starts off by examining what philosophers since Aristotle have identified as the essential subject matter of philosophy: being. As we have seen, Aristotle himself identifies being with "substance" or "essence" (οὐσία), which he thinks of as the most basic reality of things. For Aristotle, "substance" refers to the essential being or substrate of something, of which qualities can be predicated. For example, in the sentence "the horse is black," the word "horse" represents substance and "black" is the predicate. But for Hegel, "being" is merely the beginning of a long process which shows that what we call "existence" and the world "out there" is something highly mediated by our own thought processes.

Hegel takes us through his well-known dialectic, already encountered, whereby "being" gives way before its opposite, "nothing," and the two are united in "becoming." Becoming, then, is the "truth" of being and nothing, the higher unity in which they are both "sublated" (transcended and yet preserved). In this dialectical manner, Hegel examines the categories of what he designates as "objective logic" and "subjective logic," moving from the sphere of "being" through the sphere of "essence" to the sphere of the "notion" (notional thought being the highest mode of understanding, that which comprehends what is universal in an object).

The first division of the *Logic*, then, is the "Doctrine of Being." It is in the next division, the "Doctrine of Essence," that Hegel addresses the notions of "identity" and "difference." In general, the realm of Essence is a realm of "reflection" upon the realm of Being. It is the realm of "being as ideality" or being as mediated by the categories of thought, namely identity, difference, and ground. The lesser *Logic* proceeds, then, according to a schema that looks something like this:

Hegel explains that the standpoint of "essence" is that of *reflection*, whereby we pass beyond simply looking things in their immediacy and

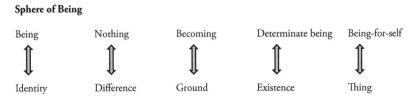

Sphere of Being

Being	Nothing	Becoming	Determinate being	Being-for-self
⇕	⇕	⇕	⇕	⇕
Identity	Difference	Ground	Existence	Thing

Sphere of Essence

view them as dependent upon something else, something that is outside of them. Essence is the sphere in which the *implicit* contradictions in the sphere of Being are made *explicit* (*Enc*, §112, *Zus*). The essence of something is defined, in part, as its permanent substratum, that which persists throughout its changing stages or relations. But we should also recall that for Hegel, the "Absolute is the Essence" (*Enc*, §112). Hegel sometimes speaks of the Absolute as God, and in this section of the Logic he affirms that the only being that has its essence within itself is God, and that whatever is finite has its essence outside itself: "All else outside God, if separated from him, possesses no essentiality: in its isolation it becomes a mere show or seeming, without stay or essence of its own" (*Enc*, §112, *Zus*).

As will emerge in a later chapter, such statements have been interpreted in a more secular sense by some commentators such as Alexandre Kojève to indicate that finite things have their essences outside of them, in their relations with numerous other things. If we wish to retain the religious underpinning, we might say that ultimately, these relations must extend outward with an infinite expansibility which achieves closure only in God. But this is not quite accurate because Hegel goes on to tell us that Essence – including God as Essence – is not somehow separate from its material embodiment or expression. As seen earlier, for Hegel, God is manifested through the progress of human history. Here is another example that Hegel offers: A person's "character" should not be thought of as some purely internal essence; rather, it is expressed through the various manifestations of her conduct (*Enc*, §112, *Zus*).

In general, "identity" in the sphere of Essence corresponds to immediate "being" in the sphere of Being: both are immediate and therefore abstract forms of self-relatedness. In other words, "being" was viewed by our sense perception as something simple and self-contained; when we move to a higher plane, mediated by thought, what appeared to our senses as simple or abstract being is now viewed by the Understanding as simple or abstract identity, as identity which is somehow self-contained (or in Hegel's terminology self-identical or self-related). As Hegel has it, identity is "Being as Ideality" (*das Sein als Idealität*) (*Enc*, §115, *Zus*; *Werke*, 8: 238). Another way of putting this would be to say that "identity" represents Understanding's view of "essence" as self-contained; or that essence as self-contained is embodied in simple self-relation or identity. So, we might view the essence of a table as contained within itself: In the sphere of Being, at the level of sense perception, we viewed the table as an independent object. In the sphere of Essence, at the level of thought or Understanding, we now view the essence of the table as self-contained, as having an independent identity.

The identity in question here – the identity questioned by so much literary theory – is "self-identity" (*Identität mit sich*). This, as Hegel explains, is identity that is treated as "quite aloof from difference." Such identity is abstract: It is formed by abstracting just one feature of something concrete and highlighting this; or by neglecting the variety of characteristics of something, and concentrating these into one (*Enc*, §115; *Werke*, 8: 236). An instance of the first kind of abstraction – as recognized, for example, by Critical Race theorists – would be to focus exclusively on my gender as a black woman and to ignore my race or color. We engage in the second kind of abstraction when we lump a group of people under the same category – for example, "Africans" – while disregarding important differences among Africans themselves or other important characteristics they may have.

We now come to the crux of Hegel's views on identity, which are often echoed by literary theories without recognizing their origin in Hegel. He challenges the so-called laws of logic or laws of thought. As seen above, the first of these is the law of identity, which states simply that "A is A"; the second is the law of noncontradiction, which stipulates that something cannot be both A and not-A; and the third, the law of the excluded middle, maintains that something must be *either* A *or* not-A. Given the sheer historical and ideological weight of these laws, given their profound and pervasive influence, we can see that Hegel's undermining of them represents on some levels a radical break with the Western philosophical tradition. It would be oversimplistic to attribute this break entirely to Hegel; no doubt it was prepared for and anticipated by Hume, Kant, and others. But it is in Hegel that it achieves systematic articulation as part of his endeavor to formulate the principles of dialectical thinking.

Hegel sees the first law, that of identity, as saying that "Everything is identical with itself." This maxim, he tells us, is not a true law of thought but "merely the law of abstract understanding" (*Enc*, §115). In other words, Understanding, which sees the world in terms of discrete and separate entities, is based upon this principle of abstract identity, which views any object or entity as self-identical and independent. But Hegel points out that the "universal experience" of humankind contradicts this abstract law, and shows that no object or existent ever conforms to it. The law is also contradicted by the very propositional form of language wherein the predicate promises to give us information that is not in the subject. For example, if we say "The man is tall," the predicate (tall) gives us information that is not in the subject (man). But, as Hegel says, statements such as "A planet is a planet" or "mind is mind" are tautologies where the predicate adds nothing to what is already contained in the subject (*Enc*, §115).

Hegel tells us then, that it is important to arrive at a proper understanding of the true meaning of identity: "we must especially guard
against taking it as abstract Identity, to the exclusion of all Difference."
He goes on to say that this is the touchstone for distinguishing bad philosophy from genuine philosophy (*Enc*, §115, *Zus*). As we will see later,
it could be argued that modern literary theory has made the reverse mistake – that of embracing abstract difference, to the exclusion of all identity. Hegel further tells us that God is "absolute identity" and that things
in the world "subsist only as the reflection of his power and glory" (*Enc*,
§115, *Zus*). Again, interpreting this even in secular terms, the implication is that finite things have only a relative identity; in other words,
they are not independent or self-identical, but rather their identity is
incomplete and finds completion only in a totality that Hegel terms the
Absolute. Finally, there is an entirely different dimension of identity, that
of the human self or human consciousness. In this respect, Hegel actually
defines identity as "self-consciousness." It is the ability to comprehend
oneself as "I" which distinguishes human beings from nature (*Enc*, §115,
Zus). We will consider this dimension of identity later.

4.4   Hegel on Difference

We now arrive at the notion that might be said to have dominated
literary theory over the last half-century or more: difference. Theory's
obsession with identity has ironically been founded upon its views of difference. But these views often have their origin in Hegel, who urges once
again that, like identity, difference is not something independent. In fact,
difference flows from identity and is already contained within it. Abstract
identity is what Hegel calls "negative self-relation," harboring an internal
distinction "between it and itself" (*Enc*, §116, *Zus*). In other words, it is
related to itself through mediation, through its connections with what is
initially presumed to be outside it. For example, at one time, my "self"
was not mediated by a spouse (though it was of course mediated by relations to other people and relatives). But now, my wife is very much a part
of who "I" am. My relationship to myself is mediated through her – and
this "mediated" self is, I hope, a little wiser for having gone beyond its
initial state and having returned to it harboring broader and more mature
conceptions of the world. Having said that, I doubt that she would ever
describe me as wise.

Hegel speaks of two broad kinds of "difference." First, there is "immediate difference" (*unmittelbarer Unterschied*), which is mere "diversity"

or "variety." In a statement that is fundamental to Hegel's thinking, and to his connections with literary theory, he explains: "In Diversity the different things are each individually what they are, and unaffected by the relation in which they stand to each other. This relation is therefore external to them" (*Enc*, §117; *Werke*, 8: 239). In other words, in this way of looking at "difference," we view the relation between two terms as external to the terms themselves, and we view the terms as independent of each other and unaffected by their relation. For example, we could view the terms "girl" and "man" as independent of each other; their relation, we would say, does not affect the essence of either. This, we recall, is the way of thinking characteristic of the Understanding that views everything as separate and independent. Hegel sees this mode of thought as predominant in the empirical sciences, which habitually employ external comparison to "reduce existing differences to Identity." For example, in geometry, two different shapes, a triangle and a quadrangle, might be seen as identical in magnitude (*Enc*, §117, *Zus*).

The second type of "difference" is what Hegel calls "implicit" or "essential" difference – for which he also uses the terms "determinate" or "specific" difference (*Unterschied an sich selbst, bestimmter Unterschied*). When we view "difference" in this light, we advance beyond mere diversity or variety to actual opposition. We now view the characteristics of things as being "in completely reciprocal relation. The one of them cannot be thought without the other ... In the case of difference ... we like to see identity, and in the case of identity we like to see difference" (*Enc*, §118, *Zus*; *Werke*, 8: 242). In this perspective, "the different is not confronted by *any* other but by *its* other ... either is stamped with a characteristic of its own only in its relation to the other" (*Enc*, §119, *Zus*). Here we have what is called the doctrine of "internal relations" whereby a relation between the two terms structures the terms themselves. If, for example, we look at the relation between "wife" and "husband," we can see that neither term can possess meaning in isolation: it presupposes the other term. The very meaning of "husband" lies beyond the term itself, in the relation which designates it.

On this basis – that relations are internal – Hegel impugns the common view of the law of the excluded middle, which he regards as a maxim of the abstract Understanding. This law demands that something be either A or not-A. The idea that something has to be "either" one of two opposites "or" the other overlooks the circumstance that these opposites exist only in relation, and that their relation is essential to either. The same argument underlies Hegel's critique of the law of noncontradiction, which states that something cannot be both A and not-A. But there is something further in his critique, namely, that the "negative" as envisioned by these laws is an abstract negative, indicating merely a contentless term in "not-A." For example, we might, in this traditional logic, view something as either blue or not-blue. But "not-blue" is merely an abstract negative, embodying contentless negation. What is "not-blue" could be rendered positive if it were designated, for example, as "yellow." In this case, we have two terms which, in relation to each other, could be both positive and negative. As Hegel puts it,

> the Negative in its own nature is quite as much Positive ... Positive and negative are supposed to express an absolute difference. The two however are at bottom the same: the name of either might be transferred to the other ... Positive and negative are therefore intrinsically conditioned by one another, and are only in relation to each other. (*Enc*, 172–3)

We have already seen the radical potential of this formulation in Margaret Fuller's characterization of the relation between the sexes, where woman and man were exchangeable in their designation as "positive" or "negative." But the more general points to emerge from all this are that, firstly, for Hegel, nothing in the actual world answers to these laws of logic: nothing possesses self-existence or independent self-identity. The world does not present us with abstract choices in terms of "either ... or." Rather, "[c]ontradiction is the very moving principle of the world," and whatever exists harbors "difference and opposition in itself" (*Enc*, §119, *Zus*). We have seen that for Hegel, finite things have their essence beyond themselves, beyond their immediate existence.

Another way of expressing the last point would be to say, as Hegel does, that all finite things are inherently contradictory: there is a lack of "correspondence between their immediate being, and what they essentially are" (*ihr unmittelbares Dasein ... nicht entspricht, was sie an sich sind*), or between their current existence and their potential existence (*Enc*, §119, *Zus*; *Werke*, 8: 247). A thing "is" only in relation to its other. Hence "black" exists only in relation to "white," and the relation itself structures the content of the terms. The second, related, point is that, in contrast with our everyday way of viewing the world as full of separate and independent objects, the "aim of philosophy is to banish indifference, and to ascertain the necessity of things" (*Enc*, §119, *Zus*). In other words, philosophy aims to abrogate the given-ness of the world, the world as it strikes us in its immediacy as composed of unrelated particular things, and to lead us to a vision of the internal and essential unity of things. In Hegel's language, we cannot rest at either undifferentiated identity or indifferent diversity but must rather "ascertain the inner unity of all existence" (*Enc*, §118, *Zus*). For Hegel, then, no entity can be rationally understood independently of its larger contexts.

4.5 Literary Theory and Identity

It was mentioned in the introduction to this book that, from one aspect, literary theory in its many modulations could be viewed as an attack on the notion of identity as something fixed, or given, or static, as something that can subsist in isolation. In general, the conceptions of identity formed by literary theory – whether they derive directly from Hegel or from the heterological stream of thought that runs from Schopenhauer through Nietzsche and Bergson to Freud, Husserl, and Heidegger – are underlain by this notion of the internality of relations. This idea is taken up by literary theory on many levels: in its treatment of identity, of subjectivity and objectivity, of history, of language, and of the very notion of Reason itself. The very concepts of hybridity, dispersal, and the so-called politics of the fragment have emerged from such reconfigurations of identity. Whether we are, like Lacan, talking about the human self or, like Foucault and Barthes, about a work of art or literature, we now tend to see these as *internally* structured by a multitude of relations in both time and place.

We view the self, the work of art, and language as intrinsically relational, and as intrinsically historical constructs. Barthes famously saw the figure of the "author" as the "epitome and culmination of capitalist ideology" in literature. Once we challenge the notion of the author as embodying some unitary identity, this opens entirely new ways of viewing the text. No longer, says Barthes, does it linearly convey some "theological" meaning from the author-god, but it becomes, rather, a "multi-dimensional space" that harbors a variety of writings that blend and clash.[4] Our newer conceptions of identity as dynamic and relational forbid us from treating the mind as separate from the body, the Orient as distinct from the Occident; from treating "woman," "man," "black woman," and "white man" as anything other than constructs, as culturally sanctioned performances.

Indeed, as seen above, the fields of Critical Race and Critical Race feminist theory furnish one of the richest discourses about identity taking place today. Critical Race feminists characteristically see identity

---

[4] Roland Barthes, *Image: Music: Text*, trans. Stephen Heath (Glasgow: Fontana, 1982), pp. 143–6.

as the intersectional site of many factors: nationality, race, skin color, ethnicity, profession, minority status, religion, gender, parental status, marital status, sexuality, class, age, disability, welfare status, and immigration status.[5] What they are urging is a holistic understanding of identity which respects its fragmentary nature, as something always dynamic and changing, always having to be performed and re-performed according to context. What my students see in my classes is merely a performance that adheres to certain professional roles. They see me elegantly dressed, emitting an exquisite fragrance, and speaking in a mild-mannered and humorous way. If they could see me working out on a kick bag, or arguing with another motorist on the road, they would be astonished. Who can say which of these selves is me? They are all equally performed. And, perhaps disturbingly, am I "performing" when I speak to God in prayer? Is "God" a performance?

All of these are questions that have been enabled by Hegel, even in the pages of his staunchest foes. As we shall see throughout this book, many literary theorists have advanced – implicitly or explicitly – notions of "difference" that rehearse or modify Hegel's views, yet refuse to constrain these notions within any kind of metaphysical or religious or even political closure.[6] In the following two chapters, I want to examine how certain theorists have responded to Hegel's notion of identity. The next chapter will seek, with the help of Michael Hardt and Antonio Negri, to assess the significance of Hegelian identity within the broader historical and economic context of capitalism and the development of liberal humanism. A further chapter will examine Jacques Derrida's treatment of identity and difference.

---

[5] Such a notion of intersectional identity is beautifully articulated, for example, by Adrienne Katherine Wing in her edition of *Global Critical Race Feminism: An International Reader* (New York and London: New York University Press, 2000), pp. 7–12.

[6] Critiques of Hegel's notion of identity have also, of course, been conducted by philosophers. Carl G. Vaught, for example, makes an interesting attempt to exhibit the presence of "non-dialectical difference" in Hegel's thought, as in the concept of space or even in the connection between subject and object, which develop in opposing directions, "Hegel and the Problem of Difference," in *Hegel and His Critics*, ed. Desmond, pp. 36–8, 41–3. Hereafter cited as *HHC*.

CHAPTER 5

Hegelian Identity and Economics

The implications of Hegel's notion of identity – as something never contained within its own immediate form, as always dispersed beyond itself into its differences from other entities, as an ongoing process – are both profound and extensive. They could be pursued in many directions, but here I will restrict myself – since this has been a persistent theme of the current book – to the implications as they intersect with Hegel's treatment and expression of capitalism and liberal-humanist thought. Let us take, then, a step back to consider what is happening here in Hegel's philosophy. Let us step back beyond Hegel's text or even his immediate biographical context to consider the broader ideological and epistemic movements of European history in the midst of which his philosophy arose. Hegel is often regarded as *the* philosopher of modernity. He is the thinker who expressed most comprehensively not only the movements and contradictions of modern bourgeois society but also the historical emergence of this society from the medieval world.

5.1   The Dialectic of Modernity

In their study entitled *Empire*, Michael Hardt and Antonio Negri suggest that European modernity was comprised by three moments. First, there was a revolutionary humanism, which affirmed the "plane of immanence" and rejected any transcendent authority over worldly affairs. Humanists were committed to a project of "recentering thought on the singularity of being" (*Emp*, 71). In other words, they regarded everything in this world as independent and as having its essence and worth within itself. It was no longer referred to as some transcendent realm (*Emp*, 73). The second, antithetical, moment was a conservative and reactionary attempt – not only by the Catholic counter-reformation, but by Descartes, who marks "the beginning … of bourgeois ideology," and by the Enlightenment itself – to impose *mediation* upon such singularity by reconfiguring transcendent authority within a worldly context. Developments in all fields were tied to "a grand narrative that European modernity told about itself, a tale told in a transcendental dialect" (*Emp*, 80).

Hardt and Negri see this reactionary impetus as climaxing in Kant, and Hegel, where the authority of God and the church was replaced by the "transcendent" authority of the state. Indeed, this last move is regarded by the authors as the third moment of modernity, which was a "temporary and partial" resolution or synthesis of this antithesis achieved through configuring the state as the locus of sovereignty.[1] According to Negri and Hardt, Hegel effectively completed the transcendental project by arguing that modern humanity could only be "free" by subordinating itself to laws, and that the "immanent goal of the multitude" is subsumed under the transcendent power of the state. In Hegel's philosophy, no given entity is just allowed to be itself, to strive, desire, or love. Its potential is always closed off, and it must always be seen in relation to the universal ends embodied in the general or state interest. The authors express this poignantly in their observation that "the analogical being of the medieval Christian tradition is resurrected as a dialectical being" (*Emp*, 82).

If such a transcendental apparatus comprises the *form* of modern sovereignty, say the authors, its *content* is "capitalist development and the affirmation of the market as the foundation of the values of social reproduction ... European modernity is inseparable from capitalism" (*Emp*, 85–6). The connection between the form and content of modern sovereignty, they aver, is "fully articulated" by Adam Smith who synthesizes the contradiction between private enrichment and public interest. In Smith's hands, the modern state's political transcendence is defined as an economic transcendence, and Smith's "theory of value was the soul and substance" of the theory of the modern state.

Such a synthesis, Hardt and Negri affirm, was effected by Hegel, who invokes the state in order to guarantee that public and private interests coincide. In Hegel, the "synthesis of the theory of modern sovereignty and the theory of value produced by capitalist political economy is finally realized ... Modern European sovereignty is capitalist sovereignty, a form of command that overdetermines the relationship between individuality and universality as a function of the development of capital" (*Emp*, 86–7). In such a state, where the synthesis of sovereignty and capital is "fully accomplished," the multitude and all singularities are subsumed

---

[1] Michael Hardt and Antonio Negri, *Empire* (Cambridge, MA and London: Harvard University Press, 2000), pp. 70–81. Hereafter cited as *Emp*.

under an ordered totality, in which social labor is produced and ordered (*Emp*, 87–9).

5.2 Hegelian Identity and Bourgeois Economy

In his extensive scholarly analysis of Hegel's debts to the bourgeois economists of the Scottish Enlightenment, Norbert Waszek has argued that Hegel's adoption of a "middle course" between liberalism and interventionism, between individual rights and the universal interest embodied by the state, was deeply influenced by Adam Smith and James Steuart.[2] We might add that Hegel's notion of identity was an important component of this dialectic between the particular or "singular" and the universal. Drawing on both Waszek's insights and the account of modernity offered by Hardt and Negri, I hope to give some indication of how Hegel's very conception of identity was at least partly informed by his struggle to express the inner economic dialectic that he saw as shaping bourgeois society.

The first point to be made in this regard is that Hegel saw in bourgeois political economy a model of interrelation, a system of complete interdependence, where no element could somehow subsist "in itself," in isolation; where the identity of everything was intrinsically dynamic, always in process, always in motion, and always depthlessly reciprocal. As Waszek notes, Hegel's first close engagement with Smith's *Wealth of Nations* occurred in 1803–4; and in his early writings, specifically in the Jena manuscripts, he reproduces Steuart's and Smith's socioeconomic model of "universal interdependence" of labor and the free exchange of its products (*SE*, 132, 160). Waszek observes that the basic elements of Hegel's model of economic life consisted of "man's particular needs, the equally particular means to satisfy them, and human labour as the dialectical mediation between needs and means; the further specifications like money and exchange ... emerge out of those basic elements" (*SE*, 147).

---

[2] Norbert Waszek, *The Scottish Enlightenment and Hegel's Account of "Civil Society"* (Dordrecht, Boston, and London: Kluwer Academic Publishers, 1988), p. 8. Hereafter cited as *SE*. The Scottish Enlightenment thinkers included the philosophers Francis Hutcheson and David Hume, the philosopher-historian Adam Ferguson, and the political economists Adam Smith and Sir James Steuart who first used the expression "political economy" in a book title as in his *An Inquiry into the Principles of Political Economy* (1767). Smith's *Wealth of Nations* was published in 1776. According to Waszek, Hegel's "foremost masters" in political economy were Smith and Steuart (*SE*, 181). It is important to recall that, as Waszek also observes, the Scottish thinkers enjoyed a wide reception in eighteenth-century Germany and their works were integrated into the teaching of political economy in German universities (*SE*, 229).

Waszek stresses that Hegel shared certain presuppositions with Smith's and Steuart's economic models concerning the "sacredness" of private property, the role of money as a "universal commodity" or universal means of exchange, and the function of contracts. Moreover, in his system of needs, Hegel "accepts and reproduces the free market economy in all its basic elements" (*SE*, 142–3, 196). Finally, as Hardt and Negri observe, the "capitalist theory of value" was integral to Hegel's thinking. To elaborate this, we might note that Waszek highlights the parallels between Hegel's and the bourgeois economists' conceptions of the value-producing function of labor; Hegel correlates the immediacy of a commodity with its "use-value" and its universality with its *possibility* of use or exchange (*SE*, 143–4). The overall point here is that, as Waszek puts it, "Hegel's individual is not alone, but is … by its own aims and wants related to other individuals" (*SE*, 147).

Having registered how Hegel's economic model was deeply influenced by the Scottish thinkers, it is equally important to identify where Hegel supersedes or sublates their ideas. Hegel's sublation or *Aufhebung* of bourgeois political economy is crucial to his expression of the dialectic of capitalism in terms of a revolutionary conception of identity. According to Waszek, Hegel supersedes the political economists in at least two important respects, namely, in his conception of "person" and his understanding of labor – both of which imply a certain notion of identity. As Waszek argues, Hegel's justification for the necessary existence of private property lies in his conception of "person," whose inner freedom finds external expression in private property; and for Hegel, a contract between persons "implies the mutual recognition of persons as property owners" (*SE*, 143). So, already we can begin to see that, in this economic and political context, Hegel's very conception of individual identity is relational and reciprocal. Hardt and Negri are surely right in suggesting that in modern thought, not least in Hegel's case, there is an intimate connection between philosophical and political-economic dispositions or outlooks. Hegel's conception of identity in his *Logic* is continuous with, and informed by, his vision of identity in the political and economic realms.

The point is that Hegelian subjectivity and identity in their very conception are mediated by the forces of the market. In the *Phenomenology*, Hegel explicitly states that the individual, in satisfying his own needs, also satisfies the needs of others. As such, he works for the whole, for which "he sacrifices himself and precisely in so doing receives back from it his own self." This is a dialectical and reciprocal process which involves a "dissolution of its [the individual's] being-for-self in the *negation* of itself and the acquisition of the *positive* significance of being *for itself* (*PS*, §351). So the individual's identity, her development from individuality to universality, is explicitly mediated by economic circumstances, both by the system of needs in which she is obliged to operate and by the "social" or universal labor that she must perform in order to become herself.

5.3 Identity through Labor

Hence, we are brought to the concept which might be seen as lying at the center of Hegel's thinking on logical, metaphysical, and political levels: labor. And here we encounter the Hegelian supersession or *Aufhebung* of the classical liberal concept of labor as a purely economic activity. In Hegel's vision, labor has a far profounder significance. We have just seen that for Hegel, it is through a certain kind of labor that we achieve a mediated identity, a developed self. Waszek notes that labor is the means whereby man transcends his animal needs in the achievement of reason and freedom, and that for Hegel free labor presupposes a state of civil society, a state of emancipation from, and rational domination over, nature (*SE*, 157–9, 168–9).

Hegel's first certain reference to Smith's *Wealth of Nations* occurred in an early Jena manuscript known as the *First Philosophy of Spirit* (1803–4).[3] His remarks on labor here indicate some of the important ways in which his vision of labor superseded that of the political economists, and how it provided at least one of the crucial frameworks for his understanding of identity. We will see in a later chapter that, in this manuscript, Hegel regards language as the theoretical means by which we negate or conquer the world – by idealizing it, by reducing it to signs, to a world of our own creation. Hegel sees language as the "outward" existence of consciousness. The practical correlate of this process is our transformation of the world through labor. Interestingly, Hegel assigns to both language and labor a universal function. The spirit of a people, he says, "realizes itself in their work." In work they "come to be themselves outside of themselves" and work is their "outwardness" (*FPS*, 243). Just as language was consciousness's mode of existing outside itself in the theoretical realm, so work embodies the "outward" existence of a people in the practical realm, and it is an activity through which they cancel or

---

[3] G. W. F. Hegel, *System of Ethical Life (1802/3) and First Philosophy of Spirit (Part III of the System of Speculative Philosophy 1803/4)*, ed. and trans. H. S. Harris and T. M. Knox (New York: State University of New York Press, 1979), p. 248 (§324). Hereafter cited as *FPS*.

supersede their own natural immediacy. Hence nature is superseded both in language and in work (*FPS*, 244).

Like speech, labor is a form of rationality "that makes itself universal in the people, and is therefore opposed to the singularity of the individual" (*FPS*, 246). Moreover, man no longer works to satisfy his own particular needs: "his labor becomes a *formally abstract universal* ... he limits himself to labor for one of his needs, and exchanges it for whatever is necessary for his other needs ... the satisfaction of needs is a universal dependence of everyone upon one another" (*FPS*, 247). The various needs reach their unifying expression in the concept of money which represents "the possibility of all things needed" (*FPS*, 249).

Strikingly, then, human identity and human subjectivity are created through a process of mediation that involves a process of negation on two levels: both language and labor negate the immediacy of nature, whether in the world or in the instinctual dimension of the self. For Hegel, language itself in this respect is a kind of labor, the very medium of the "labor of the negative," which seeks to supersede the given-ness of the world. Moreover, it is through entering the universal systems of both language and labor that one subject, after negating its own natural and immediate existence and attaining to its own universality, can engage in reciprocal recognition with other subjects.

A final point here is that this mutuality and recognition occur in an explicitly economic context of interdependent needs and an endlessly circulating system of exchange of the products of labor. In this system, no entity and no person can possibly be self-identical, i.e., ontologically independent. Nothing can exist or subsist or have meaning by itself. Everything is caught up in this dynamic system of relation and exchange. Nothing is stable; and the identity and value of each entity is always in flux, in ever-shifting connections, always in process of self-transcendence, always seeking to complete itself in layers of relation to a totality that is itself nothing more than the expression of all its moving parts. Indeed, the only universal commodity, the only universal means of exchange is money. Hence, Hegelian identity is conceived in the womb of the capitalist market.

In this view of the economic and social system, Hegel advances beyond the political economists, then, not only in the ways pertinently suggested by Waszek – in his conceptions of personhood and labor – but also in undermining the very notion of what Hardt and Negri refer to as "singularity," which is correlative with independent existence or self-identity. For Steuart and Smith, the system of exchange was indeed dynamic. But it involved exchange between fixed entities. There is no conception of the development of subjectivity itself or of the dynamic nature of identity or entities being internally shaped by one another. For the political economists, neither the human being nor the world is transformed by her labor. The system of labor and exchange is largely mechanical, and the value of any given element changes only according to the market.

By way of example, we might observe that in the chapters where Smith propounds a labor theory of value in the *Wealth of Nations*, there is a great deal of emphasis on fluctuations of the market and variability. But the variability of which Smith speaks is that of the value or price of fixed entities, such as gold and silver in their function as standards of currency. Smith essentially argues that, at all times and places, labor is "the real measure of the exchangeable value of all commodities."[4] But, since the quantity of labor is difficult to measure, he acknowledges that, at a given time and place, money is a more exact measure of the value of a commodity. Labor represents the real value and money the nominal value (*WN*, 29–32). And in a capitalist market, he acknowledges that the price of any given commodity reflects variable combinations of wages, rent, and profit whose correlative functions are embodied in the laborer, the landlord, and the owner of capital (*WN*, 44–6). Even when Smith talks about a gardener owning his own land who unites all three functions, the modification of identity that occurs here is between pre-given selves or identities, which are measured in nothing but economic terms (*WN*, 47). Identity is reduced to economic activity or status – and this is a crucial aspect of bourgeois ideology.

Indeed, according to Adam Smith, what separates "human nature" from the animals is not – as the tradition of Western philosophy would have it – reason or some higher moral or spiritual sense or even a political disposition but rather a propensity for economic activity, the "propensity to truck, barter, and exchange one thing for another" (*WN*, 12). The human being is an economic animal, *homo economicus*, whose essential nature is to trade and exchange. This propensity has profound consequences. Whereas animals are largely independent, the human being in "civilised society" depends on a great multitude of people in order to satisfy her wants "by treaty, by barter, and by purchase" (*WN*, 13). It is this trading disposition that leads to the division of labor, whereby one

---

[4] Adam Smith, *An Inquiry into the Nature and Causes of the Wealth of Nations* (New York: Alfred A. Knopf, 1991), p. 26. Hereafter cited as *WN*.

person engages in a particular occupation and exchanges the surplus of goods she makes, or services, for other goods that she needs. So, all human beings are connected within a network of economic exchange: "Every man thus lives by exchanging, or becomes in some measure a merchant, and the society itself grows to be what is properly a commercial society" (*WN*, 20). Smith sees this trading propensity as "common to all men" and as the "necessary consequence of the faculties of reason and speech" (*WN*, 12). And, over time, money became the "universal instrument of commerce" and exchange (*WN*, 24).

These statements embody the fundamental vision of bourgeois ideology, whereby the causes of economic growth and the development of commercial society into various stages of capitalism are found in human nature itself. The human being is *essentially* a merchant, a trader, and the *essence* of human nature is to trade, to participate in a system of mutual dependency and exchange. Human rationality and language subserve this fundamental disposition. The human self here is reduced to self-interest, disposed to outward interaction with others only for survival. As Adams famously puts it: "It is not from the benevolence of the butcher, the brewer, or the baker that we expect our dinner, but from their regard to their own interest. We address ourselves, not to their humanity but to their self-love" (*WN*, 13). The "invisible hand" here is the free market adjusting itself: each person directed to self-interest benefits the whole. But, noticeably, "humanity" in any larger sense is absent within this system of exchange, in which our primary and primordial bond with our fellow human beings is mediated by money.

For Hegel, in contrast, the sphere of economics, of labor and exchange, embodies just one sphere of life, namely civil or bourgeois society. As seen in an earlier chapter, Hegel does indeed see this sphere as characterized by atomistic, individual, self-interest. And he agrees with both Smith's and Steuart's "socio-economic model of universal interdependence of particularized labour and the free exchange of its products."[5] But, we recall, at one level, Hegel sees civil society as occupying the second dialectical stage between family and state. The individual in this realm is certainly caught within a larger system of needs. But, for Hegel, the individual in bourgeois society is torn between self-interest and intimations of universal interest; he is as yet not fully developed, since his identity is always changing. His identity, as conceived by Hegel, is far

---

[5] For an extended discussion of Hegel's debt here, see Waszek, *Scottish Enlightenment*, 157–62.

more comprehensive than bourgeois economics would allow – it compre-hends not only economic identity but also his participation in the larger, ethical sphere.

When literary theorists impugn the notion of self-identity, then, they are effectively rehearsing Hegel's critique, a critique that is inseparable from Hegel's critical engagement with capitalism. Hegel effectively inte-grates bourgeois ideology into his system but also sublates it, displaying its narrowness and situating it in a larger historical and ethical context. Needless to say, most theorists reject those contexts as articulated by Hegel, especially his concept of the state. But many of them nonetheless follow in Hegel's footsteps by complicating and impugning bourgeois ideology as such. And in this, they are the heirs of a liberal humanism that stands at the center of modern Western thought.

Interestingly, Hardt and Negri see Foucault's antihumanism as being continuous with the revolutionary spirit of Renaissance humanism inas-much as they both entailed an "attack on transcendence" (*Emp*, 91–2). So there are, of course, deep continuities between what was once a revo-lutionary bourgeois humanism and the post-humanism of our own era: one of these affinities is their orientation regarding the notion of identity. Of all theorists, it is perhaps Jacques Derrida who has reminded us most poignantly of what we owe to Hegel in terms of our understandings of identity and difference, and who has grappled most profoundly with these notions. We shall seek to place a wreath upon his grave in the next chapter.

PART II

Literary Theory: Reading the Dialectic

A. The Language of Metaphysics

CHAPTER 6

Hegel and Deconstruction

Where have all the deconstructionists gone? When I was a graduate student, the university was alive with them. But where are they now? It may be that searching for a deconstructionist today is rather like seeking Zaabalawi: one must be drunk and find the deconstructionist within oneself. And this, indeed, has been the fate of deconstruction: not, along with theory, to die – as has so often been gleefully proclaimed. But, rather, to remain alive in our various enterprises – feminist, Marxist, historicist, postcolonial – impelling them from within, deepening at least their appearance of subversive potential. And this potential comes largely from a certain reading of major thinkers including Nietzsche, Freud, Heidegger and, most notably, Hegel.

It was Derrida, as much as any other single figure, who deserves credit for reminding us that we shall never be finished with the reading of Hegel. In his superb introduction to a collection of essays on Hegel and Derrida, Stuart Barnett points out that despite postmodernism's "desperate attempt to be a post-Hegelian culture" in the wake of Lyotard, who viewed Hegel as the "distillation" of speculative modernity, notable thinkers including Foucault, Paul Feyerabend, and Richard Rorty have absorbed important elements of Hegelianism. Indeed, says Barnett, postmodernism is already implicit in Hegel, who is the philosopher not only of "an absolute metanarrative of the historical unfolding of an always unitary reason" but also of "difference, pluralism, relativism, and contingency," and of the "advent of historicity within rationalism."[1] Barnett affirms that it is Derrida who, uniquely, "has sought to confront the silent Hegelianism of our age," and he observes that the centrality of Hegel to Derrida has remained largely unexplored (*HAD*, 25–6). I hope that the present account might complement and continue the task

---

[1] *Hegel after Derrida*, ed. Barnett, pp. 1–4, 10–11, 20. Hereafter cited as *HAD*.

undertaken in Barnett's splendid edition of essays, on which it will occasionally draw.

The profound impact of Hegel is evident in all of Derrida's writings. But Derrida's explicit engagement with Hegel occurs most markedly in: *De la grammatologie* [*Of Grammatology*], a "science" of writing, which lays out the operations of deconstruction in the context of the history of philosophy; *L'Ecriture et la différence* [*Writing and Difference*], which contains important meditations on Hegel, as well as an essay on Derrida's neographism *différance*; *Marges de la philosophie* [*Margins of Philosophy*] (1982), which includes essays on Hegel's semiology and the use of metaphor in philosophy; *Positions* (1972), containing illuminating interviews with Derrida, detailing his attitude to Marxism, Hegel, and other issues; *Spectres de Marx* [*Specters of Marx*] (1994) which looks at the various legacies of Marx; and *Glas*, which juxtaposes Derrida's reading of Hegelian texts, in particular, the *Philosophy of Right*, with his reflections on the diaries and novels of the thief and homosexual Jean Genet.

6.1   Deconstruction as a Critique of Identity

6.1.1   Identity as Language

We need to grasp certain features of deconstruction to elucidate its connections with Hegel. Deconstruction has famously resisted any general characterization or systematization;[2] ironically, this very resistance is based on its systematic and concerted critique of identity. Deconstruction effectively rehearses Hegel's critique of identity at the level of language. More accurately, it reconceives identity in the image of language; like Hegel, Derrida views identity as part of a relational system but, unlike Hegel, he invokes language as the model or paradigm of this system. Perhaps even more accurately, he reconceives identity – and all the other terms that have conventionally preoccupied Western metaphysics, such as thought and reality, self and world, subject and object – as effects of language, as "positions" within a linguistic system. Derrida sees this deconstructive endeavor as embodying the essential impetus of modern thought across many disciplines.

---

[2] A still invaluable introduction to the subject is Christopher Norris, *Deconstruction: Theory and Practice* (London and New York: Methuen, 1982).

6.1.2   *The Metaphysics of Presence*

What exactly is implied in this rejection of identity? The identity challenged by deconstruction is *self-identity*, in other words, the notion that the identity of a given entity is somehow self-contained. Such a notion is presupposed by what Derrida calls a "metaphysics of presence." This is a type of thinking that sees the identity of any entity as contained in its immediate existence, its immediate presence. A metaphysics of "presence" would be a metaphysics of what Hegel calls self-identity: an entity's content is viewed as coinciding completely with its existence. For example, an isolated entity such as a piece of chalk would be regarded as having its meaning completely within itself, completely in its immediate "presence." Even if the rest of the world did not exist, we could say what the piece of chalk was, what its function and constitution were. Interestingly, these are the kinds of claims that were made not by Hegel – who, as we saw, interrogates such self-identity – but by philosophical realists such as Bertrand Russell.

In turn, a metaphysics of presence presupposes, according to Derrida, some kind of systematization of thought that assures the stability and self-presence of meaning, that effects a closure and disables any "free play" of thought that might threaten or question the overall structure. Such absolute self-containment of meaning must be sanctioned by a higher authority, a Logos or what Derrida calls a "transcendental signified" – a (posited) signified that transcends and stands outside the entire system of meaning – which ensures that all things in the world have specific and designated meanings. This higher authority, which stands beyond all questioning, could be God or something that is posited as the ultimate reality (substance for Aristotle, the ideal Forms for Plato, Absolute Spirit for Hegel, free trade for bourgeois economics). This reliance on a Logos or absolute authority is given the name Logocentrism by Derrida. We can see now that Derrida's attack on identity is on a broader level also an attack on the metaphysics of presence which enables it; and this, on an even more comprehensive level, is an assault on Logocentrism, which Derrida sees as the fundamental form of Western thought, reaching its highest expression in Hegel.

6.1.3   *Logocentrism*

In its ancient Greek philosophical and Judeo-Christian meaning, the Logos referred *both* to the Word of God which created the universe and to the rational order of creation itself. In other words, it is in the spoken Logos that the orders of language and reality ultimately coincide, in an identity that is invested with absolute authority, absolute origin, and absolute purpose or teleology. The Logos effectively preserves the stability and closure of the entire system. For example, in a Christian scheme, the signifier "private profit" might refer to the concept of "excess" in accumulation of wealth. And this sign as a whole, the phrase "private profit" as meaning "excess," would refer to a specific "object," which in this case might be embodied in a feudal system of economic and ecclesiastical constraints. In other words, the meaning of "profit" might be sanctioned by a hierarchy of authority, stretching back through institutional church practice, theology, philosophy, as well as political and economic theory, to the authority of the scriptures and the Word of God Himself. In the same way, all the other signifiers and signifieds in language would be constrained in their significance, making for a stable and closed system in terms of which the world and the human self could be interpreted in terms of their origins, their meaning, and purpose in life, what counts as good and evil, what kind of government is legitimate and so forth. The Logos thereby authorizes an entire worldview, sanctioned by a theological and philosophical system and by an entire political, religious, and social order.

If, now, the authority of the Logos were subverted or eroded, this would destabilize the entire order. If we are not constrained by a Christian perspective, we might attribute *other* meanings to the word "profit," meanings that may even conflict with the previously given Christian signification. For example, we might from an emerging bourgeois world view define "profit" as the legitimate fruit of labor or the reward of initiative or industry or even as the necessary condition of economic progress. We might, like the bourgeois political economists, view a propensity for profit as inhering in human nature. Various groups might give different meanings to the word so that a general consensus were lost and the semantic value of the signifier became an ideological battleground. Socialists might define it, for example, as a product of exploitation, and Romantics might see it as signifying the ambition of a utilitarian mentality. In this way, a given signifier X might be defined by a meaning attributed to signified Y. But since there is no authoritative closure to this process, it could go on ad infinitum: signified Y would itself need to be defined, and so this signified would itself become a signifier of something else; this process might regress indefinitely so that we never arrive at a conclusive signified but are always moving along an endless "chain" of signifiers, in a system of displacement that Derrida calls "metaphor."

6.1.4   Strategies of Deconstruction

One of the fundamental endeavors of deconstruction, then, is to exhibit the operation of logocentrism in all its forms, to reveal its underlying modes of construction, and to bring back these various transcendental signifieds within the province of language and textuality, within the province of their relatability to other concepts. For example, rather than merely accepting "freedom" or "profit" as intrinsic values, we might interrogate these concepts, exploring the history of their emergence and the agency of their definition, unveiling the very process of their construction and authorization.

What, then, are the strategies of deconstruction? As we have seen, its most fundamental strategy is to display the operations of logocentrism and to undermine any metaphysics of presence by infusing a linguistic paradigm into any system of thinking, by treating that system as a system of language. Let us return to my favorite example, that of the chalk. If we were to challenge a "metaphysics of presence" – a strategy in which Derrida both follows and attempts to subvert Hegel – we might argue that in fact the meaning of the chalk does *not* coincide with, and is not confinable within, its immediate existence; that its meaning and purpose actually lie in relations that extend far beyond its immediate existence.

Viewed in this light, "chalk" is not a name for a self-subsistent, self-enclosed entity; rather it names the provisional focal point of a complex set of relations. This is precisely the view of identity expressed in the second stage of Hegel's dialectic. Inasmuch as deconstruction challenges the view of identity as self-presence or immediate presence, it is impugning one of the foundations of bourgeois thought. For capitalist economics the chalk must be viewed as self-subsistent and independent, as able to be commodified and marketed, able to be valued precisely and held proportionate to a certain amount of labor; its complex connections with the learning process and other aspects of education are subordinated to the material issues of its cost, quality, and areas of distribution. Deconstruction is anti-ideological inasmuch as it reopens these suppressed or marginalized connections, and brings back the purely material considerations into a more visible relationship with other factors such as pedagogy and the entire motivational foundation of a university. But it might be argued that deconstruction is itself ideological inasmuch as it refuses to name a third dialectical stage, a third perspective, from which the principle governing the self-identity of the chalk from an economic perspective – economic viability – might be subsumed under a broader perspective that included educational and ethical considerations. Hegel, of course, is ideological in another sense, according to both Marx and Derrida: His dialectic in in its third phase, on account of its idealism, covertly sanctions this narrower economic perspective after initially negating it.

6.2 Derrida's General Characterization of Hegel

According to Derrida, Hegel "undoubtedly *summed up* the entire philosophy of the logos. He determined ontology as absolute logic; he assembled all the delimitations of philosophy as presence" (*OG*, 24).[3] Hegel's philosophy, then, embodies all of the aforementioned operations of logocentrism. Indeed, in Hegel's hands, the "horizon of absolute knowledge is the effacement of writing in the logos ... the reappropriation of difference." By "effacement of writing," Derrida refers to the fact that Hegel's Absolute Idea serves as a Logos which constrains the free play and contingency of all concepts within a closed system. Yet Derrida, rightly, sees another side to Hegel: everything that Hegel thinks within the horizon of absolute knowledge "may be reread as a meditation on writing. Hegel is *also* the thinker of irreducible difference. He rehabilitated thought as the *memory productive* of signs." In other words, Hegel saw, in his very conception of the mind's operation through its integrated faculties such memory and imagination, that thought is enabled by language. This is why Hegel was "the last philosopher of the book and the first thinker of writing" (*OG*, 26).

In his long essay "Violence and Metaphysics," Derrida does acknowledge that (Hegelian) speculative philosophy is obliged to use concepts that have a "nonspeculative ancestry," and that it must "accommodate duplicity and difference within speculation, within the very purity of philosophical meaning." He acknowledges that no one has "attempted this more profoundly than Hegel" and points to Hegel's delight in knowing that the German word *Aufhebung* (usually translated as "sublation") is intrinsically speculative since it carries two opposing meanings (to preserve and to bring to an end). What Hegel does for this concept, says Derrida, is what philosophy would need to do for all concepts (*WD*, 113–14).[4] In a sense, then, Derrida sees Hegel's philosophy as pointing beyond itself, beyond its own closure, to its own deconstruction. Hegel effectively sees the meaning of *Aufhebung* as intrinsically dialectical;

---

[3] Derrida, *Of Grammatology*, p. 23. Hereafter cited as *OG*.
[4] Jacques Derrida, "Violence and Metaphysics," *Writing and Difference*, trans. Alan Bass (Chicago: University of Chicago Press, 1978), pp. 113–14. Hereafter cited as *WD*.

in the same way, according to Derrida, philosophy must revisit and dialectize all the concepts and oppositions that comprise its own currency, treating them as containing their own subversion. For example, the oppositions of body or mind or body and soul or sense and intellect must be rethought in the light of their necessary mutual connections.[5]

This endeavor to dialectize concepts has, of course, characterized a great deal of literary theory. It was mentioned earlier that much French theory was influenced by Alexandre Kojève's anthropologistic reading of Hegel. Interestingly, Derrida sees such a reading as a "serious mistake" given that the *Phenomenology* concerns not "man" as such but the "science of experience of consciousness" (*MP*, 117).[6] Derrida points out that the critiques of humanism and anthropologism by Husserl and Heidegger (as in the latter's *Letter on Humanism*) went largely unnoticed in France. Ironically, the critique of humanism that did comprise one of the "dominant and guiding motifs" of French thought, far from seeking its own sources in Hegel, Husserl, and Heidegger, amalgamated these figures with "the old metaphysical humanism." As such, this critique overlooked "the *relève* [Derrida's translation of *Aufhebung*] of man in the thought of Hegel, Husserl, and Heidegger" (*MP*, 118–19). Derrida is surely right to suggest that, as in his own work, much of the modern antihumanist critique directed against metaphysical closure in Hegel itself stands upon a Hegelian basis. So, in Derrida's general estimation, Hegel both embodies all of the major characteristics of Western metaphysics and also points the way beyond it.

6.3 Derrida and *Différance*

6.3.1 Definitions

Perhaps more persistently than any other theorist, Derrida has rearticulated the Hegelian notion of difference so as to undermine its orientation toward closure. While Derrida rehearses Hegel's view of identity as intrinsically a relational and differential concept, he effectively reshapes from within Hegel's view of difference. In his endeavor to

---

[5] In his essay "The Surprise of the Event" and elsewhere, Jean-Luc Nancy sees a bifurcation in Hegel's thought between knowing the truth and the "event" or happening of truth, the latter offering a potential for escaping metaphysical closure. Nancy defines "surprise" as "negativity itself" but concludes that Hegel himself does not realize this potential (*HAD*, 91–3, 102–3).

[6] "Différance," in Jacques Derrida, *Margins of Philosophy*, trans. Alan Bass (Chicago: University of Chicago Press, 1982), p. 9. Hereafter cited as *MP*.

subvert the conventional priority of speech over writing, Derrida coins a term that many regard as central to his thought and especially to his characterizations of language: *différance*. The significance of this term derives partly from Saussure's concept of "difference" as the constituting principle of language: a term is defined by what it is *not*, by its differences from other terms. However, Derrida also incorporates into his term an ambivalence in the French word *différer* (and the Latin *differre*), which can mean both "to differ" and "to defer" in time. Hence Derrida adds a temporal dimension to the notion of difference. As he characterizes it in his essay "Différance," there is *"Différance* as temporization, *différance* as spacing." Moreover, the substitution of *a* for *e* in the word *différance* – what Derrida calls a "discreet graphic intervention" – cannot be *heard* in French: it is a silent displacement that can only be discerned in writing, as if to undermine not only the superior value previously accorded to speech but the very opposition between speech and writing (*MP*, 3). Elsewhere, Derrida defines *différance* as "an economic concept designating the production of differing/deferring."

So according to Derrida, *différance* belongs somewhere *between* speech and writing and "resists" all the oppositions of philosophy and indeed the very determination of being as presence, the very authority of "presence" (*MP*, 10, 21). In other words, *différance* undermines the idea that any entity or concept can somehow exist in isolation and enjoy an independent meaning. What is important in his essay on *différance* is the way he relates this notion to Saussure and to Hegel. Derrida acknowledges that most semiologists and linguists see Saussure as an "inaugurator" inasmuch as he sees semiology as founded upon two characteristics of the sign: it is both arbitrary and differential. So, signification arises from a network of oppositions, and the "principle of difference" is the condition for signification. Derrida further points out that for Saussure, language is a system in which there are only differences without positive terms. Thus, no concept, no signified, is ever "present in and of itself" but rather arises in relation to other concepts "by means of the systematic play of differences." *Différance*, then, is the very "possibility of conceptuality" (*MP*, 11). That is, signifieds (concepts) as well as signifiers arise from a process of differentiation where the differences are essential to their meaning.

What, then, is the difference (and here, I am reminded of my graduate days) between difference and *différance*? Between Saussure's "difference" and Derrida's *différance*? According to Derrida, Sausserian differences – the differences that produce language – are the effects of *différance*. *"Différance* is the non-full, non-simple, structured and differentiating origin of differences." By this he does not appear to mean that *différance* somehow precedes differences as a unitary cause. Rather it is a movement by which language is constituted "historically" as a "weave of differences" (*MP*, 11–12). In other words, Saussure's differences appear to operate on a synchronic plane, whereas *différance* also incorporates differences operating through time. Because of *différance*, says Derrida, each present element is related to past and future elements. Hence *différance* is not somehow an "event"; nor is it directed by any agency or subject, such as the Hegelian absolute.

6.3.2 Différance *and Dialectic*

This brings us to the connection of *différance* with Hegel's dialectic. We perhaps need to make an important preliminary remark here. Derrida sees the classical semiological view of the sign as both dialectical in a Hegelian sense and as embodying the "closure" of Western metaphysical presuppositions. This classical view, according to Derrida, puts the sign "in place of the thing itself, the present thing ... The sign represents the present in its absence. It takes the place of the present ... The sign, in this sense, is deferred presence." Further, the circulation of signs "defers the moment in which we can encounter the thing itself, make it ours, consume or expend it, touch it, see it, intuit its presence." In other words, classical semiology presupposes that there *is* a presence that is "original and lost" which the sign attempts to reappropriate in a "movement of mediation" (*MP*, 9). For Derrida, then, the sign itself embodies the "metaphysics of presence" that dominates Western thought. And the structure of this "classical" sign is dialectical: it begins with the positing of a simple, self-identical, presence (a "thing"). This presence is then "lost" in a network of relations where "its" sign interacts with and circulates among other signs. Finally, the movement of the sign is always toward reappropriating the lost presence, toward a consumption of the thing itself.

It is here, in the final dialectical stage, that *différance* breaks most emphatically with the classical structure of the sign and, in the same gesture, with Western metaphysics and its most powerful embodiment, the Hegelian dialectic. Since there is no "presence" prior to semiological difference, says Derrida, we can extend Saussure's view of language to the sign in general. The movement of *différance* resists any ontological reappropriation (which would be a theological gesture, as in the Logos) (*MP*, 6, 12). What this means is that we must reconceive the sign not as something that we must substitute for a thing or presence – for there *is* no presence somehow preceding the sign or language. Rather, the activity of *différance* is prior to the sign, and of course the "thing itself" is no more than a sign to begin with, never self-identical, but already a relational creation arising from the interaction of a network of signs.

As such, the activity of *différance*, says Derrida, maintains "relations of profound affinity with Hegelian discourse." It is unable to break with that discourse but can "operate a kind of infinitesimal and radical displacement of it" (*MP*, 14). The movement of *différance* effectively interrupts the movement of the Hegelian dialectic.[7] Unlike the Hegelian *Aufhebung* or sublation, says Derrida, the "character of *différance* in no way implies that the deferred presence can always be found again" – precisely because there is no original presence to begin with (*MP*, 20). The temporal dimension of *différance* is not reducible to a "simple dialectical complication of the living present as an originary and unceasing synthesis – a synthesis constantly directed back on itself" (*MP*, 21).

These statements indicate the general tenor of the relationship between deconstruction and Hegel. Deconstructive thought effectively arrests the Hegelian dialectic at its second stage – the stage where a given entity is "externalized" or diffused throughout its relations with other entities – refusing the reappropriation and reintegration of the third stage. In an interview in *Positions*, Derrida goes so far as to say:

"If there were a definition of *différance,* it would be precisely the limit, the interruption, the destruction of the Hegelian *relève* [*Aufhebung*] *wherever* it operates."[8] In this interview, he explains that it is the function of *différance* to "remain in this phase" (the second dialectical stage) and to

> inhabit philosophical opposition, resisting and disorganizing it, *without ever* constituting a third term, without ever leaving room for a solution in the form of speculative dialectics ... I attempt to bring the critical operation to bear against the unceasing reappropriation of this work of the simulacrum by a dialectics of the Hegelian type ... for Hegelian idealism consists precisely of a *relève* of the binary oppositions of classical idealism, a resolution of contradiction into a third term that comes in order to *aufheben*, to deny while raising up, while idealizing, while sublating into an anamnesic interiority (*Erinnerung*), while interning difference in a self-presence. (*Pos*, 43)

---

[7] As John Llewelyn reads it, *différance* indicates a "conflict of forces" that, unlike the "conflict of positions in dialectical contradiction, refuses incorporation ... that is to say, *différance* and dialectical difference are not dialectically opposed." "A Point of Almost Absolute Proximity to Hegel," in *Deconstruction and Philosophy: The Texts of Jacques Derrida*, ed. John Sallis (Chicago and London: University of Chicago Press, 1987), pp. 87–91.

[8] Jacques Derrida, *Positions*, trans. Alan Bass (1972; rpt. Chicago and London: University of Chicago Press, 1982), p. 40. Hereafter cited as *Pos*.

Hence the entire project of deconstruction is to destabilize philosophy from *within*, not only by undermining its "classical" oppositions but also by resisting the third phase of the dialectic, by refusing to advance to any synthesis of those oppositions within some larger unity. The "conflictuality" of *différance* "can never be totally resolved" (*Pos*, 44). What is interesting here is that this second dialectical stage, as we shall see, is also where Marx breaks with Hegel. Derrida in fact acknowledges that, like Marxism, his own project could be described as a "critique of idealism" inasmuch as idealism is the "most direct" representation of Logocentrism (*Pos*, 51, 62).

Derrida indeed sees his work as operating in "infinitesimal and radical displacement" in relation to Hegel but not by passing to some "totally exterior" terrain. He acknowledges and cautions: "We will never be finished with the reading or rereading of Hegel." Derrida characterizes Hegel's text as "necessarily fissured" since it exceeds the "circular closure of its representation." That text needs to be reexamined in terms of the movement whereby it "exceeds its meaning, permits itself to be turned away from, to return to, and to repeat itself outside its self-identity" (*Pos*, 77–8). Those last words in a sense sum up the overall project: philosophy, Hegel's text, the dialectic – these must be made to "repeat" themselves outside their self-identity, in the sphere of play, of contingency, of pure difference. And this by an internal operation: not by impugning them from the outside – for there is no outside, no possible externality – but by miming their very gestures from within. Hence the gestures of the *Aufhebung* are mimicked without leading to any synthesis or definite conclusion.

One example of a classical "opposition" subjected to a deconstructive reading might be that between mind and body. In the philosophies of both Schopenhauer and Nietzsche, the Cartesian dualism between mind and body is severely undermined. These thinkers show that what we call "neutral" and "rational" thought is intrinsically attuned to our bodily instincts of survival and aggression. The dualism becomes further undermined in much modern thought, as in Freud's work or feminism, where thought is seen as deeply conditioned by the body, by one's specific situation in an intersecting complex of place, time, ideology, race, and class. And in Lacanian psychoanalysis, this sublation of the mind–body dualism reaches a further depth, where language itself infuses the very fiction of the unconscious. Gender studies takes this *Aufhebung* even further, locating localized interactions of thought and physical sensation in *performance* or performative moments in need of constant repetition in order to simulate conceptual identity as an effect.

6.4   Derrida on Hegel, Saussure, and Logocentrism

It's clear, then, that Derrida sees an intrinsic connection between the classical structure of the sign and Logocentrism, the former serving effectively as the means of the latter, which governs and closes all discourse. The main vehicle of metaphysical closure, according to Derrida, is the Hegelian *Aufhebung*, whose operation occurs explicitly in Hegel but also implicitly in nearly all other thinkers. He sees Saussurian linguistics and structuralism as participating in the movement of closure effected by the Hegelian *Aufhebung*. He claims that Saussure's view of the arbitrariness of the sign occurs *within* the framework of a presumed "natural" relationship between the voice and sense in general.[9] Derrida sees this arbitrariness as constrained by Saussure's subordination of writing to speech, which is seen as more immediately embodying "sense" or meaning (*OG*, 44–6). Derrida aligns Saussure and Hegel in their belief that there is a distinction between sign and symbol: for both thinkers, a "sign" exists in virtue of an arbitrary relationship whereas a "symbol" embodies a "natural" relationship with what it signifies (as, in Hegel's example, where clouds might be a symbol of rain) (*PM*, §457–8).[10] In fact, Derrida explicitly sees Saussurian linguistics and structuralism generally as occupying the same logocentric episteme as Hegel, in which true difference is sublimated within a larger, theological, totality (*OG*, 70–1, 99).

Derrida's view of Hegel's place in the history of the "metaphysics of presence" is rather interesting. Before Descartes, he says, the idea of presence was contained in objective modes such the Platonic Forms or Aristotelian substance. But Descartes inaugurated a new model of presence in the *cogito*, whereby the subject's self-presence was located within consciousness or feeling. In other words, when Descartes argued that *cogito ergo sum* or "I think, therefore I am," he was identifying the existence or "self-presence" of the human subject with thought. In a sense, says Derrida, this paves the way for the Hegelian sublation of difference: objectivity now takes the form of the "modification of a self-present substance" (*OG*, 97–8). What Derrida means by this is that, after Descartes, objectivity was no longer viewed as something independent, existing

---

[9] Derrida's imputation of this view to Saussure has been characterized as a misreading based on an editorial insertion into Saussure's text. See, for example, Beata Stawarska, *Saussure's Philosophy of Language as Phenomenology: Undoing the Doctrine of the Course in General Linguistics* (Oxford: Oxford University Press, 2015), p. 82.

[10] Hegel's *Philosophy of Mind: Being Part Three of the Encyclopaedia of the Philosophical Sciences* (1830). Trans. William Wallace. Oxford: Oxford University Press, 1971. Hereafter cited as *PM*.

outside human subjectivity. Rather, it was a "modification" of subjectivity itself; both Locke and Hume denied that we could have any knowledge of an independent external world and affirmed that all we can know is the *effect* of that world on our sensations; what we know are "impressions" and "ideas," which are functions (or "modifications") of our own sensibility, not of the external world.

In proclaiming the *cogito*, Descartes affirmed a sharp dualism between mind and body; the latter was a part of the material world and not strictly a dimension of human existence. Derrida states that Descartes expelled the sign (as an element of the material, bodily world) from the *cogito*, and saw "clear and distinct ideas" as immediately present to the mind. Similarly, Hegel "reappropriates the sensible sign to the movement of the Idea" (*OG*, 98). In other words, like Saussure, Hegel "contains" the arbitrariness he acknowledges in the sign within a broader movement of closure. Even when Hegel proclaims the unity of opposites, such as absence and presence, or nonbeing and being, dialectics continues to be "a movement of mediation between two full presences" (*OG*, 246).

Derrida's overall point seems to be that, whereas the Cartesian subject remains static and isolated (both from the sensible world of language and from other selves), the Hegelian subject escapes itself, into otherness, into externality, into language, only to return to itself, to reconstitute itself as presence, a mediated but composite identity. Derrida asserts that the epoch of logocentrism has "effaced" the signifier: philosophy has attempted to restore presence so that "being" can be "signified in its brilliance and glory" (*OG*, 285–6). In other words, the movement of Western metaphysics has been to reconnect with, and reaffirm, some reality which exists prior to language. As such, Derrida's project, in one sense, is to reinstitute the signifier against the "dominant authority of the signified" (*Pos*, 82). We can consider later the post-humanistic character of this project, but for now we must consider how the foregoing critiques of Hegel are *enacted* (not merely expounded) in an altogether unique fashion by Derrida.

6.5 *Glas*

Derrida's most striking engagement with Hegel occurs in *Glas*, which is undoubtedly his most brilliant and innovative accomplishment. This volume – which comprises a subtle critique of capitalism – contains Derrida's meditations on Hegelian texts, especially the *Philosophy of Right*, in the left-hand column of each page, while the right-hand column contains extracts from the diaries of the thief Jean Genet as well as Derrida's reflections on these and other texts such as those of Saussure. Interspersed alongside these in smaller print are often quotations from the German texts of Hegel, detailed entries from various dictionaries, and "marginal" comments. But the book undertakes far more than the mere exercise of intertextuality. It examines the "name" of Hegel. Who is he, this eagle (*aigle*) of the strange name? What are the connections between the various aspects of his work, personal and philosophical, earlier and later?

Glas examines implicitly Derrida's own name and the very field of autobiography and life-writing. Its very form undermines any distinction into separate genres. It examines connections among religion, philosophy, the political state, gender, and language. Overall, it is a beautifully written meditation on the contours of Hegel's thought, which places itself into question, into participation in a larger polysemy of voices, staging its own lack of control over these, over any of the connections implied between those voices or their own implied extension beyond the boundaries of this book. In some ways, Derrida's book embodies a return to traditions of medieval glossary, whereby a "text" was presented not in isolation but surrounded by commentary from various traditions or schools. But the text is also a *Glassary*, also looking forward to the era of hypertextuality and the digital potentials of the word. As such, it enacts textuality as a process deeply rooted in temporality and tradition while destabilizing these notions by forcing them into relation with contemporaneity.

Hence, the larger register of the book juxtaposes Hegel's *Philosophy of Right* – which is based on the concept of *Recht* or "right" as it is embodied in property, a concept that Hegel saw as central to a modern capitalist economy – with the journal and other literary output of a thief. On the one side we have a text devoted to the ethical and legal orientation of so-called civilized life, such as family, civil society, and the state; a book that, as we have seen, expresses the inner dialectic and contradictions of capitalism. On the other side, we are immersed within the perspective of an outcast, a homosexual, who glorifies and sanctifies criminality. And the contrast, at least on its surface, is sharpened by the fact that Derrida relates the ethics of the family, for example, to the notion of the Christian Trinity in Hegel's early theological writings. But this level of interaction between broad registers, of course, is self-deconstructing. I say that the contrast is superficial because when these texts are explored in more depth, when the names and signifiers "Hegel" and "Jean Genet" are probed beneath their conventional associations, we might, for example, see Genet as an advocate for gay rights, for racial equality, for justice in various political conflicts, and as a voice against police brutality, a spokesperson for the global ills of capitalism. And, equally, we might see Hegel as propounding the "rationality" of a state where women are suppressed, where the poor are left unacknowledged, and where war and imperialism are extolled as necessary to the sustenance of the bourgeois world. The juxtaposition, even as self-deconstructing, is stark.

It is not that somehow the tables are simply turned; it is, rather, that the one discourse – intimate, intensely personal, full of passion, alive with overt sexuality – is coerced into relation with the other – which is majestic, dry, impersonal, distant, and parades itself as rational – so that both exist in mutual reverberation as part of a larger discourse, a larger dialectic yet to be formed. For example, despite all the Hegelian focus on the structural movement from *Moralität* or individual morality to social morality or *Sittlichkeit*, his own biography, his own letters – dragged by Derrida into Hegel's legal text – begins not so much to undermine it but to force that text into relation with a larger, conventionally unacknowledged, context. Hegel's text is "repeated" in play: beyond any boundaries it can control or by which it might be controlled. The gleaming pages of Absolute Spirit are obliged to turn alongside a spiritualization of the physical: the depraved, fallen physical, the world of pimping, murder, and homosexuality that cannot be sublated or integrated. In our search for meaning in the text, we go back, forward, between, within, and without. This is liberal humanism staging its own confusion, its desperate oscillation between conflicting registers, straining to hear its own death-knell from deep within itself.

Given that *Glas* is such a comprehensive exercise in virtuosity, I cannot pretend to do it justice here – that would take a separate book.[11] My strategy will be to use Derrida's text to illuminate the crucial issues already discussed, by showing how the semantic registers of *Glas* enact the operation of the Saussurian sign in the light of Hegel's understanding of the Logos.

6.6 *Glas*, the Saussurean Sign, and Hegel's Logos

Derrida introduces the word *glas* in the right-hand column of his text, where he is analyzing Genet, in relation to the notion of death. Genet, observes Derrida, writes for the dead, "the dead who have never been

---

[11] For some extremely insightful and specialized analyses of *Glas*, see the essays by Simon Critchley, Heinz Kimmerle, Kevin Thompson, and Henry Sussman in *Hegel after Derrida*.

alive."[12] In Genet's inverted world, where saintliness is achieved through murder, where murder embodies a kind of consecration of life whereby existence is attained only in death. Hence it follows, says Derrida, that "I am ... sounds its own proper *glas*, signs itself its own death sentence" (*G*, 79). In the main right-hand column, Derrida appears to use *glas* as a metaphor: "This work of mourning *is called* – *glas*" (*G*, 86). He points out the various meanings of *glas*, which can also refer to the signal of a trumpet destined to call, or convoke or gather together. He proceeds to give two pages of dictionary definitions of *glas* and its Latin roots, which span the meanings of "fleet," "class," "ringing noise or clamor," "slow ringing of a church's bell to announce someone's death-struggle, death, or interment" (*G*, 87–9).

In these maneuvers, Derrida effectively sets up a number of interacting registers, foregrounding the almost inexhaustible contexts in which "death" in Genet's text might be understood. The point is precisely not to allow any single interpretation or set of interpretations but to resist any avenue toward closure: the listing of dictionary definitions in their original dictionary format is an index of this refusal to choose, of allowing the reader to traverse for herself the various meanings of *glas* and to situate herself within their fathomless relation to Genet's text, as well as Derrida's self-situation within an endlessly intertextual process.[13] The word *glas* becomes a metaphor for the very process of metaphor. At the very most, one might pounce – rather arbitrarily – upon certain themes and nodal points, such as death (as I have just done), and relate the recurrences and mirror-imagings of these.

Derrida now – still in the right-hand column – suggests that the concept of *glas* allows us to pursue "a grammatological reading" of Saussure (*G*, 90). Here we need to observe that Derrida takes the title of his book from Saussure. In his lectures gathered as *Course in General Linguistics*, after Saussure has explained the arbitrary nature of the sign, he cites some possible objections to this view. One is the figure of onomatopoeia whereby the sound of a word might appear "naturally" to mimic its meaning. The word *glas* is one of the examples used by Saussure, who says:

> Words like French *fouet* "whip" of *glas* "knell" may strike certain ears with suggestive sonority, but to see that they have not always had this property

---

[12] Jacques Derrida, *Glas*, trans. John P. Leavey, Jr., and Richard Rand (1974; rpt. Lincoln and London: University of Nebraska Press, 1986), p. 79. Hereafter cited as *G*.

[13] Henry Sussman suggests that Derrida sees Genet as deflowering the pieties based on the bourgeois notion of the family and the morality of Western modernity as embodied by Hegel (*HAD*, 280).

we need only to examine their Latin forms (*fouet* is derived from *fagus* "beech-tree," *glas* from *classicum* "sound of a trumpet") ... As for authentic onomatopoeias (e.g. *glug-glug, tick-tock,* etc.), not only are they limited in number, but also they are already chosen somewhat arbitrarily, for they are only approximate and already more or less conventional imitations of certain noises ... In addition ... these words ... are drawn into the same evolution ... that other words undergo ... obvious proof that they lose something of their original character in order to assume that of the linguistic sign in general, which is unmotivated.[14]

Derrida suggests that Saussure's procedure here begs a number of questions concerning his formulation of "arbitrariness" and that the "whole work of the *glas* could, at the least, provide material for the reelaboration of these questions" (*G,* 91). To begin with, Saussure presupposes a knowledge of "authentic onomatopoeias," which embodies yet another "recourse to a pure origin" (*G,* 92). As the notion of "authentic onomatopoeia" slips away, it takes with it "all the oppositions that follow or proceed." Moreover, this notion presumes a simplified structure of imitation, between the noise of the thing and its sound in language. Derrida observes that perhaps there are "morsels" of *fouet* and *glas* in each word. And if arbitrariness and unmotivation can supervene upon the "original character" of authentic onomatopoeias, then surely some kind of remotivation could "draw in the allegedly arbitrary again." If the arbitrariness were pure, this would not be possible (*G,* 93). Once again, Derrida's criticism of Saussure is that his notion of arbitrariness is *contained,* that it is redintegrated within a framework of meaning, just like Hegel's notion of the sign; both are examples of the redintegrative momentum of the *Aufhebung.*

Which brings us back to Hegel. While all this is going on in the right-hand column, the analysis of Hegel has continued relentlessly in the left. Derrida has been discussing Hegel's account of the Gospels, and his understanding of the Logos: *Im Anfang war der Logos.* Hegel "translates John into German" (*G,* 75, 78). Meaning? That Hegel sees in John, from his own German speculative perspective, a Jew writing of the Logos in Greek. The German Protestant philosopher feels the strain of attempting to oppose what he sees as Judaic and Greek "analytic, intellectualistic formality" which, according to him, cannot comprehend the living connection between God and the world, between God the father and God the son. This connection appears to the analytic understanding as

[14] Ferdinand de Saussure, *Course in General Linguistics,* trans. Wade Baskin (New York: Philosophical Library, 1959), p. 69.

a contradiction. For Hegel, the "Jewish principle," as Derrida explains, sees the two sides of the Logos as subsisting in contradiction: an objective side, as the world in its individual parts; and a subjective side, the Logos as reason, as the universality of thought. This effectively posits "a relation of death between God and the world" (*G, 76*). Hegel's anti-Semitic and anti-Islamic orientations, as well as his impugnment of Kant's conception of the divine, rest upon the same basis.

John is struggling to "slide [*glisser*] the Christian semanteme" into Jewish culture – in a language not ready for this. One must understand the Logos, the relation of God to humankind, as a filial relation, a *living* relation, not a relation between "dead" concepts. In the family, there is a "living relation of living beings" (*G, 80*). Derrida quotes Hegel as saying that "a tree which has three branches makes up *one single* tree (*einen Baum*) ... but every son of the tree, every branch ... is itself a tree" (*G, 81*). The Logos as the Christian Trinity can be expressed only in speculative, dialectical, language – which was not available to John, who struggles to express this unity in the terminology of the Understanding. As Derrida says, the expression of this unity "requires a kind of metaphoricity" (*G, 80*). According to Hegel, as Derrida reads him, the language of the Jews (like the language of the Muslims) was "incapable of metaphor" (*G, 73*). And the Logos as metaphor, says Derrida, "stands, like life ... beyond the dead concept" (*G, 81*). Further, according to Hegel, the "dead language" of the Gospel text must be animated by the reader to be understood in its metaphoricity, in its living meaning.

Hence, the reader must relive the text, must engage in its "living repetition," bringing her own spiritual activity into it; otherwise, she will see "only formal contradictions." As Hegel says: "This always objective language hence attains sense and weight only in the spirit of the reader" (*G, 76*). So, the objective language of the text must be *repeated* within the reader's subjectivity; this alone can bring it to life; this alone can do justice to its speculative meaning. The relation of reading occurs not between the letter and the abstract understanding but between spirit and spirit, the one recognizing itself in the other (*G, 85*). We understand the Logos as Incarnation by reading *ourselves* into its weave. Thus, "the Hegelian system," says Derrida, "commands that it be read as a book of life" (*G, 83*): a rather beautiful explanation of the process of reading, that we might implement in our own classrooms.[15]

---

[15] In his important essay "Eating My God," Stuart Barnett brilliantly extends the implications of the reading process to Hegel's treatment of the last supper where the materiality of Jesus' status as a

6.7 Summary of *Glas* as a Hegelian Self-Reflection

In this volume, then, Derrida has ushered into mutual conversation under the signifier *glas* a number of discourses from various cultures and traversing many eras concerning not only "death" in all its dialectical splendor – as the very presupposition behind life – but death as a metaphor, not only for the Logos in its revolutionary "calling to" a new era of spirituality (from the Judaeo to the Christian, from law to criminality, from ethics to moral exile) but also for the sign itself, its own death knell, its own refusal to cooperate with any given system, its own unmaking. All of these moves effectively embody an *Aufhebung*, a sublation of the Hegelian text, a repetition of it outside itself, in the field of play. What Derrida evokes is Hegel's understanding of the Logos as undergoing a historical transformation, from a Jewish to a Christian perspective, into the Absolute Sign, the absolute unity of thought and reality, reason and sense, history and meaning, signifier and signified. This impetus toward unity prefigures the integrative movement of the entire Hegelian system which distils away the very arbitrariness of the finite, human sign by investing it with self-transcendence, by viewing it in relation to the infinite, the all-encompassing movement of Absolute Spirit.

On the other "side," the right-hand column, we have the discourse of that which refuses assimilation, the discourse of the "depraved," a discourse of self-exile from conventional values, a discourse of theft and "illicit" irreducible love between males, which subverts the Absolute Sign, highlights and provokes the arbitrariness within its closed gates. Male-on-male fellatio – so ecstatically evoked in Genet's poetry in its imputed embodiment of beauty, sanctity, and mutual recognition – is incapable of integration into the Hegelian system in any of its movements: logical, ethical, historical, or aesthetic. But again, it is not a question of simple opposition between these registers. Their relation is complicated by a further, meta-discourse: Saussure's theorizing of arbitrariness and Derrida's own theorizing of the metaphorical nature of Saussure's strategies, which echoes the metaphoricity, at its core, of even the Absolute Sign. The same erasure of the filial relation that marks the Trinity for the Understanding (unable to grasp father and son as one) marks Genet's spiritually exalted criminals, such as Our Lady of the Flowers, who affirms that he is fatherless and generated from the Holy Spirit, that he *is* his father, mother,

---

sign must be destroyed and consumed in order to perpetuate the spirit of Christianity (*HAD*, 132–4, 140–4).

son, and himself (*G*, 82). He stands aloof from all designable relation by the sign. He, like the Logos, like Hegel and Genet, like Derrida himself, is the unsignable. *Glas* is the weave, the irreducible sound, the signifier knelling its own death (and that of all signs), that punctuates and actu-ates the mutual sliding of these discourses within one another. It is the absolution of the Absolute.

6.8   Epilogue

Glas is symptomatic of Derrida's general endeavor to open up Hegel's thought to its own subversive and dynamic potential. By way of a provi-sional conclusion, we might ask: what does it mean to arrest the dialectic at its second stage, to interrupt the movement of the *Aufhebung*, to with-draw from the momentum of the Absolute Idea and to spill one's idea-tional seed, like Onan, onto the ground? We thereby deny the dialectic its offspring, its continued lineage, its very survival. And our reward, like Onan's, will be death, pure negativity. It will be the womb of difference, a darkness and a light we have yet to explore, where the Other can roam freely without answering to us, without our recreating her in our image, without our pinning her wriggling on walls that we have erected. Yes, this is the realm of death, where we find out finally who we are. And who will condemn us? All the subalterns, all the enforcers of the Absolute Idea, from the high priests of various religions through feudal hierarchies of power to the global coercions of contemporary capitalism. So, clearly, any endeavor to halt or challenge the dialectic – which, as we have seen, is inherently imperialistic in its impulse to conquer all forms of otherness – is not just academic: it has real, and often terrible, implications. This decon-structive gesture, it might be said, is the archetypal strategy of all literary theory, which inevitably arrests the dialectic at its second stage.

The early Derrida, or at least deconstruction in its earlier formulations, was often seen as abstract and apolitical, implying no commitment to any particular ideological stance. But even perspectives that have profound political resonance – such as those of feminism, gender theory, some new historicism and reader–response theory, and postcolonialism – still occupy, like deconstruction, this second dialectical stage.[16] While they

---

[16] Fredric Jameson defines theory as the attempted "outside" of "philosophy as such," as that which attempts to grasp the limits of philosophy. Theory is the "perpetual and impossible attempt to dereify the language of thought." And deconstruction is the "very paradigm" of a theoretical pro-cess of undoing terminologies which itself "becomes a philosophy and an ideology in its own turn

incorporate elements from deconstruction, deriving these from the same source (Hegel), they differ from it in that the object of their critique is explicitly political. But, like deconstruction, they cannot move beyond this second stage (Marxism's third stage, that of a classless, socialist society that has done away with both private property and the state, has generally been abandoned as a viable transition to a third stage, even by Marxists). The *only* totality that any of our theories posit (or can posit) is capitalism as a world system, but as *internally* reformed, to accommodate more desirable notions of gender, class, and power.[17]

This, surely, is the archetypal lesson of deconstruction that is recapitulated in all theory. In this reading, deconstruction becomes the paradigm for all critiques of capitalism conducted under the aegis of "theory." Such critiques operate from the inside, and they all acknowledge their complicity, their own rootedness, in the very ideological and epistemic structures they impugn. When we come to Derrida's reading of Hegel's master–slave dialectic in a subsequent chapter, we can consider more closely how a deconstructive critique impugns the basic presuppositions of bourgeois ideology. But what is certain is that deconstruction is not dead, since it always needs to be killed, and since certain types of death are needed for the renewal of life.

---

and congeals into the very type of system it sought to undermine." This is the hopelessness of theory's nonetheless "unavoidable" aim to escape the "reifications of philosophy as well as the commodification of the intellectual marketplace today" (*VD*, 9). My interpretation of deconstruction's paradigmatic status for theory is, I think different from, but does not entirely conflict with, Jameson's reading. Fredric Jameson, *Valences of the Dialectic* (London: Verso, 2010).

[17] This is certainly not to deny the value or power of theories (such as critical race theory or queer theory) that insist on the intersectional nature of identity.

CHAPTER 7

Hegel on Language

One of the persistent endeavors of deconstruction and much literary theory, as seen in previous chapters, has been to challenge the notion of stable and fixed identity – whether based on Aristotelian substance or Platonic Forms or God. A crucial strategy in this undermining of identity was an insistence that what we call reality is constructed by language, a propensity to see reality as modeled on language as a relational system, where no entity has an independent identity. What we need to understand here is that this entire endeavor was articulated by Hegel who not only challenged the notion of self-identity but also anticipated contemporary views of language. We will see that language is the very form of the dialectic. Language, for Hegel, is intrinsically an instrument of negation and supersession of the world and the self as given; as such, it mimes within itself and is correlative with the larger historical dialectic in which feudalism is superseded and the revolutionary and imperialistic spirit of capitalism is born. Most bourgeois philosophers paint a picture of the mind that accepts the world as it is, a world that foists impressions and ideas on us. For Hegel, in contrast, the very process of knowing is both linguistic and imperialistic: it is transformative.

The ideas that language is integral to thought and that signs are somehow arbitrary or conventional are usually traced by literary theorists to Saussure.[1] However, not only are these insights ancient – going back to the pre-Socratics and the Greek rhetoricians[2] – but they are also

---

[1] For example, Jonathan Culler states: "The arbitrary nature of the sign lies at the root of modern theory," and traces this to Saussure's *Cours de linguistique générale* (1916), *The Literary in Theory* (Stanford: Stanford University Press, 2006), p. 117.

[2] For example, Sophists such as Antiphon viewed words as having no permanent reality behind them and speech as composed of "conventional and arbitrary signs." See George Alexander Kennedy ed., *Cambridge History of Literary Criticism: Volume I: Classical Criticism*, (Cambridge: Cambridge University Press, 1989), pp. 82–3. Also, there is a famous example in Plato's *Cratylus*, (384d) where Hermogenes, possibly a disciple of Parmenides, urges that names are conventional and their relationship to reality arbitrary: "there is no name given to anything by nature; all is convention and

replicated in much modern philosophy, such as that of Herder, Locke, Hume, and Rousseau. These notions in fact have also a Hegelian provenance. Indeed, it has been well-documented that the so-called linguistic turn of the early twentieth century has its roots in a much earlier linguistic turn that occurred in the late eighteenth and early nineteenth centuries.[3] As Jere Surber notes, the founder of modern comparative linguistics, W. von Humboldt, was a contemporary of Hegel, and Hegel's reflections on language supervened upon an entire series of debates concerning the connections between language and philosophy which involved both the German idealists and their empiricist opponents. Hegel's own views of language were forged in relation to the ideas of Schelling and Fichte (*HL*, 3–10). But Surber also points out that Hegel did not formulate any coherent philosophy of language and that his work could furnish the bases of several approaches to language.[4]

The present account of Hegel's views of language is strictly limited in its scope and is intended primarily (a) to offer a clear exposition of those views for the nonspecialist reader, and (b) to highlight the ways in which Hegel anticipates many of the insights of modern literary theory. Given Hegel's consistent insistence that entities are intrinsically related, it is hardly surprising to find that in his system, language and the processes of thought are internally connected with each another: They do not merely subsist in some kind of external relation, where, for example, a word expresses a concept. Rather, the two realms – of thought and language – internally shape and condition each other, and their relation is what enables them both. It is predictable, then, but also remarkable that in Hegel's *Encyclopaedia* – and specifically in his *Philosophy of Mind* which contains his most extensive treatment of language[5] – he views language as intrinsic to the dialectical process; or, we might say that the dialectic is intrinsic to language; or that language, as conceived dialectically, is intrinsic to thought.

---

habit of the users," *Collected Dialogues of Plato*, ed. Edith Hamilton and Huntington Cairns (Princeton, NJ: Princeton University Press, 1969), p. 383.

[3] See, for example, the superb anthology *Hegel and Language*, ed. Jere O'Neill Surber (New York: State University of New York Press, 2006). Hereafter cited as *HL*. Many writers – including Gadamer, Kojève, Hyppolite, Derrida, Kristeva, and Deleuze – have dealt with Hegel's views of language, and a few of these will be considered in Chapter 8.

[4] Jere O'Neill Surber, Rev. of Jim Vernon, Hegel's *Philosophy of Language*, *Notre Dame Philosophical Reviews*, (November 5, 2007): https://ndpr.nd.edu/news/23221-hegel-s-philosophy-of-language/

[5] For an excellent account of Hegel's developing views of language, see Jere O'Neill Surber, "Hegel's Philosophy of Language," in *A Companion to Hegel*, ed. Stephen Houlgate and Michael Baur (Oxford: Wiley Blackwell, 2011), pp. 245–58.

7.1 Hegel's First Philosophy of Spirit

Before looking at Hegel's *Encyclopaedia*, it is worth pausing to consider one of his earlier manuscripts on social theory entitled the *Philosophy of Spirit* (1803–4). This contains some revealing anticipations of his later views of language. These earlier expositions in fact may help us to see more clearly Hegel's connection to modern literary theories. In this earlier text, Hegel sees the "Idea" as divided into the two moments of "body" and "Spirit." Nature is the body of the Idea, whereas Spirit is ultimately expressed in the collective life of a people and also in the State. So the philosophy of Spirit follows from the philosophy of Nature, tracing the development of consciousness from its beginnings in sensation through the various phases of cognition to conceptual life and the practical implementation of this in the institutions of the state. What is fascinating, in both earlier and later texts, is the central and mediating role that language plays in this overall development.

7.1.1 *Hegel's Definition of the Sign*

In the *First Philosophy of Spirit*, Hegel offers an interesting definition of the sign, which anticipates the use of this term in much literary theory. He regards consciousness as a kind of "middle" or mediation between subject and object. As this middle, he says, consciousness is "a *sign* in general."[6] When we use something as a sign, we abstract from its existence as a *thing*: "it means something other than it is, it is posited as something other than it is on its own account; [it is] contingent for that of which it is the sign." So, for example, we might say that "red" means "stop." But the idea of stopping has no intrinsic connection with redness. And therefore the meaning of the sign is arbitrary, in that it is wholly dependent upon *us*, upon the subject: "the meaning of the sign is only in relation to the subject ... the sign does not have its absolute meaning within itself" (*FPS*, 221). In other words, we are not interested in the redness in itself. What Hegel is basically describing is the process whereby we have a sense-experience of some aspect of the world. Our minds receive this sensation (of what will eventually be discerned as an object), and they classify and reproduce it. Our memory takes the sense-intuition and internalizes it,

---

[6] Hegel, *System of Ethical Life (1802/3) and First Philosophy of Spirit (Part III of the System of Speculative Philosophy 1803/4)*, p. 220 (§286). Hereafter cited as *FPS*.

abstracting it from its original setting in space and time, and giving it an existence in the mind's *own* ideal realm. Its existence here takes the form of a sign, a name; hence in memory external things are posited "implicitly as other than themselves. In this [product] consciousness gains for the first time a reality ... The idea of this existence of consciousness is *memory*, and its existence itself is *speech*" (*FPS*, 221). To put it another way, the ideal realm exists as memory, and speech or language is its external form.

What's striking here is that language is not merely the medium in which consciousness exists. It *is* the existence of consciousness itself. We recall, previously, that Hegel defined consciousness as the sign in general. As he envisions it, the mind receives the world initially as sensation and turns it into language, into speech, into the medium in which consciousness literally "exists," the medium of consciousness's mediation between itself as subject and the world or object as sensation. For Hegel the world as merely given must be "negated" so that we can discern its rational core. Negation in this manner is the first phase of the dialectic. Language is the very means of this negation.

We all know of Adam's naming activities in the Garden of Eden. But it takes perhaps an impossible leap of historical imagination to see Adam as the first Hegelian. Here is Hegel:

> The first act, by which Adam established his lordship over the animals, is this, that he gave them a name, i.e., he nullified them as beings on their own account, and made them into ideal [entities]. This sign was previously, qua [natural] sign, a *name* which is still something else than *a name* on its own account ... In the name the *self*-subsisting reality of the sign is nullified. (*FPS*, 222)

So, negating the world through language is an act of subjugation (and we will see that language is equally integral to the master–slave dialectic). Naming the animals is not merely an act of categorization but of domination, of control. For it abolishes their independent existence, their being as "natural" signs, their status as *things*. And it recreates them as *ideas* in the mind, in an ideal world where their original connections and contexts in the world are *replaced* by whatever connections and contexts the mind chooses to invoke. But once the name is created, once the act of naming is accomplished, the name itself now persists, as something concrete, as something that might outlive its creator and indeed the very thing it named ("dinosaur" – which actually "names" our way of looking at the world). "Adam," of course, is a metaphor – for a community, for historical development; for no one person could have the power to name.

7.1.2   *Language as a Relational System*

Long before literary theorists and linguists examined the connection between the material or physical qualities of a word and its meaning, Hegel characterized the sign as marked by "duality," which itself could be grasped only in a relational context. He states that the "name exists as *speech*. Speech is the existing concept of consciousness, so that it does not fixate itself, but immediately ceases to be, when it is." Speech is "absolutely external to itself" and has "universally communicative existence" (*FPS*, 222). In other words, the meaning or signification of speech is external to its own materiality or material embodiment, and this meaning is what has communicative power, not the material dimension. The meaning of the word "rose" is external to its sound and resides in a consensual understanding of the relation of this sound to other sounds. Hegel acknowledges that sound has meaning but only because it represents something ideal: "Speech as articulated sounding is the voice of consciousness, because every tone within it has meaning, i.e., because there exists in it a name, the ideality of an existing thing; [in other words] the immediate non-existence of the thing." Importantly, Hegel says that the various sounds or tones are not independently "determinate distinctions" but are determined "through the preceding and following tone" (*FPS*, 222). So the value or significance of any given sound is relational and is achieved only through its connection to other sounds.

Hence we come to Hegel's emphasis on language as a relational system. He effectively redefines speech:

> The name as such is just the name of the single thing; speech is the *relating* of names, or once again it is the *ideality* of the multiplicity of names, and it *expresses* likewise this *relation*, the achieved universal (*das gewordene Allgemeine*); in other words it becomes *understanding*. In the universal element of speech names [are] only formally ideal in themselves, they express the concrete determinate [thing]; but the unity of the element in which they are, posits them equally as these determinate [things], i.e., as different from one another, [it posits] their relation, or themselves as absolute particulars, which means that in their determinacy they are likewise self-suspending. (*FPS*, 222–3)

So speech is the universal element, the unifying element, which posits names as both self-standing and related in their difference from one another. A name has a merely "formal" ideality, an ideality which has yet no content; it is only within the system of speech that this ideality of names – this elevation to the plane of universality and relatability through supersession of mere singularity – is realized. In other words, it is realized as a *concept* of the understanding, relatable to other concepts. The negating power of consciousness, as always, is a power to negate what is merely given, and to raise it to the level of universality and differentiability on which it can be seen as part of a system.

7.1.3 Language and Reality

In *First Philosophy*, Hegel has an interesting approach to the connection between a name or sign and reality. He questions the antithesis of realism and idealism which assert respectively that, for example, "color" is grounded in the object or the subject of perception. He suggests that color exists in three "potencies" or levels of manifestation: first, in sensation as a determinate color, then in imagination as a concept, and subsequently in memory as a name that is related to other names or concepts. Both realism and idealism sunder "this essential totality of the three levels of determinacy" (*FPS*, 225). So, for Hegel, what we call, for example, the color "blue" is not something that is either already out there in the world or something merely imposed by our minds upon the world. Indeed, it is not a thing at all but a *process*, which emerges from our initial sensory engagement with our surroundings through increasingly refined levels of comprehensiveness.

Hegel puts the matter in terms of spirit's interaction with nature: "Spirit *as sensing is itself animal*, submerged in nature; in the progress upwards to the relating and distinguishing of colors, and to their coming forth as color, as concept, the nature of color itself becomes spirit" (*FPS*, 225). So the transition or transformation occurs not just in nature but in our minds also. Hegel's insight here is quite astonishing. Initially, *we ourselves* exist only in the mode of sensation, indistinguishable from the color; the color gets distinguished and universalized and related only insofar as our minds become internally differentiated through their various faculties to rise to this universalizing capacity. So, what is progressing "upwards" is color as a function of both our minds and the world, until color itself becomes spirit, until color becomes part of our conceptual manner of apprehending the world and ourselves. Color is one of the multifold ways in which the unity of our minds and the world is expressed; both realism and idealism falsely isolate a respective side of this antithesis, spuriously supposing that color can subsist or exist exclusively in either the perceiving subject or the perceived object.

Hegel states that even when sensation is elevated to memory and speech, it is not fully a concept of consciousness, since the singular sensations that are posited (or recreated) as ideal by memory form a multitude of idealities, a multitude which is not yet a unity and must "raise itself to connection" or relatedness, and "their connection, the concept, must be what is posited" (FPS, 226). So in a concept, sensations are posited as related, as part of a system. Likewise, says Hegel, "Speech that elevates itself to understanding ... supersedes the *singular* spoken name – the concept itself, like everything else, falls within speech, and [it is] absolutely communicative. The suspended name [is] posited not according to its singular being, but only according to its relation" (FPS, 226). This is Hegel's way of saying (a) that a name has a kind of dual existence, both as an entity in itself (a material part of language) and as "suspended," as pointing beyond itself, in its meaning; and (b) that language can arise only as a relational process, only as a relating of names which suspends or supersedes their singularity. The concept is intrinsically and "absolutely communicative" inasmuch as it too is orientated toward communication, toward relationality, rather than toward independent existence. In its very nature, it is a self-transcendence of individual existence. We see here how language is at the very heart of the process whereby immediate identity and singularity are negated, are superseded. Language itself has an inherently imperialistic impetus. To understand the world is to conquer it – through both language and labor.

7.1.4   Consciousness as Language

Let's recall once again that Hegel defines consciousness as the sign in general. Through the process of positing the name, of positing language, as pure relation, as pure negativity, the mind establishes itself as purely negative, as an empty, individual unit that contains nature – which was originally confronted as composed of discrete and separate entities – "as its absolutely negative side" (FPS, 227). In other words, consciousness exists as the capacity to negate nature by means of language, to divest nature of its discreteness and singularity and to reconfigure it as ideal. This step will be important in understanding the life-and-death struggle in the master–slave dialectic. For consciousness has now reached the point where it can give up any dependency on nature: "every determinacy by which he [a consciousness] should be gripped he can cut away from himself, and in death he can realize his absolute independence and freedom [for] himself as absolutely negative consciousness" (FPS, 228).

In its capacity to raise nature to the level of ideality, to rethink original sensations in terms of signs and concepts, the mind has recreated nature on its own ideal level, independent of the world of nature as originally given. It confronts that world in its capacity as a negating power, a power to transform that world. But this power is still abstract; it is still merely a power of language, a power to organize and assimilate and essentialize. It is merely a negative power and cannot transform the world as such. Moreover, it still confronts that world in its capacity as an individual consciousness. To act on the world, it must become "practical consciousness, consciousness as existing thing against [other] existing things" (*FPS*, 228). For Hegel, this means that consciousness must first overcome or supersede its own singularity and must interact with other consciousnesses.

Before moving to Hegel's account of language in the *Encyclopedia*, it is worth stressing that the process Hegel describes here – whereby we effectively recreate the world as language – has profound ideological resonance. For example, this is exactly the process of orientalism, as Edward Said describes it: The negation of the "Orient" as based on knowledge derived from sensation and actual experience, and its recreation according to conceptions of the Other that might sustain certain images of the self. Hence the Orient was characterized as backward, irrational, and sensuous in order to complement Europe's self-image as progressive, rational, and moral. Of course, the process is not quite this simple, for there is no original Orient, unmediated by language or categories of thought. It's a question of various ways in which the Orient is constructed. It could be argued that this imperialistic strategy, of negation and recreation, is integral to our understanding of the world at every level, ranging from broad ideological structures to the most intensely personal psychological experience.

7.2 Language in Hegel's *Philosophy of Mind*

Indeed, Hegel's views of language form an integral part of his account of the process of cognition and can't be understood without grasping that account. In the *Philosophy of Mind*, Hegel describes the various stages by which our mind knows an object in the external world. What is significant, as will emerge later in this chapter, is that he sees the "sign" as mediating *both* the mind's self-development and its relation to the world. Hegel begins by distinguishing his approach from that of psychology, which studies the "facts of human consciousness, merely as facts, just as they are given," without any attempt to discern an underlying reality or unity (*PM*, 186–7). Mind achieves full freedom, says Hegel, when the so-called facts of consciousness are shown "to be *acts* of mind, to be a content which *it* has posited" (*PM*, 182–3). Hegel states that, as consciousness "has for its object the stage which preceded it, so mind has or rather makes consciousness its object" (*PM*, 184).

Hence there is an important difference between mere consciousness and mind. Consciousness relates to objects merely as they are immediately given. Mind must remove not only the immediacy of the object but the "*illusory appearance* of its own immediacy" (*PM*, 191). In other words, mind must seek the rational, ideal, core not only of the object but of its *own* contents, which it cannot take as merely given (*PM*, 191). We can see here that the dialectical process involves two simultaneous negations, the one of an internal and the other of an external, situation.

7.2.1   *Language and Cognition*

It's within this larger, cognitive process, then, that we must place Hegel's account of language. He divides the process of cognition into three stages. The first is "intuition" (*Anschauung*), where the mind confronts an immediate object; the second stage is that of "mental representation," where the mind withdraws itself from its relation to the single object and relates the object to a universal category; in the final stage, that of "thought," the mind understands the concrete universal nature of the object, as something determined by its (the mind's) own subjectivity (*PM*, 192). We might elucidate this by giving an example. When we experience a particular object, we first confront it as a mass of sensation, which our intuition distinguishes from other objects that produce a different sensation. In the second stage, our mind removes the sensation from its unique or isolated situation and brackets its particular characteristics, instead subsuming it under a universal category, such as "table" (always the philosopher's favorite example); in the final stage, we understand the object in its essential character, in what essentially constitutes it as a table – an operation of our minds which situates it within a vast system of objects – in short, we now rise to the level of "thought" and understand the table as a *concept*. We are beginning to see here how, for Hegel, the very process of understanding is intrinsically a linguistic, and even imperialistic, process. This is basically what Hegel means by the process of cognition, as it goes through the phases of intuition, representation, and thought. To appreciate the significance of language for Hegel, we need to understand this process in detail, starting with intuition.

7.2.2   The Phases of Cognition

In the phase of intuition, the mind itself exists as mere feeling, and possesses merely a "vulgar subjectivity." It has attained to a feeling of Self, apprehending itself as an "I." Mind, in this stage of mere feeling, exists as individual, in the form of "casual particularity," shut up in its "own isolated subjectivity – [its] private and particular self" (*PM*, 193–4). But it is in feeling that we stand in closest contact with any given content in the world. Indeed, Hegel goes so far as to say that in "feeling, there is present the whole of Reason, the entire content of mind. All our representations, thoughts, and notions of the external world, of right, of morality, and of the content of religion develop from our feeling intelligence ... men have formed their gods out of their feelings and passions" (*PM*, 194–5). Hence, all our knowledge is implicitly contained in feeling, whose content, as it is progressively unfolded and explicated, becomes more and more explicitly rational.

Feeling then progresses to the stage of "attention." The mind now defines the content of sensation as something external to itself, projects it into space and time, as an object (*PM*, 195). This stage involves (a) identifying the object by abstracting it from everything else, (b) a "negation of one's self-assertion" and a correlative surrendering to the object, and therefore (c) a division into subject and object, self and world (*PM*, 196). Ironically anticipating Russell and other analytic philosophers, Hegel summarizes the process of attention when he states that it involves a "transformation of what is sensed into an object existing outside of us" (*PM*, 197). Notwithstanding his "realism," Russell admitted that what we *know* is not the object itself but our sense-experience of it. Hegel is suggesting that our sense-experience occurs initially as a unity of self and object, which is subsequently divided into the two realms of subjectivity and objectivity. On another level, Hegel here anticipates the psychoanalytic theories of Lacan and Kristeva, who both see the infant as initially inhabiting a unified realm where distinctions between itself and the external world (including its mother) have not yet been formed.

Our mind now, according to Hegel, reaches the level of "intuition" proper, where I am implicitly aware of the distinction between the object and myself. I no longer relate to the object as something isolated and individual but am aware of it as rationally determined, as "a totality, a unified fullness of determinations" (*PM*, 199) Such intuition grasps "the genuine substance of the object," but this is only the beginning of cognitive awareness since that substance remains unexplicated and still immersed in inessential or accidental circumstances (*PM*, 199–200). In intuition I have the entire object before me, but my cognition must apprehend the object in its *essential* nature and relations before the object can once again confront me as "an articulated, systematic totality" (*PM*, 200).

Hegel gives a pertinent example of this dialectical process – which will be echoed by Wordsworth: a poet may start off with some intuition; but this needs to be informed by meditation and reflection so that the subject-matter is freed from all contingent or accidental associations. In this way, the poet's intuition is developed organically, by proceeding from an apprehension of the object as something immediate and isolated, through viewing it in its essential relations, to a view of it as once again individual but as embodying those relations. The poet begins with immediate intuition and traverses thought or reflection to end with "mediated" intuition. For example, I may have a sensuous intuition of a tree, as an object in its accidental surroundings, which might include a waterfall and a mountain. When I reflect on this intuition, I may view the tree as part of a broader system of nature infused with a divine spirit. I then come back to the tree with a fuller, more mediated intuition of it, viewing it as a symbol of life and regeneration. This is the kind of development that Wordsworth describes in "Lines Composed a Few Miles Above Tintern Abbey."

For Hegel, the next general stage after intuition is "representation," which is essentially intuition recollected or internalized (*PM*, 201). Whereas in intuition the emphasis is on the object (to which I "surrender"), in representation, subjectivity withdraws into itself, "in an externality of its own" (*PM*, 201). Again, this is a striking insight. Subjectivity *displaces* the original externality of the object with its own "externality," that of a representational image, an externality which *it* has reshaped. Hegel here anticipates many notions of literary theory, including the view of reality as constituted by or modeled on language. But at this early stage, the representations are not wholly independent and are still tied to the "ready-found material of intuition" with which they form a kind of synthesis. They attain independence fully only at the stage of "thought" (*PM*, 202).

Representation consists of three phases: recollection, imagination, and memory. In the first phase, that of "recollection," the content of an intuition is internalized, or reproduced identically within the mind in the form of an image. This content is thereby "recollected" or posited as mine, as belonging to me (*PM*, 202). Hegel states that the mind recollects the intuition or feeling, and places its content "in a space and time of its own." In this way, that content becomes "an *image* or picture, liberated from its original immediacy and abstract singleness ... and received into the universality of the ego" (*PM*, 203). The content of feeling is lifted out of the particularity of space and time and transposed into the mind's ideal or "universal" space and time.

7.2.3 The Three Phases of Representation

7.2.3.1 Recollection: The Mind as an Unconscious Pit

An image from the past no longer exists except in the mind. In the early phase of recollection, it is "stored up out of consciousness." In other words, it is stored *unconsciously* in the mind. Hegel characterizes the mind in this phase as a "night-like mine or pit in which is stored a world of infinitely many images and representations, yet without being in consciousness" (*PM*, 203–4). This early intelligence is a "subconscious mine" in which any image contains only the germ of universality, only the *potential* to be differentiated. At this stage of cognition, I do not as yet have "full command over the images slumbering in the mine or pit of my inwardness, am not as yet able to recall them at will" (*PM*, 205).

The overall point here is that in the early phase of recollection, the content of intuition is (a) internalized into an image, (b) transposed into the mind's ideal space and time, and (c) received as such into the mind's unconscious store of images. To enter the phase of recollection proper, the image in our mind needs to be referred to an *actual* intuition. Numerous images are submerged in "the blank night" of our initial intelligence. I may, for example, have a vague image of a former student Angela in my mind. If I now encounter that person and have a *present* intuition of her, this will help me relate the image that already exists in my mind to an actual intuition, thereby authenticating it. For something to be retained in my memory, for me to undertake recollection proper, I must have "repeated intuitions" of it. To use Judith Butler's language from another context, the intuition must be "performed" repeatedly.

In referring the mental image to the intuition, I am subsuming "the immediate single intuition (impression) under what is ... universal, under the representation (idea) with the same content." So, for example, the sensation of "table" is subsumed under the (general) idea of "table" – the content is the "same" but apprehended on differing levels. In this way, the image is distinguished both from the original intuition (relating to the external world) and from "the blank night" of the unconscious mind. Hegel states that the mind "disperses the night-like darkness enveloping the wealth of its images and banishes it by the luminous clarity of a present image" (*PM*, 208). He defines this synthesis of the internal (mental) image with the recollected existence as "representation proper" (*PM*, 205).

7.2.3.2 Imagination

In "recollection" we first internalize the content of an intuition, the represented content being identical to the intuited content. In the second phase, imagination works on this content, drawing out its universal or general features, thereby creating a representational image that is now *different* from that which was originally intuited. The intuited content is now regarded merely as a "sign" of the content shaped (imaged) mentally by imagination (*PM*, 202).

Hence imagination connects the images by dissolving their merely given empirical connections and subsuming the image under the idea, the particular under the universal; or, in Hegel's language, by the idea "making itself into the image's soul" (*PM*, 209–10). In the mind, the general idea is the inward side and the image the external side. It is imagination that effects their unity. In achieving this unity of universal and particular, of representation and intuition, imagination embodies the nature of art in general, which represents the idea "in the form of sensuous existence, of the image" (*PM*, 210). For example, whereas philosophy will treat concepts on a purely discursive level, an imaginative work of literature, such as Spenser's *Faerie Queene*, will concretely personify virtues and vices such as holiness and duplicity. This production of *signs* by the creative imagination forms the transition to memory (*PM*, 208).

What Hegel now does is little short of astounding (Derrida will call it scandalous). He explains that, at the stage of creative imagination, "intelligence makes itself *be* as a *thing*" (*PM*, 211). In other words, the mind gives *existence* to its own ideas, as signs, in the dimension of language. Hegel adds that the image of an object produced by the imagination (the associative imagination) up to this stage is a "bare mental or subjective intuition: in the sign or symbol it adds intuitability proper." The "it" here refers to the creative imagination, which lifts the mind from "the vague mine" (or "pit") of unconsciously stored images and "elevates the internal meaning to an image and intuition" (*PM*, 211). In other words, creative imagination gives "being" or "existence" to a general idea (the "internal meaning") by "imaging" it as a sign in language. In this way, the general idea is able to be "intuited" – and in this way, the mind replaces or rather sublates the original sensuous intuition, which was caught up in its accidental or contingent surroundings, with an intuition of ideality itself, with something *material* which now represents the object as it has been worked on by the mind, distilled into a precise meaning extricated from those accidental circumstances, and relatable to other objects that have been similarly rationalized.

So, for Hegel, the very process of intuition is sublated or superseded: Not only is the sensuous world as it comes to us transformed and ideally reconfigured by the mind, but the mind now has intuitions of this ideal-ized content *itself*. Again, this has resonance for the workings of ideology. Even what might seem to be a "natural" process such as lovemaking is actually infused with techniques that have been idealized and constructed through a long cultural history, but we appear to "intuit" them in this idealized form. The same will apply to ideals of beauty – *ideals* that are intuited, that strike us with the force of sensuous intuitions.

7.2.3.2.1 Symbols and Signs Hegel makes a distinction between symbol and sign. Symbolic imagination is still guided by the sensuous content of its images, and is only relatively free (*PM*, 212). For example, a cloud might be said to symbolize rain, and this is dependent upon a pre-given or natural connection. Truly creative imagination attains a total independence from the original image and its given import. Hence, for example, the use of "cloud" in the technological application i-cloud bears no relation to this natural connection (*PM*, 213).

So, the use of signs rather than symbols indicates a progression in the mind from merely a subjective authentication of the general idea (by referring it to the image, with which it is naturally connected) to an objective authentication in an external world of its own creation: the world of the sign, the world of language. Hegel states that:

> [T]he general idea, liberated from the image's content, in making its freely selected external material into something that can be intuitively perceived, produces what has to be called a sign – in specific distinction from symbol. The sign must be regarded as a great advance on the symbol. Intelligence, in indicating something by a sign, has finished with the con-tent of intuition, and the sensuous material receives for its soul a significa-tion foreign to it. Thus, for example, a cockade, or a flag, or a tomb-stone, signifies something totally different from what it immediately indicates. The arbitrary nature of the connection between the sensuous material and a general idea occurring here, has the necessary consequence that the significance of the sign must first be learned. This is especially true of lan-guage signs. (*PM*, 212)

Hegel calls the sign "an independent representation" that is now united with an intuition; but the content of the intuition as first given (as with the flag) is made to represent something else: "It is an image, which has received as its soul and meaning an independent mental representation. This intuition is the *Sign*" (*PM*, 212–13). This formulation, as we shall see, is strikingly similar to Roland Barthes's description of myth as a second-order language, which empties the content of a sign to replace it with some other, arbitrary – and ideologically motivated – meaning.

The sign, says Hegel, "is some immediate intuition, representing a totally different import from what naturally belongs to it; it is the pyramid into which a foreign soul has been conveyed, and where it is conserved" (*PM*, 212–13). Sound, or the "vocal note" – and its systematization in language – gives to sensations, intuitions, and conceptions a "second and higher existence than they naturally possess – invests them with the right of existence in the ideational realm" (*PM*, 214). So, language is an externalization of the mind's ideas as something concrete, as signs that can be intuited. But again, it is not that the mind has ideas which are then somehow expressed; rather, they are created or formulated in their very expression.

So, we can see that the mind has not simply stripped the sensuous matter of its immediacy and particularity and raised it to the level of generality; the mind has also removed from the image anything extraneous to its own universalizing and semantic intentions, and has then replaced this mental image with a sign whose connection to it is wholly arbitrary. The relation between the sign and the mental image is merely conventional. What was received as sensuous matter is processed first into an intuition and then into an image or idea and then into a sign. What enters the mind as *matter* leaves as a *sign*. In dialectical terms, the received matter is sublated by intuition; and the intuition is sublated by the image which in turn is sublated by the sign. Each of these is a stage; and each stage both transcends the previous stage while retaining what is considered to be universal and relevant to the mind's rational purpose. Language is the means whereby the mind "gives its own original ideas a definite existence" (*PM*, 213). Language is the very medium of sublation and, indeed, of the dialectical process itself.

7.2.3.3 Memory

In the third phase, that of "memory," the sign is internalized within the mind, yet retains the "form of something external and mechanical, and, in this way, a unity of subjectivity and objectivity is produced which forms the transition to thought as such" (*PM*, 203). So the content of the external intuition is internalized as a sign of that content as mentally refined (by the imagination) to its generalizable, rational core. The unity of subjectivity and objectivity thereby produced is the mind's connection with the external world as reduced to signs. In other words, it is the mind's connection with an externality that it has created to replace the original externality of the world. This, the mind's externality to itself, is the world of signs, of language. It is this which mediates the transition to the level of thought and, as we can now summarize, for Hegel, language is indeed intrinsic to the very process of thinking.

7.3   Language as Integral to Thought

Once again, the sphere of language for Hegel is a form of externality, but an *ideal* externality, the mind's representation to itself of the external world as filtered through its own operations (*Enc.* § 462). Language is the form in which the sensory aspects of the world and their representation in images is raised to the level of thought, which can operate independently of the original sensations and their original processing in the mind. Hegel is emphatic that language is integral to the very process, and the very possibility, of thought:

> The true, concrete negativity of the language-sign is *intelligence*, since by this the sign is changed from something outward to something inward and as thus transformed is preserved. Words thus attain an existence animated by thought. This existence is absolutely necessary to our thoughts. We only know our thoughts, only have definite, actual thoughts, when we give them the form of objectivity, of a being distinct from our inwardness, and therefore the shape of externality, and of an externality, too, that at the same time bears the stamp of the highest inwardness. The articulated sound, the *word*, is alone such inward externality. To want to think without words ... is, therefore, a manifestly irrational procedure ... the word gives to thoughts their highest and truest existence ... Just as the true *thought* is the very thing itself, so too is the *word* when it is employed by genuine thinking. Intelligence, therefore in filling itself with the word, receives into itself the nature of the thing. (*Enc.* §462 *Zus*)

There are a number of important points here. Language is the objective form of thought, or its "outward" side. This does not mean that we first have thoughts and then find words to express them. Rather, as Saussure was later to imagine the connection between thought and word as occurring on reverse sides of the same sheet of paper, so language is the other "side" of thought. Ironically, this externality (language) expresses the "highest inwardness." It has the same degree of externality as objects in the world, which is why it can give "objective" existence to thought, but it is an externality manufactured by, and thus "animated" by, thought. The word's "inward externality" is what mediates between our mind and the externality of the world.

It would be a mistake to view Hegel's statement that "true thought" and the "word" are "the thing itself" as voicing a referential view whereby words refer to actual things in the world. The "thing itself" for Hegel is of course neither the Kantian nor the realist "thing in itself." Rather, it is the object as already apprehended in its essence, in its ideality, by thought (*Enc.* §464). In other words, the mind finds its objective existence in language, whose "externality" falls within the realm of ideality itself. Indeed, Hegel characterizes "thought" – the last main stage in the development of mind – as the stage where intelligence "knows itself to be the *nature of the thing*" The mind at this stage is "recognitive" in that the intuitions it cognizes are already its own, and "in the name it rediscovers the fact" (*Enc.* §465). Hence the "fact" is now filtered through the mind's own operations and is transformed by the mind into language. The content and object of thought is nothing but itself, its own operations.

The foregoing demonstrates that most of the innovative ideas of literary theory concerning language were anticipated by Hegel. He sees language as a system of signs in necessary relation. More than this, he articulates intricately how language is integral to the very process of thought. Language is the medium in which consciousness effects a negation of the world – and its own contents – as these are immediately given, raising both to the form of universality and rationality. Language is effectively the medium of the dialectic. Where literary theory diverges from Hegel, as we will continue to see in Chapter 8, is precisely in its refusal to ascribe universality or rationality to the linguistic frameworks in which the immediacy, the given particularity, of the world is sublated, in its reluctance to move to the third stage of the dialectic.

CHAPTER 8

Hegel, Language, and Literary Theory
Saussure, Barthes, Derrida, Deleuze

8.1 Saussure, Barthes, and the Structure of the Sign

While we can't say that Hegel's views of language directly influenced all literary theorists, it's clear that those views anticipate some of the fundamental concepts of language on which much literary theory is founded. For example, Saussure's very definition of the sign is dialectical. In his lectures published as *Course in General Linguistics*, Saussure states: "I propose to retain the word *sign* [*signe*] to designate the whole and to replace *concept* and *sound-image* respectively by *signified* [*signifié*] and [*significant*]: the last two terms have the advantage of indicating the opposition that separates them from each other and from the whole of which they are parts."[1] The sign is the synthesis of signifier and signified, and it is this synthesis that "refers" to the object. The indifferent externality or "thing" is constituted as an object not by the fact of reference but by the *relation* of this reference to the reference of other signs, a relation that structures other "objects" as part of an overall network. In other words, the system of objects is actually *internal* to the network of signs, each sign shaping or prefiguring its object.

Hence, in this system there is no object beyond the sign; this is not to say that the sign somehow *creates* its object (whether this be physical, like a "table," or psychological like "love"). Rather, the object has significance in the light of the sign. But it is the same process which creates subjectivity – not any individual subjectivity but a cumulative, historical, communal, subjectivity. Hence language is the *form* of both subjectivity and objectivity, which are created at the same time and are effectively coterminous, the difference between them being one of viewpoint or emphasis. Language is the medium of their creation. In this sense, subjectivity becomes linguistic. Whatever categories we hold subjectivity to

---

[1] Saussure, *Course in General Linguistics*, p. 67. Hereafter cited as *CGL*.

comprise – as in Kant's case, substance, causality, relation, etc. – are not just categories but concepts in language. Kant saw the "external" world as actually shaped by our subjective apparatus: by our intuitions of sensibility, whereby we see everything in space and time; and by the twelve categories of our Understanding, whereby we see everything in terms of quantity, quality, relation, causality, etc. But whereas Kant saw subjectivity as fixed, we can, if we view these categories as merely concepts related to other concepts in language, withdraw from them their privileged or universal status and see them as interacting with, or even replaceable by, other concepts.

When we say that the concepts are necessarily in interaction with other concepts, we have moved to a Hegelian standpoint; when we recognize, with Saussure, that these concepts are part of the system of language, we have effectively reformulated the insights of Kant in terms of language. Whereas he addressed the connection between thought and reality, we, like Hegel, are interposing language into that connection – not as a mere relation but as an *internal* relation that contributes to the constitution of both terms. In other words, language internally structures both thought and reality.

The French structuralist (and poststructuralist) Roland Barthes was effectively expressing this "linguistic turn" embodied in Hegel when he remarked that "it is human history which converts reality into speech."[2] Hegel, we recall, held that the world comes to us as sensation and is transformed into a world of language. According to Barthes, what mythical speech presupposes is a "signifying consciousness" and every object in the world can "become speech" (*Myth*, 111). Myth belongs to semiology, the general science of signs initially postulated by Saussure. Like Derrida, Barthes sees an entire province of contemporary research – including psychoanalysis, structuralism, and some kinds of literary criticism – as concerned not with facts but with signs. And, reminiscent of Hegel's definition of his *Logic*, Barthes sees semiology as "a science of forms" (*Myth*, 111). Indeed, the explanation of mythology, for Barthes, entails what Engels called a "dialectical coordination" of particular sciences: mythology is a part of both semiology and ideology, and cannot be explained by a one-sided omission of either of these domains (*Myth*, 112).

What's fascinating here is that Barthes's definition of the sign, like Saussure's, brings out its dialectical structure. He begins by

[2] Roland Barthes, *Mythologies*, trans. Annette Lavers (London: Collins, 1973), p. 110. Hereafter cited as *Myth*.

acknowledging that "semiology postulates a relation between two terms, a signifier and a signified." However, "we are dealing, in any semiological system, not with two, but with three different terms. For what we grasp is not at all one term after the other but the correlation which unites them ... the signifier, the signified, and the sign, which is the associative total of the first two terms." Barthes offers an example: if I use roses to signify my passion, we do not (except for analytical purposes) have merely a signifier (roses) and a signified (my passion); we have only "passionified roses" (*Myth*, 113). The point is that neither signifier nor signified have any meaning independently of the totality, the unity, the synthesis, that they mutually comprise.

What Barthes calls this "tri-dimensional pattern" is operative, as he observes, in many other thinkers besides Saussure. For example, in Freud's analysis of dreams, there are actually three terms: manifest content, latent content, *and* a "correlation of the first two: it is the dream itself in its totality." For Freud, a dream is "the functional union of these two terms." For Sartre, the signified is comprised by "the original crisis in the subject ... Literature as discourse forms the signifier; and the relation between crisis and discourse defines the work, which is the signification" or sign (*Myth*, 113–14). In all these cases we are dealing with a dialectical structure whereby the initial positing of any term already presupposes not only another term whose relation to "it" defines it (or, in Hegelian terms, brings it into being) but a totality which must be understood as a concrete unity of the terms. The identity of each exists only in relation to the totality which itself presupposes the openness of its parts toward mutuality of completion.

Interestingly, the notion of discourse as the "signifier" brings to mind Kojève's influential reading of Hegel's Absolute Idea as "discourse." And in subsequent passages, Barthes effectively reiterates this idea, not as specifically applied to Hegel, but in more general terms. In myth, he says, the tri-dimensional pattern forms a second-order semiological system, a meta-language. In mythical language, what was the totality of the sign in the first-order language becomes merely one component – merely the signifier – in the second-order system. So what was a totality in the first system becomes merely a part in the second. This is effectively the dialectical process reconceived in terms of language, with one totality being superseded within a larger framework, and with the process of sublation embodying a move to a higher level, a more comprehensive perspective. In this sense, also, the function of Absolute Spirit is usurped by language – which does not necessarily rob the movement of its unifying tendencies but denies any absolute authority to those tendencies, relocating them – within language – as immanent, as ideologically motivated, and as sustained only by their connections within the larger (human) network of signs. We can use the example that Barthes himself gives: a Negro soldier saluting the French flag on one level has an obvious significance, one of Frenchness and militarism, and a particular person's nationalistic orientation. But, at a higher "mythical" level, this entire sign of the first system (the entire combination of signifier and signified as denoting Frenchness) itself becomes the first term, the signifier of the second, mythical, order of signification: it portrays and posits "Frenchness" as a universal concept, one that commands the willing allegiance of even former colonials or their descendants. And in this broader mythical signification, the personal traits and history of the Negro are entirely suppressed, a strategy that makes the order of myth ideological (*Myth*, 122). This is a revealing example of how the dialectical process is never arrested; for its third term, the synthesis or mediated unity it posits can always be regarded as the first term, the given or immediate unity, of a further development.

In fact, for Barthes, the function of Absolute Spirit is effectively supplanted by myth. For it is myth that gives "historical intention a natural justification" (*Myth*, 142). It is myth that has the "bourgeois" ideological function of erasing "the historical quality of things: in it, things lose the memory that they once were made." In other words, myth suppresses any historical dialectic, substituting this with an idealized dialectical process. "The world enters language as a dialectical relation between activities, between human actions; it comes out of myth as a harmonious display of essences" (*Myth*, 142). This, as we will see later, was almost exactly Marx's critique of the Hegelian dialectic: that it substituted for the real world a panorama of essences, of ideas. And Barthes himself sees this process of myth as "exactly that of bourgeois ideology." Myth is "*depoliticized speech*" (*Myth*, 142).

For Barthes, the term "political" signifies "the whole of human relations in their real, social structure, in their power of making the world" (again, Marx's account of "labor" in Hegel comes to mind). But what myth does is to abolish the "complexity" of human acts; it "gives them the simplicity of essences, it does away with all dialectics ... it organizes a world which is without contradictions ... it establishes a blissful clarity: things appear to mean something by themselves" (*Myth*, 143). Again, this is strikingly similar to Marx's critique of Hegel's dialectic as first acknowledging the contradictions of the bourgeois world but then resolving these in a synthesis engineered by Absolute Spirit, in a reaffirmation of the alienated vision of religious thinking which retracts the reality of the world into the sphere of pure essences. Barthes in fact cites Marx's view that "the most natural object contains a political trace," a trace that has been suppressed or superseded. Barthes effectively identifies the dialectic as a kind of culmination of bourgeois ideology, with its characteristic instrument being myth as that which reconciles, naturalizes, and brings all into a harmonious totality.

Where I would differ with Barthes is in this: it is not bourgeois ideology as such which does the work of harmonizing and naturalizing; this, rather, is the function of liberal humanism. It is liberal humanism that writes the narrative of bourgeois ideology. Bourgeois ideology is the "patient," reeling off the details of her own economy, her own immediate material needs and requirements, as yielded by her short-term calculations for the future. "I desire this and this and this; I would sell this, and exchange that. I want to work in this way, and would be compensated. But I am not happy. In fact, I am not just alienated but utterly confused and conflicted. And I have a history of abuse, at the hands of my father." Liberal humanism is the psychoanalyst, piecing together these fragments, shored against its own ruins, into a narrative, restoring history, bringing back into visibility originating circumstances as well as a reminder of other aspects of the patient's life, ethical, moral, aesthetic – into what can be only a labored coherence, a provisional totality. Bourgeois ideology represses the dialectic of its own making; liberal humanism attempts to restore, to bring back, this dialectic – however imperfectly configured – and as such, must begin with a critique of Hegelian restoration. And of course, many modes of literary theory, including deconstruction (as we have seen) and Deleuzian "Schizoanalysis" (as we shall see) comprise a critique of this liberal humanist critique, citing psychoanalysis as part of the problem – and, more fundamentally, the ego and the very concept of "man."

The work of Saussure and Barthes exhibits how Hegel's views of language anticipate some of the founding notions of literary theory. We can now examine in detail specific readings of Hegel on language by two profoundly influential theorists, Jacques Derrida and Julia Kristeva.

8.2 Jacques Derrida: Language and Difference

Derrida's reading of Hegel on language might be seen as one aspect of his general critique of the dialectic as logocentric, as presupposing the authority of a Logos which enables a closed, totalizing, and unified metaphysical system. Essentially, Derrida sees the sign as central to Hegel's dialectical process, whereby (a) mind or the self is posited as an immediate unity, (b) it engages with the otherness of the external world or nature, and (c) it negates this otherness and returns to itself as a mediated unity. We saw in the previous chapter that Hegel sees the mind as receiving the external world in the form of sensations and reconfiguring it as language. Derrida's reading of Hegel can be summarized as follows. The sign for Hegel is the vehicle of mind's engagement with, and negation of, the world. The sign thus mediates between two "presences," two states of the self, hence the sign is viewed as essentially "psychological," as a part of our mental experience. So Derrida sees the sign in Hegel as the contradictory site of oppositions embedded in the mind's interaction with the world – between sense and intellect, same and other, internal and external. The sign is sustained in this function by the privilege Hegel grants (as do most philosophers, according to Derrida) to speech over writing, where the sign as *sound* is central to the mind's *Aufhebung* or sublation of nature and the external world. The mind converts its sensuous intuitions of the world into its own internal images or representations. It is the sign, as sound, which gives "external" form to these representations, thereby giving mind or intelligence an objective existence. According to Derrida, Hegel's phonocentrism here rests upon the privilege Hegel accords to the "name" in his account of language. In the following section, we can pursue the details of Derrida's argument.

Like Saussure and Barthes, Derrida sees the sign itself as dialectical in its very structure. In a renowned essay on Hegel, he makes the general observation that metaphysics has treated the sign only as a "transition" between "two moments of full presence," acting as provisional reference of one presence to another. "The process of the sign has a history ... between an original presence and its circular reappropriation in a final presence ... Always, from the outset, the movement of lost presence already will have set in motion the process of its reappropriation."[3] Derrida is referring here to the Hegelian dialectic, which moves from an initial identity or presence to "lose" itself in external relations, and is finally "reappropriated" into a higher identity or presence. So metaphysics in general, and Hegelian metaphysics most powerfully, has been based on "presence," and has given the sign a merely transitional status in the

[3] Jacques Derrida, "The Pit and the Pyramid: Introduction to Hegel's Semiology," in *Margins of Philosophy*, trans. Alan Bass (1972; rpt. Chicago: University of Chicago Press, 1986), pp. 71–2. Hereafter cited as *PP*.

potential opening up or "losing" of that presence or identity in difference, in a network of relations. This status is transitional because the function of opening up is abrogated by a larger presence which incorporates and negates both difference and relation – at least, this is Derrida's understanding. Hegel himself might argue that the third stage does not merely negate difference but integrates it into a more comprehensive conception of identity, namely "identity-in-difference."

What is the place of semiology in Hegel's system? According to Derrida, Western metaphysics has always located semiology within psychology – the "non-natural science of the soul." Derrida notes that in general Hegel's philosophy is divided into three parts: Logic, which deals with the Idea "in and for itself"; the philosophy of Nature, which treats the Idea "in its otherness"; and the philosophy of Spirit, which is "the science of the Idea come back to itself out of that otherness" (*PP*, 73). What is significant here for Derrida is that Hegel's theory of the sign belongs to the third of these moments: The sign is "the agency or essential structure of the Idea's return to self-presence." It is part of the movement of the Idea's relation to itself (*PP*, 74). To locate the place of semiology still more narrowly, Derrida observes that, for Hegel, semiology is "a chapter" in psychology (*PP*, 75).[4] In Hegel's speculative semiology, Derrida explains, the sign is understood according to the structure and movement of the *Aufhebung*. By means of sublation, Spirit elevates itself above nature in which it was submerged, and it both suppresses and retains nature, sublimating nature into itself, and presents itself to itself (*PP*, 76). In other words, the sign is instrumental in the mind's process of reducing the other, the world of nature, to itself.

8.3   Pit to Pyramid: A Circular Journey

Derrida elaborates the mechanism of this reduction. For Hegel, he notes, semiology is a part of the theory of imagination. Mind or intelligence sublates the content of an intuition and creates an *image* which, in being freed from its original immediacy, is effectively mind's way of creating "an externality of its own." The image enables the passage from the intuition originally given to conceptuality. The image, as seen earlier, is internalized

---

[4] As Catherine Kellogg notes, such a placing of the discussion of the sign under psychology "mobilizes an entire metaphysical tradition that privileges speech over writing," "The Three Hegels: Kojève, Hyppolite, and Derrida on Hegel's Philosophy of Language," in *Hegel and Language*, ed. Surber, p. 209. Hereafter cited as *HL*.

in memory and preserved in an "unconscious dwelling" or "pit." Derrida proposes to follow the path leading from this "pit" to the "pyramid" or sign. This path, he claims, "remains circular," and "the pyramid becomes once again the pit that it always will have been" (*PP*, 77). Intelligence (as Derrida reads Hegel) can draw from this pit or reservoir, synthesizing the internal image with recollected existence to create representations. But this first process is merely the province of "reproductive" imagination which is still constrained, passively, by what is given to us in intuition (*PP*, 78).

Derrida notes that in the next stage, that of "productive" imagination, this limit is passed, since imagination now creates without recourse to external intuitions. Intelligence is externalized and "produced in the world as a thing. This singular thing is the *sign*" (*PP*, 78). Derrida sees this process, which externalizes an internal content and produces intuitions from itself, as "scandalous," implying that the observer spontaneously produces what she observes. The "scandal," apparently, is not just that the mind manufactures the world from within itself, but that it appears to produce *intuitions* from within itself. We recall Hegel's view that sensations, even when transformed and idealized by the mind, could nonetheless be *intuited* – as signs. Derrida likens the status of Hegel's productive imagination to Kant's transcendental imagination: They are both intermediaries between sensibility and Understanding, and so the sign in its very nature is an inherent contradiction. It is "*both* interior and exterior, spontaneous and receptive, intelligible and sensible, the same and the other, etc., the sign is none of these" (*PP*, 79). It is none of these because it is caught between each of these oppositions.

8.4 The Sign as Dialectic

Here, Derrida raises a more fundamental question concerning the very nature of the dialectic: "Is this contradiction dialecticity itself?" The question of the sign, notes Derrida, would soon become confused with the question of dialectics (*PP*, 80). What Derrida appears to mean here is that, if the sign is an element in psychology, it serves as the vehicle whereby the mind achieves self-relation; or, to put it crudely, whereby the human self-achieves realization, progressing from immediate self-identity to mediated identity. The sign, being "double" in its nature, being both material (as a sound or inscription, a signifier) and ideal (a meaning, a signified), is the site where the sensible and intelligible intersect. And this is also the site of the dialectical process: the sensible is first transformed into the intelligible (as the content of sensuous intuition is idealized by the mind); then, this idealized content, the mental image, is again given a sensuous form in the sign, which is the mind's way of representing itself, of giving itself an "external" existence. The sign is therefore integral to the dialectic whereby we create ourselves and the world (as structured by ideality or our mental operations). We saw earlier that, for Derrida, the Hegelian sign is dialectical in its very structure; it now emerges that the dialectic in its very nature is semiotic.

The "scandal" here concerns the relation of the sign to reality, and to truth. Hegel's productive imagination which produces the sign and presides autonomously over its own creations is indifferent to truth as such. We must ask, says Derrida, "why truth … is announced as absence in the sign" (*PP*, 80). In other words, the sign as produced by the productive imagination is by definition distanced from reality since it is "freely" created, independently of any actual intuition, of any actual engagement with the world.

In his somewhat indirect attempt to answer this, Derrida notes that for Hegel the sign is created by a process of kenosis, of emptying, of the significance of an original intuition, and replacing it with another significance. So, says, Derrida, "we have … a kind of intuition of absence, or more precisely the sighting of an absence through a full intuition." He quotes Hegel's statement that the "sign is some immediate intuition, representing a totally different import from what naturally belongs to it … it is the *pyramid* into which a foreign soul (*eine fremde Seele*) has been conveyed" (*PP*, 83). Derrida claims that this conception of the "pyramid" fixes a number of essential characteristics of the sign. The first of these is arbitrariness, the "absence of any natural relation" between the signified (the representation, *Bedeutung*) and the signifier (the intuition). He sees this arbitrariness in the fact that the "soul" (meaning) conveyed into the "pyramid" (the material signifier) is foreign. It's not hard to agree with Derrida up to this point. But he then goes on to state that the "irreducibility" between a sound or signifier and what it means (the signified) "amounts to the irreducibility of the soul and body, of the intelligible and the sensory, of the concept or signified ideality on the one hand, and of the signifying body on the other, that is, in different senses, the irreducibility of two *representations*" (*PP*, 84). So Derrida sees an "irreducibility" or disjunction between all the registers in which a signifier exists – body, sense, matter – and the registers in which the meaning or signified exists – soul, intellect, ideas.

8.5   Some Problems with Derrida's Reading

On the foregoing points we could perhaps take issue with Derrida. The arbitrariness here is for Hegel not a function of irreducibility (of whatever type) but of the *suspension* or *abrogation* of the natural import of an intuition. It surely does not concern any kind of distance or incommensurability ("irreducibility") between intellect and sense or body and soul or signifier and signified. The arbitrariness lies simply in the fact that the intellect is free to assign any meaning it likes to the intuition. Derrida further claims that this "irreducibility" is the reason that the signifier "*represents an entirely other content*" (than what is given in intuition); but again, the reason is not irreducibility but rather – as seen in the previous chapter – the raising of the content of the given intuition to generality. The "meaning" of arbitrariness, asserts Derrida, is freedom: "the production of arbitrary signs manifests the freedom of the spirit ... In the sign spirit is more independent and closer to itself." This is why the sign has "an essential place" in the development of psychology and logic (*PP*, 86). Derrida notes that Saussure will later make a similar observation, saying that signs are wholly arbitrary, and that Saussure will "realize better than the others the ideal of the semiological process" (*PP*, 86, n). But as we have already seen, this is not quite what Hegel says. What he argues is that signs have a necessary place in "the economy of intelligence." in other words, in the process of understanding the world, from the initial encounter with sensation in experience to conceptualization of that experience.

Derrida is essentially arguing that for Hegel the sign suppresses "truth" or external reality – whereas Hegel himself argues that the sign expresses that reality *as mediated by the mind*. Is there a difference? Unlike Hegel, Derrida does not differentiate between immediate and mediated absence. For Hegel, the sign is a means of suppressing immediate presence and of awakening-mediated presence – which fulfills the true identity of the original presence, and proclaims its affiliation with other signs in a relational system of presence. Derrida's larger point concerning the semiotic nature of the dialectic is perhaps that the mind or the self effectively reproduces the world in its own image; that the very process of negation, the very process of thought as enlisting the sign is imperialistic, conquering all the rich variety of sensuous otherness in the world and reducing it to sameness within a predetermined ideal framework. The rich "presence" of reality is always converted into, always reconfigured as, *re*-presentation – of the mind to itself. Mind effectively substitutes language – the outer form of its own existence – for reality. It substitutes the world of signs for the external, sensuous world.

8.6   Language and Machines

Hegel's views of language have profound implications for human subjectivity and its interaction with the world, its production of the world through signs. An important element in the way that humans connect to the world in most of the phases of capitalism is their reliance on machines and the precise function that machines are made to bear. What exactly is a machine? This has been the focus of theorists such as Deleuze and Guattari. Anticipating their work, Derrida uses the notion of a machine to draw out certain implications of Hegel's linguistics. He points out that when Hegel criticizes attempts by Leibniz and others to create a universal language on mathematical models, he is stipulating the limits of a "machine." Derrida defines a machine here as embodying a "mute writing, released from the voice and from every natural language," as well as of the mathematical symbolism which proceeds according to the operations of the abstract or formal understanding. The silence of this writing, says Derrida (i.e., its disembodiment, its dislocation from the human body and from speech) would "interrupt the movement of the *Aufhebung*, or in any case would resist the interiorization of the past (*Erinnerung*), the *relevant* idealization, the history of the spirit, the reappropriation of the logos in self-presence and infinite parousia" (*PP*, 105). In other words, the machine disrupts the movement of Hegel's dialectic at all levels.

Calculation, the machine, and mute writing, says Derrida, all fall outside of any possible redintegration into an Hegelian identity. This prompts him to ask: "What might be a 'negative' that could not be relevé?" In other words, what might be a negative content that cannot be sublated or appropriated into service of the overall system? His answer is: "Quite simply, a machine ... A machine defined in its pure functioning, and not in its final utility, its meaning, its result, its work." What Hegel could never conceive is a machine that would work without being "governed by an order of reappropriation." It could not serve as the Other, the opposite, the non-thought, for any thought. The machine, working by itself, would constitute pure externality, an outside that could not be internalized. Derrida sees in the Hegelian system a "structural incapacity to think without relève." Yet the sign "cannot completely do without the machine" (*PP*, 107).

So, for Derrida (as I understand him here), the "external" mode of thought implicit in calculation and in the machine – which is an embodiment of externality – is somehow unable to be seen by Hegel as a true "other" of thought proper, and therefore unable to be integrated into any teleological or purposive scheme. But again there is a problem here. Derrida's understanding of "externality" is spatial and does not answer to Hegel's own view of it. What Hegel means by saying that arithmetical calculation – as conducted by a machine – is "external" is simply that its elements are externally, additively, cumulatively, related; there is no internal unity or coherence or purpose shaping them from within. The machine performs this, if you like, in a purely mechanical way. However, for Hegel, this kind of externality – whether performed mechanically by a human being or an actual machine – cannot somehow be placed "outside" of thought; it is simply another, inferior, level of thought. To say that the machine somehow represents an absolute externality is to take literally its ability to think "outside" the living thought of a human being. The "external" thinking employed by the abstract understanding, according to Hegel, is used in many fields and characterizes certain historical periods; it represents a lower stage of thought which is nonetheless internal to, and integral to, the overall progress of thought, whether considered as the thought of an individual, an entire culture, or an epoch.

8.7   Epilogue: Deleuze, Guattari, and the Language of Capitalist Machines

The issues raised here are significant, for machines play an increasingly vast role in our world, specifically as harnessed by the productive forces of capitalism in its most technocratic and digital phases. What if we interpreted "machine" in the sense attributed to it by Deleuze and Guattari? In their major work *Anti-Oedipus*, these thinkers offer a vision explicitly directed against the Hegelian dialectic of integration and totality. They regard the world as composed not of subjects and objects, but of "machines" in interaction with "partial objects."[5] In this anti-humanist

---

[5] This was a concept originated by Melanie Klein, who saw the infant's undeveloped subjectivity as relating not to a composite person but merely to one part, initially the mother's breast. Lacan extended the implications of the concept to suggest that partial objects in general are incapable of being represented completely and cannot be integrated into the subject's self-image as complete. Deleuze and Guattari interpret the concept even more generally to indicate the necessary incompleteness of all "objects" since these are immersed in a network of "flows" and "breaks" where all identity is shifting.

vision, human beings are not composite entities but are, like everything else, machines – eating machines, loving machines, and most fundamentally, desiring machines. There is no distinction between man and nature. The human body is reconceived as the "body without organs," which is no longer a composite and hierarchical organism, with the brain directing the remaining parts. Rather, it is undifferentiated, unhierarchical, unorganized, and indifferent. All the flows of desire pass through it freely.[6]

Deleuze and Guattari define the machine as "a *system of interruptions* or breaks *(coupures)*." Every machine is part of a continual material flow that it cuts into. The anus is a machine that cuts off the flow of feces; the mouth cuts off the flow of milk or air. These are "desiring machines." Each machine that interrupts this flow is connected to another machine that produces it; and this second machine, in turn, is an interruption or break only in relation a third machine that "produces a continuous, infinite flux" (*AO*, 36). This is almost an inverted dialectical process. It is a vision of the world where the human body does not compose any kind of unity but is a site of several, mutually interacting machines, whose functions are sometimes specific and sometimes transferable. The "self" here is but a residue, an appendage, within this "grid of disjunctions" (*AO*, 38). The subject, existing as merely a residual break alongside a machine, has no specific or personal identity. It is born anew with each of the states through which it passes (*AO*, 40–1). There is no whole or totality or purpose within which these machines operate, except the totality of "matter" – air, sound, space, parts of bodies, parts of objects – which represents an unbroken flow always interrupted by machines. And these desiring machines, as we shall see later, are invested in the larger social machine which regulates desire and indeed, in our present era, in the all-consuming capitalist machine.

The question here is how these machines relate to language. Each machine, say Deleuze and Guattari, has a code built into it. They see machines as interacting according to these codes. But these codes are not linear. Using Lacan's model of the code of the unconscious as comprised of several chains of meaning, they see the machinic codes as open-ended and polyvocal, resembling "not so much a language as a jargon" (*AO*, 38). No chain is homogeneous and the chains resemble a series of characters

---

[6] Gilles Deleuze and Félix Guattari, *Anti-Oedipus: Capitalism and Schizophrenia*, trans. Robert Hurley, Mark Seem, and Helen R. Lane (1972; rpt. London: Athlone Press, 1984), pp. 2–5, 9–11, 15. Hereafter cited as *AO*.

from different alphabets, with each chain capturing fragments of other chains. This system of writing "is a great disjunctive synthesis" where the "one vocation of the sign is to produce desire, engineering it in every direction" (*AO*, 39). So, as I understand this, the language of machines is, like the language of the unconscious, open, polyvocal, and related to desire on a preconscious level – before desire itself becomes regulated by social codes "where a despotic Signifier destroys all the chains, linearizes them" (*AO*, 40). It is the task of the rebel or "schizo" – who could, one imagines, be a socialist, a gender rights activist, an artist, or simply some weed-smoking Beckett-reading nihilist – to detach words and concepts from their stability of meaning and to recapture the polyvocity that is the code of desire (*AO*, 40).

"Writing has never been capitalism's thing. Capitalism is profoundly illiterate." The death of writing, Deleuze and Guattari tell us, is like the death of God or the death of the father: the news is slow to reach us (*AO*, 240). Writing is really an archaism in capitalism and, inasmuch as it is still used, is "adapted to money." What the capitalist machine employs is a "language of decoded flows" as opposed to "a signifier that strangles and overcodes the flows." In this "nonsignifying language," no type of sign is privileged, whether it be phonic, graphic, or gestural. Electronic language and data processing do without voice or writing, and the computer "is a machine for instantaneous and generalized decoding" (*AO*, 240–1). The "productive essence of capitalism" speaks "only in the language of signs imposed on it by merchant capital or the axiomatics of the market" (*AO*, 241). In other words, the authors seem to be suggesting that "despotic" language, or language where signs are despotically reduced to fixed meanings, belong to overtly repressive regimes of the past, where a given language – embodying a given view of the world and certain definite values – was stabilized by recourse to some ultimately authoritative and despotic Signifier, whether this be God, the divine right of kings, or the cosmological hierarchy.

However, according to Deleuze and Guattari, capitalism also *recodes* these flows, investing its own codes and regulations into desire, in a system where, as Marx observed, money becomes the measure of "meaning" in every sense. The value, function, and purpose of any entity must accrue from its place in the market. As I understand their thesis, even language or writing here becomes a commodity, directly saleable or, for students, a means to a monetary end. Its "meaning" – whatever other value is accorded to it by specific professions such as academia – cannot escape ultimate determination by the larger forces and codifications of the market.

Even the styles of writing predominantly encouraged within pedagogy under capitalism – concise, containing an unambiguous thesis, discernible progression through paragraphs, and a summarizing conclusion – are geared to the demands of the corporate world. We don't generally encourage our students to use metaphor, repetition, symbols, and allusions – there are separate creative writing programs within which the nurturing of such skills is "contained" and directed toward further modes of entry into the market such as publishing. In this overall scenario, language as such has ceased to function as a relation with the world, a means of self-expression or self-exploration or seeking knowledge. The meanings of its signifiers are "recoded" according to the demands of the market economy. As Deleuze and Guattari see it, art becomes subversive in its use of language when it disrupts this system of recodification, and, in a sense, returns to modes of exploration of desire.

Indeed, according to Deleuze and Guattari, language as used in capitalism – as a disjunctive linguistics of decoded and recoded flows of desire – is not expressed by Sausserian linguistics, which is a "linguistics of the signifier," in which signifiers retain a "minimal identity" throughout their variations in the overall system. The capitalist "linguistics of flows" is embodied more nearly, they suggest, in the work of the Danish linguist Louis Hjelmslev, who engaged in a "destruction of the signifier" (*AO*, 243). Hjelmslev's linguistics, being a more open-ended system than what Saussure offered, is "the only linguistics adapted to the nature of *both* the capitalist *and* the schizophrenic flows" (*AO*, 243).

What is interesting here is that both Derrida, on the one hand, and Deleuze/Guattari on the other, view Sausserian linguistics as ultimately a linguistics of "closure." But whereas Derrida correlates Saussure's linguistic with Hegel's views of language in a metaphysics of presence which represents the culminating expression in Western thought of the movement and contradictions of capitalism, Deleuze and Guattari see capitalism as having superseded the historical era of the "despotic Signifier" and its expression in Saussure, and needing the more open linguistics of Hjelmslev. So all these thinkers would agree on the correlation of Hegelian metaphysical "closure" with Saussure's closed linguistic system. But Deleuze and Guattari presumably – for they don't appear to address this issue directly – see capitalism as having superseded its expression in Hegel. Or do they? It is also clear that they see capitalism as riven by a broad contradictory movement, between the releasing of schizophrenic energies and an apparatus of repression. This insistence on the constituting nature of this contradiction may well comprise a rejection of any dialectical synthesis. But it is above all in their notion of the machine that they posit a world that is inexplicable in the terms of Hegelian or Sausserian linguistics. Again, this is a thesis that will be disputed later in this book, for it assumes that Hegel's system, as well as Saussure's, must be read as enforcing closure.

Equally, Derrida imputes to Hegel – to the dialectic, to the *Aufhebung*, to his concept of the sign – a greater absoluteness than his system needs to bear. We may recall, for example, that in *First Philosophy of Spirit*, Hegel saw the meaning of sounds as emerging only in relation to other sounds, and the "name" not as something absolute but as a "self-suspending" particular, whose ideality or fullness of identity was realized only in a relational system of speech. I would argue that it is not the sign, nor language in general, that is the vehicle of closure in Hegel's system. These are an integral part of the dialectical process; the often-cited instruments of closure – teleology, the state, freedom, Absolute Spirit – arise from within the dialectic, and they themselves cannot be extricated from the weight of their own immersion in semiosis, from their own internal structuring by the operations of the sign.

CHAPTER 9

Language and the Unconscious

Kristeva

Derrida, Deleuze, and Guattari raised some crucial issues impinging on the role of language in Hegel's philosophy, and more generally in late capitalism. These included the "closed" nature of the Hegelian dialectic, the basis of this closure in Hegelian/Sausserian linguistics, and the dual tendency in capitalism both to institutionalize this closure and to enable its puncturing by recourse to schizophrenic "desire" and bodily drives. The work of Julia Kristeva approaches these connections – between language, subjectivity, bodily drives, and the repressive institutions of capitalism – in a somewhat different way.

To begin with, Kristeva's theory of language is founded on a reconception, rather than an outright rejection, of Hegelian negativity. Moreover, whereas Deleuze and Guattari posit a machinic universe where both objectivity and human subjectivity are abrogated, Kristeva posits a "split" subject, divided between its respective orientations toward conscious and unconscious realms. And, like Derrida, she sees the Hegelian dialectic as effecting closure; but, unlike Derrida, she stages a recasting of this dialectic so as to include the protagonistic role of the unconscious. Hence, finally, while her entire endeavor, like that of Deleuze and Guattari, can be read most fundamentally as a critique of capitalism based on the reinvestments of desire it unleashes, for Kristeva subjective agency – in a broadened conception as renewing its suppressed connections with pre-Oedipal drives – is integral to both this critique and its practical implementation.[1]

---

[1] For a more general comparison of the ideas of Deleuze and Guattari with Kristeva's, see Estelle Barrett's "Materiality, Language and the Production of Knowledge: Art, Subjectivity and Indigenous Ontology," *Cultural Studies Review* [Online], 21.2 (2015): 101–19. Web. June 29, 2016.

9.1   The Signifying Process

Essentially, Kristeva sees the signifying process as composed of two modes, the semiotic and the symbolic, and subjectivity as emerging from their interaction.[2] The semiotic process includes "drives, their disposition, and their division of the body, plus the ecological and social system surrounding the body, such as objects and pre-Oedipal relations with parents." The realm of the symbolic encompasses the emergence of subject and object as well as the constitution of meaning, structured according to categories of the social order (*RPL*, 86). Poetic language is "revolutionary" and has a subversive potential inasmuch as it threatens to reach back into the semiotic *chora*, to release energies and drives that have been thwarted by the conventional structure of the symbolic, disrupting the symbolic from within and reconceiving its notions of subject, object, and their connections. In the signifying practices of late capitalism, according to Kristeva, only certain avant-garde literary texts, such as those of Mallarmé and Joyce, have the ability to transgress the boundaries between semiotic and symbolic; such texts can open up new possibilities of meaning, new modes of signification.

9.2   Semanalysis as the Child of Hegel

The most significant of Kristeva's theoretical undertakings is her attempt to define language in general and the sign in particular as a *process* rather than as a static entity or system. In her essay "The System and the Speaking Subject," Kristeva urges the creation of a new science of the sign, which she designates "semanalysis."[3] As we will see shortly, she regards this new science as the descendant of the Hegelian dialectic. Semiotics, she says, is currently modeled on the science of linguistics, which rigidly focuses on language as a social code, a homogeneous structure that cannot grasp anything which belongs "not with the social contract but with play, pleasure or desire," which it relegates to the realms of rhetoric or poetics (*SS*, 26).

In contrast, semanalysis must treat language as a signifying *process*, recognizing its heterogeneous nature. To do this, it must begin from a theory of meaning that is a "theory of the speaking subject." But this theory

---

[2] Julia Kristeva, *Revolution in Poetic Language*, trans. Margaret Waller (New York: Columbia University Press, 1984), p. 24. Hereafter cited as *RPL*.

[3] Julia Kristeva, "The System and the Speaking Subject," *Times Literary Supplement*, October 12, 1973. Reprinted in *The Kristeva Reader*, p. 28. Hereafter cited as *SS*.

must go beyond generative grammar's rehabilitation of "the Cartesian conception of language as an *act* carried out by a *subject*" (*SS*, 27). In this view, meaning is the act of what Husserl called a "transcendental ego," which, Kristeva notes, is "cut off its body, its unconscious and also its history." It is the "Freudian revolution," she urges, which enables us to theorize the speaking subject "as a divided subject (conscious/unconscious)" and to specify the kinds of operation characteristic of the two sides of this split, namely the bio-physiological processes that Freud called the drives, on the one side, and on the other, the social constraints effected by family structure and modes of production (*SS*, 28).

In other words, though Kristeva wishes to view signifying as a practice, as a process grounded in the speaking subject, this subject is not the subject that has been posited by much of the philosophical tradition since Descartes and his dualism of mind and body; it is not a subject that is disembodied and somehow treated as an abstract mind, above time, space, and history. Rather, it is a subject that is very much part of a body, a body imbricated in specific, not to say unique, material contexts of gender and class. And this subjectivity is composed partly by an unconscious play of drives and instincts, which of course are even more deeply rooted in its bodily processes. It's important to understand here that Kristeva is grounding the very process of the unconscious in a material, concrete historical context, viewing it as the product of specific circumstances.

Hence the signifying process is a dialectic between these two orders: the drives are constrained by the social code and the "symbolic law" of language and convention, yet they continually – through their "semiotic disposition" – transgress that law to refashion and renovate it (*SS*, 28-9). The true nature of semiotics, according to Kristeva, can be preserved only in concrete signifying practices, such as poetry, music, dance, and even experiences with drugs. All of these release heterogeneity, reordering the psychic drives, and fracturing the symbolic code, which can no longer contain or constrain its speaking subjects (*SS*, 30). Released in such ways, Kristeva's speaking subject serves the same subversive function as the "schizo" posited by Deleuze and Guattari.

In these ways, semanalysis demystifies the operations of traditional logic and conventional epistemes. Semanalysis effectively reveals "the negativity which Hegel had seen at work beneath all rationality." Kristeva goes so far as to say that "*semanalysis* can be thought of as the direct successor of the dialectical method" (*SS*, 31). However, whereas Hegel subordinated negativity to absolute knowledge, this new dialectic "will at last be genuinely materialist since it recognizes the *materiality – the heterogeneity* – of that negativity whose concrete base Hegel was unable to see and which mechanistic Marxists have reduced to a merely economic externality" (*SS*, 31). Hence, this new dialectic will rehabilitate heterogeneity in the system of meaning and will call into question the transcendental subject. By "concrete base" Kristeva appears to mean that the dialectic is grounded not in a movement of ideas but in the very formative process of subjectivity itself as it emerges from the interaction of the drives and the symbolic order. It is in this way, by grounding subjectivity in the very interaction that gives rise to language, that semanalysis undermines the transcendental subject.

9.3   Semanalysis Contra Marxism

Kristeva seems to imply that this materiality is somehow more comprehensive, reaching into the very formation of subjectivity, than the mechanistic materialism of some Marxist thinkers who grounded the movement of the dialectic in purely economic factors, a procedure that leaves intact the notion of subjectivity as a transcendental ego. A less "mechanistic" Marxist might reply that one of the fundamental claims made by Marx and Engels is that the human subject, like anything else, is a product of specific historical conditions. In fact, Kristeva states that the present "mutations" of capitalism, and the reemergence of the civilizations of India and China, have "thrown into crisis the symbolic systems enclosed in which the Western subject, officially defined as a transcendental subject, has for two thousand years lived out its lifespan" (*SS*, 31). Marxism, while powerful in grasping the economic determinants of social relations, lacks an adequate theory of the subject, she says, effectively continuing its homage to Feuerbach's "humanistic standing of the dialectic on its head" (*SS*, 32).

Semanalysis, suggests Kristeva, might help to address this gap in dialectical materialism by establishing "the heterogeneous logic of signifying practices" and locating them and their subject within "historically determined relations of production" (*SS*, 32). The subject of semiotic metalanguage must emerge from the "protective shell of a transcendental ego" and restore her "connection with that negativity – drive-governed, but also social, political and historical – which rends and renews the social code" (*SS*, 31).

This is where Kristeva's ideas display some convergence with those of Deleuze and Guattari. In an essay entitled "The Ethics of Linguistics" (1974), she observes that ethics used to be a matter of coercion, custom, and repetition.[4] Now, however, "the issue of ethics crops up wherever a code ... must be shattered in order to give way to the free play of negativity, need, desire, pleasure, and jouissance." She avers that linguistics is still caught in a "systematics" whose ethical foundations and epistemology are "helplessly anachronistic." As such, linguistics must change its object of study to "a consideration of language as articulation of a heterogeneous process." This would establish poetic language as the primary object of analysis, a language that continually threatens the boundaries of language as a social code or system (*DL*, 24–5). Poetry, she says, is a "practice of the speaking subject," a practice that oscillates between system and its subversion – in much the same way, we might add, that Deleuzian schizophrenia operates within capitalism's oscillation between desire and its repression.

In *Revolution in Poetic Language*, Kristeva's explanations of these ideas show more specifically what she owes to Hegel. She stresses Lenin's understanding of Hegelian negativity as "the liquefying and dissolving agent that does not destroy but rather reactivates new organizations and, in that sense, affirms" (*RPL*, 109). Yet Kristeva sees the supersession that occurs within the Hegelian dialectic (as in the supersession of being and nothing by becoming) as amounting to an "erasing of heterogeneity." Nonetheless, Hegel equates negativity with freedom, and Kristeva sees this negativity as liberating. "Hegelian negativity," she maintains, "prevents the immobilization of the thetic, unsettles doxy, and lets in all the semiotic motility that prepares and exceeds it."[5] In other words, it forestalls the rigidity of the thetic or propositional realm. Indeed, Kristeva points out that Hegel defines this negativity as the "fourth term of the true dialectic: triplicity is only an appearance in the realm of the Understanding" (*RPL*, 112–13). But, whereas the "theology" inherent in Hegel's metaphysics results in an affirmative negativity that "erases ... the moment of rupture," we must dare to conceive negativity "as the *very movement of heterogeneous matter*, inseparable from its differentiation's symbolic function" (*RPL*, 113).

---

[4] Julia Kristeva, "The Ethics of Linguistics," in *Desire in Language: A Semiotic Approach to Literature and Art*, trans. Thomas Gora, Alice Jardine, and Leon S. Roudiez (New York: Columbia University Press, 1980), p. 23. Hereafter cited as *DL*. This essay was first published in *Critique* 322 (March 1974).

[5] Kristeva makes a fundamental distinction between the "semiotic," which is the pre-Oedipal realm of unconscious drives, and the "symbolic," which is the realm of signification, propositions, and judgment. Her point is that the symbolic is already permeated from within by the semiotic.

Even when Hegelian negativity appears as "force," as in the *Phenomenology*, says Kristeva, even when it is "closest to what we have called a semiotic chora,"[6] its freedom from thought, its "powerful moment" of "scission that exceeds and precedes the advent of thetic understanding" is closed off and superseded by an idealist dialectic that effectively reduces force, reduces radical negativity, to mere expression in language. What made the "materialist overturning" of this dialectic possible was the notion of "drives" in Freudian theory (*RPL*, 114–16). Indeed, according to Kristeva, the concept of negativity "registers a *conflictual state* which stresses the heterogeneity of the semiotic function and its determination, and which dialectical materialism, reading Hegel through Freud, will posit as instinctual (social and material)" (*RPL*, 118). Kristeva appears to be saying that the "materialist overturning" of the dialectic consisted in grounding the dialectic not solely on the interplay of concepts in language, but also, and more formatively, in the conflict between instinctual drives and the coercive or regulatory social order. At this point, we need to understand some of the Freudian concepts that structure Kristeva's thinking.

9.4   Hegelian Negativity and Freudian Rejection

We might recall here that in the mirror stage, the infant begins to distinguish between itself and objects in the external world, and enters the realm of the symbolic, as what Kristeva calls a "speaking subject," with its own identity and its own place in the system of signifiers. This movement into independence, whereby the child separates itself from and rejects the mother is known as "abjection." Much of Kristeva's work is premised on the dialectical exchange between these two orders – the semiotic, which is the prelinguistic realm of the drives and of immediate connection with the mother, and the symbolic, which is the realm of social structure and masculine authority. The subject, who is effectively constituted within this dialectic is what Kristeva calls the subject "in process/on trial."

Rejection (Kristeva's term for negation) is the "key moment," she says, that shatters unity (the unity in which child subsists with mother). It is "a step on the way to the object's becoming-sign, at which the object will be detached from the body and isolated as a real object." Rejection is

---

[6] Kristeva defines the *chora* as "a nonexpressive totality" comprising the bodily drives and the primary processes of the unconscious such as displacement and condensation. It has no fixed identity and precedes the linguistic sign. Kristeva associates the prelinguistic semiotic process with the mother's body (*RPL*, 25–6).

also a step on the way to the imposition of the superego (*RPL*, 151). The acquisition of language, which occurs at the mirror stage, is the acquisition of a "capacity for symbolization through the definitive detachment of the rejected object" (*RPL*, 152). There are two "signifying modalities" that harmonize and affirm the "shattering brought about by rejection." The first is oralization or a reunion with the mother's body, which is now viewed as "vocalic," signifying the real. The second is the reunion with the bodies of brothers in a homosexual "phatry." These two modalities point to the two sides – poetic and mastering – of texts that are "situated on the path of rejection" in their disruption of the "superego and its linear language" (*RPL*, 153–4).

Kristeva notes that Hegel's version of rejection (negation) is subordinated to the symbolic function, whereas Freud makes rejection or expulsion "the essential moment in the constitution of the symbolic function" (*RPL*, 158). Hegel simply cannot envisage a subversion of the unity that posits itself as other and returns to itself: "The ideational closure of the Hegelian dialectic seems to consist in its inability to posit negativity as anything but a repetition of ideational unity in itself" (*RPL*, 159). In contrast, aesthetic productions do not neutralize negation or rejection but restage the "dialectical moment of the generating of significance" (*RPL*, 164).

Kristeva effectively reconceives Hegelian negativity in terms of Freud's notion of "rejection." To begin with, she cites Frege's insight that in the realm of thought, negation is merely a type of affirmation: It aims to destroy the predicate of a judgment, but it is in fact part of judgment, and is "merely a variant of the *positive predicate*" (*RPL*, 119–21). Negation is thus part of the thetic, syntactic, symbolic function. We need, she says, to understand negation not as a logical process, within judgment, but "as something economic" – something that is prior to and produces the symbolic function – by means of a theory of the unconscious (*RPL*, 121–2). In other words, negation and negativity are, in their profoundest significance, not merely movements in logic. Rather, they characterize the very formation of the ego, which also marks the formation of the symbolic order – the external world and its representation through a system of signs. Specifically, in Kristeva's eyes, we need to grasp "the process of rejection which pulsates through the drives in a body that is caught within the network of nature and society" (*RPL*, 122–3). In short, when we reject something, this isn't just a matter of rational judgment but mobilizes our entire being, a large part of which is composed of unconscious drives.

Indeed, according to Kristeva, when we express negativity in logic by making judgments in language (about the subject and predicate), this doesn't express its true dynamic character but merely a static "series of differences." In poetic language, and various kinds of psychosis such as schizophrenia (again reminding us of Deleuze), this static kind of negation, and the stasis of "syntactic structure" within which it is imprisoned, become disturbed, transformed into a new "psychotic discourse" that expresses an "economy of drives" and a transformed relation of subject and predicate (*RPL*, 124). This is true "negativity" rather than mere negation: it disturbs "the normative rule of lexical oppositions" by displacing them with a trajectory of primary processes such as displacements and condensations. And this occurs because rejection resists "the *locking* of significance into *units* of meaning" and "oppositional pairs" (*RPL*, 125). Again, negativity is an act or an orientation that goes far beyond simply negating a logical premise from a neatly oppositional stance: It involves the entire being and results in a transformation of the very terms of a question.

So this kind of rejection or negativity undermines mere logical negation; it "destroys the pairing of opposites and replaces opposition with an *infinitesimal differentiation*" (*RPL*, 125–6). In other words, each term of a linguistic opposition effectively subsumes a potentially infinite variety of difference and arbitrarily delimits one range of that variety, separating this range from another, equally delimited range. For example, when we talk of an "opposition" between "black" and "white," we are subsuming under the terms "black" and under "white" an infinite range of shades. We could have a range of shades of black and gray, whose variety we elide in calling the entire, arbitrarily restricted range, "black." We do the same with "white," and we then oppose one arbitrarily delimited range to the other, as "white" and "black." And these reductive terms, of course, are charged with centuries of cultural significance. But the negativity that characterizes our unconscious drives both undermines such linguistic negation and also enables its emergence. In psychosis, it is the very struggle – the Hegelian, dialectical struggle which is here grounded in the unconscious – "between thesis and rejection" that actually makes possible the symbolic realm (*RPL*, 126).

We need to understand here that the realm of the thetic, the symbolic, is the realm where the Hegelian *thesis* can meet its *antithesis*. But Kristeva's reading of Hegel through Freud recasts the drama of dialectic onto a more primordial stage, one that both gives rise to the possibility of the symbolic realm of language as embodying social convention and simultaneously furnishes the ground of its subversion.

We recall that Kristeva began with Hegelian negativity. What is astonishing here is that she grounds the dialectic in its deepest significance within the very mechanisms of the unconscious mind. In doing so, she opens up the potential of the dialectic to reflect upon the constraining of its own terms by their necessary formulation in language – terms whose formalization into mere "opposition," for example, elides the infinite richness of relation that they might otherwise enjoy. To give another example: Instead of designating "woman" and "man" as two polarized ends of a static opposition, we would see the relation between them as composed along a path of infinitesimal differentiations, a path on which the allegedly mutually exclusive components of those terms might actually meet and overlap. Even more remarkable is that, in Kristeva's vision, language is *born* as a dialectical process, in which the body both separates itself from the external world and – in Hegelian fashion – replaces that world (which becomes an absence) with signs, with language. To recover this deeper dialectic is to begin to reconceive the subject's relation to both the language and the world. It is to enter the psychosis of revolution. Kristeva effectively recasts Hegel's theory of language on a stage where the unconscious plays an almost Antigone-like role, reminding the social order of its profoundest origins in the underworld.

9.5   Freud on Negation

So Kristeva sees negativity or rejection as giving rise to the symbolic realm. She states that negation "is a symptom of syntactic capacity" and that negation in judgment "puts the subject in a position of *mastery* over the statement as a structured whole, and in a position to generate language" (*RPL*, 124). To grasp these statements, we need to refer to some of Freud's characterizations of the process of thinking, as well as of neurosis. In his essay on "Negation," Freud describes how we immediately reject certain ideas that come to us: the "person in the dream ... [is] *not* my mother."[7] But, as long as an idea is *rejected* or negated, it can make its way into our consciousness, and we can accept it in its negated status: "Negation is a way of taking cognizance of what is repressed." Freud sees this mode of dealing with repression as "the psychological origin ... of intellectual judgment" since the function of such judgment is to affirm or negate the content of thoughts. Indeed, a "negative judgment is the

[7] "Negation," in Sigmund Freud, *Complete* Works (online edition), p. 4140. Hereafter cited as *CW*. http://freudforscholars.com/Freud_Complete_Works.pdf

intellectual substitute for repression" (*CW*, 4141). Freud goes so far as to say that the ability to make a judgment is not even possible until "the creation of the symbol of negation has endowed thinking with a first measure of freedom from the consequences of repression and, with it, from the compulsion of the pleasure principle" (*CW*, 4143).

So thought needs negation to enrich itself by freeing itself from "the restrictions of repression." Here we can begin to understand Kristeva's claim that negativity gives rise to the symbolic realm. But, according to Freud, thought also needs to orientate itself to the world through the "reality-ego" rather than the "pleasure-ego." The function of judgment has two kinds of concerns: the first is the instinctual impulse either to eat something or spit it out, to take whatever is good into oneself and to eject whatever we perceive as bad. But this impulse, guided by the pleasure-principle, must be constrained by the second function of judgment which is to determine whether or not a "presentation" in the ego, let us say an idea or image in the ego, *also* has an existence in reality. It is this function of judgment and thought, according to Freud, that generates the fundamental antithesis between subjective and objective. This antithesis arises only because thinking possesses the capacity "to bring before the mind once more something that has once been perceived, by reproducing it as a presentation without the external object having still to be there" (*CW*, 4142). Interestingly, Freud uses the word "presentation," and stops short of using the word "sign" (which Hegel and Kristeva use).

We can now understand the passages quoted earlier from Kristeva suggesting that the separation of one's body from the world, and the (re)creation of the object as an absence, as a sign, take place at the same time. More importantly for grasping Kristeva's account of Hegelian negativity, Freud says:

> Judging is a continuation, along lines of expediency, of the original process by which the ego took things into itself or expelled them from itself, according to the pleasure principle. The polarity of judgment appears to correspond to the opposition of the two groups of instincts ... Affirmation – as a substitute for uniting – belongs to Eros; negation – the successor to expulsion – belongs to the instinct of destruction. (*CW*, 4143)

We can see here the roots of Kristeva's reconception not only of Hegelian negativity but of the Hegelian dialectic in general. "Expulsion" or "rejection" is Kristeva's preferred term for negativity. The very act of expulsion from oneself, of negating what is undesired, is what opens up the space between subjectivity and objectivity. The "polarity of judgment" – which characterizes the dialectical process – has its foundation at the level of the instincts in the interplay between the unifying impulse of affirmation and the divisive impulse of negation, i.e., between the primordial impulses of life and death.

It is because negativity has its profoundest roots in the unconscious, for Kristeva, that it possesses such transformative and subversive power. She sees negativity or rejection as characteristic of the subject in process/ on trial "who succeeds ... in remodeling the historically accepted signifying device by proposing the representation of a different relation to natural objects, social apparatuses, and the body proper." The subject moves through all of these "texts" and uses the very linguistic network it subverts to show that the network "does not represent something real posited in advance" but is itself tied to the instinctual process and the drives. The subject is not a fixed point, a subject of enunciation that somehow stands over and controls the perception of the world as a prefabricated linguistic subject-predicate structure, but rather "acts *through* the text's organization" which represents the *chora (RPL,* 126). Again, the subject on trial or in process might be compared with Deleuze's schizophrenic.

9.6   Hegelian Desire and Freud on Paranoia

Furnishing a further parallel with Deleuze and Guattari, Kristeva treats the notion of negativity in terms of desire. For Hegel, the most fundamental form of self-consciousness is desire, as given in his statement in the *Phenomenology* that "self-consciousness is *Desire* in general" (*PS,* 105).[8] Desire is the medium through which we abrogate the foreignness of the object and make it ours. It is through such possession and transformation of the external world that self-consciousness asserts and recognizes itself. It is by abolishing the independence of the object that it achieves "certainty of itself" (*PS,* 109). Quoting the passage containing these statements of Hegel, Kristeva characterizes desire as "the negation of the object in its alterity" as an independent existence, as well as the "supersession of its heterogeneity," and the "assumption" of this alterity into the certainty of self-consciousness (*RPL,* 133). Kristeva sees this very process of subject-construction as paranoid, as producing a paranoid subject or self-consciousness. If self-consciousness comes into being through the supersession of the heterogeneous other, "Desire is this very supersession." Having always been on the path of desire, self-consciousness "becomes its Other, without, however, giving itself up as

[8] Hegel's *Phenomenology of Spirit,* trans A.V. Miller (Oxford: Oxford University Press, 1979), §167.

such. The movement of scission continues and is the very essence of self-consciousness, corresponding to Desire." In Hegel, as Kristeva observes, this "dividedness is subordinated to the unity of the self in the presence of the Spirit [*Geist*]" and desire is the agent of this unity by negating the object (*RPL*, 133).

Reading "between the lines in Hegel," Kristeva finds a fundamental truth about the nature of the subject: "*The subject is a paranoid subject constituted by the impulse of Desire that sublimates and unifies the schizoid rupture.*" She arrives at the remarkable conclusion that not only "is paranoia therefore the precondition of every subject – one becomes a subject only by accepting, if only temporarily, the paranoid unity that supersedes the heterogeneous other – but paranoia also lies close to the fragmenting that can be schizoid." The very fluidity of differences that constitute self-consciousness threaten that unity (*RPL*, 134). So Kristeva locates the dialectic within an individual subjectivity torn from any Hegelian unifying context of totality or teleology.

9.7   The Hegelian Subject and Capitalism

According to Kristeva, Hegel's idealist dialectic expresses this primordial division or rupture which constitutes the subject as paranoid at its very foundation: The subject returns from otherness into itself, having abrogated that otherness, having converted the otherness of the world to itself, or in Hegelian terms, having converted the world as "substance" to "subject." This is the potential of the Hegelian dialectic. However, as Kristeva sees it, Hegel himself does not realize that potential, for he "posits division, movement, and process, but in the same move dismisses them in the name of a higher metaphysical and repressive truth, one that is differentiated but solely within the confines of its unity: Self-Consciousness and its juridical corollary, the State." This state, moreover, is "the bourgeois State," created by the French Revolution (*RPL*, 135). So Hegel "glimpsed the splitting of the ego" and its negative relation to the material and social formations of capitalism; he had "one of the most lucid visions of the loss of subjective and metaphysical unity and of ... jouissance," but, anxious to overcome this loss, his dialectic "closes up the movement of negativity within unity" – and this is precisely the definition of desire (*RPL*, 135).

In Kristeva's eyes, theological and metaphysical revivals of Hegel – even those such as Feuerbach's and Marx's which claim to be materialist – take up both this notion of desire and the idea of man as a unity. In other words, their materialist overturning of the dialectic is accomplished at the cost of "a blindness to the Hegelian dialectic's potential ... for *dissolving* the subject." This unifying of the signifying process under the unitary concept of "man" betrays Feuerbach's "pious atheism." The human subject, thus shorn of negativity, is reduced to a "desiring" subject whose "status as a speaking signifying being" can never be negated. The desiring human being is the mainstay of religion since the archetypal object of desire is God. Moreover, it is desire that unifies man and binds him to others, serving as the foundation of anthropomorphism, and the human foundation of community and the state. Feuerbach "attenuates the driving force of the dialectic" in declaring that man's essence is contained "in community, in the unity of man with man" (*RPL*, 136). Kristeva's point is that this "materialist overturning" of the Hegelian dialectic effectively reveals that the bourgeois family, civil society, and state are "founded on the unitary subject and his desire." Indeed, Feuerbach sees the state as the realization of the human essence. As such, this overturning amounts to an "anthropomorphization of Hegelian negativity" (*RPL*, 137).

So, whereas Marx argued that Hegel saw the human subject as alienated under capitalism but superseded this alienation by means of religion, which provided an overarching totality in which all divisions could be abrogated, he himself, according to Kristeva, views this subject, both in its alienation and its overcoming of alienation, as unitary, never as *internally* divided. The subject is always a "speaking signifying being," always a subject that is already situated in the symbolic order of language and convention. Both Marx and Feuerbach overlook Hegel's insight – which he himself did not pursue – that under capitalism the human subject is not just "externally" divided from the social order outside herself, but *internally* divided, exhibiting in attenuated form the essential features of what Freud saw as a pathological condition. In other words, the division is rooted in the very unconscious, the deepest psyche, of the subject.

Interestingly, Freud states that the conscience of a paranoic confronts him "as a hostile influence from without" and that the self-criticism conducted by this conscience "coincides with the self-observation on which it is based." This "internal research," says Freud, is the "very material required for the intellectual operations of philosophy," as shown in the "characteristic tendency of paranoics to construct speculative systems" (*CW*, 2949). If we were to take the word "speculative" here in a Hegelian sense – and of course Freud himself does not – we might say that Hegel's system is the archetypal example of a paranoid meditation, one that projects the contents of subjectivity outward and integrates all externality into the subject. For Kristeva, this paranoid system is the historical product and corollary of capitalism.

According to Kristeva, both Marxism and subsequent revolutionary movements aimed to transform the structure of the state and relations between men, but they overlooked this fundamental "dividedness of the unitary subject" as rooted within an unconscious shaped by the social configuration. In the apparatuses of state and religion, "capitalism requires and consolidates the paranoid moment of the subject: a unity foreclosing the other and taking its place" (*RPL*, 139). For Kristeva, the failure of both Marxism and deconstruction to address the semiotic and its potential to disrupt the symbolic order is a failure to capitalize on the potential of Hegel's critique of capitalism, inasmuch as this articulates a divided subject, in process of dissolution and capable of radical reconfiguration (*RPL*, 141–2, 144). Such a failure leaves incomplete any Marxist or deconstructive critique of what Hegel saw as the foundational institutions of capitalism – the family, civil society, and the state – since their presupposition of a subjective unity and humanistic agency is left intact.

9.8   Epilogue: The Ends of Language

Overall, then, what can we make of Kristeva's encounter with Hegel? This encounter is mediated by Marx and Lenin, Freud and Lacan, as well as Derrida. Most fundamentally, we might say that Hegelian negativity is crucial to Kristeva's account of ego formation. Kristeva sees Hegelian negativity as disrupting any stabilization within the symbolic order. But she also insists on a "materialist overturning" of Hegel's dialectic, and sees its negativity reaching far beyond the thetic and symbolic into the realm of the *chora* and the Freudian drives. What is crucial here is that Kristeva sees the ego itself as both linguistic and dialectical: The body's separation from the world and the creation of the object as an absence – a sign – occur at the same time. The human subject is nothing more than a "speaking subject," nothing more than the process and practice of language, which converts the world as it is given or immediately experienced into signs.

Such an account of language bears an important similarity to Hegel's narrative whereby our mind receives the world as sensation and transmutes it into signs. This is the Hegelian negation in which language plays such an important role. But for Kristeva, the process of language creation is not rational nor wholly "thetic" as it is in Hegel. She reconceives Hegelian negativity as reaching into the depths of the semiotic, and the eruption of the semiotic within the symbolic resists any reappropriation into a higher unity. It's worth invoking here a larger historical context where Kristeva sees her own work as continuing a nineteenth-century revolution against the rational and the thetic, conducted archetypally by symbolist poets like Mallarmé against what she calls the signifying practices of capitalism. Capitalism sustains its ideological stasis by excluding poetic language, a figurative and semiotic language that undermines the kind of denotative precision aspired to by bourgeois philosophers such as Locke.

It is here that Marxists might take issue with Kristeva, in her insistence that poetic language is intrinsically subversive. As part of the *Tel Quel* group, Kristeva saw some radical promise in Mao's China, but her subsequent disillusionment led her to withdraw her interests from any overtly political program to a deeper, psychoanalytic understanding of the individual. In an article of 1977 she went so far as to say that the public intellectual is caught in a master–slave dialectic whereby she is imbricated in the very structures she challenges, and, more strikingly, that true dissidence lies in the realm of thought and language.[9] Moreover, she has distanced herself from the insistence of much feminism that the personal is the political. Again, it is easy for cynics to deride Kristeva's position: I have one colleague, an analytic philosopher, who caricatures Kristeva's idea of revolution as people sitting around smoking legalized marijuana and reading Bukowski.

In the face of such criticisms, one could respond that Kristeva sees the subversive traits of much feminism as already inscribed in her own view of the "feminine" as existing only within the order of signification, as comprised only by the signifying process itself. Again, it's arguable that for Kristeva, the feminine is located within the semiotic and not within the symbolic order and is therefore not subject to conventional social codes. It is through reaching back to the *chora*, to the semiotic, that, for example, literature and art can point toward a reconstitution of the conventional subject as a subject in process/on trial. But most importantly, we might recall that, in her reconception of Hegelian negativity as extending into the unconscious, she sees the unconscious itself as grounded in a material context, as actually shaped by given social configurations. She recognizes that Hegel articulates a paranoid subject as

[9] Julia Kristeva, "A New Type of Intellectual: The Dissident," in *The Kristeva Reader*, ed. Toril Moi (New York: Columbia University Press, 1986), pp. 293–4, 299–300.

a product, a correlative, of capitalism. But she reconceives this division within the subject as grounded in the unconscious.

This subject – and language – are born in the same dialectical process: Kristeva effectively recasts Hegel's drama of language, as transmuting the world into signs, onto a stage where the unconscious plays a leading role: this shaping of the world into signs creates both an internally divided subject as well as an alienated object (the world). It's by recognizing this reaching of language into the semiotic, this grounding of language within the unconscious, that we can recognize the subversive power of "poetic language" – which of course serves as a metaphor. The reconception of language necessarily entails the reconception of the human subject – which is entirely consumed and constituted by linguistic practice. This subject under capitalism is already deeply divided; Kristeva's point is that we can harness this division, drawing on the subject's semiotic elements to infuse dissolution and reconfiguration into its symbolic elements, to create a new kind of subject. Today, for example, the very notion of gender and gendered subjects is being transformed – not just in theory but in legal rights and political practice as well as uses of language. Hence, to transform language, to transform the signifying structures of capitalism, is not only to engender a new subject but also to transform the object, the world that is conceived through the categories of language. It is to enable a transformation of the political order.

B. The Politics of Recognition

CHAPTER 10

The Master–Slave Dialectic

Why are we so full of rage when we are on the road? People who in face-to-face interactions are courteous and deferential suddenly become steeled in defiance when relating to one another from the confines of a car. What is the difference? When we interact with people directly, we inhabit a realm where recognition has already been established. We recognize one another's rights and there is no competition in this respect, no struggle to obtain recognition, at least of our basic rights. But once you put us all in cars, we revert to a kind of state of nature, where we must each assert our rights again.[1] So much so that sometimes this struggle for recognition becomes a life-and-death struggle: we forget who we are, we forget the speech and manners appropriate to our station, we forget that we have families and children, and we are suddenly prepared to risk everything in this battle on the tarmac.

Most of us certainly don't want to kill or be killed. But we must show that we are willing to risk this, to risk both the giving and taking of life. The person who wins this struggle becomes the "master" of the road, and the person who backs down becomes like a "slave" who must meekly follow behind. But the slave here is actually the one who can negotiate the world better and will end up being more successful, realizing that she can earn recognition not in one instant of bravado but rather by the work she does in the world. The master, on the other hand, who displays a triumphant recklessness on the road, will find that his attitude is mired in ignorance of the world and its customs. Eventually he will become subordinate to the very person over whom he enjoyed a fleeting triumph. If we understand this scenario, we have understood the basic outlines of Hegel's master–slave dialectic, which is a dialectic of *recognition*, and

---

[1] Of course, there are established rules that govern our interactions on the road; yet the phenomenon of road rage shows how easily these are forgotten, and how readily we can regress to a more primitive scenario.

which shows that human subjectivity is not conceivable in isolation but only in interaction with other human beings. Indeed, one can achieve humanity only through social interaction.

Hegel broke with the Cartesian psychological way of viewing the human self. Descartes viewed the self as an isolated, atomistic entity. He even proposed a sharp mind–body dualism, whereby the mind as a "thinking substance" is in its very nature distinct from the body which exists in a material world of spatiality and extension. Hegel also reacted sharply against empiricist notions of the "I" as a mere convention or assumption, an assumption formalized in Kant's notion of the transcendental ego. The idea behind this notion is that in order for our diverse empirical experiences to be unified, we must presuppose some transcendental "I" standing behind these experiences, an "I" to which all those experiences belong. Yet Kant's ego is still an independent entity, and remains a mere presupposition. In Hegel's deeply contrasting vision, the self cannot even emerge as a human self in isolation, nor can it emerge in independence from the material world of which it is a part. Humanity, and the human self, must arise through social interaction, through struggle, and their status as such is attained only through reciprocal recognition.

Whereas Descartes, Kant, and nearly all the Enlightenment philosophers formulated their notions of the human self as an isolated being, Hegel insisted that human identity and consciousness are in their very nature social and historical. It is this insight that emerges most clearly – albeit somewhat metaphorically – in the master–slave dialectic. This dialectic embodies the archetypal scenario whereby the self-achieves its identity through encountering the Other. Such a view of the self as inherently relational, as a highly *mediated* existence arising through shifting relations and struggle – with itself, with its own past, with others, with the material world, and with larger historical forces – underlies almost all modern versions of selfhood, in fields ranging from structuralism and psychoanalysis through feminism and gender theory to postcolonialism and global studies.

Throughout Hegel's writings there are a number of accounts of the master–slave dialectic. The most renowned of these occurs in the *Phenomenology*, and this is the one that has been taken up by many branches of modern theory. Hence, in the present chapter, we'll try to offer a clear exposition of this rather difficult account, since it has been so influential.

10.1 The Master–Slave Dialectic in Hegel's *Phenomenology*

In the *Phenomenology*, Hegel expounds the various forms taken by human consciousness and ways of knowing as they progress toward what Hegel calls "Absolute Knowing." The dialectic of master and slave represents the transition from mere consciousness to self-consciousness. To understand the context of this dialectic, we need to visit briefly an early section of this text, entitled "Self-Certainty." Here, Hegel examines what he considers to be the three initial forms of consciousness: sense-certainty, perception, and understanding. These, he says, are not self-subsistent views of the world but *moments* or phases of self-consciousness. For Hegel, the most fundamental form of self-consciousness is desire. As he puts it, "self-consciousness is *Desire* in general" (*PS*, §167). Desire is the medium through which we abolish the foreignness of the object and make it ours. It is through such possession and transformation of the world that self-consciousness asserts and recognizes itself. It is by destroying the independence of the object that self-consciousness achieves "certainty of itself" (*PS*, §174). For example, a sculptor might find in her world a block of marble, which is entirely indifferent to her existence. By chiseling it into a statue, she impresses upon this part of the world her own subjectivity; the statue, if only implicitly, speaks with her voice.

However, self-consciousness can achieve satisfaction only through *recognition*, which an object in the world is unable to give explicitly.[2] This recognition can only be given by another self-consciousness. We may recognize ourselves in an object that we transform and possess so that it is stamped with our character, but in such an object we merely recognize ourselves *implicitly*. For true self-recognition, we need the mirror of another self-consciousness, in which we can see ourselves objectively affirmed – as subjects. As Hegel puts it, self-consciousness can achieve satisfaction and recognition "*only in another self-consciousness*" (*PS*, §175). And this, as he states at the beginning of the master–slave section, is his major contention: "Self-consciousness exists ... only in being acknowledged" [*es ist nur als ein Anerkanntes*] (*PS*, §178).[3] When we interact with another human being, she speaks with her own voice; being human in

---

[2] As Robert R. Williams states, the object is transient and has no independence, *Tragedy, Recognition, and the Death of God: Studies in Hegel and Nietzsche* (Oxford: Oxford University Press, 2012), pp. 34–5.

[3] *Phänomenologie des Geistes, Werke*, 3: 145.

this context is to speak and to listen, to allow this dialogic interaction to shape us both.[4]

Hegel now posits his famous scenario where two self-consciousnesses meet, each seeking recognition. He says that when they initially confront each other, each loses its own self and finds itself as an *other* being: it has sublated that other and "sees its own self in the other." In other words, each self-consciousness must sublate or supersede the other self-consciousness as an independent being but must also "sublate its own self, for this other is itself" (*PS*, §179–80).[5] When we recognize an "other" as our self, we effectively see that we share in something universal. Consciousness

> finds that it immediately is and is not another consciousness, as also that this other is for itself only when it cancels itself as existing for itself, and has self-existence only in the self-existence of the other. Each is the mediating term to the other, through which each mediates and unites itself with itself ... They recognize themselves as mutually recognizing one another. [Sie *anerkennen* sich als *gegenseitig sich anerkennend*] (*PoM*, 231; *PS*, §184; *Werke*, 3:147)

So my consciousness can exist only as something mediated by another consciousness.

Hence, self-consciousness cannot somehow arise in isolation. One's own identity as a human being is not something immediately given; it must be achieved, through recognition. And this recognition must be mutual. I become myself only through the mediation of an other. I must negate or sublate not only the other's material existence but also my own; we must both recognize that it is in the realm of pure consciousness, unfettered by material existence, that we each find our "self-existence" affirmed only in the self-existence of the other. Our bodies may be entirely different, and these are what divide us; our "consciousness" is what we have in common.

Another way of expressing this is to say, as Hegel does, that when the two self-consciousnesses initially confront each other, they do so appearing "in their immediacy ... they are for each other in the manner of

---

[4] For an excellent account of all these themes, see *Hegel's Phenomenology of Spirit: A Critical Guide*, ed. Dean Moyar and Michael Quante (Cambridge and New York: Cambridge University Press, 2008), esp. pp. 63–111.

[5] G. W. F. Hegel, *The Phenomenology of Mind*, trans. J. B. Baillie (London and New York: George, Allen & Unwin/Humanities Press, 1977), p. 229. Hereafter cited as *PoM*. For purposes of clarity, my exposition draws on both the standard English translations of the *Phenomenology*, the one by A. V. Miller, cited earlier, and this one by J. B. Baillie. I have often cited references to both texts. I have kept citations of the German text to a minimum.

ordinary objects. They are independent individual forms that have not risen above the bare level of life." So they confront each other as *objects* but must rise to an interaction whereby they see each other as *subjects*. They must reveal "themselves to each other as existing purely for themselves," i.e., as pure self-consciousness, free from this imprisonment in materiality (*PoM*, 231; *PS*, §186). This insight is crucial to many of our own endeavors today, where we need to treat others as subjects – each with her own perspective – rather than as objects to be "worked upon."

There now ensues the famous "life-and-death struggle." In this, each self-consciousness must prove that "it is fettered to no determinate existence, that it is *not* tied up with life." In other words, we must prove that we don't care about the world our bodies inhabit – about our survival, our security, our material ambitions. This "proving oneself" involves a twofold action: each must seek the death of the other, and must also risk its own life:

> [I]t is solely by risking life that freedom is obtained; only thus is it tried and proved that the essential nature of self-consciousness is not bare existence, is not the merely immediate form in which it at first makes its appearance, is not its mere absorption into the expanse of life ... the other's reality is presented ... as an external other, as outside itself; it must cancel that externality. The other is a purely existent consciousness and entangled in manifold ways; it must view its otherness as pure existence for itself or as absolute negation. (*PoM*, 233; *PS*, §187)

A rather interesting question now arises: what is meant by "death" in this context? A literal, physical death of either combatant would not serve Hegel's purpose, of course; for that would bring the entire scenario to an end.[6] But we must remember that this is not a literal scenario, and we could argue that the "death" of which Hegel speaks is an ideal death, or even death *as* ideality. This death is equated with the "absolute negation" of material existence, and in the next paragraph, Hegel effectively transmutes the notion of death into this ideal status: if the two combatants were to die, he says, that would be "abstract negation, not the negation characteristic of consciousness, which cancels in such a way that it

---

[6] This, as we can see later, is precisely the scenario on which Bataille and Derrida focus. Jack Reynolds indicates that "death" must be taken metaphorically when he observes that "one cannot be acknowledged or recognized by a corpse," "The Master-Slave Dialectic and the 'Sado-Masochistic Entity': Some Deleuzian Objections," *Angelaki: Journal of the Theoretical Humanities* 14.3 (2009): 13. The same point had been made by Edward S. Casey and J. Melvin Woody, "Hegel and Lacan: The Dialectic of Desire," in *Hegel's Dialectic of and Recognition: Texts and Commentary*, ed. John O'Neill (New York: State University of New York Press, 1996), p. 229.

preserves and maintains what is sublated, and thereby survives its being sublated" (*PoM*, 234; *PS*, §188). So Hegel must assume that, unlike Eteocles and Polyneices, his combatants do not kill each other.

In this struggle, nonetheless, one of the combatants does indeed risk his life, showing his disdain for his (and all) material existence, while the other, who refuses to engage such a risk and clings on to his materiality, becomes the slave. In Hegel's terms, the result of this struggle is a "dissolution" of the initial "simple unity" of each "simple ego" as "absolute object." There now results, on the one hand, a "pure self-consciousness" (the master), and on the other hand a consciousness

> which is not purely for itself, but for another … consciousness in the form and shape of thinghood. Both moments are essential … they stand as two opposed forms or modes of self-consciousness. The one is independent, and its essential nature is to be for itself; the other is dependent, and its essence is life or existence for another. The former is the Master, or Lord, the latter the Bondsman [*jenes ist der* Herr, *dies der* Knecht]. (*PoM*, 231; *PS*, §189; *Werke*, 3:150)

The master is the "pure" self-consciousness because he is free of the material world, while the slave has not superseded his dependence on material existence.

Hegel tells us that the consciousness of the master "is mediated with itself through an other consciousness, i.e. through an other whose very nature implies that it is bound up with an independent being or with thinghood in general." So the master is both "an immediate relation of self-existence" and "at the same time mediation, or a being-for-self which is for itself only through another" (*PoM*, 234–5; *PS*, §190). So, firstly, Hegel again stresses that the master's identity is *mediated*: It achieves self-existence or self-relation only through mediation of another existence. Secondly, what subordinates the slave to the master, his "chain," is that the master relates to him in this mediated way whereas the "essential character" of the slave's consciousness is "thinghood," since the slave has failed to attain an identity as a mediated subject. The master has engaged in a "pure negation" of the thing (i.e., thinghood or material existence). As a result of his dominance, his ability to engage in mediation, the master "relates himself to the thing [the world] mediately through the bondsman." The master has effectively "interposed" the bondsman between himself and the world, which he now enjoys without reserve. But the bondsman must work, must labor, upon the thing, the world (*PoM*, 235; *PS*, §190).

However, an interesting twist or reversal arises here. As Hegel reminds us, the slave *also* is "in a broad sense" nonetheless a self-consciousness, and he "also takes up a negative attitude to things and cancels them." But, since the "thing" (material existence, the world) is "independent" for the slave (in the sense that he does not control it, being dependent on it), he cannot "with all his negating, get so far as to annihilate it outright ... he merely works on it" (*PoM*, 235; *PS*, §190). So in fact, there is not after all merely a simple or outright opposition between master and slave; for all the slave's inability to shun material existence, both master and slave are forms of self-consciousness and *both* are engaged in negating the world. The difference is that the master's negation is seemingly instantaneous and "outright," whereas the slave's negation must be achieved through labor. But this common activity of negation contains the seeds whereby the overall scenario will be reversed.

How does this reversal come about? After he is victorious in the struggle, the master exists "only for himself"; that is his "essential nature." He is the "negative power," a power to which the "thing" means nothing. As such, he gets his recognition from the slave, who confirms his own "unessential" nature both by working upon the thing and by being dependent upon "determinate existence." However, there is a problem here. The recognition that the master gets from the slave is not sufficient to confirm his own (the master's) humanity; it is a recognition that Hegel calls "one-sided and unequal" [*ein einseitiges und ungleiches Anerkennen*; *Werke*, 3:152], a recognition that is not forged in reciprocity (*PoM*, 236; *PS*, §191). The master gets his recognition from an "object" that "does not correspond to its notion." In other words, the slave has not realized his own essence, his own status as an independent *subject*, by freeing himself from his own material existence. Hence the recognition he gives cannot be the full recognition that might be given by an equal. So, after all, the master is "not assured of self-existence as his truth," and indeed he learns that his truth "is rather the unessential consciousness." His truth "is accordingly the consciousness of the bondsman" (*PoM*, 237; *PS*, §192–3).

As readers of literature, we may recall a graphic illustration of this point in Frederick Douglass's *Autobiography*. What we witness there, on numerous occasions, is a master failing to treat his slave like a human being, failing to give her recognition. As a result, not only is the slave dehumanized, but the master himself is shown to be less than human.[7] This is a lesson that in our own era we have not finished learning: When

---

[7] Margaret Kohn argues that Douglass's "life-and-death struggle" with the reputed slave-breaker Edward Covey was a turning point that led to his self-recognition, "Frederick Douglass's Master-Slave Dialectic," *Journal of Politics* 67.2 (2005): 500, 511.

we treat others as objects instead of subjects, we effectively denude ourselves of subjectivity and humanity, reducing ourselves to objects. Any
kind of oppression denies humanity to both oppressor and oppressed.

Now Hegel shows us that just as lordship ends up being the reverse of
what it desired, so bondage passes into "the opposite of what it immediately is" and will blossom into "real and true independence" (*PoM*,
237; *PS*, §193). The first element in this transformation is "fear." During
the life and death struggle, the slave's consciousness experienced not
just some localized fear, but "was afraid for its entire being; it felt the
fear of death, the sovereign master." In that experience it was "melted
to its inmost soul" and suffered an "absolute dissolution of all its stability into fluent continuity." What is striking and surprising is that Hegel
actually equates this "dissolution," this fear of death – which was the
slave's reason for not risking death, for *failing* to adopt a negative attitude toward material existence – with "the simple, ultimate nature of
self-consciousness, absolute negativity, pure self-referent existence." This
total dissolution does not comprise the slave's consciousness merely in
an abstract or general way. In "serving and toiling the bondsman actually carries this out. By serving he cancels in every particular aspect his
dependence on and attachment to natural existence, and by his work
removes this existence away" (*PoM*, 238; *PS*, §194). By working on the
world, by transforming it, the slave overcomes his dependence on it. The
seed of the slave's eventual transformation, then, lies in his subservience
to an even higher force, the "sovereign master" Death [*Todes, des absoluten Herrn; Werke*, 3:153], which represents a "negativity" (a potential to
negate the "thing" or world) even more profound than that which actualized the local master's superordination.

Such dissolution, ironically, engenders a "feeling of absolute power,"
which is realized both in general, and also through service. Hegel reminds
us of the Old Testament adage that "the fear of the lord is the beginning of
wisdom" (the word for "lord" – *Herr* – has referred in this text to the victor of the life and death struggle, to Death, and to God). However, what
fear alone gives is merely "dissolution implicitly," which does not yield
an independent, self-existent consciousness. It is through work and labor
that "this consciousness of the bondsman comes to itself." The master's
satisfaction in and enjoyment of the "thing" rests on the master's desire
purely negating the object and is therefore "only a state of evanescence,
for it lacks objectivity or subsistence." The slave's labor, on the other hand,
is "desire restrained and checked, evanescence delayed and postponed; in
other words, labour shapes and fashions the thing" (*PoM*, 238; *PS*, §195).

The point is that the master's negativity was exercised for immediate gratification, whereas the slave's negativity is compelled to be disciplined and deferred because it finds actual objectification in the world. Hegel states that the slave's negative relation to the object "passes into the form of the object, into something that is permanent and remains." Moreover, this "negative mediating agency, this activity giving shape and form, is at the same time ... the pure existence of that consciousness, which now in the work it does is externalized and passes into the condition of permanence." The slave's consciousness thereby attains "the direct apprehension of that independent being as its self" (*PoM*, 238; *PS*, §195). So the slave's labor enables his "self" to be embodied in the products into which he transforms the world or "thing."

Indeed, in shaping the thing (the world), the slave's consciousness becomes aware of

> its own proper negativity ... through the fact that it cancels the actual form containing it. But this objective negative element is precisely alien, external reality, before which it trembled. Now, however, it destroys this extraneous alien negative, affirms and sets itself up as a negative in the element of permanence, and thereby becomes for itself a self-existent being ... in fear self-existence is present within himself ... Thus precisely in labour where there seemed to be merely some outsider's mind and ideas involved, the bondsman becomes aware, through this rediscovery of himself by himself, of having and being a "mind of his own." (*PoM*, 239; *PS*, §196)

So, ironically, the very condition – fear – that generated the slave's subordinate status proves *also* to be the ground of his own "negative" power, which is realized on a gradual but more permanent basis than the master's negating power, which is instantaneous but ephemeral. This fear – embodying subordination to a higher master, Death or Negativity itself – leads to the burden of labor for another, which eventually becomes labor for oneself and the transformation of the world to reflect oneself.

For this "reflection of self into self," says Hegel, there are required not only the two moments of fear and service, but also the discipline of obedience and, above all, "formative activity ... Without the formative activity shaping the thing, fear remains inward and mute, and consciousness does not become objective for itself" (*PoM*, 239; *PS*, §196). What is astonishing about this dialectic is that, as in Aristotle's vision of Greek tragedy, the very ground of victory for the master and defeat for the slave is also the ground whereby this status is reversed. The slave's very imprisonment in materiality, his very inability to negate his own material existence, is occasioned by his fear, which is itself the ground of a more permanent negative power in himself, which will negate the world objectively and find itself in this transmuted world. And the master's negative power emerges into its true light as an act of bravado, achieved through risk, to be sure, but embodying a negativity exercised toward the very subordination that cannot reflect back an image of him as an independent and fully realized self-consciousness.

It might be worth summarizing the essential features in the overall movement of the master–slave dialectic:

1   The form of self-consciousness is desire; it is through desire that we transform and possess an object, making it our own, and giving it the stamp of our own character.
2   But a mere object in the world cannot truly reflect back to us our own status as a subject. This can be achieved only through another subject. In other words, self-consciousness exists only in being *recognized*, with each consciousness negating what is purely material and contingent both in itself and in the other.
3   Hence we have a scenario in which two consciousnesses confront each other, each seeking the aforementioned negation or "death."
4   One consciousness shows that she is "free" of material existence by risking her life, by a fundamental act of negation. She thereby becomes the "master." The other consciousness is unwilling to take this risk, showing that he remains dependent on material existence; he is the slave (this scenario looks increasingly like my own marriage).
5   However, the master cannot get the recognition he needs (in order to be a fully developed subject or human being) from the slave, since the latter is not a fully developed self-consciousness. This is the beginning of the περιπέτεια or reversal.
6   The slave, like the master, has a negative orientation toward the world. Moreover, the slave has experienced a profound fear, the fear of death, of absolute negativity. As such, she is *actively* engaged in negating the world.
7   The master's desire can be immediately gratified since the slave works for him and since his connection to the world is mediated by the slave. But the slave's desire is restrained and deferred. Her desire embodies a negativity that finds actual objectification in the world, transforming it through her labor.
8   Hence, through fear as embodied in and motivating her service, through the discipline of obedience, and above all through

her formative activity upon the world, the slave achieves the negative power requisite to the realization of a fully developed self-consciousness.

One might be tempted to read the stages of the master–slave dialectic as elements in the plot of a Greek tragedy, moving from an initial conflict and climax to a change of fortune through reversal and recognition. The "recognition" here, however, is of a different nature. Nonetheless, this dialectic is essentially a drama of both recognition and negativity, stressing that we achieve our humanity through conflict, through social interaction, through labor, and most importantly, through negating contingency in both ourselves and the world.

What do we learn from this dialectic? We find, most basically, that the consciousness of oneself that comprises our humanity cannot possibly arise in isolation. Nor can it arise in a relationship of subordination. It can emerge only through mutual recognition. And recognition can only be exchanged between equals, between two subjects, not between two objects, nor even between a subject and an object. If I treat someone as an object, that person's recognition of me will be inadequate for me to attain the status of subject, of humanity.

An even more crucial lesson is one that applies across a broad range of inquiries including feminism, gender studies, and postcolonialism: the status of subordination, of forced discipline and obedience is something that rests ultimately on a kind of "fear" which dissolves our worldview, our very being. We are forced to adopt a negative or negating attitude toward the world as it immediately confronts us. Take, for example, a Muslim woman who is denied certain rights in a given country. She, through years of servitude, will be forced to reassess the very alleged "rules" that subject her; she will be disposed to rethink her position in the world, and if she is able to collaborate with others who are thus subordinated, she may be able to transform parts of that world so that it does begin to reflect her "self." This "logic of reversal" could obtain with any subordinated or suppressed group, whether a subordinated class, or any group marginalized on account of religion, gender, sexual preference, race, or geography. In each of these cases, there is a more fundamental, existential, fear than merely fear of the oppressive or ruling group: it is a "fear" that is correlative with the attainment within oneself of pure negativity, which is both a willingness and an absolute need to transform the given that confronts us – whether this given be in the world or in our own minds.

The Master–Slave Dialectic in Literary Theory

Gilles Deleuze, Jacques Derrida

There have been many renowned and influential readings of Hegel's master–slave dialectic. The views of the Hegelian Marxist Lukács will be considered later. Two particularly striking interpretations were advanced by Jean Paul Sartre and Simone de Beauvoir. In his earlier work, *Being and Nothingness*, Sartre acknowledged that people struggle for recognition, but, viewing the self as essentially solitary, he rejected the idea that reciprocal recognition could be achieved. His later works do accept this idea of intersubjective recognition, but he located the struggle in concrete historical and political contexts. Similarly, Beauvoir identified the struggle between master and slave as a political and social one, concerning, among things, gender. In general, a number of traditions have sought to explore the philosophical and political possibilities of the master–slave dialectic: a Hegelian-Marxist tradition; a French tradition, which has run through Kojève, Hyppolite, Sartre, and Lacan; a German tradition that has included, beyond Lukács, figures such as Habermas and Gadamer, as well as the later scholars Shlomo Avineri and Henry S. Harris. In recent times, there has also been a "psychoanalytic turn" in approaching the master–slave dialectic, as exemplified by Edward S. Casey and J. Melvin Woody, who build on Lacan's grounding of psychoanalysis in a Hegelian intersubjective tradition as opposed to the Cartesian tradition of the isolated, atomistic self mentioned earlier.[1]

In the last chapter, it began to emerge how the master–slave dialectic might have profound ramifications for our own world and our own endeavors to rethink the concepts of subjectivity and recognition. My argument has been that the Hegelian dialectic in general must be understood as an integral part of his expression and critique of capitalism and modernity. This applies equally to the master–slave dialectic, whose

[1] For a more detailed account of these tendencies, see the superb volume *Hegel's Dialectic of Desire and Recognition: Texts and Commentary*, pp. 2–17. Hereafter cited as *HDD*.

broader implications must be grounded in Hegel's own historical context. In this chapter we can analyze critically two extraordinarily rich readings of this famous Hegelian scenario, as offered by Gilles Deleuze and Jacques Derrida, which, following in the spirit of Kojève, are "allegorical" readings.[2] That is, they take the master–slave dialectic to signify certain broader conflicts – concerning, for example, the notions of difference, metaphysical closure, and subversive uses of language and art. I will argue that these readings are all in some sense "creative misreadings," which each shed a different light on how Hegel's ideas might both continue to shape our understanding of capitalism and to furnish the conceptual means whereby we can address its problems and dilemmas. Our first task, however, is to look briefly at Kojève's seminal reading.

11.1 Alexandre Kojève on the Master–Slave Dialectic

Of the various streams mentioned above, the tradition most germane to literary theory is the French tradition, in particular, as shaped by Alexandre Kojève. It was Kojève who functioned as a major vehicle for the transmission of Hegelian ideas to an important and seminal generation of thinkers and literary theorists, including Sartre, Merleau-Ponty, and Jean Hyppolite. It is worth recalling that Kojève taught both Derrida and Foucault, while a number of other important figures including Bataille, Lacan, and Levinas attended his lectures.[3] The master–slave dialectic was central to Kojève's influential reading of Hegel. Kojève saw this dialectic as integral to man's humanity. What marks human identity,

---

[2] It should also be mentioned that Andrew Cole and Susan Buck-Morss have offered "historical" readings inasmuch as they relate the master–slave dialectic to particular historical circumstances or frameworks. I acknowledge that the difference articulated here between "allegorical" and "historical" readings is merely strategic and does not represent a rigid distinction. In his groundbreaking study of the connections between these modes of reading, Thomas Kemple explains how Max Weber's work provides a "sociological allegory," whereby we view sociological speech and writing as not merely a scientific enterprise but as a rhetorical craft. This kind of allegory allows us to understand given texts not just in terms of what they say about their own time but also their application to "other times and places, purposes, and contexts." This is exactly what I mean by "allegory" here. See Thomas Kemple, *Intellectual Work and the Spirit of Capitalism* (London: Palgrave Macmillan, 2014), pp. x, 3. See also my article on "Allegory" in Kocku von Stuckrad and Robert A. Segal (eds.), *Vocabulary for the Study of Religion* (Leiden, The Netherlands and Boston: E. J. Brill Academic Publishers, 2013).

[3] The field of Recognition theory is vast and much of it, of course, diverges widely from Hegel's account. Levinas, for example, views recognition as a process whereby the otherness of the other is left intact and communication achieved via an exchanging of "worlds" through language. See Emmanuel Levinas, *Totality and Infinity: An Essay on Exteriority*, trans. Alphonso Lingis (1961; rpt. Dordrecht, Boston, and London: Kluwer Academic Publishers, 1991), pp. 194–226.

according to him, is desire. It is desire that impels us to transcend the given, to transform our world. My desire moves me to action, to transform an object, to internalize it, and to "destroy" it.[4] Desire is human, says Kojève, only if one desires not the body but the desire of an other, if one "wants to be ... 'recognized' in his human value." In other words, to be truly human, human desire must win out over animal desire, over the desire for mere self-preservation. Hence our humanity emerges only if man risks his life for the sake of his human desire: "It is in and by this risk that the human reality is created ... All human Desire ... is, finally, a function of the desire for 'recognition.'" (*IRH*, 6–7).

The second important point is that Kojève sees human history as the "history of the interaction between Mastery and Slavery: the historical 'dialectic' is the 'dialectic' of Master and Slave." But this interaction, insists Kojève, must "finally end in the 'dialectical overcoming' of both of them," of both mastery and slavery (*IRH*, 4). For Kojève, Hegel's insistence on the service that the slave performs is vital. It is through this service that the slave "creates a real objective world, which is a non-natural World, a cultural, historical, human World." It is only by work, says Kojève, that "man realizes himself objectively as man ... he is 'objectivized' History" (*IRH*, 25–6). It is because the slave has experienced fear – the "fear of death," we recall – that he gives himself up to such service. He must work in a world that is not his: "the given World in which he lives belongs to the (human or divine) Master, and in this World he is necessarily Slave" (*IRH*, 29).

The only way that the slave can free himself, says Kojève, is through revolution, that is, through revolutionary transformation, negation of the world as it is given. In transforming the world by his work, the slave transforms himself. He creates the new conditions in the world that allow him to take up once more the fight for recognition that he initially refused (*IRH*, 29). Hence, Kojève's reading of the master–slave dialectic effectively opens it up to very broad application. It is a dialectic of recognition that enables our very humanity and as such must be fought out in several spheres, including those of gender and ethnicity, class and power, race and empire. But this struggle for humanity, this struggle for recognition, necessarily has a historical dimension. Not only is such struggle in its various forms the driving force of history but, as such, it conditions the very nature of our theorizing, our philosophizing, which must be

---

[4] Kojève, *Introduction to the Reading of Hegel*, p. 4. Hereafter cited as *IRH*.

dialectical, itself embodying conflict as its integral feature.[5] In what follows we can examine how the foregoing issues are treated in a number of prominent critiques of Hegel's master–slave dialectic, beginning with the "allegorical" readings of Deleuze and Derrida.

11.2 Allegorical Readings of Master and Slave

11.2.1 *Gilles Deleuze and Nietzsche: Mastery and the Slavish Dialectic*

A rather provocative critique of Hegel's master–slave dialectic was conducted by Gilles Deleuze, via his treatment of Nietzsche.[6] In essence, Deleuze sees Nietzsche as fundamentally opposed to Hegel's dialectic, yet he does point to similarities between their respective notions of mastery and slavery. What is interesting is that, like Derrida later, Deleuze extends the implications of his assessment of the master–slave dialectic into a critique of Hegelian thinking in general. Deleuze, in fact, reads the notions of mastery and slavery into the Hegelian dialectic itself. What Deleuze sees as the "most ferocious enemy" of the dialectic is pluralism, and this is why, he asserts, we must "take seriously the resolutely anti-dialectical character of Nietzsche's philosophy."[7]

According to Deleuze, the most important feature of the dialectic is the role of the negative. Hegel's dialectic is essentially a "dialectic of appropriation or the suppression of alienation" (*NP*, 8). In other words, the negative – at least as Deleuze explains it – is already present in the "essence" of any positive term that we might initially posit. We might recall our previous example from the *Logic*, where Hegel initially posits "being" and then

---

[5] Stuart Barnett astutely observes that Kojève's emphasis on the connection between phenomenology and social being, as well as on the necessity of social struggle in the achievement of humanity effectively formulated the version of Hegel who stood behind Lukács and Lenin. Moreover, in emphasizing the master–slave dialectic, Kojève drew attention to the fact that Hegel made social and political struggle intrinsic to philosophy itself. Hence Hegel's work became the primary basis for articulating the relation between Marxism and phenomenology; it made possible "the advent of historicity within rationalism." *Hegel after Derrida*, ed. Barnett, pp. 19–20.

[6] A number of other attempts have been made to relate Hegel's master–slave dialectic to Nietzsche's concepts of mastery and slavery. See, for example, William Callison, "Nietzsche and Hegel: Identity Formation and the Master/Slave Dialectic," *Gnosis: A Journal of Philosophic Interest*, 9.3 (2008), 3, 11–12. The most pioneering treatment of Hegel's connections with Nietzsche is Stephen Houlgate's *Hegel, Nietzsche and the Criticism of Metaphysics* (Cambridge and New York: Cambridge University Press, 1986), which argues that Hegel's dialectic and rationalist critique of metaphysics is profounder than Nietzsche's critique, since the latter merely opposes to metaphysics the contingency of life, pp. 89–140.

[7] Gilles Deleuze, *Nietzsche and Philosophy*, trans. Hugh Tomlinson (1962; London and New York: Continuum, 2002), p. 8. Hereafter cited as *NP*.

sees "nothing" as the negative of this, while this opposition is superseded in the notion of "becoming." Deleuze's point seems to be that we should not treat "nothing" as the mere negative of "being." Rather, we should stress its *own* substantial nature; we should treat it as an "active force" and should positively commit ourselves to the "affirmation of its difference" (*NP*, 9). So, according to Deleuze, for Hegelian "speculative ... negation, opposition or contradiction Nietzsche substitutes the practical element of *difference.*" In this "Nietzschean empiricism," Nietzsche's "yes" is opposed to the dialectical "no," "affirmation to dialectical negation; difference to dialectical contradiction." In this scenario, says Deleuze, each human consciousness or will wants to *affirm* its difference (*NP*, 9).

Hence the Hegelian dialectic, according to Deleuze, is premised on a negative force which is "exhausted" and does not have the strength to affirm its own difference. It "makes this negation its own essence and the principle of its own existence" (*NP*, 9). And this is entirely the opposite of what Nietzsche describes as the "masterly" or noble mentality. The latter develops from a "triumphant affirmation" of itself, while a "slave morality from the outset says No to what is 'outside', what is 'different'" (*NP*, 9–10). And this why, for Nietzsche, the dialectic represents the mentality of the slave. In this mentality, one's posture is that of reaction rather than action, revenge and *ressentiment* rather than aggression and affirmation.

Moreover, says Deleuze, in Hegel's dialectic, power is conceived not as will to power but rather the representation or *recognition* of power. And Nietzsche, as Deleuze characterizes him, views this as the slave's conception of power. Indeed, it is the slave who "dialectises" the relation between himself and the master. As such, concludes Deleuze, Hegel's portrait of the master is a "portrait which represents the slave" (*NP*, 10). Here is Deleuze's characterization of this process:

> This is the slave's conception, it is the image that the man of *ressentiment* has of power. The slave only conceives of power as the object of a recognition, the content of a representation, the stake in a competition, and therefore makes it depend, at the end of a fight, on a simple attribution of established values. If the master–slave relationship can easily take on the dialectical form, to the point where it has become an archetype or a school-exercise for every young Hegelian, it is because the portrait of the master that Hegel offers us is, from the start, a portrait which represents the slave, at least as he is in his dreams, as at best a successful slave. Underneath the Hegelian image of the master we always find the slave. (*NP*, 10)

The master here is effectively the idea of him formed by the slave, when he imagines himself as taking over the master's place (*NP*, 81). The mania for being represented is "common to all slaves" and presupposes established values that such slavish wills seek to have attributed to them, rather than exercising any true will to power that might actually *create* new values (*NP*, 81–2). Indeed, observes Deleuze, Hegel's master himself depends on the slave for recognition (*NP*, 83).

A crucial difference between Hegel and Nietzsche is that the latter's idea of "mastery" is anything but reciprocal. Deleuze quotes Nietzsche's statement in *Beyond Good and Evil* that "It is the intrinsic right of masters to create values" (*NP*, 84). Moreover, Deleuze points out that the slave for Nietzsche is a figure of *ressentiment*. This word, stresses Deleuze, does not merely indicate a desire for revenge or a desire to rebel and triumph (*NP*, 116). Rather, it refers to a reversal of the "normal relation of active and reactive forces ... *Ressentiment* is the triumph of the weak *as* weak, the revolt of the slaves and their victory *as* slaves" (*NP*, 117). According to Deleuze, it is the "will to nothingness" that allows reactive forces to triumph (*NP*, 148). It is here that Deleuze attempts to generalize his insights such that they apply to the Hegelian dialectic itself (not just the master–slave dialectic). He claims that:

> the whole of the dialectic moves within the limits of reactive forces, that it evolves entirely within the nihilistic perspective ... the will to nothingness ... expresses itself in the labour of the negative. The dialectic is the natural ideology of *ressentiment* and bad conscience. It is thought in the perspective of nihilism and from the standpoint of reactive forces. It is a fundamentally Christian way of thinking, from one end to the other; powerless to create new ways of thinking and feeling. The death of God is a grand, noisy, dialectical event; but an event which happens in the din of reactive forces and the fumes of nihilism. (*NP*, 159)

It seems that, even though according to Deleuze's own definition, the two types of nihilism cannot coexist (one cannot both extol and deny the supersensible world), he is attributing *both* types to Hegel. Moreover, Deleuze claims that the nihilistic stance of Hegel's dialectic is "fundamentally Christian." But this identification contains a further problem inasmuch as a Christian worldview can hardly be nihilistic in Deleuze's second, "reactive" sense, since it affirmatively posits a supersensible world.

And what of that "noisy, dialectical event," the "death" of God? This is the concrete example that Deleuze gives of the essential difference between Hegel's dialectical thinking and Nietzsche's anti-dialectical, empirical impulse. According to Deleuze, Hegel sees the death of God as "an event possessing its meaning in itself." Hegel interprets the "death of Christ" as representing "superseded opposition, the reconciliation of finite and infinite, the unity of God and individual, of changeless and particular." Deleuze argues that Nietzsche, on the contrary, speaks of "forces which give the death of God a sense that it did not contain in itself, which give it an essence determined as the magnificent gift of exteriority" (*NP*, 156–7). Deleuze's point seems to be that Hegel sees in Christ's death a principle (the unity of finite and infinite) which then directs and subsumes subsequent historical developments: all appearances are subsumed under this development of Spirit.

Indeed, says Deleuze, Hegel's dialectic, proceeding as it does by "opposition or contradiction and solution the contradiction ... is unaware of the real element from which [historical] forces ... derive." The "sham oppositions" of dialectic overlook the "far more subtle and subterranean ... differential relations of forces." As such, opposition "ceases to be formative, impelling and co-ordinating: it becomes a symptom, nothing but a symptom to be interpreted" (*NP*, 157). The whole dialectic, says Deleuze, "operates and moves in the element of *fiction* ... There is no fiction that it does not turn into a moment of spirit, one of its own moments." Deleuze sees Nietzsche as "directed against the dialectic" for three reasons: it misinterprets both sense and essence as well as change because it does not take account of the actual nature of forces and merely works with "abstract and unreal terms" (*NP*, 158). Deleuze suggests that all these deficiencies have a "single origin," namely, an ignorance of the question "which one?" When Hegel claims to reconcile God and man, Deleuze asks "who is Man and what is God? ... he who is Man has not changed: the reactive man, the slave, who does not cease to be slavish by presenting himself as God, always the slave, a machine for manufacturing the divine" (*NP*, 158). Deleuze's point seems to be that in Hegel's dialectic, all that changes are the positions of the terms, terms that are themselves abstract and bear little relation to the complexity of life or the complexity of actual historical development. It is this self-imprisonment of the dialectic, characterized here as progressing only through the internal reconfiguration of its elements, that perpetuates its "slavish" character.

Given that Deleuze's critique focuses on this allegedly abstract nature of the dialectic and its divorce from history, it is ironic that his critique itself appears to lack any historical grounding. Significantly, his later, more renowned work on capitalism and schizophrenia mentions Hegel only twice, in passing.[8] As such, it might be instructive to place both Nietzsche's

---

[8] In one of these references, the authors praise Bernard Pautrat for pointing out that "Nietzsche, in contrast to Hegel, causes the master–slave relationship to go by way of language and not by way of labor." Deleuze and Guattari, *Anti-Oedipus*, p. 207, n.

views on mastery and slavery as well as Deleuze's reading of Hegel those views in a broader, historical setting. Let us begin by asking the question that Hegel fails to ask (according to Deleuze): Which one? Who?

Who is Nietzsche's "master"? Who exactly is this admirably undialectical figure? In *Beyond Good and Evil*, Nietzsche makes a distinction between "master" morality and "slave" morality. The master morality is that of the ruler, the "noble human being." He determines his own values, with no need of approval. In fact, his morality is a mode of "self-glorification." It is he who determines what counts as goodness and justice. His "ruling" morality reveres tradition and is "most alien and painful to contemporary taste."[9] This "master" is a figure of the feudal past: he is aristocratic, stern, warlike, and his morality is "firmly fixed beyond the changes of generations" (*BGE*, 181). This "noble" soul, says Nietzsche, accepts the subordination and sacrifice of others as a "fact of its egoism" and as "part of the natural condition of things" (*BGE*, 185). Nietzsche asks: what is noble? His answer is that nobility consists in "some fundamental certainty which a noble soul possesses in regard to itself, something which may not be sought or found" (*BGE*, 196). Such a master requires no recognition. He himself is unilaterally the source of all value.

We might argue that Nietzsche's "master" figure, since he is defined by spiritual traits, cannot be correlated directly with a feudal (or ancient) aristocracy or nobility. But Nietzsche also attributes to this figure the *power* to impose his own views on his subordinates and explicitly states that this power is viewed as something naturally endowed, part of the world as it is "given" – by the past, by tradition, by a hierarchy of power. This, if you like, is very much a part of Nietzsche's "empiricism."

And what is Nietzsche reacting against? We might well concede to Deleuze that, even though Nietzsche does not mention Hegel in these discussions, he is reacting *implicitly* against Hegel's views. But we might also do well to recall the larger context of this reaction. What Nietzsche is *explicitly* reacting against, of course, is emerging bourgeois society and the trend throughout Europe toward democratic capitalism. *This* is Nietzsche's own master–slave dialectic, which works itself out not merely as a development of consciousness but as a movement of history. For, according to Nietzsche, what emerges with the growth of capitalism is precisely the "slave morality." Like Shelley, Schiller, and some of the other Romantics, Nietzsche sees the "slave" as devoted to a

---

[9] Friedrich Nietzsche, *Beyond Good and Evil: Prelude to a Philosophy of the Future*, trans. R. J. Hollingdale (Middlesex: Penguin, 1978), p. 177. Hereafter cited as *BGE*.

narrow utilitarianism: "slave morality is essentially the morality of utility." Significantly – since we are contrasting him with Hegel – he also sees this morality as imbued with a "longing for *freedom*" (*BGE*, 178).

What gave rise to this slavish hankering after freedom, democracy, and a capitalist utilitarian ethic? Ironically, Nietzsche's "empiricism" seems to take less account than Hegel's "idealism" of what Deleuze calls "real forces." Nietzsche attributes the "rise of the democratic order of things" to the "mixing of the blood of masters and slaves" (*BGE*, 180). In contrast with this rather vague metaphorical explanation, Hegel – as many writings of his amply attest – had a detailed, if not always accurate, grasp of his contemporary historical conditions. Nonetheless, Nietzsche's account is worth detailing. As a result of this "mixing," he says, the originally noble and masterly impulse to "ascribe a value to oneself on one's own account" will be spread more widely. More people will be inclined to value their own opinion. But, says, Nietzsche, in these same people the even older, slavish inclination, will cause them to seek out favorable opinions of themselves from *others,* regardless of their truth or falsehood. And Nietzsche emphatically states that much "slave" still "remains in woman" (*BGE*, 180). Is this also, we might ask, what Deleuze extols as Nietzschean "empiricism"?[10]

What Nietzsche goes on to say, however, somewhat matches Hegel's description of bourgeois society. He suggests that we now live in an era of a new, unrestrained individualism, with each individual "reduced to his own law-giving" as well as his own stratagems of self-preservation, enhancement, and redemption. In this age, Nietzsche observes, everything is transient, and "nothing can last beyond the day after tomorrow" except the incurably mediocre: "The mediocre ... are the men of the future" and the only morality left is "this morality of mediocrity!" (*BGE*, 182). It is well known that Nietzsche sees humankind as developing into "the similar, ordinary, average, herdlike" (*BGE*, 187). We live, he warns, under the "overcast sky of the beginning rule of the rabble," and everywhere in Europe there is a cult of "unmanliness" (*BGE*, 196–8). But here the similarities with Hegel end. In Nietzsche's vision, with the arrival of

---

[10] It should be pointed out that Hegel also sees both mastery and servitude operating *within* the progress of any given consciousness. In his important essay "Notes on Hegel's 'Lordship and Bondage,'" George Armstrong Kelly suggests that to view the master–slave dialectic as a purely social phenomenon is one-sided. He suggests that it should be viewed from three perspectives: (1) social; (2) psychological, as concerning the "shifting pattern of psychological domination and servitude within the individual ego"; and (3) as a fusion of these two processes, as in the "interior consequences" wrought by the "external confrontation of the self and the other" (*HDD*, 257–8).

a bourgeois way of life, the tables are now turned, and we approach the conclusion of Nietzsche's own master–slave dialectic: "today," as he says in *Thus Spoke Zarathustra*, the petty people have become lord and master." That which is "womanish," that which stems from "slavishness" and the mob – "*that* now wants to become master of mankind's entire destiny – oh disgust!"[11] The slave has become the master, and the masters are the "masters of the present," the mob that exclaims "we are all equal" (*Z*, 297–8).

The difference between the two visions, the two characterizations of capitalist society, are striking. Nietzsche sees the emergence of the bourgeoisie into hegemony as the victory not merely of the slave but of the slave mentality or morality as such. He derides the freedom sought by this mentality, which he regards as a freedom that encourages mediocrity and a herd mentality. But Nietzsche's model of mastery and slavery excludes the human, the all too human dependence on mutuality and interaction. It is a model that speaks from the depths of feudal hierarchy, a vision of the natural order of things, a frozenness of social relations, absolute unaccountability, and, above all, a profoundly static and intransigent irrationality. It is not that Hegel's and Nietzsche's accounts of what capitalist society contains necessarily conflict. They both see it as rife with a potentially destructive individualism. And if Hegel's master–slave dialectic is taken as a metaphor for the ultimate victory of the bourgeoisie over feudal convention and caprice, then the two thinkers are also in agreement that what triumphs is not just the slave but the slave mentality as such. But the significance they attach to this mentality is very different.

The difference is that, for Hegel, the slave's victory is meritorious and indeed historically necessary. Even in the earlier context of the master–slave dialectic as described in *Phenomenology*, historical development proceeds through the consciousness of the slave.[12] As Lukács puts it, the subsequent developments "scepticism, stoicism and the unhappy consciousness (primitive Christianity) are without exception the products of the dialectics of servile consciousness" (*YH*, 328). The point is that for Hegel it is the slave consciousness which impels historical progress. It is the bourgeoisie, the revolutionary class – if you like, the "servile" class rebelling against the authoritarianism and provinciality of its feudal

---

[11] Friedrich Nietzsche, *Thus Spoke Zarathustra: A Book for Everyone and No One*, trans. R. J. Hollingdale (Middlesex: Penguin, 1982), p. 298. Hereafter cited as *Z*.

[12] But we should not forget that the master has also played his part. As George Armstrong Kelly states, "both principles are equally vital in the progress of the spirit ... the slave will invent history, but only after the master has made humanity possible" (through showing that he can relinquish dependence on the material world) (*HDD*, 270).

masters – which brings industrial development, technological progress, and political freedom – where freedom is defined as rational citizens participating in a rational state. It is the revolutionary, servile class that brings about a society based on Reason. We have already seen the importance of labor in Hegel's master–slave dialectic. Hegel's conception of labor, derived partly from Adam Smith, is integral to his view of both the success and the limitations or contradictions of bourgeois society.[13] The slave consciousness is superior to the masterly consciousness, in Hegel's eyes, because its negation of the world is mediated – through labor.

Among the many lessons of Hegel's master–slave dialectic is surely this: it is through labor that we transcend our merely natural or immediate existence and attain to our universality, our fully human status as beings able to engage in reciprocal action on this universal level. Nietzsche's "master" is indeed Hegel's master: he is the one who, having triumphed in the initial struggle, now lives a life where he gratifies his instincts immediately. But, in Hegel's terms, this merely annihilates the object without transforming it. There is no future for the master, for he merely consumes (as Hegel characterizes the feudal nobility); he does not know how to work on his world and to transform it into his own image – which would also be to transform and create himself. Like Hegel, Nietzsche of course is aware that such "mastery" is in a state of decay; the difference is that the one thinker laments its passing while the other sees this as enabling a new world. From a Hegelian perspective, Nietzsche's master never really escapes the kind of competitive egotism characteristic of a state of nature; nor does he truly understand his world or the forces of upheaval within it, which will shake it to its foundations. In essence, because his "mastery" is unilaterally achieved, dismissing the need for reciprocity or recognition, he does not understand what it is to be human.[14]

Hence, where Nietzsche extols some master fading within the mists of history, a master who is vanished beyond some speculative return as an *Übermensch*, Hegel is busy analyzing and integrating into his philosophical system the economic categories that underlie the newly emerging bourgeois world created by the slave. Hegel saw economics as the most immediate expression of human social activity, and while he attended

---

[13] Lukács stresses that for Hegel, economics was the "most immediate, primitive and palpable manifestation of man's social activity," Lukács, *The Young Hegel*, p. 321. Hereafter cited as *YH*.

[14] In his Jena lectures of 1805–6, known as the *Jenenser Realphilosophie II*, Hegel provides an extensive treatment of these economic issues. Here, Hegel goes so far as to view human existence itself as intrinsically relational, *Hegel and the Human Spirit*, p. 123.

fully to the higher categories of political economy such as exchange, commodity, value, price, and money, he accepted Smith's view that labor was the "central category of bourgeois political economy" (*YH*, 321, 334). It is no accident that labor is also the central category of the master–slave dialectic, and central to Hegel's thinking as a whole: the "labor of the negative" plays a driving force in the dialectic, from our initial confrontation with an object of sense to the dialectic of world history. Thus, Hegel's dialectic of the economic process, whereby humans labor on the world to transform both it and themselves, is the core of his dialectic concerning the development of capitalism and indeed of his dialectic in general. The master–slave dialectic furnishes an archetypal scenario in this respect, because for Hegel the very process of labor is fundamental in many respects to the capitalist world.

It is on his analysis of labor that Hegel's essential insights into the nature of capitalist society rest, not only in economic terms but in the very way that human subjectivity is constructed. Significantly, for Hegel, labor is discussed, as in the *Realphilosophie II*, under the general heading of "Recognition." We remember that the slave's "desire" is deferred. Hegel tells us that desire becomes universal only when it is considered as the desire of all; and this is why "Labor is of all and for all, and the enjoyment [of its fruits] is enjoyment by all. Each [one] serves the other and provides help. Only here does the individual have existence, as individual" (*HHS*, 120). In other words, labor is the means through which recognition is achieved. Labor itself is intrinsically reciprocal. In society, we don't labor for merely our own individual needs (the self that does this is not fully developed). Rather, we labor to satisfy the desires and needs of all. This is what Hegel calls abstract labor, and it is doing this that we achieve a social personality. Through division of labor and technical innovation, productivity and wealth are increased, but these very mechanisms also create an alienated world where subjectivity becomes mechanized, where a person cannot see herself in what she creates, and where many other evils, such as poverty, are rampant.[15] In such an economic setting,

---

[15] In the *Jenenser Realphilosophie II*, Hegel observes that, as human needs become multiplied and diversified so that no one person can satisfy her own needs but must labor to satisfy a small portion of the overall need, there arises an ever increasing division of such labor, augmented by a perpetual search for innovation and mechanization, leading to a diminution of subjectivity, as well as an increasing gap between rich and poor. The individual becomes "more mechanical, duller, spiritless ... The power of the Self consists in a rich [all-embracing] comprehension; this power is lost," *Hegel and the Human Spirit*, pp. 139–40. These insights of course anticipate much of Marx's analysis of alienation.

Hegel sees that human beings themselves are torn, divided between various loyalties, as well as between self-interest and communal good. The point is that Deleuze is right: As much as Nietzsche may have frowned upon it, Hegel's master–slave dialectic is truly a dialectic of the slave, a dialectic of revolution.

11.2.2   Jacques Derrida: Lordship and Sovereignty

As seen in an earlier chapter, the arresting of the Hegelian dialectic at its second phase marks and underlies much of Derrida's thought. He specifically addresses the movement of the Hegelian *Aufhebung* or sublation in his long essay entitled "From Restricted to General Economy: A Hegelianism without Reserve." Here, Derrida grounds his own reading of Hegel's master–slave dialectic in Bataille's reading of this episode in Hegel's *Phenomenology*. Derrida characterizes Bataille's interpretation as engaging in a "simulated repetition" of the Hegelian discourse whereby "a barely perceptible displacement disjoints all the articulations" of the original text.[16] The same might be said of Derrida's reading of Bataille's account, which draws out its deconstructive implications.

We might have noticed in the previous chapter a precarious moment in the master–slave dialectic. For Hegel, "lordship" indicated an ability to confront death, to *risk* death. Hegel correlated this ability with negativity, the capacity to overcome one's attachment to particularity, one's immersion in material existence. Bataille-Derrida point out that Hegel's word for "lordship," *Herrschaft*, can also be translated as "sovereignty." In some English translations "sovereign" is the word attributed to Hegel's characterization of "death" ("death, the sovereign master"), emphasizing that for Hegel death is correlative with negativity (the expression that Hegel uses is *Todes, des absoluten Herrn*) (*PS*, §194; *Werke*, 3:153). Bataille-Derrida use this alternative translation – "sovereignty" instead of "lordship" – to indicate an alternative path for the master–slave dialectic, one which diverges from the itinerary of the Hegelian *Aufhebung*.

The "precarious moment" that both Bataille and Derrida seize upon, the moment that might destabilize the entire dialectic, is predictable: we recall that the one consciousness becomes master or lord by risking her life. But while she must *risk* it, she cannot afford to *lose* it. If she actually

---

[16] "From Restricted to General Economy: A Hegelianism without Reserve," in Jacques Derrida, *Writing and Difference*, trans. Alan Bass (Chicago: University of Chicago Press, 1978), p. 260. Hereafter cited as *WD*.

underwent death, this would result in absolute loss (of meaning) and the entire dialectic would die. Hegel sees this scenario as embodying "abstract negation" rather than the required "negation characteristic of consciousness, which cancels in such a way that it preserves and maintains what is sublated, and thereby survives its being sublated" (*PS*, §188).

This paragraph in the *Phenomenology* is effectively what both Bataille and Derrida call a "scandal." Hegel simply circumvents the possibility that both combatants might die by saying that his argument, in order to proceed, cannot accommodate it. If both were to die, "there vanishes from the play of change [*dem Spiele des Wechsels*] the essential moment, viz. that of breaking up into extremes with opposite characteristics" and the two combatants would "let one another go quite indifferently, like things" (*PS*, §188). This is the point at which, for Bataille-Derrida, there is "a certain burst of laughter" at Hegelian discourse, the point where Hegelian lordship "collapses into comedy" (*WD*, 253, 256). Indeed, for Bataille-Derrida, it is laughter alone that exceeds the dialectic, and laughter (along with poetry and sacred speech) is absent from the Hegelian system (*WD*, 256).

As Derrida says, the difference between Hegel and Bataille is the difference between lordship and sovereignty (*WD*, 254). Hegelian lordship cannot afford to take an *absolute* risk: its project is to seek recognition and to *work* at the creation of a system of meaning. As Derrida puts it, the risk that lordship takes is "a moment in the constitution of meaning" (*WD*, 254). As such, lordship does not *really* confront death. What is "laughable" about this, for Bataille-Derrida, is that Hegel's dialectic can brook no real risk; it engages merely in a *simulation* of risk (*WD*, 256). In other words, lordship itself is "servile," like the slave who refuses to face death. Lordship represents a "submission" to the self-evidence of meaning (*WD*, 256). In Hegel's own account, we recall, the slave eventually becomes the master, servility becomes lordship and, in Derrida's words, lordship retains "the trace of its repressed origin" (*WD*, 255). Hence, for Derrida, not only is self-consciousness mediated through the servile consciousness, but self-consciousness is *itself* servile – where "servility" betokens desire for meaning, and "work" the creation of meaning. The entire history of meaning is represented by the figure of the slave (*WD*, 262, 276). What, then, is the difference between "lordship" and "sovereignty"? For Bataille-Derrida, sovereignty is "the absolute degree of putting at stake" – it risks everything, including the absolute loss of meaning (*WD*, 256). So "sovereignty" would represent the *actual* taking of the risk of death.

Sovereignty, as Derrida sees it, operates within a "general" economy which accommodates play and chance and the possibility of absolute loss. There is an excess or "reserve" which is not somehow assimilated and is simply useless (*WD*, 270). But at the heart of "lordship" is the Hegelian *Aufhebung* – which Derrida calls "the speculative concept par excellence," which appropriates all negativity and works "risk" into an "investment," an investment in absolute meaning. Bataille-Derrida call this "the comedy of the *Aufhebung*" (*WD*, 257, 275). The absolute negativity represented by sovereignty cannot be converted into positivity, into something affirmative, some positive system of meaning. But Hegelian negativity is in effect an "expenditure without reserve" – there is nothing outside it, nothing that it cannot assimilate. As such, this negativity is always the underside and accomplice of positivity. Hegel interprets negativity as labor, as work – the work of signification, which produces discourse, meaning, and history, and which elides risk, chance, and play (*WD*, 260). The comedy of the *Aufhebung*, the comedy of Hegelian lordship, is that it becomes servile, it enslaves itself when it starts this work, when it enters into dialectic. It is servile because it operates within a "restricted" economy, never exceeding the closure of the circle of absolute knowledge, and always being limited to the established meaning and value of objects, the absolute "circuit of reproductive consumption." The Hegelian *Aufhebung* is the victory of the slave (*WD*, 256, 271, 275).

How, then, or where can sovereignty be expressed? Bataille-Derrida urge that sovereignty does not somehow escape the dialectic but *inhabits* it without treating risk as an investment. They talk of two forms of writing. The one is "servile" writing, which operates entirely by means of "significative discourse," always seeking to assimilate the other, always seeking to "reconstitute presence" (*WD*, 265). The other form is "sovereign" writing, which interrupts the "servile complicity" of speech and meaning and inscribes within the discourse of absolute knowledge "a space which it no longer dominates." It exceeds the history of meaning and the project of absolute knowledge "by simulating them in play." It makes that entire discourse "slide." Hence, the project of Hegel's *Phenomenology* is not overturned, but its "restricted" economy is situated, is inscribed, within a "general" economy (*WD*, 266–71).

Derrida effectively sums up these subversive and disruptive strategies by explaining that Bataille uses "the empty form of the *Aufhebung*, in an analogical fashion" that forces this "speculative concept par excellence" to designate a transgressive movement which exceeds "every possible philosopheme" (*WD*, 275). The use of the term "analogical" is instructive: Centuries earlier, the theologian Aquinas had stated that we can talk of God not by reference to his actual characteristics, which we cannot know, but only in terms of "analogy" with human qualities. The project of Bataille-Derrida, in introducing "play" and genuine "risk" into the discourse of Western metaphysics, is explicitly anti-theological. In fact, what they both do is to take Hegel's master–slave dialectic, which Bataille regards as the "center" of the Hegelian discourse, as a metaphor for the all-appropriating and self-closing nature of Western metaphysics, regarded as reaching its culmination in Hegel.[17] Anticipating Žižek's later reading of Hegel, they see Western philosophy as "devouring" everything in its path, reducing every form of otherness to something sublatable into its own image, able to be incorporated into the overall system, which remains essentially unchanged and therefore closed.

11.3 The Master–Slave Dialectic in Our World: Economics and Liberal Humanism

The "risk" of which Bataille and Derrida speak embodies an acknowledgment that there are forms of otherness that cannot be reductively assimilated, which could destabilize the entire system, whereby we are forced to reconceive it.[18] An example of this might be the theory of the "melting pot," whereby all "others," all different races and religions are accepted. But the problem is that they all go into the melting pot in their diversity and come out with the character of the predominant social group. Bataille and Derrida – and almost all literary theorists – reject the Hegelian notions of *Aufhebung* and difference underlying this kind of self-confirming and coercive normalization. What they want is a notion of difference as unassimilable to the same, a difference that resists

---

[17] Judith Butler resists the idea that the *Aufhebung* is as totalizing, appropriative, and dominating as Derrida suggests. It actually contains a comical element in that at each stage of the *Phenomenology* what is dramatized is a false arrival of the absolute, an ongoing need for subjectivity to reassess itself (*HHC*, 175). Indeed, she rejects Derrida's characterization that what is external is assimilated back into some self-identical subject. Drawing on Nathan Rotenstreich's characterization of the structure of Hegelian self-consciousness as "insistently impelled outside itself," she rejoins that, for Hegel, "the act of assimilation is simultaneous with a radical revision of the subject itself." Moreover, Derrida fails to realize that the totality described at the end of the *Phenomenology* is not a static and closed totality (*HHC*, 176). All of this, contends Butler, undermines Derrida's distinction between mastery, as *appropriation*, as designating "an economy of ever-circulating resources," and sovereignty as *expenditure*, as designating a "metaphysics of unlimited funds." The *Aufhebung* designates both appropriation and expenditure (*HHC*, 176–7).

[18] This notion of encountering the "absolutely-other" is also explored in Derrida's essay on Levinas "Violence and Metaphysics," in Derrida, *Writing and Difference*, pp. 94–109.

sublation, that is irreducible to ultimate identity. Hence, although these issues may seem remote and "purely" theoretical, they have very profound practical and political implications. As we have seen earlier, it is here, at the second stage of the dialectic, that literary theory is intent on arresting the movement of the *Aufhebung*.

Indeed, Derrida's later book *Specters of Marx* shows graphically how Hegelian discourse generally, and the master–slave dialectic in particular, might illumine the economic power structures that govern our world. This book arose out of a conference convened in 1993 in the context of the collapse of communism and Francis Fukuyama's claim that the end of history was nigh, marked by the global triumph of pluralist democracies and capitalist free market economies. This conference, and Derrida's book, were dedicated to examining the various theoretical and practical legacies of Marx, his various "specters." Derrida notes that Fukuyama's vision of the triumphant liberal state is "not only that of Hegel, the Hegel of the struggle for recognition," but is also that of a Hegel who privileges the "Christian vision."[19] He also observes that Fukuyama credits Kojève with identifying the "important truth" that "postwar America or the members of the European community constituted the embodiment of Hegel's state of universal recognition." Derrida explains that it is in the name of a "highly Christianized ... outline of the master–slave dialectic" that Fukuyama proposes to "correct" Marx's materialist economism (*SM*, 61–2). Fukuyama saw both Hegel and Marx as "masters of the end of history." For Hegel this was the liberal state and for Marx, communism. Fukuyama chose the former (*SM*, 66). Derrida sees a dual "risk" here. There is the risk of a perpetuated Eurocentrism, in which recognition is sought only among "equals," with the other serving merely to reinforce self-identity. This, for Derrida and Bataille, would be the sham risk of "lordship." Then there is the "genuine" risk, the risk of "sovereignty" whereby Eurocentrism risks its own death by truly recognizing the other.

What is striking about Derrida's reading of the master–slave dialectic is its persistent recourse – via Bataille – to the terms and metaphors of bourgeois political economy. Derrida suggests that in the life and death struggle of the master–slave dialectic, the risk of death of both combatants (the risk Hegel overrides) is the risk of losing the "profit" of meaning (*WD*,

---

[19] Jacques Derrida, *Specters of Marx: The State of the Debt, the Work of Mourning, and the New International*, trans. Peggy Kamuf (1993; rpt. New York and London: Routledge, 1994), p. 60. Hereafter cited as *SM*.

255). For Hegel, this risk is turned into an "investment" that "*amortizes* absolute expenditure" (*WD*, 257). Hegelian speculative thought, says Derrida, reappropriates and overcomes all negativity, all risk. In this situation, he argues, comedy is the anguish experienced by the dialectic when confronted by "expenditure of lost funds," by the absolute sacrifice of meaning "without return and without reserves" (*WD*, 257). Sovereignty, on the other hand, is attached to nothing and does not "collect the profits from itself or from its own risk" and cannot be defined as a "possession" (*WD*, 264). For Derrida, sovereign "writing" is "absolutely adventurous" and yields "no certitude, no result, no profit" (*WD*, 273).

What Derrida-Bataille have done here is to view language itself as a system of capitalist accumulation, where the "risk" (of negativity) is undertaken only as an investment in meaning. And within this system, it is philosophy that does the "work of signification," the work of creating stable meaning, and of excluding everything embodied in laughter. Bataille calls this the "world of work," with its disciplinary prohibitions of free play (*WD*, 256, 275). Derrida even quotes a passage from Bataille that explicitly equates a "restricted" economy with political economy, which is characterized as "restricted to commercial values" (*WD*, 270). Such an economy, says Derrida, is "limited to the meaning and the established value of objects, and to their *circulation*." It is a "*circuit of reproductive consumption*" (*WD*, 271). Hence language itself – and therefore thought itself, philosophy itself as embodied in the Hegelian *Aufhebung*, is shaped from within, is modeled on, a bourgeois work ethic, one that demands discipline, compensation (of meaning) for intellectual labor, and a return on one's investments.

Above all, this restricted economy is an economy of the "same": It reduces all otherness, all difference, all newness, to itself. It sees the world in its own image, and converts the world to its own image. We saw in an earlier chapter that for Hegel language and labor are mutually correlative. Language enables the theoretical negation or transformation of the world in the mind, reducing the external world to signs. Labor effects the practical transformation of the world. For Hegel, language is a form of labor, the labor of the negative. But for Bataille-Derrida, labor – with all the wealth of its correlative terms such as production, profit, and value – is a form of language. It is what creates and regulates meaning, in a system of circulation and exchange. This is perhaps as profound a critique of capitalism as we might find anywhere in literary theory – where the very process of signification and indeed of thinking is seen as determined inwardly in the image and terminology of bourgeois economics.

For all its brilliance, though, Derrida's insight here is achieved at a high cost (to continue the economic metaphor). Unable to escape the "totality" which is comprised by the economic regime of capitalism, deconstruction introjects all the elements of the capitalist market – production, consumption, profit, possession, labor, exchange, expenditure, investment, amortization – into the province of language, where alone they can be resisted, where alone they can be situated within the broader perspectives (which, nonetheless cannot be named and are abstractly symbolized by the term "general economy"). In other words, the struggle between the restricted (political) economy and a general economy is itself retracted from the sphere of economic reality into the sphere of language, into the sphere of reflection – not even speculation – where the lance of justice hurtless breaks.

Hence, the terms of the capitalist market can now be seen, in Derrida's reading, as structuring internally the very process of meaning, as inhabiting the very relations between words, as enabling concepts at their profoundest level, as determining what is thinkable. Alternatively, we might say that the very terms of the restricted economy comprise the necessary ground of their own attempted subversion in the general economy. Even the terms of our attempt to think beyond capitalism are dictated ultimately by its own foundational elements. Marx saw Hegel's passing to a third dialectical stage as abstract and idealistic, which in effect left everything intact in the second dialectical stage, leaving the status quo of an alienated subjectivity – and an alienated world. In refusing the totality of a third dialectical stage, deconstruction effectively does the same thing, leaving everything frozen in the second dialectical stage, leaving the status quo as merely abstractly impugned and never actually superseded.

It should be said that the endeavor to "exceed" a restricted (commercial) economy is actually a conventional strategy of liberal humanism, which has typically sought to problematize the atomistic subject and the narrow categories of bourgeois economics. We remember Arnold's attempt to situate philistinism – what he regarded as the narrow, commercially minded outlook of the middle classes – within the broader ethical demands of "culture." And we can go back further, through many of the Romantics who aimed not only to situate a bourgeois utilitarian mentality within a wider conception of humanity but to situate the very notion of reason itself, regarded as a utilitarian faculty, within a more comprehensive scheme of human faculties at whose pinnacle stood the supremely integrative faculty of imagination.

What is interesting here is that this problematization of bourgeois thought occurs in the pages of bourgeois thinkers themselves. It can be traced back, for example, to Adam Smith's own earlier work, *The Theory of Moral Sentiments* (1759), which effectively propounds a model of human nature that some scholars have found to be very different from, and possibly irreconcilable with, the *homo economicus* modeled in the later *Wealth of Nations*, published some seventeen years subsequently in 1776. The later text famously propounds the notion that each person pursues her own economic self-interest and in doing so unwittingly benefits the whole. It is not so much that the earlier text contradicts this notion; rather, it situates self-interest within a much larger ethical scheme that rests on principles of moral sympathy founded on prudence, benevolence, and justice.[20] Smith argues here that "in acting according to the dictates of our moral faculties, we necessarily pursue the most efficient means for promoting the happiness of mankind" and are thereby "co-operating with the Deity and advancing as far as we can the plan of Providence."[21]

---

[20] The possible contradiction between these two texts of Adam Smith – which the German Historical School of economic thought, dating back to 1843, saw as *das Adam Smith Problem* – has been the subject of a longstanding controversy. While many nineteenth-century German economists did see this rift between Smith's earlier and later work, with the emphasis moving from "sympathy" to "self-interest," Michael Novak impugns such a reading. In *The Spirit of Democratic Capitalism* (1982), Novak argues that Smith's last revision of the early work occurred in 1790, some fourteen years after his *Wealth of Nations* was published, indicating that he did not modify his earlier opinions. Others, such as David D. Raphael and Alec A. Macfie, have seen this issue as a "pseudo-problem," yet the debate continues into the present day. I am arguing that there is not a contradiction between the two texts but rather a narrowing of focus in the later text, whereby self-interest acquires a more prominent role in a primarily economic context. I am not aware that Hegel anywhere explicitly referred to *das Adam Smith Problem* – nor do Waszek and other writers on the subject appear to cite any such reference – but his situating of bourgeois or civil society within a broader ethical framework can be seen as addressing this kind of "problem" or contradiction. It should be noted that, like Hegel, the German Historical School saw economics as a broad science related to ethical and political issues, as *Nationalökonomie* combined with a *Staatswirthschaftslehre*. For a full discussion, see Leonidas Montes, "*Das Adam Smith Problem*: Its Origins, the Stages of the Current Debate, and One Implication for Our Understanding of Sympathy," *Journal of the History of Economic Thought*, 25.1 (2003), 63–90. Significantly, Montes's one mention of Hegel is unrelated to the Smith problem.

[21] Adam Smith, *The Theory of Moral Sentiments*, edited by Knud Haakonssen (Cambridge: Cambridge University Press, 2002), p. 87. Hereafter cited as *TMS*. Smith even talks of human nature as possessing a "universal benevolence" and suggests that the wise and virtuous person is "always willing for his own private interest to be sacrificed to the public interest of his own particular order or society" (*TMS*, 125). Indeed, a benevolent action is especially virtuous if it is performed in defiance of some strong motive from self-interest" (*TMS*, 125). Even in this text, Smith talks of an "invisible hand" whereby life's necessities are shared out despite the selfish intentions of the rich (*TMS*, 91). Smith does say, however, that while we have an innate sympathy for others, self-interest is appropriate when we pursue "important objects" such as position, territory, and profit in business (*TMS*, 91). And he acknowledges that society can be held together without any mutual love, and merely on the basis of "mercenary exchange" (*TMS*, 47).

In general, bourgeois thought, as Hegel recognized, contains many levels of self-contradiction. Bourgeois ideology always needs liberal humanism as its self-contextualization, sometimes as its conscience. Where the tradition of liberal humanism always posits a third dialectical stage, a broader vision to encompass any narrow utilitarian model of humankind – for the Romantics, "nature," for Arnold, "culture," for Hegel, Absolute Spirit – deconstruction equally rejects this narrow conception of human nature but refuses to articulate or posit anything broader. It refuses both closure and humanism – which it sees as integrally related. The only universal it posits is language, paradigmatically conceived as a refusal of universality, as a system of endless relationality, an infinity of networks and connections that can never be stopped, that can never be closed. Such a gesture is post-humanistic insofar as it sees subjectivity and objectivity as positions or effects within language. The deconstructive critique of Hegel and of philosophy is resolutely focused on resisting any transition to the third stage and on exposing the mechanisms whereby such transition is claimed.

C.   Hegel and Marxism

CHAPTER 12

Hegel and Marx

It is sometimes thought, quite reasonably, that Hegel's master–slave dialectic furnished a kind of model for Marx's vision of the struggle of the proletariat against the ruling class. Contrary to popular belief, however, this dialectic as such does not figure in Marx's writings. But the issues it raises – the nature of subjectivity and its relation to the state, the mutual recognition of rights, the competitive or antagonistic relation between people and classes, and the connection of economics with the ethical order – preoccupy much of Marx's thought.[1] Because it has addressed these issues in depth, Marxism has played a foundational role in literary theory's encounter with capitalism. In fact, deconstruction and Marxism represent the two archetypal forms of abrogating Hegel's dialectic that have shaped much literary theory from within. Deconstruction arrests the dialectic at its second stage, the stage where "difference" predominates as the protagonist, the stage of openness, where no conceptual deus ex machina is allowed and where no particular direction or teleology is necessarily embraced.[2] The emphasis of deconstruction's critique of the

[1] In general, as Ian Fraser and Tony Burns usefully suggest, we might identify three broad strands of commentary on the Hegel-Marx connection. The first sees Marx as having demystified Hegel's thought in order to effect a materialist "appropriation" of it. Recently, a variant of this approach, which Chris Arthur has termed the "new dialectics" school, rejects the dialectical materialism of Engels and orthodox Marxism, and returns directly to the thought of Hegel. Practitioners of this approach include Arthur himself and Tony Smith. The second has effectively sought to "purge" Hegelianism from Marxism altogether (as with Bernstein and Althusser). And the third general approach rejects the notion that Hegel and Marx stand opposed in terms of idealism and materialism. Focusing on Hegel's social thought rather than his metaphysics, it sees Hegel as more materialist than idealist, and regards Marx as essentially inheriting the substance of Hegel's dialectic rather than needing to invert it, Ian Fraser and Tony Burns, "Introduction: An Historical Survey of the Hegel-Marx Connection," in *The Hegel-Marx Connection*, ed. Tony Burns and Ian Fraser (London and New York: Macmillan/St. Martin's, 2000), pp. 1, 20–1. See also Chris Arthur, "Hegel's *Logic* and Marx's *Capital*," in *Marx's Method in Capital: A Reexamination*, Fred Mosely (Atlantic Highlands, NJ: Humanities Press, 1993), pp. 63–87.
[2] There are of course many ways of reading deconstruction's relation to the dialectic. We could argue that deconstruction actually refuses the *first* stage of the dialectic; and that, rather than freezing the

dialectic is on language, on undermining metaphysical presuppositions, and on exposing transcendental signifieds as well as the coercive force of binary thinking.

The influence of Marxism on the various areas of literary theory has in some ways been even more profound. The traditions of Marxism have long undermined the orthodoxies that the law is somehow natural or eternal, that the values of the bourgeoisie are universal or represent the interests of an entire nation, or that the modern state is truly democratic. They have also fostered a recognition that the oppression of women and minorities, as well as the entire project of imperialism, are grounded in economic pressures structurally integral to capitalism. And Marxism's insights into language as a social practice with a material dimension, its awareness that truth is an interpretation based on certain kinds of consensus, its view of the world as created through human physical, intellectual and ideological labor, and its insistence that the analysis of any given phenomenon must be informed by historical context, were articulated long before such ideas made their way into modern literary theory. All these insights are enabled by the fact that Marxism brings to the analysis of all phenomena a dialectical way of thinking that is rooted in, but crucially modifies, Hegel's thought.

It's worth observing that Marxism and deconstruction are by no means entirely mutually exclusive. Though some of their elements are undeniably irreconcilable, they share certain features. We might say that, even before the advent of deconstruction, Marxism inherited from Hegel certain deconstructive features, such as an emphasis on negativity, on negating the world as given. We might also allow that deconstruction enlists powerful strategies for undermining bourgeois ideology in all its variants, strategies that have served Marxism well.[3] Indeed, many branches of feminism and gender studies draw valuably on a potent combination of Marxist and deconstructive insights. We saw in an earlier chapter that the reconception of Hegelian negativity underlying Julia Kristeva's views of language was mediated by both Marxist and deconstructive notions (as well as notions from Freud and Lacan).

---

dialectical "space of contradiction," it opens it up to the potentially infinite, a gesture apparent in Derrida's proximity to negative theology. Perhaps, again, deconstruction could be said to open up "difference" to a radical alterity that is ethical, as enunciated in Derrida's readings of Levinas.

[3] For an extended account of this connection, see Michael Ryan, *Marxism and Deconstruction: A Critical Articulation* (Baltimore: Johns Hopkins University Press, 1984); see also the chapter "Marxism and Deconstruction" in Eagleton, *Walter Benjamin*.

As I have been arguing throughout this book, in order for us to understand literary theory's engagement with contemporary culture as shaped by capitalism, we need to grasp the foundations of this engagement in the relevant seminal thinkers themselves. In an earlier chapter, we examined in some detail Hegel's dialectic as it emerged from his own assessment of capitalism. This is the dialectic that has enabled both deconstruction and Marxism. The connection between Marx and Hegel has been the subject of an enormous amount of commentary, much of it highly technical and confusing for many readers. But it's important to understand what Marx himself says about Hegel. So, my aim here will be to provide a clear account of Marx's often difficult commentaries, an account whose only claim to originality is that it brings together in a concise analysis the most important of his numerous reflections on Hegel. As such, this chapter will offer a detailed assessment of Marx's own critique of Hegel's dialectical treatment of capitalism. That critique addresses the structural features of capitalism – such as private property, the classes within society, and the nature of the political state – that continue to be crucial and contentious issues in our world and have increasingly informed the focus of literary theory as it grapples with the ethical and ideological dilemmas inhering not only in "literature" as narrowly defined but also in the contemporary "texts" which surround us – including social and digital media, journalism, and all the elements of popular culture.

12.1   Marx on Hegel: An Overview

After Hegel's death in 1831, his immediate legacy ran through two fundamentally opposed groups, the so-called "right" Hegelians, who interpreted his philosophy in a conservative manner, and the "left" Hegelians, who used his thought to articulate more radical theological and political perspectives. There was also (an often ignored) movement of "center-Hegelianism," represented by such followers of Hegel as Rozenkranz and Michelet.[4] However, it is the group of left Hegelians that interests us here; it included David Strauss, whose groundbreaking work *The Life of Jesus* appeared in 1835, a radical reinterpretation of Christ that was clearly influenced by Hegel's own theology and methods. The left Hegelians also included Bruno Bauer who viewed Hegel as a covert atheist, as well as Moses Hess and Arnold Ruge who both linked Hegelianism

---

[4] John Edward Toews argues that this was in fact the dominant group, *Hegelianism: The Path toward Dialectical Humanism, 1805–1841* (Cambridge: Cambridge University Press, 1980), p. 206.

with political activism and radicalism (at that time, liberalism).[5] Karl
Marx was deeply involved in the endeavors of this group.

Marx's attitude to Hegel no doubt declined from his initial youthful
enthusiasm. But even in his mature years, he recognized his own debt
to Hegel, as indicated by his renowned comments in the "Afterword"
(1873) to the second German edition of *Capital*:

> My dialectical method is, in its foundations, not only different from the
> Hegelian, but exactly opposite to it. For Hegel, the process of thinking,
> which he even transforms into an independent subject, under the name of
> "the Idea," is the creator [demiurgos] of the real world, and the real world
> is only the external, phenomenal form of the Idea. With me, the reverse
> is true: the ideal is nothing else than the material world reflected in the
> human mind, and translated into forms of thought.
>
> The mystifying side of Hegelian dialectic I criticised nearly thirty years
> ago, at a time when it was still the fashion. But just as I was working at the
> first volume of *Capital*, the peevish, arrogant, and mediocre epigones
> ['Επ'Ειγονοι] who now talk large in educated German circles, began to
> take pleasure in treating Hegel in the same way as the good Moses
> Mendelsohn treated Spinoza in Lessing's time, namely, as a 'dead dog'.
> I therefore openly avowed myself the pupil of that mighty thinker, and even
> here and there, in the chapter on the theory of value, coquetted with the
> modes of expression peculiar to him. The mystification which the dialectic
> suffers in Hegel's hands by no means prevents him from being the first to
> present its general forms of working in a comprehensive and conscious
> manner. With him it is standing on its head. It must be turned right side
> up again, if you would discover the rational kernel within the mystical
> shell.[6]

These words have provoked volumes of debate, much of it highly contentious.[7] Nonetheless, it's worth examining the salient aspects of these

---

[5] For a detailed account of Hegel's early followers, see the superb collection of essays in *The New
Hegelians: Politics and Philosophy in the Hegelian School*, ed. Douglas Moggach (Cambridge:
Cambridge University Press, 2006), especially chapters 2–7.

[6] Karl Marx, *Capital: A Critique of Political Economy: Vol. I*, trans. Ben Fowkes (Middlesex: Penguin,
1992), pp. 102–3. I have retained one or two phrases from an older translation: Karl Marx, *Capital:
A Critique of Political Economy: Vol. I*, trans. Samuel Moore and Edward Aveling (London:
Lawrence & Wishart, 1977), p. 29. Hereafter cited as *Cap*.

[7] In the last few decades scholars such as Joseph McCarney, David MacGregor, and Ian Fraser have –
to some extent following Marcuse – challenged the "myth" of Hegel as an idealist whose thought
had to be "inverted" and have affirmed the continuity between the dialectics of Hegel and Marx.
See David MacGregor, *Hegel and Marx: After the Fall of Communism* (Cardiff: University of Wales
Press, 1998), pp. 2–4; Ian Fraser, "Two of a Kind: Hegel, Marx, Dialectic and Form," *Capital and
Class*, 61 (1997), 103. Robert Fine insists that we should not read the Hegel-Marx connection simply through Marx's own account, and he offers the immensely productive suggestion that we should
read Hegel and Marx together – which is what I have tried to do here – since their insights are

passages in their context, a context that has all too often been ignored. If we looked at merely the first paragraph, we might be tempted to say – as many commentators have – that Marx simply mischaracterizes Hegel's dialectic. Marx is essentially following Feuerbach when he says that for Hegel, thought itself is the "subject" which creates its "object" or the "real" world as an externalization of itself. As against Marx's reading, it could be argued that what Hegel actually says is that thought – which itself is initially at a primitive stage – confronts the external world as merely given, as pure otherness, and eventually, over a long historical process, it sees its own operations as the rational core of that externality. This rational core, and its harmonization with the historically developed rational subject, comprises "reality."

It's in the second paragraph above that Marx reveals his insight into the dialectic when he suggests that, notwithstanding his idealist orientation, Hegel was the first to present the "general form" of the dialectic in "a comprehensive and conscious manner." But what did Marx understand by "dialectic" here? Earlier in this Afterword, he quotes a review of *Capital,* which states that the scientific value of Marx's inquiry "lies in the disclosing of the special laws that regulate the origin, existence, development, death of a given social organism and its replacement by another and higher one." Marx sardonically praises this reviewer for grasping his "dialectic method" (*Cap,* 28). And what is at the heart of this method? For Marx, it's the Hegelian notion of "sublation," the transcendence and partial preservation of a given condition or state. Marx insists that what distinguishes him from the classical political economists, who are trapped within "the bourgeois horizon," is that they view "the capitalist regime ... as the absolutely final form of social production, instead of as a passing historical phase of its evolution" (*Cap,* 24). In other words, for Marx, Hegel's dialectic furnished a model for analyzing political economy as a series of historical *phases,* and for viewing the capitalist mode of production as but a stage which was destined to be transcended.[8]

---

mutually complementary in our understanding of capitalism.[1] See Robert Fine, "The Marx-Hegel Relationship: Revisionist Interpretations," *Capital and Class,* 25 (2001), 73. This last approach, of reading Hegel and Marx in conjunction, is very skillfully articulated by Allen Wood who suggests that we should focus on the points where the two thinkers agree (Wood, "Hegel's Ethics," pp. 422–36).

[8] It might be pointed out here that other philosophies of history, such as those of Adam Ferguson, Kant, Herder, and Fichte, had treated history in terms of stages, and that to some extent both Hegel and Marx were following them.

Did Marx misunderstand Hegel? He remarks that the "mystified" form of dialectic became the fashion in Germany because it "seemed to transfigure and to glorify the existing state of things." This statement indicates that Marx was the originator of a further misconception of Hegel – namely, as an apologist for an authoritarian Prussian state.[9] But it also shows what Marx valued about the dialectic:

> In its rational form it is a scandal and abomination to bourgeoisdom ... because it includes in its comprehension and affirmative recognition of the existing state of things, at the same time also, the recognition of the negation of that state, of its inevitable breaking up; because it regards every historically developed social form as in fluid movement, and therefore takes into account its transient nature not less than its momentary existence; because it lets nothing impose upon it, and is in its essence critical and revolutionary. (*Cap*, 29)

This embodies a more insightful understanding of the dialectic than Marx is usually given credit for. He recognizes the dialectic as a method of regarding the world as a process, as in movement; of viewing social forms as historically developed; and of viewing a given state of affairs as containing its own negation. Crucially, Marx sees the dialectic as in its essence "revolutionary" since it enables him to theorize the abrogation of capitalism as part of a historical process. We shouldn't forget that, in Hegel's time, the bourgeoisie was the revolutionary class.

Much earlier, in 1858, Marx had written to Engels that the categories in Hegel's *Logic* had helped shape his (Marx's) treatment of capital, and in a letter of 1868 he insisted that Hegel's formulation of the dialectic – shorn of its idealism – must be retained as the basis of dialectics. There are at least three other crucial documents where Marx engages in some depth with Hegel's thought. The first of these was the *Critique of Hegel's 'Philosophy of Right'*, written in 1843 but unpublished during Marx's lifetime. The next was the *Economic and Philosophic Manuscripts of 1844*, which presents Marx's most sustained and focused treatment of Hegel's dialectic. Both of these, published in 1932, inspired a radical reappraisal of Marx, leading to characterizations of him as a humanist or even an existentialist. Finally, there is the *Grundrisse* (1857–8), which David McLellan

---

[9] As Allen Wood pointed out to me, this was a fashionable misreading of Hegel based on the Preface to the *Philosophy of Right* and the polemic against it by Paulus, Fries, and others. The element of truth in it is that Hegel was trying to protect himself against the newly ascendant reactionary censorship. He had reason to want to protect himself, since the content of *Philosophy of Right* aligns it with the Prussian reform movement, which the reactionaries sought to suppress – as seen in an earlier chapter.

calls "the most fundamental of all Marx's writings."[10] This profoundly Hegelian text became available in the West only in 1953 and hence was entirely neglected by many earlier writers who had taken sides on the question of Marx's connection to Hegel. Louis Althusser, for example, argued strongly that Marx's later "scientific" disposition led him to abandon Hegel, but Althusser never mentioned the *Grundrisse* in the context of his polemic.[11] I now propose to examine each of these texts in turn, to help us assess what exactly Marx took from Hegel's dialectical thinking.

12.2 Marx and Hegel

12.2.1 Marx on Hegel (I): The 1843 Critique of Hegel's Philosophy of Right

The manuscript of Marx's critique of Hegel's *Philosophy of Right* was written in 1843 but never published in Marx's lifetime. Marx intended to revise it for publication and wrote an introduction to the proposed revision. While the introduction was published in 1844, the revision was never undertaken; instead Marx channeled the substance of this *Critique* into various other projects. But it's generally agreed that the *Critique* was an integral part of Marx's work between 1843 and 1847, which laid out a critical program that Marx continued to develop for the rest of his life. This manuscript shows that some of Marx's fundamental notions – concerning the significance of private property, the role of the proletariat, the need for universal suffrage, the connections between economics and the political state – came out of his engagement with Hegel's political and social thought.[12]

What's essentially wrong with Hegel's philosophy of the state, according to Marx, is that it's merely an "allegorical" and "mystical" account of

---

[10] Terrell Carver contextualizes this judgment within McLellan's own project to "make Marx Marx." In his essay of this title, Carver explores how Marx's persona was carefully created by himself and others during his lifetime. Professor Carver was kind enough to share with me the unpublished manuscript of his essay.

[11] See *Marx's Grundrisse*, ed. David McLellan (London: Macmillan, 1971), pp. 2–3. Hereafter cited as *MG*.

[12] Karl Marx, *Critique of Hegel's Philosophy of Right*, ed. Joseph O'Malley (1970; rpt. Cambridge: Cambridge University Press, 2009), pp. li–lii. Hereafter cited as *CPR*. The ensuing analysis develops some of the excellent insights in O'Malley's extensive introduction, but it adopts a rather different approach, focusing on Marx's critique of Hegel's dialectic as "allegorical." Moreover, as Terrell Carver has pointed out to me, Marx was using Hegel's *Philosophy of Right* as a way into political economy and social theory (which Hegel had taken on from other sources, notably Sir James Steuart).

how political society comes into being. He says that for Hegel, the subject of this process, what *drives* it, is something abstract – the Absolute Idea; and that the major social institutions – family and civil society – are merely moments or phases in what Hegel sees as merely a *logical* development. In other words, as Marx sees it, the transition from family and civil society into the political state is not derived by Hegel from the actual nature of these institutions but merely from the categories of his *Science of Logic* (*CPR*, 10). Marx is here echoing Feuerbach's critique that Hegel inverts the positions of subject and predicate: he makes the Absolute Idea subject and he treats the *real* subjects, such as family and state, as the predicates or attributes of this Idea. In Hegel's hands, political realities are viewed as logical-metaphysical determinations. As Marx puts it: "Logic is not used to prove the nature of the state, but the state is used to prove the logic" (*CPR*, 18).

In Marx's eyes, it is this "speculative" nature of Hegel's dialectic – whereby reality is adapted to thought rather than thought comprehending any actual reality – that leads his political theory everywhere into self-contradiction. But Marx does see Hegel's philosophy, in exercising this defect, as accurately expressing the contradictory nature of the modern political state under capitalism (*CPR*, 50, 72, 108, 136). In what follows, I want to analyze three of the most important issues where Marx finds Hegel's accounts to be riven with such "speculative" self-contradiction: monarchy, the connection of Hegel's bureaucracy with the estates, and the role of private property. As we shall see in this chapter and the next, these issues are still with us today and have served as the focus of much Marxist literary and cultural theory in its critique of capitalism.

12.2.1.1   Constitutional Monarchy

Hegel sees the constitution or political state as comprising three elements: legislature, executive, and monarchy. One of Marx's aims in this critique was to impugn the notion of constitutional monarchy, and he finds in Hegel's idea of sovereignty a prime example of "speculative mysticism" and self-contradiction. Hegel had stated not only that the monarch is the "ultimate self in which the will of the state is concentrated" but also that a given individual is "raised to the dignity of monarchy in an immediate, natural fashion, i.e. through his birth in the course of nature" (*PR*, §280). In other words, becoming a monarch is basically an *accident*. Marx essentially responds by saying that Hegel's monarch represents an exercise of arbitrary will: "The monarch is personified sovereignty, sovereignty become man, incarnate state-consciousness, whereby all other persons are thus excluded" (*CPR*, 26, 22–4). The monarch is the "mystical" subjectification or personification of the state. As before, in Marx's eyes Hegel reverses subject and predicate, regarding sovereignty or the essence of the state as the subject and the true elements of sovereignty – the legislature, the will of the people, etc. – as predicates of this abstract Idea (*CPR*, 23–4). Instead of conceiving the state as the ultimate social reality of man, Hegel presents one man – conceived as the incarnation of the Idea – as the ultimate reality of the state. This, observes Marx, is effectively an incarnation of God, and is pure allegory. As Marx puts it, we encounter "at all levels an incarnation of God" (*CPR*, 39–40).

12.2.1.2   Hegel's Bureaucracy and the Estates

Marx acknowledges Hegel's "great advance" lies in intending to consider the political state as an organism, as a totality whose (universal) interests harmonize with the (particular) interests of its constituent spheres (*CPR*, 40). But despite this intention, he sees Hegel's political structure as harboring a major contradiction. For Hegel, the corporations are supposed to represent the collective private economic interests of civil society, and the "universal" class (the bureaucracy of civil servants) is meant to embody the wider interests of the state. But both of these, says Marx, are compromised by their mutual relation, and in effect, as Hegel himself says, the interests of civil society must be subordinated to those of the state (*PR*, §288–9). Marx points out that in Hegel's bureaucracy, "the state's interest becomes a particular private interest opposed to the other private aims" (*CPR*, 48). The state bureaucracy is sunk in "passive obedience" to higher officials, trust in authority, mechanical acceptance of fixed principles and traditions, and a careerist devotion to the state as its private end, whereby the civil servant himself is torn between universal and particular interests (*CPR*, 47, 53). The issue raised here resonates profoundly with us today: what is or should be the connection between large business interests and the state bureaucracy? In an age where government policy is largely shaped by super PACs, it seems impossible that any class could represent the "universal" interests of the state. Indeed, the resulting "schism" within the individual has been well theorized by many theorists, including Lacan, Kristeva, and Deleuze.

12.2.1.3   Private Property

Marx also impugns Hegel's assessment of the role of primogeniture, the tradition whereby landed property is passed invariably through the lineage of first-born sons.[13] Such property can't be divided among other members of the family nor is it subject to the vicissitudes of the market, like the wealth generated by business. Hegel's argument concerning primogeniture is essentially that the class most suited for political position – by birth, like the monarch – is the hereditary landed nobility. According to Hegel, this class possesses an independent will (less likely to be corrupted by particular aims) because "its capital [inherited landed property] is independent alike of the state's capital, the uncertainty of business, the quest for profit, and any sort of fluctuation in possessions" (*PR*, §306). As such, this class is "entitled to its political vocation by birth without the hazards of election" (*PR*, §307).

This very "independence" that Hegel touts as a desirable qualification for political office is criticized by Marx as yet another form of externality, another expression of the undialectical and unharmonized nature of Hegel's state. As Marx sees it, inherited landed property exists *beyond* the sphere of state capital, the sphere of property established by the social will. Because such property is inalienable, its "social nerves have been severed" and it is isolated from civil society. Hence the opposition that Hegel develops, says Marx, is between private property and state capital. What Hegel presents is "the power of private property over the political state" (*CPR*, 104). Hegel effectively makes political citizenship a function of private property (*CPR*, 111). The issue raised here is again vital in our own time: The institution of private property, exerting inordinate power over the political state, effectively forecloses the democratic process.

12.2.1.3.1   General Significance of Marx's *Critique*   Overall, we can see that Marx's engagement with Hegel in this text is crucial to the further development of his ideas. It's here that, like Feuerbach, he articulates his humanism, asserting the primacy of man, of his social being, as the premise of economic and political life, which transforms his world through labor – something that he and Engels will develop in the various polemics later assembled as *The German Ideology*. And it's here, in interrogating Hegel's notion of the bureaucracy as the universal class that he begins to develop (in the 1844 introduction) the idea of the proletariat as the truly universal class in whose emancipation lies both German emancipation and the "redemption of humanity" (*CPR*, 141). Finally, it is here that he addresses what he calls (in the subsequently written introduction

---

[13] It should be mentioned that primogeniture took various forms; Prussia and England, for example, did not have the same system when Hegel was writing.

to the text) a "major problem of modern times," the relation of industry and wealth to the political world (*CPR*, 134–5). In his assault on primogeniture, he begins to examine the role of private property in the political state. In pointing out the contradictions in Hegel's conception of sovereignty and the estates, he lays the groundwork for his own notions of democracy and his own communism by undermining the Hegelian notions that other writers found so appealing. All these ideas are further developed in Marx's 1844 manuscripts and *Capital*.

What underlies all these critiques is Marx's relentless and often bitter attack on Hegel's "mystical" dialectic which, he claims, merely furnishes an *allegory* of the real situation.[14] Moreover, this dialectic, beginning with the Absolute Idea as subject, fails to live up to its intentions, and fails to resolve the contradictions of the modern state. But we shouldn't forget either that Marx credits Hegel with accomplishing the "most logical, profound and complete ... critical analysis of the modern state" and its deficiencies (*CPR*, 136). Marx's own social and political theory was worked out within the framework laid down by Hegel.[15] It's in his very self-contradictions that Hegel expressed the unresolved dilemmas of the modern capitalist world, which still overwhelm us today: the opposition between civil society and state, between each of these and family, the irrationality of the legislature, the power that wealth and property wield in politics, the state as a set of private interests, and the resulting profundity of schism within human beings themselves.

12.2.2   *Marx on Hegel (II): The Economic and Philosophic Manuscripts of 1844*

Many of these issues – private property, communism, the religious mystification of actual conditions – are further developed in Marx's *Economic and Philosophic Manuscripts of 1844*. It's actually here that Marx offers his most comprehensive and focused engagement with the Hegelian dialectic. It's a difficult but instructive analysis, where Marx once again takes as his starting point Feuerbach's critique of Hegel to formulate what he calls an "atheistic humanism." In our era, literary theory has positioned itself against humanism generally and liberal humanism in particular. But Marx's

---

[14] As Terrell Carver suggested to me, Marx's attack was directed primarily against contemporary Hegelians, such as Bauer, Stirner, and Grün, who appealed to this outlook as authoritative.

[15] Again, Marx's critique of Hegel was part of his polemic against Hegelians, which laid the groundwork for Marx's thinking about social class and other questions.

critique here reminds us of the radical nature of his humanism, founded as it was upon a subversion not only of recent traditions of German idealism, but of centuries of Western thought that had shaped those traditions. What Feuerbach and Marx discern at the depth of Hegelianism is not only idealism but ancient and medieval Neoplatonism and Christian theology, a hierarchical system of subject and predicate whereby the "human" is always an afterthought, a mere appendage, an adjective, of the Divine or the One, or some ultimate governing Principle of the Universe.

Humanism is radical and subversive in this context because it allows the human to emerge from its darkened status of mere predication into the light of self-subsistence, as *subject*, as agency – of its own development, of the historical process. In a sense, this humanism – like the humanism of the Enlightenment – represents a reaffirmation of Renaissance humanism whose spirit was itself compromised and subverted not only in neoclassicism but even in many philosophical systems from Descartes to Hegel. In Marx's reading, Hegel affirms the value of the individual – as emerging through a long historical dialectic – but then betrays this affirmation by reintegrating the individual within a spiritual totality, and by defining freedom as harmony (or, more cynically, conformity) with the universal interests of the state. In our era this dilemma – of how the individual relates to the universal – increasingly plagues almost every ethical and political and cultural issue we confront. And, as we can elaborate later, our modes of challenging humanism are becomingly increasingly problematic.

12.2.2.1 *Hegel's Inversion of Humanism*

Feuerbach's great achievement, thinks Marx, is to show that both philosophy and religion, as Hegel expounds them, are merely forms of "estrangement" of the essence of man. In other words, Hegel views the essence of the human as external to humankind itself, as merely a phase in the self-development of God or Absolute Spirit. In contrast, says Marx, Feuerbach establishes "true materialism" by founding his theory on the actual "social relationship" between human beings. As Marx sees it, the third stage of Hegel's dialectic effectively reaffirms the estrangement of the human in the second stage by viewing this estrangement as merely a phase in the achievement of God's self-identity. Feuerbach, however, displaces this "negation of the negation" with a new, positive basis – the social character of humankind.

Marx finds a "double error" in Hegel. On the one hand, though Hegel sees the institutions of wealth, religion, and state power as estranged from the human being in capitalist society, these institutions are for Hegel merely "thought-entities," and Hegel's vantage-point, that of the philosopher, is itself estranged. In other words, the entire external world, for Hegel, is merely the world as comprehended in thought; the world of nature is merely the externalization of thought (*EPM*, 129–30). On the other hand, Hegel also reduces the human being to self-consciousness, to pure thought, to a merely "*thinking being*," so that the distinct forms of estrangement appear only as various forms of consciousness. Hegel fails to view such estrangement in the realm of thought as a mere expression of *real* human estrangement (*EPM*, 133–4, 143). For Hegel, the "*human character* of nature and of the nature created by history – man's products – appears in the form that they are *products* of abstract mind and as such, therefore, phases of *mind – thought-entities*" (*EPM*, 131). So, according to both Feuerbach and Marx, Hegel replaces actual history with an abstract, logicized, and speculative history. Hegel's logic embodies alienated thinking because it is "totally indifferent to all real determinateness" (*EPM*, 129).

12.2.2.2   *Hegel on Labor and Alienation*

On the positive side, Marx sees Hegel's dialectic as grasping two important features of capitalism: that humankind's self-creation occurs essentially through labor; and that the bourgeois world is estranged or alienated. On the first of these, Marx observes that the "outstanding achievement" of Hegel's *Phenomenology* is its "dialectic of negativity" in which "Hegel conceives the self-creation of man as a process, conceives objectification as loss of the object, as alienation and as transcendence of this alienation ... he thus grasps the essence of *labour* and comprehends objective man – true, because real man – as the outcome of man's *own labour*" (*EPM*, 132). This describes the dialectical process whereby "Man" – initially presumed to be self-identical – objectifies himself through labor; his being is alienated or dispersed among objects in the world; and then, he resumes a broader identity or human selfhood which overcomes this alienation and integrates into itself the objective features of his existence. In this way, man achieves his identity as a "species-being," characterized (according to Marx) by consciousness, will, and freedom. In other words, Hegel's dialectic *is* the dialectic of capitalism: It sees that the "external" world and the human self are created by labor, which is a process of negation, of transforming what is immediately given in either case.

Secondly, "Hegel grasps man's self-estrangement, the alienation of man's essence, man's loss of objectivity ... Hegel conceives labour as man's act of *self-genesis* – conceives man's relation to himself as an alien being and the manifestation of himself as an alien being to be the emergence of *species-consciousness* and *species-life*" (*EPM*, 143). This is of course Marx's rewriting of Hegel's dialectic which, as modified, grasps that the human being – initially in isolation from an indifferent world – creates her world through labor, a world from which she is then estranged or alienated, after which she overcomes that estrangement to find her true self in her emergence as a species-being. But Hegel's own dialectic, says Marx, annuls in its third stage not only estrangement or alienation[16] but also objectivity itself. Hegel overcomes this alienation of the human being and objectivity only in the realm of thought. This means that all the existing institutions – wealth, religion, state power – are left exactly as they are, in their alienated condition. This is what Marx calls the "uncritical" or "false" "positivism" of Hegel's dialectic, which embodies a dissolution and restoration of the existing empirical world merely in the realm of philosophy, of abstract thought (*EPM*, 130, 140–1).

Looked at in a broad historical context, Hegel's philosophy accommodates the then revolutionary spirit of capitalism and of bourgeois humanism. But, as we have seen, the profundity of his vision also comprehended the contradictions and dilemmas of the capitalist world and its modes of thought. Hegel saw that the atomism and individualism of civil society led to insoluble contradictions. Hence he endeavored to redeem such atomism and particularism by undermining the very self-subsistence won for them by humanism, by reinvesting them with the status of finitude – derived from Plato, Aristotle, Christian theology, and Neoplatonism – and thereby with the imperative to find their true realization and self-completion in totalities that transcended them – the state, the ethical community, the Absolute Idea. This, at least, is how Marx reads Hegel. Thus the role of Hegelian *Aufhebung* or sublation is simply to *confirm* the actual world – the world of capitalism – in its alienation instead of actually overcoming alienation. In Hegel's *Phenomenology*, as Marx understands it, the realm of civil law is sublated by morality which in turn gives way to family, civil society, and the state; but all these *remain*, says Marx, though now no longer viewed as independently real or objective but only as *moments* in the evolution of Absolute Spirit (*EPM*, 140).

Marx views both religion and private property as the primary causes and symptoms of estrangement. But Hegel's dialectic does not supersede

---

[16] Marx does not differentiate these terms.

these institutions, merely their *concepts*, which means that the actual objects or institutions are left intact in the real world. They are super-seded only as objects of knowledge. Marx states that this "lie is the lie of Hegel's principle" (*EPM*, 140–2). Indeed, the *subject* of Hegel's dia-lectic is not the human being but God. As Marx eloquently puts it, the dialectic is not centered on human life; rather, it is "a divine process ... the divine process of man, a process traversed by man's abstract, pure, absolute essence that is distinct from itself." The subject of this process is God or Absolute Spirit, while "[r]eal man and real nature become mere predicates – symbols of this hidden, unreal man and of this unreal nature" (*EPM*, 143). Again, the implication is that Hegel's system is mystical and Neoplatonic, viewing the human not in its reality but merely as an "emanation" or phase of the divine. Yet, in this very gesture of mystification, Hegel accurately expresses the fundamentally alienated nature of the bourgeois world.

If "man" is never conceived by Hegel in anything other than an estranged fashion – as merely a phase, an externalization, of the divine, this Absolute subjectivity, says Marx, is engaged in "a pure, *incessant* revolving within itself" (*EPM*, 144). In a sense, this is the circle of "meta-physical closure" that Derrida and many other theorists have impugned. But Hegel has effectively and perhaps unwittingly shown, says Marx, that "abstract thought is nothing in itself; that the absolute idea is nothing in itself; that only *nature* is something" (*EPM*, 145). Interestingly, in a footnote, Marx credits Hegel with highlighting the "act of abstraction which revolves in its own circle" and with bringing together the abstract concepts of various philosophers, thereby creating "the entire compass of abstraction as the object of criticism" (*EPM*, 146, n). Hence Hegel has shown that intrinsic to capitalism are not only the processes of self-creation and world creation through labor, but even that the very process of thought under capitalism is alienated inasmuch as it sees the world only through the system of concepts it has inherited, a close and circular system insulated from any authentic engagement with reality.

12.2.2.3 *Humanist Rewriting of the Dialectic*
Where Hegel makes God or the Absolute Idea the subject of the dialecti-cal process, Marx again follows Feuerbach in displacing this divine sub-ject with the human subject. The human subject for Marx is not merely consciousness but "a human and natural subject endowed with eyes, ears, etc., and living in society, in the world, and in nature" (*EPM*, 146, n). We know what Deleuze and Guattari think of this: They see "eyes"

and "ears" as machines divorced from any notion of human subjectivity. Marx might reply that ears and eyes per se cannot have political agency. Can machines? Indeed, what Marx advocates here is a humanism on both theoretical and practical levels. It's worth remembering, again, that in this context, such humanism was revolutionary. On the theoretical level, estrangement or alienation is embodied in religion: positing God as the subject of dialectical evolution is already an estrangement of man's essence, which is regarded not as self-grounded but as having its ground beyond itself, in absolute dependence upon the divine.

On the practical level, alienation is embodied in private property, which is a structural cause of man's separation from the world as a product of his own labor. Hence, as Marx says, "atheism, being the supersession of God, is the advent of theoretical humanism, and communism, as the supersession of private property, is the vindication of real human life as man's possession and thus the advent of practical humanism" (*EPM*, 142). Marx thereby rewrites the dialectic in humanistic terms, with the human as the subject of the process: "[A]theism is humanism mediated with itself through the supersession of religion, whilst communism is humanism mediated with itself through the supersession of private property." In this way, "*positive* humanism" – to displace Hegel's "positive reason" or Speculation – comes into being (*EPM*, 142). Unlike Hegel's Speculation, atheism and communism represent no flight into abstraction; rather, they "are but the first real emergence, the actual realization for man of man's essence and of his essence as something real" (*EPM*, 143). What is striking here is that Marx sees the two forms of humanism – theoretical and practical – as mutually inextricable. The alienation embodied in the institution of private property in capitalist society is inseparable from an ideological appeal to "God" – perhaps a metaphor for any ruling ideological imperative such as "economic freedom" or "profit-making" – some power that, once again, transcends the human and abrogates human agency, as might be said of Foucault's concept of power.

Marx's reformulating of the dialectic has certain distinct premises. First, Man is an "*active* natural being" endowed with vital powers which "exist in him as tendencies and abilities – as *instincts*." Second, "the *objects* of his instincts exist outside him, as *objects* independent of him; yet these objects are *objects* that he *needs* – essential *objects*, indispensable to the manifestation and confirmation of his essential powers." So man is "a *corporeal*, living, real, sensuous, objective being" who can "only *express* his life in real, sensuous objects" (*EPM*, 136). This leads directly to the third premise, which is Marx's view of objectivity and thinghood. Marx is at some pains to point out, as in the quotations above, that objects are "real" and "sensuous" (i.e., are perceptible by the senses) and exist independently of the human subject. Indeed, he remarks that, for Hegel, the object is "something negative, self-annulling – a *nullity*." Objectivity is merely something that has to be superseded and is finally integrated into consciousness. For Hegel, objectivity itself is something negative; it is the fundamental mode of estrangement (*EPM*, 138).

Marx observes that, in Hegel's eyes, the object of knowledge for consciousness is knowing itself, i.e., *self*-consciousness, and that it "has *no* objectivity outside the knowing" (*EPM*, 139). For Hegel, "thinghood" is merely alienated self-consciousness; it is without independence or essentiality, and only has the semblance of real substance (*EPM*, 135). Likewise, nature, for Hegel, represents merely "an externality which has to be annulled" (*EPM*, 147). Marx states that for Hegel, externality itself is alienation, a mistake or defect (*EPM*, 148). The implication in nearly all of these statements is that Hegel reduces things in the world to their generalized essence, depriving them of their uniqueness and specificity. He effectively reduces everything to a thought entity, something that has its true being in thought, as opposed to the sensuous external being that is regarded as a mere appearance or phenomenal manifestation of this underlying reality.

Having said all this, Marx clearly cannot be described as a naïve realist or materialist or positivist who believes that objectivity and the world are simply "out there," independently of all human interaction.[17] In fact, he makes this explicit:

> [M]an is not merely a natural being: he is a *human* natural being. That is to say, he is a being for himself ... Therefore, *human* objects are not natural objects as they immediately present themselves, and neither is *human* sense as it immediately *is* – as it is objectively – *human* sensibility, human objectivity. Neither nature objectively nor nature subjectively is directly given in a form adequate to the *human* being.

There may appear to be some sleight of hand in Marx's strategy here. For this paragraph seems to contradict what he has said concerning the independent externality of the object and of nature. Perhaps we can say that, while Marx claims to reject Hegel's account of the connection between

---

[17] In "Ludwig Feuerbach and the End of Classical German Philosophy" (1886) Engels criticized the vulgar, "metaphysical," and ahistorical materialism of Büchner, Vogt, and Moleschott who based their thought upon eighteenth-century mechanistic models of natural science which investigated both dead and living things as finished objects (Marx, Engels, 1968, 597–9, 610–12).

subjectivity (the categories of thought) and objectivity, whereby the latter is shaped by the former, he himself sees objectivity as molded not by thought but by labor, and this is precisely the difference between their two accounts (in Marx's view): For Hegel, labor is *"abstractly mental* labour" (*EPM*, 132). It is the labor of the development of thought, whereas for Marx, labor is a practical activity, whereby the material world is shaped – not in the sense of its underlying reality merely being grasped or understood by thought – but in that its initial indifference is transformed into something human and its human reality *created*. Hence, the "estrangement" that Hegel sees as a universal feature in the progress of thought is something that Marx wishes to ground in historically specific conditions.

Marx might also have directed this critique to much literary theory, whose "negation" of the ethics and ideology of the capitalist world he would have seen as purely theoretical. Many theorists might respond that in order for Marx to propose a practical overcoming of alienation, he must presuppose an essence of humanity. And Marx might reply that the nature of man-woman, as a species being, is not somehow given in the world but is always created by its own labor in specific historical conditions, and can realize its true nature and full potential only by reorienting itself through political agency. Having said all this, there is less difference between Hegel's and Marx's views of human self-creation than Marx is willing to acknowledge.

12.2.3   *Marx on Hegel (III): The* Grundrisse

The final major text to examine as we consider the main lines of Marx's engagement with Hegel is the *Grundrisse der Kritik der Politischen Ökonomie* (Outlines of the Critique of Political Economy). This was a huge set of manuscripts left aside by Marx in 1858, when he began again drafting his critique of political economy, dealing with various aspects of the economic process. It has sometimes been seen as a "rough draft" or outline of *Capital* (1867–83), but its scope is actually far more extensive than the later, well-known work. The *Grundrisse*, apparently unknown to Engels, was discovered in 1923 and not published until 1939–41 in Moscow. It deals not only with subjects such as capital and labor, property, money, and trade, but also with alienation, individual freedom, leisure time, and the universal tendencies inhering in capitalism. McLellan sees a continuity between this and the Paris manuscripts of 1844, especially in terms of their Hegelian disposition (*MG*, 12). According to McLellan, the most striking passage in the *Grundrisse* in this respect is the draft plan that Marx lays out for his *Economics*, which, he says, is "typical" of large parts of the *Grundrisse*. Those scholars, notes McLellan, who argued for a "radical break" between the young and the old Marx did so largely on the grounds that the conception of alienation, which was so central to the earlier work, is absent in the later writings. But given that alienation is indeed important in the *Grundrisse* and also figures more in *Capital* than these writers acknowledge, their notions about the influence of Hegel on Marx need to be revised (*MG*, 12).

The section of the *Grundrisse* that outlines the projected *Economics* actually forms part of Marx's General Introduction of 1857 to his critique, a text he "set aside" when he drafted a preface in 1859 to his published "part-volume," *A Contribution to the Critique of Political Economy*. Needless to say, any analysis of the *Grundrisse* lies far beyond the scope of the present book. I propose to analyze one passage that crucially indicates the nature of Marx's method in order to furnish some insight into the *nature* of Hegel's influence.

In this introduction Marx offers a critique of various political economists, examining their methodology and philosophical assumptions. From this critique emerges Marx's own method and approach to the subject of political economy. He works out the logic of the economic categories – production, consumption, distribution, exchange – in terms that derive from Hegel. Terrell Carver remarks that Marx formulates these categories in the form of a Hegelian syllogism. Indeed, as Carver notes, Marx even presents the views of the political economists he criticizes in Hegelian terms.[18]

It's worth bearing in mind these important general directions of Hegel's influence on Marx's introduction to the *Grundrisse* as we analyze the following specific passage from this text, where Marx makes some general comments about his procedure:

> The further back we go into history, the more the individual and, therefore, the producing individual seems to depend on and belong to a larger whole: at first it is, quite naturally, the family and the clan, which is but an enlarged family; later on, it is the community growing up in its different forms out of the clash and the amalgamation of clans. It is only in the eighteenth century, in "civil society", that the different forms of social union confront the individual as a mere means to his private ends, as an external necessity.

---

[18] *Karl Marx: Texts on Method*, trans. and ed. Terrell Carver (Bristol and New York: Blackwell/Harper & Row, 1975), p. 115.

> ... Whenever we speak, therefore, of production, we always have in mind production at a certain stage of social development ... we must either trace the historical process of development through its various phases, or declare at the outset that we are dealing with a certain historical period, as, for example, with modern capitalist production.
>
> (*MG*, 18)

The Hegelian "influence" on this passage is subtle, operating in Marx's *mode* of thought on a number of levels. First, the need to locate individuals in a larger social context derives from Hegel, who derives it from Aristotle. In fact, the above paragraph is very similar to a statement in Marx's *A Contribution to the Critique of Political Economy* where he explicitly invokes Aristotle. But the language, and the mode of thought it embodies – "belong to a larger whole" – is from Hegel. Not only that, but the need to situate the "individual" within a historical context, within the evolving history of that term, derives from Hegel. So it is with the notion of "production." Marx upbraids the bourgeois economists for treating production – especially capitalist production – as subject to "eternal laws independent of history" (*MG*, 20). Then, at the level of content, Marx's evocation of the individual as developing from the family through the antagonisms of clan into a "civil society" of self-interested individuals embodies a schema derived, as we have seen, from Hegel's *Philosophy of Right*. Hence the mode of thought here is relational and historicist, viewing present conditions as a *result* of a long process of development, a process fraught with conflict and antagonism. We cannot say that this kind of thinking exactly replicates Hegel's dialectic, but it does invoke its general movement. While Marx's thinking is hardly totalizing in the sense that Hegel's is, he has recourse to the language of totality, relation, mediation, and historical movement in his understanding of any phenomenon.

Overall, Marx sees the "identity" of production and consumption as mediated through three stages: direct identity, mediation of the other, and finally creation of the other "and itself as the other" (*MG*, 26–7). This sounds very much like some versions of the Hegelian dialectic. Marx goes on to say that production is "the act in which the entire process recapitulates itself. The individual produces a certain kind of article and turns it again into himself by consuming it; but he returns as a productive and self-reproducing individual" (*MG*, 27). Again, this reads like a very succinct exposition of the dialectical process, which involves a "recapitulation" of the entire process in which a subject (here, the individual) loses itself in otherness and "returns" to itself on a higher plane. The Hegelian language here is arguably integral to the very process of Marx's thinking. Marx further states, for example, that "production *in its one-sided form* is in its turn influenced by other elements" (*MG*, 33). Again, this organic view of the relations between various phenomena derives ultimately from Aristotle, but Marx receives it as it is refracted through Hegel. For example, the notion of "one-sidedness" is deeply Hegelian: It implies an intrinsic finitude and partiality, an intrinsic variability and openness in any phenomenon, whose nature displays itself in different lights as it is refracted through the prism of its own relation to varying larger contexts or totalities in which alone it can complete its meaning.

12.3 Epilogue: Marx and Literary Theory Today

Without Marx's reading of Hegel, the formulations quoted above would not have been available to him. Most of the worldviews outside Hegelian perspectives at Marx's time – including rationalism, materialism, empiricism – either tended to see the world atomistically, as composed of discrete entities independent of one another and of any history or, like Romanticism, posited a totalizing transcendent unity that was spiritual and explicitly irrational. Both Hegel and Marx took over elements from all these modes of thought, as well as from thinkers such as Herder and Adam Ferguson who advanced historical views of social development. Moreover, we can't say that Marx took over the exact form or movement of Hegel's dialectic. But his constant recourse to the principles underlying it does appear to structure his thinking from within, so that its broad framework is organic, relational, and historical. Whatever phenomenon he examines, he views not as discrete but as integrally related to other phenomena; not as static but as always in process, in movement; not as fixed or timeless but always as in a process of struggle or contradiction and always dependent on a particular historical context and historical evolution. What Marx most fundamentally inherited from Hegel was a *mentality*, a way of thinking, a form of cognition – furnishing a relationship with his predecessor deeper than mere imitation or reaction, attainable only by the profoundest immersion in his philosophy.

These characteristics have deeply informed literary theory – not just Marxist theory but all theory. And it's important for us to remember that they emerged in Marx's thought through his critique of Hegel as a philosopher of capitalism, through his critique of the dialectic as expressing the overall historical movement of capitalism as well as its inner contradictions, including the contradictory nature of the human self. The philosophies of Hegel and Marx summarize and integrate much previous thought into visions of the world which are still with us today. Literary theory is still concerned with the fundamental issues that Marx wrestled with in Hegel: the nature of subjectivity and objectivity, the relation of property, wealth, and big business to ethical life and the political world, the contradiction between civil society and the state, the relation between idealism and materialism, and not least, the connection between what we call "history" and the categories of thought. Indeed, it was Marx who made the archetypal criticism that Hegel "logicizes" history and reality in general. Literary theory today is – to its credit – deeply embroiled in all these themes.

It could be responded that much literary theory derived these orientations from figures such as Schopenhauer or Nietzsche or Heidegger. Inasmuch as this is true, it needs to be qualified by acknowledging that, as Deleuze, Derrida, Žižek, and others have shown, the ideas of Schopenhauer and Nietzsche themselves were born as subversions of Hegelian notions. Literary theory has effectively rehearsed in various guises their critique of Hegel. And if we simply stop at these thinkers in tracing the development of various branches of literary theory, without an understanding of what exactly they were reacting against, we will not grasp the substance and motivation of their critiques nor will we see the ways in which we might adequately develop them. Again, it was Marx who furnished the archetypal critique of Hegel's dialectic, and the elements of this critique have been diffused and disseminated throughout literary theory as it continues to struggle against the ramifications of capitalism.

Above all, Marx articulated a humanism whose power flows from its imperative to actualize in practice its theoretical revolution. The radical potential of that humanism has itself been diffused through the various registers of "posthumanism" in which theory has situated itself. Despite the many proclamations that theory is somehow dead, that we live in a post-theoretical world, we can no longer deny that when we teach literature today, we are not merely addressing in an abstract manner issues of style and theme. In analyzing textuality and language, we are addressing almost every aspect – ethical, ideological, economic, historical, technological – of the very teaching situation in which we find ourselves with its inescapably economic implications, and of the very world of global capitalism in which our students must, against overwhelming odds, struggle to find forms of "labor" through which they can create themselves.

CHAPTER 13

Hegel and Marxist Literary Theory (I)

Horkheimer, Adorno, Benjamin

The Hegelian dialectic has enjoyed a rich and varied life in the traditions of Marxist theory as formulated by Engels in his *Anti-Duhring* (1878), V. I. Lenin in his *Philosophical Notebooks* (1933), and Georg Lukács's *History and Class Consciousness* (1923). Lukács's book traces a direct line of descent from the Hegelian dialectic to historical materialism, relegating the intermediary role of Feuerbach to the background.[1] Its analysis of class consciousness, and particularly of alienation as central to the critique of capitalist society, exerted a profound influence not only through Marxist theory but in other areas such as French existentialism. Lukács's extraordinarily intricate work *The Young Hegel* (1938) attempted to define more closely the connection between Hegel's economics and dialectics. Lukács saw both the potential and limitation of Hegel's dialectic in Hegel's economic thought, in both its grasp of the contradictions of capitalist society and its failure to move beyond the parameters of idealist thought. Hegel was, in essence, a bourgeois philosopher.[2]

The Frankfurt School of Critical Theory, whose leading exponents were Max Horkheimer, Theodor Adorno, and Herbert Marcuse, produced a number of philosophical and cultural analyses informed primarily both by Hegel's work and by Freud. These theorists, as we shall soon see in more depth, saw modern mass culture as regimented and reduced to a commercial dimension, and they saw art as embodying a unique critical distance from this social and political world. Walter Benjamin argued in "The Work of Art in the Age of Mechanical Reproduction" that modern technology has transformed the work of art, stripping it of the "aura" of uniqueness it possessed in earlier eras. However, this

---

[1] See especially "The Antinomies of Bourgeois Thought," in Georg Lukács, *History and Class Consciousness: Studies in Marxist Dialectics*, trans. Rodney Livingstone (1968; rpt. London: Merlin Press, 1971), pp. 110–49.
[2] Lukács, *The Young Hegel*, pp. 564–5.

new status of art, thought Benjamin, also gave it a revived political and subversive potential, a potential he articulates in relation to Hegel in his work on the "dialectical image." As Benjamin conceives it, the dialectical image does not embody some smooth transition from a continuous past to a continuously emerging present; rather, a moment from what "has been" is preserved, brought out from its mythical slumber precisely by its unpredictable affiliation with a present reduced from its conventional continuity to the distinctness of a moment – a moment of insight, of revolutionary insight, of insight that can subsist only in language.[3] It is the fusion of two moments, which each independently would be lost in mutually unrelated slumber, that awakens them into unity. It is not a fusion of opposites nor of two elements constrained by a unity exceeding and superseding them. This is how Benjamin reconceives Hegel's dialectic. Interestingly, Susan Buck-Morss observes that Benjamin uses the same term as Hegel – cunning (*mit List*) – to refer not to Reason's use of unwitting individuals for its own historical purposes but to designate rather the capacity to "outwit history."[4]

In Benjamin's vision, historical materialism brings the history of the victor to a standstill, to a moment of self-assessment, a moment sufficiently external to history to evade its flow and its alleged progress. It seeks to define the present in the light of its affiliation with elements of an oppressed (and suppressed) past, thereby both rescuing or redeeming that past and using that past to define its own present – a present that has not resulted causally from the alleged march of historical events, a present that escapes the dialectic which has trampled over the defeated, the oppressed, the superseded, in what Eagleton called its "triumphant sublation."[5]

As we have seen, in France the philosopher Alexandre Kojève offered an interpretation of Hegel that widely influenced literary theory, focusing on Hegel's master–slave dialectic and the importance of labor, seeing these as the basis of Marx's revolutionary ideas. Also influential was Jean Hyppolite, who stressed the notion of alienation in Hegel and the importance of this for Marxist thought. Henri Lefebvre and Jean-Paul Sartre also viewed Hegel as the source of Marx's dialectical views of

---

[3] Walter Benjamin, *The Arcades Project*, trans. Howard Eiland and Kevin McLaughlin (Cambridge, MA and London: Harvard University Press, 1999), pp. 459–63. Hereafter cited as *AP*.
[4] Susan Buck-Morss, *The Dialectics of Seeing: Walter Benjamin and the Arcades Project* (Cambridge, MA and London: MIT Press, 1989), pp. 272–3. Hereafter cited as *DS*.
[5] Eagleton, *Walter Benjamin*, p. 83. Hereafter cited as *WB*.

labor, alienation, and history. Subsequent thinkers, however, attempted to purge what they saw as Hegel's idealism from Marxist thought in an endeavor to present Marxism as unambiguously materialist and scientific. These included Galvano Della Volpe, Lucio Coletti, and Eduard Bernstein. Marxist cultural and literary theory, such as that of Louis Althusser, Lucien Goldmann, and Pierre Macherey, also turned away from Hegel and was heavily influenced by the structuralist movements of the earlier twentieth century, which stressed the role of larger signifying systems and institutional structures over individual agency and intention. Louis Althusser argued for the later Marx's "epistemological break" from his own earlier humanism, stressing Marx's scientificity and his departure from, rather than his debt to, Hegel. Althusser's structuralist Marxism, as stated in his *Pour Marx* (*For Marx*, 1965) and his often-cited "Ideology and Ideological State Apparatuses," rejected earlier humanist and historicist readings of Marx, as well as literary critical emphases on authorial intention and subjective agency.

The American Marxist critic Fredric Jameson outlined a dialectical theory of literary criticism in his *Marxism and Form* (1971), drawing on Hegelian categories such as the notion of totality and the connection of abstract and concrete. Such criticism recognizes the need to see its objects of analysis within a broad historical context, acknowledges its own history and perspective, and seeks the profound inner form of a literary text. Jameson's *The Political Unconscious* (1981) attempts to integrate this dialectical thinking with insights from structuralism and Freud, using the Freudian notion of repression to analyze the function of ideology, the status of literary texts, and the epistemological function of literary form. In subsequent work such as *Postmodernism, or the Cultural Logic of Late Capitalism* (1991), Jameson performed the valuable task of extending dialectical insights into the central role of postmodernism in determining the very form of our artistic and intellectual experience. Finally, in his *Valences of the Dialectic* (2009), Jameson offers an "open" and "pluralistic" interpretation of the dialectic which allows him to find "dialectical moments" in non-dialectical thinkers.

In his later work, the most important Marxist British critic Terry Eagleton moved beyond Althusser's influence and acknowledged the lasting value of Lukács (whom he called the greatest Marxist aesthetician) (*WB*, 84). Eagleton, in fact, has always affirmed the dialectical character of Marxism, as, for example, his insistence that the "power of the negative ... constitutes an essential moment of Marxism" (*WB*, 142). Significantly, Eagleton helps us to contextualize Benjamin's rewriting of the Hegelian dialectic. In what follows we can look at a particularly interesting example of how Marxist thinkers have "appropriated" this dialectic, namely Adorno and Horkheimer's *The Dialectic of Enlightenment*.

13.1   The Dialectic of Enlightenment: Adorno and Horkheimer

Writing in 1944, just before the end of the Second World War, Adorno and Horkheimer were highly attuned to what they called "the present collapse of bourgeois civilization." They saw Hitler's fascism, along with totalitarianism in general, as a structural consequence of capitalism. Following Marx, they asserted the need for a "true humanism."[6] In the previous chapter, we saw that, in Marx's eyes, Hegel's dialectic expressed some of the profound contradictions of capitalism. The most basic of these was between civil society and the state, founded largely on the inordinate influence of private property and wealth on the political process. Marx critically analyzed Hegel's view of the connection between business interests and ethical life, seeing the former as predominating over and shaping the latter. He saw the representatives of Hegel's civil society as inwardly compromised, by conforming to the state conceived as a series of private interests. As a result of these structural contradictions, according to Marx, a profound schism arose in capitalist society within the individual herself – not only as torn between private and public interests, but as fundamentally alienated from herself, from the products of her own labor, and from the world in general. Marx viewed individuals as enslaved under a power alien to them, namely the world market, and the relation between people as reduced to commercial relations (Marx, Engels, 1973, 47). We also saw that Marx criticized Hegel's "logicized" view of history and reality.

All of these insights inform *The Dialectic of Enlightenment*, where Horkheimer and Adorno develop them into an argument that mass culture has become the primary instrument of ideology and of both political and economic domination. Even more importantly, it is mass culture that effectively creates both the subjectivity of consumers and the objectivity of the external world. The logical categories that subjugate history and reality are here actuated not by the Absolute Idea but by the controllers of production. Horkheimer and Adorno trace the foregoing

---

[6] Max Horkheimer and Theodor W. Adorno, *Dialectic of Enlightenment*, trans. John Cumming (1944; rpt. New York: Herder and Herder, 1972), pp. x–xi. Hereafter cited as *DE*.

contradictions of the modern capitalist world back to what they called the "dialectic" of the Enlightenment.

13.2   Enlightenment as Positivism

What was this dialectic? In order to understand this, we need to recall that Hegel had viewed the sphere of civil society as the realm of individualistic economic competition, in need of regulation by higher ethical interests. Horkheimer and Adorno see the Enlightenment as expressing the movement of civil society, both in its economically atomistic orientation as well as in its modes of thought. Hegel had seen civil or bourgeois society as embodying the "external" mode of thought characteristic of the Understanding, which views the world atomistically as an assemblage of particular things. This is a mechanistic kind of thinking which classifies, divides, and organizes, without seeing any internal unity between these discrete objects or situating them within any larger totality. Hegel regarded mathematics as the archetypal example of such thinking, focused on the notion of number.

Horkheimer and Adorno are evidently drawing on these views of Hegel when they characterize the Enlightenment as equating thought with mathematics, and as stressing formal logic and number in order to ensure the calculability of the world (*DE*, 7, 18). Thought is here restricted to a tool of organization and administration, and bourgeois philosophy in general has viewed the mind as an instrument of power and self-mastery in the service of a stringent work ethic (*DE*, 28). To be sure, the explicit program of Enlightenment was to liberate human beings from fear and to establish their sovereignty by "disenchantment of the world," by dissolving all myths and substituting knowledge for superstition and fancy. But the essence of this knowledge in a bourgeois economy was technology, used in part to calculate the effectiveness of techniques of production and distribution, but primarily deployed for the purpose of domination (*DE*, xvi, 4).

Such domination was enabled by the fact that Enlightenment degenerated into an enforced positivism, a compulsion to accept things as they are. Here, the Enlightenment was distinguished from Hegel, say the authors, by its insistence on sober factuality.[7] Thought, as science, was fettered to blind economic tendencies (*De*, 32), and the investment

---

[7] Max Horkheimer and Theodor W. Adorno, *The Dialectic of Enlightenment: Philosophical Fragments*, trans. Edmund Jephcott (Stanford, CA: Stanford University Press, 2002), p. 18. Hereafter cited as

of thought with mathematical and scientific authority helped to generate a fear of departing from "facts" already molded by the "dominant conventions of science, commerce, and politics" (*DE*, xiv). Any genuine novelty of thought, any authentic engagement with the world, was thereby proscribed. Whatever was unassimilable or irrational was "fenced in by mathematical theorems." The world of mathematics and science was "cut loose ... turned into an absolute authority," a world of ideality which could subjugate the external world and mold it in its own image. Thought was "reified as an autonomous, automatic process, aping the machine it has itself produced, so that it can finally be replaced by the machine." In this way, positivism assumed the office of Enlightenment reason (*De*, 18–19). This, then, is the dialectic of Enlightenment: a dialectic between progress and regression, between the advancement of knowledge, and its stultification or conversion into positivism. Horkheimer and Adorno summarize this dialectic in this way: "By sacrificing thought, which in its reified form [is] mathematics, machinery, organization ... enlightenment forfeited its own realization" (*De*, 33).

In his book *Reason and Revolution* (1941), a fellow member of the Frankfurt School Herbert Marcuse had attributed the rise of positivism to a conservative reaction against Hegel's "negative" and revolutionary philosophy. Instead of negating the given state of affairs, positivism or "positive" philosophy wished to affirm it (hence its name). What is interesting here is that Horkheimer and Adorno trace the roots of positivism back to the Enlightenment, treating it not as a movement that reacted against Hegel but rather a movement against which Hegel himself reacted. In this reading, the later positivism (of figures such as Comte) of which Marcuse speaks becomes a crucial reaffirmation of bourgeois philosophy, which in fact had been positivistic all along. Hegel's dialectic subjected the world of the Enlightenment – the world in its immediacy, as immediately given – to a process of negation and mediation. But for Horkheimer and Adorno, as for Marx, the problem with Hegelian negation is that it results in a merely abstract Absolute, thereby, like the Enlightenment, lapsing into the very mythological and mystified form of thinking against which both Hegel and the Enlightenment had initially challenged (*De*, 18). As such, Hegel remains, like the Enlightenment philosophers, within the horizon of bourgeois thought.

De. In this account I have referred to both earlier and later translations of this text, selecting each respectively where it seems clearer.

So, in effect, Horkheimer and Adorno equate Hegelian negation (which is merely abstract) with Enlightenment positivism. Hegelian mediation ends up reaffirming what the Enlightenment asserted by its "mathematical" arresting of thought in its immediacy: the world as it is, as it immediately confronts us, the world created by blind economic forces, is the only reality. Reason becomes "merely an aid to the all-encompassing economic apparatus. Reason serves as a universal tool for the fabrication of all other tools" (*De*, 23). In other words, Reason affirms the given. Truth is equated with regulative thought and all that knowledge can do is repeat itself, in an endless circle, confining itself to apprehending the previously known reality of things (*DE*, 14–15; *De*, 19).

As Horkheimer and Adorno appear to see it, Hegelian mediation has allowed its own function to be appropriated by the mediation of the capitalist market. Bourgeois society is "ruled by equivalence." It annihilates difference and uniqueness. Its science and logic assimilate everything by reducing it to abstract qualities, in a scheme of "universal interchangeability" (*DE*, 7–10). All difference between human beings, say the authors, is equalized in the sense that the Enlightenment dissolves the old (feudal) injustice of unmediated lordship but perpetuates it in the new form of the "universal mediation" of the market, which now governs the hierarchical relation between people and between all things. The market does not inquire after birth, but the circumstances of our birth dictate where and how we are inserted into the market (*DE*, 12; *De*, 8–9). In dialectical thinking, no thing is self-identical; it is itself and something else (*De*, 11).

Reading Marx – and even Hegel – back into the Horkheimer/Adorno text, we might say that this universal interchangeability and mediation whereby everything is itself and something else is no longer given by a thing's intrinsic finitude (as in Hegel) where it must complete and realize itself in a larger totality (for example, an individual realizing herself first in family, then in civil society, then in the state). Rather, the instrument of such interchangeability is money, which measures the value of everything as mediated by the market. In other words, everything is always "itself" *and* exists as a commodity. But its being as a commodity always structures what it is in itself. So its existence can never be defined independently of the market.

By way of example: most historians would say that E. P. Thompson's *The Making of the English Working Class* has more value as history than a ghost-written book by Bill O'Reilly on a historical subject such as *Killing Lincoln*. But the latter, as its ghost author boasts, sells two million copies, while (as he claims) most eminent historians toil in relative obscurity. The market determines not only monetary value but the range of influence, power, and authority. It is the book written specifically for the market, the book whose very existence is structured from within by the market – and not the book seeking to advance knowledge – that becomes part of the machine that defines the world, that defines objective reality. Each of these books is a historical text, but it is also something else, a commodity. And its status as a commodity, its point of insertion into the capitalist market, determines what else it can be. We academics hope that the true historian's work will endure. But nowadays, who can tell? This entire phenomenon embodies what Marx might have called Hegelian mediation come down from heaven to earth.

13.3　The Suppression of the Individual

Hence objectivity, the world itself, is a creation of the market which harnesses reason as its coercive instrument. And what is the fate of the individual, of subjectivity, in this broad movement encompassing the decline of Enlightenment into positivism? This, if you like, is the other side of the dialectic of Enlightenment. As Horkheimer and Adorno describe it, the individual disappears before the economic apparatus that she serves: the "unity of the manipulated collective consists in the negation of each individual" (*DE*, xiv, 13). In other words, the countless agencies of mass production and its culture shrink the individual to "nodal points" of conventional behavior, which is determined by the values endowed upon commodities. Not only this, but individuals define themselves as "things" and measure their own self-preservation by their successful adaptation to the "objectivity of their function" (*De*, 21).

Horkheimer and Adorno acknowledge that in a bourgeois economy, the individual's work is mediated by the "principle of self." But as self-preservation depends increasingly on the bourgeois division of labor, this enforces the self-alienation of individuals who must "mold themselves to the technical apparatus body and soul." In fact, in this endeavor toward self-preservation, the last remnants of subjectivity are abolished and replaced by the "automatic mechanisms of order" (*De*, 23). Indeed, the fundamental ethic of bourgeois civilization is "obedience and work," in the service of which the self has been molded into something "identical, purpose-directed, masculine" by the repression of instincts, pleasure, and even art (*De*, 26). Under this repression of subjectivity and individuality, the masses are unable to "hear with their own ears what has not already been heard, to touch with their hands what has not previously been grasped" (*De*, 28). Through the mediation of the "total society, which encompasses all relationships and impulses, human beings are being turned back into ... mere examples of the species, identical to one another ... It is the concrete conditions of work in society which enforce conformism" (*De*, 29). Hence, the mass of the population are reduced to mere objects of administration, which "preforms every department of modern life right down to language and perception" (*De*, 30). Even when I express my deepest feelings, I will typically do so through a Hallmark card which is not only a commodity profiting from and constraining those feelings but contains a message that is mass-produced "poetic" sentiment.

We recall Marx's statement that the individual stood perplexed by the world market. Horkheimer and Adorno see the individual's stance here as paradoxical. On the one hand, they state that, to the individual, "domination appears to be universal: reason in actuality" (*DE*, 22). On the other hand, the "tangled mass" of institutions that ensure the status quo is "impenetrable to each individual" (*De*, 30). In either case, through the division of labor, individuals realize and repeatedly reproduce the rationality of the whole (*DE*, 22). Even as I write on the Hallmark card, I am re-performing and reconfirming not only the self that has been created for me but the very "reason" operating through the state's institutions. To understand this process in a little more depth, it's worth looking more closely at the workings of the "culture industry" as envisioned by Horkheimer and Adorno.

13.4   The Culture Industry

This industry, according to Horkheimer and Adorno, is a dialectic between two types of subjectivity. The first is the "subjectivity" of the culture industry itself, which as a whole gathers together as "culture" the creations of the human spirit and neutralizes them (*DE*, 130–1). This broad subjectivity governing human affairs is no longer God or Absolute Spirit or some abstract overarching Consciousness; rather it is comprised, in part, by "the consciousness of the production team" which churns out "hit songs, stars, and soap operas" in "cyclically recurrent and rigidly invariable types" (*DE*, 125). In this homogenization, change is merely apparent, not real, and in all domains, replete as these are with ready-made clichés and formulae, the details are interchangeable (*DE*, 125). This subjectivity of the culture industry is driven from within by economic interests: "[T]he objective social tendency is incarnate in the hidden subjective purposes of company directors, the foremost among whom are in the most powerful sectors of industry – steel, petroleum, electricity, and chemicals. Culture monopolies are weak and dependent in comparison. They cannot afford to neglect their appeasement of the real holders of power" (*DE*, 122–3). One thinks here of vulnerable organizations such as the NEA. In fact, an economic criterion – the "triumph of invested capital" – supplants all other criteria of art as "the universal criterion of merit." The budgets of the culture industry bear no relation to "factual values" or to the "meaning of the products themselves" (*DE*, 124).

On the other side, there is the subjectivity of the consumers, which is an equally manufactured subjectivity, and equally as uniform as the products it consumes. Those with leisure must "accept what the culture manufacturers offer" (*DE*, 124). Interestingly, the authors allude to Kant's model of perception, whereby the faculty of imagination synthesizes the data of sense-experience as given in our intuitions. They are effectively stressing Kant's view that we ourselves contribute to the manner in which we "receive" or perceive the external world; we ourselves supply the intuitions of space and time, and the various categories of the understanding such as quantity, quality, and relation. This is why we see the world as being in space, and why we view objects in the aspects of quality and relation. But Adorno and Horkheimer imply that this process of subjectivity is somehow interrupted by the mechanisms of the culture industry. This industry "robs the individual of his function. Its prime service to the customer is to do his schematizing for him." The very process of understanding and perception – the very process of subjectivity – is molded by "those who serve up the data of experience, that is, by the culture industry" (*DE*, 124).

At first sight, the analogy seems far-fetched: Kant was talking of the universal constitution of human subjectivity, of the most fundamental forms of the way in which we engage with the world of phenomena. How could the very form of subjectivity be somehow invaded or interrupted by a historically specific phenomenon such as the culture industry? However, there is a coherence in the analogy with Kant's general account of perception. For, according to Adorno and Horkheimer, the "whole world is made to pass through the filter of the culture industry," allowing "the illusion to prevail that the outside world is the straightforward continuation of that presented on the screen ... Real life is indistinguishable from the movies" (*DE*, 126). If this is indeed the case, if the culture industry creates not only film but by extension reality itself, it does this through supplanting the subjective categories through which we view the world, with its own categories.

This is a process that involves the remanufacturing not only of our subjectivity – now viewed as historically specific and changeable in its content – but also of the so-called external phenomenal world, the world that appears to our senses. A film

> leaves no room for imagination or reflection on the part of the audience, who is unable to respond within the structure of the film, yet deviate from its precise detail without losing the thread of the story; hence the film forces its victims to equate it directly with reality ... sustained thought is out of the question if the spectator is not to miss the relentless rush of facts. (*DE*, 127)

We can infer that this stunting of the audience's response is not achieved by one film, but by an entire history of film-viewing which has taught the viewer what to expect, where to fill in certain gaps and the meanings of various cinematic techniques. This history of film-viewing, then, has effectively recreated reality through technical effects, and through the "true meaning" of both film and reality as "the triumph of invested capital." Consumers "consume" not only film but reality – and in doing so, submit to the "creation" of themselves.

Hence, the very subjectivity through which a subject contributes to the construction of her reality is itself a fiction, a cultural and ultimately an economic product, manufactured by the culture industry. Whatever potential for development was possessed by individual subjectivity is – virtually from birth – supplanted by a subjectivity whose essential lineaments and responses are entirely manufactured as a mass product: "no scope is left for the imagination," and no space is left for individuality (*DE*, 127). The authors state that the culture industry "has molded men as a type unfailingly reproduced in every product" (*DE*, 127). Hence, the labor through which men should produce a human world has been alienated in several ways. Men are indeed united with what "they" produce, but only in an estranged mode. Their own subjectivity has been manufactured by a larger cultural and ultimately economic subjectivity, and the objective world they inhabit is itself produced by this alienated subjectivity. So men, in their alienation, are indeed reproduced in every (alienated) product.

It would have been interesting to know how Adorno and Horkheimer might have regarded the Internet. Would this represent for them a step beyond merely passive consumption? Many writers have shown how the digital media, for example, in the Arab revolutions, was "actively" deployed and was continuous with activism and political protest on the streets, helping to disseminate, organize, and foment it. But Adorno and Horkheimer might also have observed how the Internet is increasingly being subjected to various ideologies which are themselves ultimately hierarchized through economic interests. They might also have noticed that the kinds of responses brought to debates on the Internet are usually not individual but are themselves manufactured, and represent pre-given stances into which consumers can neatly slot themselves.[8]

Hence the culture industry imposes a "ruthless unity" not only upon its own products but upon the audience that receives these products: "The might of industrial society is lodged in men's minds" (*DE*, 127). But there is a further aspect to the subjectivity of the capitalist culture industry as Adorno and Horkheimer conceive it: like Hegelian subjectivity, it is all-devouring and all-encompassing. It possesses the ability to integrate all dissent and opposition into an increasingly broadened vision of itself. The "otherness" embodied in protest or dissent or difference is itself subsumed, categorized, domesticated, so as to confirm the validity of the system. Above all, it *assimilates* what is different: "Every detail is … firmly stamped with sameness" through the use of "calculated mutations" and of experts who find a place for anything, including gags, effects, and jokes (*DE*, 128). The culture industry "crushes their insubordination and makes them subserve the formula, which replaces the work" (*DE*, 126). Hence, not only does the subjectivity of the culture industry remanufacture the subjectivity of the consumer, and the objectivity of the "real world," but it also remolds the objectivity of art, reconfiguring it as a mere series of effects. But in contrast with Hegel's dialectic, this subsumption of all things – including dissident objects or subjectivities – into its own subjectivity is without even any attempted philosophical rationale: "The so-called dominant idea is like a file which ensures order but not coherence. The whole and the parts are alike; there is no antithesis and no connection. Their prearranged harmony is a mockery of what had to be striven after in the great bourgeois works of art" (*DE*, 125–6, 130).

So the culture industry is effectively part of a broader movement that has stripped things from their generalizable contexts, and reduced the world to that of a series of surfaces without depth. The great works of

---

[8] On the other hand, some might see the Brexit vote as a refutation of the claim by Adorno and Horkheimer that the hegemony of the ruling class and the mass culture industry entirely conditions the responses of a majority of people.

art strove to be iconoclastic, to "create truth by lending new shape to the conventional social forms" (*DE*, 130). But this oppositional function of art has been ended by the "totality of the culture industry" (*DE*, 126). On the other hand, the "inferior work" – produced under various cultural formulae – "has always relied on its similarity with others – on a surrogate identity" (*DE*, 131). The identity produced here – of the consumer, the external world, of art, and of the culture industry itself – is what Hegel would call an abstract identity, aloof from any genuine interaction with oppositions; it is "surrogate" because it is manufactured, it supplants and recreates individual identities in its own image.

13.5   Epilogue

In general we can see that, as envisioned by Horkheimer and Adorno, the Hegelian dialectic has here collapsed: Perhaps the most brutal fact of the late capitalist world is that there is no truly unifying vision which can subsume and integrate the world of particular things – of particular human beings and particular objects. All is reduced to the level of particularity, of irreducible particularity; the only logic that subsumes this particularity is the abstract logic of economic interests. These have no bearing whatsoever on the merit of a work of art or the truth of a particular philosophy or the moral value of a certain set of actions. That is why there is no genuine relation, no genuine dialectic, between general and particular. The distinction between general and particular, whole and part, is abrogated. The great bourgeois works of art, as Lukács observed, strove to represent general truths by depicting a particular situation.

We might add, finally, that, on the one hand, the colonization of the very construction of subjectivity and objectivity by the mechanisms of mass culture entirely distorts the import of Hegel's concept of labor as a process whereby we create both ourselves and the world. Indeed, Marx saw such distortion as inherent in the bourgeois division of labor which subjects individuals to mind-numbingly repetitive specialized tasks. On the other hand, as we saw in an earlier chapter, Hegel himself under the influence of Adam Smith arrived at this insight into the drudgery of mechanized labor. And, as we have also seen, he acknowledged that there were several dilemmas inherent in civil society, in the world of capitalism, which could not somehow be resolved by recourse to the state or any incarnation of the Absolute Idea. So Horkheimer and Adorno are developing not only Marx's ideas here but also the aporia or impasses explicitly encountered by Hegel.

Nonetheless, the picture of the capitalist world as projected by these theorists of the Frankfurt School remains haunting in its enduring pertinence to our era. And its portrayal of the coercive uniformity of that world – repressing uniqueness, pleasure, and all aspects of subjectivity that cannot be harnessed by the narrow ethic of work, commodification, and consumerism – helps explain the near-obsessive insistence of literary theory on "difference," on the preconscious drives and instincts, on jouissance, and, above all, on irreducible particularity. The problem is that this emphasis is itself, as seen above, a product and reflex of capitalist culture. That culture harbors a fundamental contradiction: it *already* presents the world as atomistically composed of particular things, and as unable to be generalized, and as unintelligible except in utilitarian, economic terms. Yet this utilitarian "universality" establishes the bland identity or sameness of which Horkheimer and Adorno speak.

Literary theory effectively inhabits this contradiction, articulating it in ever new guises: the human self and its world are but irreducible sense-impressions; they are mere functions or effects of language; they are rooted in unassimilable unconscious drives; they are finite centers or discrete units of experience; they are machines; and now, they are performances. It is the same contradiction posed by the bourgeois philosophers such as Locke and Hume and articulated formally by Kant: We know only our own ideas and impressions, which are utterly imprisoned in particularity; but somehow these relate to an "externality," which we build up through generalization into a world. It is the reductive nature of this generalization, effected as it is through the register of economic imperatives, which literary theory has resisted in its tenacious adherence to particulars and its recalcitrance from universals. As we have seen, Hegel's was the most articulate endeavor of bourgeois philosophy both to formulate and resolve this contradiction, this mutual incommunicability of universal and particular. In situating itself at the second stage of dialectic, theory inhabits the space of the contradiction itself.

Marxist theory itself has not escaped this dilemma, this strategy of undermining capitalism from within, often ensconced within a residual idealism persisting through its engagement with Hegel's dialectic. Terry Eagleton suggests that Western Marxism turned back to its idealist resources (as argued by Perry Anderson) essentially because it was aloof from mass revolutionary practice. Marxist theory, notes Eagleton, has often been obliged to incorporate bourgeois humanism, whether in the language of Hegel or positivism or Kantian idealism (*WB*, 82–3). Indeed, aesthetic contemplation offered "a lonely enclave of estrangement" within the tyrannical and timeless enclosure of late monopoly capitalism. This was especially true of members of the Frankfurt School, who were "theoretically and practically divorced from the working-class movement" (*WB*, 91). Eagleton identifies the "positive" moment of Hegelian Marxism with Lukács, for whom Marxism itself was "the triumphant sublation of the bourgeois humanist heritage" (*WB*, 83). Adorno and the Frankfurt School embody the "negative" moment of Hegelian Marxism, viewing bourgeois hegemony as liable to subversion only through "silence, negation and estrangement" (*WB*, 91).

This, as I have been arguing, is the archetypal silence of theory itself, which refuses to advance beyond the negative moment – the moment of contradiction, difference, and particularity – except into further modes of particularity. As Eagleton puts it, Lukács fetishized the "totality" and the Frankfurt School the "particular." The elements of the dialectic were mutually dirempted (*WB*, 97) – hence we can see that Marxist theory also inhabits the contradiction named above.

CHAPTER 14

Hegel and Marxist Literary Theory (II)

Žižek

We now fast-forward from the Frankfurt School, which deployed Hegel to make sense of capitalist culture after the Second World War, to a contemporary East European intellectual from the Slovenian Lacanian school, who effects an equally radical reconfiguration of Hegel's dialectic for our own era. Slavoj Žižek has persistently engaged with the thought of Hegel in his major works, which include *The Sublime Object of Ideology* (1989), *Tarrying with the Negative* (1993), and *Less Than Nothing: Hegel and the Shadow of Dialectical Materialism* (2013). He published a self-interview entitled *The Metastases of Enjoyment* in 1994. Žižek draws heavily on Hegel – as sometimes reconfigured through Lacan – to assess what Lacan calls the "Real," in order to offer a critique of ideology and the system of capitalism itself.

We might begin by sketching the broad context of Žižek's reinterpretation of Hegel's dialectic before addressing the details of that reading. In *The Sublime Object of Ideology*, Žižek argues that traditional Marxism sees a basic social antagonism – premised on economics and class – as underlying all other antagonisms of race, gender, and political systems. He himself essentially agrees that a revolution in the economic sphere would resolve all these antagonisms.[1] The basic feature of so-called "post-Marxism," he says, is a break with this logic: for example, some feminists argue that gender is more fundamental than class and that inequalities in this sphere must be addressed first. But it is Lacanian psychoanalysis, insists Žižek, that advances decisively beyond the usual post-Marxist anti-essentialism in "affirming the irreducible particularity of particular struggles" (*SOI*, xxvii). Crucially, Žižek sees the first post-Marxist in this respect as none other than Hegel, whose dialectic comprehends the inherent contradictions of capitalism, such as the fact that a radical or

---

[1] Slavoj Žižek, *The Sublime Object of Ideology* (1989; rpt. London and New York: Verso, 2008), p. xxvi. Hereafter cited as *SOI*.

pure democracy is impossible. For Žižek, Hegelian dialectics embody an acknowledgment of antagonism: far from being a "story of its progressive overcoming," Hegel's dialectic expresses the failure of all radical attempts at revolution, and his notion of absolute knowledge accepts contradiction "as an internal condition of every identity" (*SOI*, xxix). What we find in Hegel, Žižek claims, is "the strongest affirmation yet of difference and contingency." This Hegelian heritage, as "salvaged" by Lacan, will allow a new approach to ideology, one that resists post-modernist traps such as the illusion that we live in a "post-ideological" age (*SOI*, xxxi).

14.1   De-constipating the Dialectic

14.1.1   *The Idea and Nature*

Žižek's most fundamental argument concerning Hegel's dialectic is expressed in his powerful and iconoclastic meditation, scatologically entitled "Hegel and Shitting." Here, he dramatically challenges what he takes to be the standard reading of the Hegelian Absolute Idea as "a voracious eater that 'swallows' every object upon which it stumbles."[2] This view, says Žižek, "constructs the Hegelian Absolute Substance-Subject as thoroughly *constipated* – keeping in itself the swallowed content" (*HI*, 221).[3] It derives partly from Hegel's own remarks to the effect that whatever a human does to an object must be grounded in the nature of the thing itself. For example, if "I eat an apple, I destroy its organic self-identity and assimilate it to myself." This means that the apple in its nature is "subject to destruction" and has "in itself a homogeneity with my digestive organs such that I can make it homogeneous with myself." Such remarks, says Žižek, are grasped as a "lower version of the cognitive process itself" (*HI*, 221). In other words, the process of knowing, for Hegel, is usually seen as the subject devouring/knowing the object, whose nature is to be devoured or known. This idea, we might add, derives in part from Kant's view of "purposiveness" whereby the world in general is viewed as conformable to our faculties of knowing.

Žižek wants to reverse this digestive metaphor: "What about the countermovement, the Hegelian shitting excrementation?" Surely, he says, the Hegelian subject of Absolute Knowing is an "*emptied* subject, a subject

---

[2] "Hegel and Shitting: The Idea's Constipation," in *HI*, p. 221.
[3] *Hegel and the Infinite: Religion, Politics, and Dialectic*, ed. Slavoj Žižek, Clayton Crockett, and Creston Davis (New York: Columbia University Press, 2011).

reduced to the role of pure observer, witnessing the self-development of the content itself" (*HI*, 222). The Idea "freely releases itself" into nature, discarding nature and thereby liberating it. So, for Hegel, says Žižek, there is no "violent reappropriation" of the externality of nature. Rather, there is a "passive ... observer" who watches "nature sublate its own externality" (*HI*, 222). In the same way, Hegel's God "freely releases" Himself into temporal existence in Christ; and art, as it progresses historically, progressively frees itself from visual or other media, releasing nature or material existence from the burden of expressing Spirit or Idea (*HI*, 222–3).

It is not a question, says Žižek, of first eating, then shitting. Rather, we must see that "[s]hitting is the immanent *conclusion* of the entire process." In other words, following Catherine Malabou, Žižek is asserting that the aim or end of excrementation structures the entire process; it is not merely a "remainder" that is expelled at the end. True cognition for Hegel, says Žižek, is not only a conceptual appropriation or conquering of the object but, when complete, a letting go or "liberation" of it. Žižek cites Badiou's view that the subject has to "subtract itself" to set the object free. And the released part, says Žižek, is not merely an excremental remainder or waste but the very "ground out of which further development will grow" (*HI*, 223). The subject now merely observes the object develop according to the object's own immanent concept. In this (where Hegel follows Kant, according to Žižek), the subject is passive but also active inasmuch as it takes "strenuous effort" for the subject to erase herself and to act as a "neutral medium." The agent of the process is not the subject but the "system of knowledge" itself (*HI*, 224). The Idea's absolute (*absolvere*) freedom consists in "absolving" or letting go the moment of its own particularity. This act of releasing the other, says Žižek, is "thoroughly *immanent* to the dialectical process ... the sign of the conclusion of a dialectical circle" (*HI*, 224).

The "key passage" for Žižek's argument is from Hegel's *Science of Logic* (though he misattributes it to the third part of Hegel's *Encyclopedia* entitled *The Philosophy of Mind*). Here, according to Žižek, Hegel argues that the Idea releases "Nature out of itself":

> The Idea, namely, in positing itself as absolute unity of the pure Notion and its reality and thus contracting itself into the immediacy of being, is the totality in this form – nature.
>
> ... the pure Idea in which the determinateness or reality of the Notion is itself raised into Notion, is an absolute liberation for which there is no longer any immediate determination that is not equally *posited* and itself

Notion ... The passage is therefore to be understood here rather in this manner, that the Idea *freely releases* itself in its absolute self-assurance and inner poise. By reason of this freedom, the form of its determinateness is also utterly free – the *externality of space and time* existing absolutely on its own account without the moment of subjectivity. (*HI*, 225)

According to Žižek, Hegel argues here that this "absolute liberation" is very different from the standard dialectical transition. In this case, the other is set free after it has been completely internalized. This is possible, says Žižek, because Hegel's subject, like Lacan's, is a divided subject; in fact, both the particular subject and the universal substance embodied in "collectivity" are divided, and this division is what unites them (*HI*, 225). It is unclear what Žižek means by this; perhaps that what is united is a split subject and a split object. In any case, the connection of this statement with Hegel's difficult passage above remains obscure, and I will shortly offer an alternative interpretation of that passage.

To simplify things: Žižek's overall point seems to be that, contrary to postmodern readings of the dialectic which see it admitting antagonisms and splits only to "resolve them magically in a higher synthesis-mediation," Hegel – as Marx noted – does not resolve these antagonisms in reality but only in thought. Žižek's point is that this is deliberate, so that antagonisms are thereby perceived in their "positive" role (*HI*, 225). According to Žižek, while Hegel does dissolve reality "into its notional determinations," his true point is a radical materialist one, namely, that a *fully* developed notion or concept of an entity (such as God or money) recognizes that material reality has already been conceptualized, that it is in fact a concept (*HI*, 226–7). With a Hegelian conception of truth, says Žižek, one "compares a statement with itself," not with any external reality. Žižek is rehearsing here Alain Badiou's notion of a "truth-event" that lacks any neutral objective criteria (*HI*, 228).

14.1.2 *The Language of Universal and Particular*

How, then, asks Žižek, do we read the Hegelian "concrete universal," the identity of opposites as in that of universal and particular? The universal is not a form imposed upon an independent empirical content; it does impose necessity upon the "multitude of contingent content, but *it does so in a way that remains marked by an irreducible stain of contingency.*" The universal genus "encounters itself among its particular-contingent species" (*HI*, 228). Language, thinks Žižek, provides "the ultimate example" of this dialectical unity of opposites. The opposition in language is between the "universal content" of meaning and its expression in a contingent particular form, the signifier. In other words, as Malabou states (whom Žižek here quotes), the essential is "said" precisely through the accidents of language (*HI*, 229).

Žižek infers that the starting point of thought has to be the contingency of language, as the "substance" of one's thinking. Language is "one's unsurpassable substance." But because language is the medium of the fixed distinctions of the Understanding, it ossifies our thoughts. Hence, we must think "*against* the language in which thought is encompassed, but we can do this only *within* language; there is no other option" (*HI*, 229). Where do we find, in language, a ground for thinking against it? Hegel's answer, according to Žižek, is in that which lies beyond the formal system of language – in what is inconsistent, contingent, idiosyncratic, in the elements of wordplay that Lacan designates *lalangue*. Hegel's "great example," according to Žižek, occurs when he observes the three disparate meanings of *Aufhebung* (sublation) as to cancel, preserve, and elevate. But sublation, says Žižek, is conventionally thought to signify the Hegelian operation whereby all external contingency is overcome and integrated into the universal concept or notion. Against this, he remarks, the fashionable postmodern rejoinder is to insist that there is a "remainder" of contingency and particularity that cannot be integrated or *aufgehoben* (*HI*, 230). Žižek's point is that there is no conceptual clarity without *lalangue* as a starting point: necessity does not somehow preexist contingent appearances as their ground but emerges out of contingency. Critics of Hegel, says Žižek, emphasize the first aspect, while neglecting the second.

So, Žižek concludes, Hegel was not a "sublimated coprophague," as the usual understanding of the dialectic would have us believe. The dialectic comprises not "excrementation-externalization followed by reappropriation" or swallowing up of the externalized content. Rather, it is appropriation followed by the "excremental move of dropping it, releasing it, letting it go" (*HI*, 231). Hence externalization is not alienation but the highest point of *dis*alienation: we reconcile ourselves with external content not when we still try to master and control it but when we can afford the "supreme sovereign gesture" of releasing it from ourselves, of setting it free. In this way, says Žižek, Hegel opens up a space for ecological awareness, since the implication is that we should not aim to *master* nature but let it follow "its inherent path." Hence, in the Hegelian system, there is no "mega-Subject" who controls the dialectical process. Rather, that system "is a plane without a pilot." In fact, suggests Žižek, the Hegelian dialectic is the most radical version of a process without a subject. When Hegel states that we must "grasp the Absolute not only as Substance, but also as Subject," this means that the emergence of a pure subject is correlative with the notion of "system" as the "self-deployment of the object itself." What critics of Hegel's "voracity" need, suggests Žižek, is "a dosage of good laxative" (*HI*, 231).

14.2   Problems and Promise in Žižek's Reading

14.2.1   Creative Misreading of a Key Passage

The foregoing ideas are appealing and perhaps have potential as a way to salvage some of Hegel's thought for future application; and though they have little foundation in Hegel, they represent another important direction in which theory has creatively misread his work. Indeed, this vein of interpretation of Hegel is not new and was conducted, for example, much earlier by Georges Batailles. The two passages in Hegel that comprise the total evidence for Žižek's argument are both misattributed,[4] and one of them, being notoriously difficult, is hardly susceptible to the kind of one-sided reading to which Žižek reduces it. I want to look again at what Žižek calls the "key passage" that allegedly sustains his argument. The end of the passage, as Žižek quotes it, reads (he does not quote the subsequent, crucial, sentence):

> [T]he Idea *freely releases* itself in its absolute self-assurance and inner poise. By reason of this freedom, the form of its determinateness is also utterly free – the *externality of space and time* existing absolutely on its own account without the moment of subjectivity.

Žižek reads this to mean, "I set the Other free after I completely internalized it" (*HI*, 225). But what does it mean to set the other free? In Žižek's reading, after the Idea goes out into the other, it sees in this other its own operations, returns to itself or incorporates into itself an "ideal" version of this other, and then lets the other be, in its independence. But is this what Hegel has in mind? What he says in this passage is not, as Žižek would have it, that the Idea releases the other but that it releases *itself*. At a lower level of thought, in the sphere of being – as Hegel says in the previous paragraph, the "Notion appears as a knowing in a subjective

---

[4] In his sixth endnote, he attributes a passage to the *Philosophy of Nature* when in fact it comprises the last paragraph (§244) of the *Logic*; and in his seventh endnote he attributes the "key passage" discussed here to the *Philosophy of Mind* when it is actually the very last paragraph of the *Science of Logic* (pp. 843–4).

reflection external to that content." In other words, the "moment of subjectivity" occurs when the Idea is working on a more primitive level, viewing its object as external to it. But the Absolute Idea – the title of this last section of the *Science of Logic* – has *itself* for its object; hence there is no distinction between subject and object: according to Hegel, every "immediate determination" of the Idea or Notion in the sphere of "outside" existence or being has itself been raised to the level of nationality, to the status of a notion or concept.

Hence, as Hegel says, "the simple being to which the Idea determines itself remains perfectly transparent to it and is the Notion." This is where we need to be clear: The "externality" of space and time is "utterly free" precisely because it is no longer external but is itself notional.[5] This is why there is no longer the "moment of subjectivity," the condition of a subject apprehending an external object. In the very next sentence – which Žižek does not quote – Hegel explains that insofar "as this externality presents itself only in the abstract immediacy of being and is apprehended from the standpoint of consciousness, it exists as mere objectivity and external life; but in the Idea it remains essentially and actually [in and for itself] the totality of the Notion" (*SL*, 843–4). In other words, the object is external when apprehended by human consciousness, but in the Absolute Idea – in the complete system of knowledge – it attains its true, notional, actuality. Hence, the "freedom" of the form of space and time, or of any object, lies *not* in its externality but in its very *integration into* – not *excretion from* – notionality. This is precisely the opposite of what Žižek claims.

As Hegel states earlier in this section of the *Science of Logic,* in the Absolute Idea, "the objective ... is posited in its identity with the subjective Notion" (*SL*, §1785). In Hegelian language, to attain the status of a notion is to be freed from material contingency and to be understood in terms of universality and necessity. The form of space and time achieves independence and freedom precisely by *becoming* conceptualized, by becoming notion or idea. Indeed, in the lesser *Logic* – in the very paragraph to which Žižek alludes – Hegel states that Nature is "the Idea as Being" (*LL*, §244).[6] In other words, Nature is the self-externalization of

---

[5] For a detailed attempt to explain this passage, which also (contrary to Žižek) sees Nature as an externalization of the Idea, see Robert M. Wallace, *Hegel's Philosophy of Reality, Freedom, and God* (Cambridge: Cambridge University Press, 2005), pp. 268–70.

[6] *Hegel's Logic: Being Part One of the Encyclopaedia of the Philosophical Sciences (1830)*, trans. William Wallace (Oxford: Oxford University Press, 1982).

the idea. It intrinsically, therefore, cannot make sense to view this externality as independent. In the *Philosophy of Mind* – again, in a paragraph cited by Žižek – Hegel states that Nature, far from being independent, is but a "transition-point and negative factor," the second term of a syllogism that moves from Logic through Nature to Mind (*PM*, §575).

Hegel also makes these insights clear in his *Philosophy of Nature*, where he states that

> Spirit finds in Nature its own essence, i.e. the Notion, finds its counterpart in her. The study of Nature is thus the liberation of Spirit in her, for Spirit is present in her in so far as it is in relation, not with an Other, but with itself. This is also the liberation of Nature; implicitly she is Reason ... Thus Nature is the bride which Spirit weds.[7]

Again, what is liberated is not Nature *from* the Idea or Notion; the liberation of Nature consists in her *attaining* notional status. She is liberated *into* the Idea. So Nature is not simply used and discarded by Spirit, as Žižek argues; nor is she consumed and excreted. She is treated with the highest reverence, as a being whose essence is implicitly identical with Spirit itself. She is treated as a permanent bride, as a soul-mate, not a casual acquaintance.[8]

The paragraph that Žižek designates as the "key passage" comprises the end of the *Science of Logic* and the end of the section entitled "The Absolute Idea." Hegel's explanations of the dialectical process throughout this section militate against Žižek's reading. Hegel states that the Idea "contains *all* determinations within it, and its essential nature is to return to itself through its self-determination or particularization" (*SL*, §1782). The point here is that Nature represents the second stage of the dialectical process and is *essential* in all its determinations to the realization of the Idea. The third stage of dialectic will abrogate those determinations, but it will also "restore them in their truth and in the consciousness of their right, though also of their limitations" (*SL*, §1793). Hegel even says that the first stage is "essentially *preserved* and *retained* even in the other," the second stage (*SL*, §1795); the first stage, that of immediacy, is the subject, while the second stage, that of mediation, is the predicate (*SL*, §1796). The second stage essentially designates a *relation*, a mediation

---

[7] *Hegel's Philosophy of Nature: Being Part Two of the Encyclopaedia of the Philosophical Sciences (1830)*, trans. A. V. Miller (Oxford: Clarendon Press, 1970), §246, *Rem*. Hereafter cited as *PN*.
[8] This and subsequent paragraphs allow Hegel's sexist language to stand, purely for ease of explanation, but there is no reason that we should not think of Spirit as female and Nature as male, or both as neither.

between first and third stages (*SL*, §1797, 1800); hence the idea that it can somehow be set free, or excreted, cannot comprehend the way in which the dialectic operates, at least in Hegel's hands. This dialectic entails that the universal is shown to be "the *identity of its moments*" (*SL*, §1803). It does not leave those moments behind.

The only way, I think, in which we might make sense of Žižek's argument is as follows: Spirit "consumes" Nature inasmuch it internalizes it, which is also to say that it pervades it, raising it to notionality, to a consciousness of its universal and essential traits; what Spirit "excretes" and leaves behind is a "remainder." But this remainder is not, as Žižek claims, the ground of further dialectical progress. It is simply Nature as originally given, as a mass of contingent matter, an aggregate of objects related to one another only externally without any underlying rationale. But this, surely – notwithstanding Žižek's spatial terminology – represents a transition in *perspective*, from lower to higher: We progress from viewing Nature as an incoherent assemblage of objects to a rationally organized system. It's true that Hegel sees this process as discovering the inherent reason and universality *within* Nature itself (*PN*, §246, *Rem*), but the point is that the two sides of this process can't be separated. While objects in Nature might be regarded as "free" and as achieving their own notional self-determination, this freedom is realized only *through* the process of (increasingly rational) thought. In Hegelian terms, it's the notional apprehension of objects and terms that "brings out their dialectic" (*SL*, §1794). Again, Nature is not simply left "free" in Žižek's sense, as unpervaded by conceptuality; this, for Hegel, would be anything but a condition of freedom or liberation.

14.2.2　Dialectical Method

Even if we don't agree with Žižek's flamboyant assertions, perhaps they can help us formulate a more accurate description of how Hegel's dialectic does operate. There is one particular paragraph in the *Science of Logic* which shows that, far from becoming "constipated," the dialectic in its advance continually *expands*. Each dialectic, says Hegel, moves into a new dialectic. As "cognition rolls onwards from content to content," progressive determinations become "ever richer and more concrete." Here is how Hegel characterizes this progress:

> The universal constitutes the foundation; the advance is therefore not to be taken as flowing from one other to the next other. In the absolute method the Notion maintains itself in its otherness, the universal in its

particularisation, in judgment and reality; at each stage of its further
determination it raises the entire mass of its preceding content, and by its
dialectical advance it not only does not lose anything or leave anything
behind, but carries along with it all it has gained, and inwardly enriches
and consolidates itself. (*SL*, §1809)

Žižek's argument presupposes precisely – contrary to Hegel – that the
Idea moves from "one other to the next other," leaving each behind once
it has internalized it. But this is not how Hegel views his own dialectic;
he sees one "other" not only as *remaining* but as enriched by subsequent
determinations of otherness. Each advance, each successive determination, enriches the *entire* preceding content. The entire system reverberates
in self-adjustment, like T. S. Eliot's notion of "tradition." True, Hegel does
say that each further determination "is also a withdrawal inwards, and the
greater extension is equally a higher intensity" (*SL*, §1810). But here, in
another dimension of Hegel's argument overlooked by Žižek, we observe
in the dialectic a movement deriving from Neoplatonism whereby, as
Hegel states, each step of the advance "from the indeterminate beginning is also getting back nearer to it" in a process where the retrogressive
grounding of the beginning and the progressive further determining of it
coincide, in a movement that comprises a circle (*SL*, §1812).

Hegel often uses Neoplatonic terminology in this section, stating that
the circle of this method is "a circle of circles, for each individual member as ensouled by the method is reflected into itself, so that in returning
into the beginning it is at the same time the beginning of a new member.
Links of this chain are the individual sciences [of logic, nature and spirit],
each of which has an *antecedent* and a *successor*" (*SL*, §1814). This reads
much like the procession from the primal One described by Proclus,
whereby each level gives rise to a lower level, which itself "expansively"
generates ("ensouling") an even lower level while itself aspiring to the
"intensity" of previous levels. In this way all levels progressively descend
into increasingly *expansive* elaboration and particularity, containing the
memory and archetype of previous levels, which infuses the whole with
an *intensive* impulse to return to the source, the One. The point is that
in this system, nothing is left behind, and that each level is a mode of
mediation, having both a successor and an antecedent. And this is also
the movement of the Hegelian dialectic. To talk of it being "constipated"
is to presuppose that certain levels can be mutually isolated; that what is
sublated or abrogated is *content*, rather than form and perspective; and
that the universal is not realized through its particular embodiments or
manifestations. Also, it doesn't make sense to talk of a moment or stage

of *mediation* as somehow liberated or independent. This wresting of moments into independence was indeed, as we saw, an important part of Benjamin's project – but this was explicitly a subversion of Hegel, not a presumed expression of his own ideas.

Moreover, Hegel distinguishes between what he calls a "practical" approach to Nature, which is merely concerned with "using and mastering" and "consuming" individual products of nature, and a theoretical approach, which seeks knowledge of the universal aspects of Nature – its forces, laws, and genera. The theoretical approach regards Nature as "free in her own peculiar vital activity" but nonetheless does not leave Nature as it is; rather, it gives Nature "the form of something subjective, of something produced by us, and belonging to us in our specifically human character" (*PN*, §246, *Rem*). The theoretical attitude *begins* with a disinterested attitude that "lets things exist and go on just as they are" – without consuming them – allowing a duality of subject and object. But the overall intention is to "comprehend Nature, to make her ours." However, the universal aspect of things is not merely subjective; it is "the true, objective, actual nature of things themselves" (*PN*, §246, *Rem*). And this universality "proceeds [again, Neoplatonic terminology] from the Notion." So, while cognition stands in a negative relation to the things of Nature and "assimilates them to itself, it equally finds individuality in them and does not … interfere with their free self-determination" (*PN*, §246, *Rem*). Žižek's argument does not comprehend the fact that these two sides, practical and theoretical, are for Hegel united and presuppose each other. Nature is "left free" precisely by being assimilated to thought. It is only *in* this assimilation that Nature is free; in its mere externality, "Nature exhibits no freedom in its existence" (*PN*, §246, *Rem*).

Would it be unfair to say, then, that Žižek is full of shit? That he has willfully constipated himself with error, with a flamboyant but groundless reading of Hegel? I think it would indeed be unfair. We need to acknowledge the subtlety of Žižek's endeavor. He has provided us with a misreading that is so profound and so rooted in such numerous and glaring distortions of Hegel that these can only be deliberate. Žižek is effectively attempting to redefine "Hegel" to signify a potential that bursts beyond the conventional boundaries of this name, of this concept.

14.3   Hegelian Subjectivity and Capitalism (Again)

Let's recap the broad outlines of Žižek's argument so far. He rejects the "standard notion" of Hegel's famous assertion that substance becomes subject. For one thing, he says, with Hegel, this "subjectivization of the object" always leaves a "remainder" which not only eludes subjective mediation but is "correlative to the very being of the subject" (*TN*, 21).[9] We recall that Žižek sees the dialectic as a process without a subject. An essential part of this argument concerns the nature of Hegelian subjectivity, which we can now consider. The subject, says Žižek, is the very "nothing," the "purely formal void" that is left over after the substantial content has been worked on, the empty form of a container that remains after all its content is subjectivized (*TN*, 21). In this reading, the Hegelian subject is wholly formal and abstract like Kant's transcendental ego, lying above and beyond but organizing the content of experience. Žižek describes this "split" in the Kantian subject as the "very kernel of his self-identity" (*TN*, 25).

What's interesting is how Žižek sees this empty subject as an index of capitalist economics. We have seen that he rejects the interpretation of the Hegelian dialectic as a "closed economy," and he traces this "misreading" back to Marx. For Marx, says Žižek, the proletariat represented a "substanceless subjectivity," an abstract subjectivity "freed from all substantial-organic ties," yet dispossessed and obliged therefore to sell his labor (*TN*, 25–6). The proletarian revolution for Marx is a materialist version of the "Hegelian reconciliation of subject and substance," reestablishing the unity of the subject (labor force) with the objective conditions of production. As against this, urges Žižek, "the time has come to raise the inverse possibility of a Hegelian critique of Marx." Hegel enables us to see the "perspective-illusion" in Marx's revolutionary "dialectical reversal" whereby the "subject reappropriates the entire substantial content." But such a reversal, says Žižek, is precisely what Hegel precludes, for Hegelian "reconciliation" does not designate the moment when substance becomes subject but rather the acknowledgment that "subjectivity is inscribed into the very core of Substance in the guise of an irreducible lack which forever prevents it from achieving full identity." There is an ontological "crack" in substance itself. The notion of Hegel as absolute idealist is "a *displacement* of Marx's own disavowed ontology" (*TN*, 26).

Again, these statements have little grounding in the texts of either Marx or Hegel. In Žižek's hands, the relation of subject and substance is turned into a metaphor for the connection of the proletariat with the productive apparatus. The metaphor is deliberately incoherent, as is its

---

[9] Slavoj Žižek, *Tarrying with the Negative: Kant, Hegel, and the Critique of Ideology* (Durham: Duke University Press, 1993).

continuation in the idea of substance as "cracked" – as containing a void somehow filled by subjectivity (the latter reducing what is in Hegel a transition in viewpoint to a spatial relation). But, again, this is deliberate because it allows Žižek to create his own language, or at least, a new register within, but resistant to, conventional language, where he can engage in a kind of metaphysical conceit that not only frees itself from any basis in what Hegel and Marx actually say, but is internally inconsistent (the proletariat as subject is a "crack" in substance as the productive process). The overall aim of the metaphor, in all its paraded incoherence, is to show how Hegel's dialectic, in resisting Marx's attempt to correct or "reverse" it, expresses the empty and merely formal subject in capitalist society.

Žižek extends the metaphor or conceit through a further level of incoherence, where substance is now aligned not with production but with capital. He sees Marx's "ambiguous" relation to Hegel as reflected in Marx's attempt to delineate the nature of capital by means of the categories of Hegel's logic. On the one hand, for Marx, capital is the alienated substance "which reigns over the atomized subjects." Through revolution, the "historical Subject appropriates to himself his alienated substantial content, i.e., recognizes in it his own product." On the other hand, Marx sees "Capital as Substance which is already in itself Subject," which reproduces itself through self-mediation. He defines capital as "money which begets more money ... in short, Capital is Money-which-became-Subject." Hence Hegel's logic provides the "notional structure" behind the movement of capital (*TN*, 27).[10] If the Kantian subject is a "void of absolute negativity," says Žižek, it is a void that emerges from the economic structure of exchange mediated by the modern notion of paper money, which replaces the relation between a bank and an individual with money's relation to itself as a commodity (*TN*, 28). The link to any concrete individual was cut loose, and an anonymous "bearer" becomes "the very subject of self-consciousness," designating a neutral universal function (*TN*, 29). And so, through all these distortions, all these misreadings, and a broad incoherent metaphor, we arrive at a striking and powerful conclusion: The true Absolute Subject of the dialectical process in capitalism, the true ultimate shaper of both subjectivity and objectivity, is money.

Money is the real subject, in the service of which the human being is reduced to an abstraction. It's precisely this reproach, says Žižek, that

---

[10] As we saw in Chapter 12, a number of Hegel scholars have already analyzed in great detail this connection between Hegel's logic and Marx's analysis of capital.

Feuerbach and Marx direct against Hegel: that he replaces "actually exist-ing individuals" with an abstract "subject." He transposes the multitude of relations between concrete individuals into, firstly, a relation of *the* individual (as subject) to society (as Substance), and, secondly, a relation of Substance to itself (*TN*, 29). What Žižek wants to point out is that in reducing the subject to a "subordinated moment of the Substance's self-relating," we encounter a distinction in Hegel between the "indi-vidual" and the "subject." The Hegelian subject is merely a name for "the externality of the Substance to itself, for the 'crack' by way of which the Substance becomes 'alien' to itself, (mis)perceiving itself through human eyes as the inaccessible-reified Otherness" (*TN*, 30).

Žižek points to Lacan's "elegant" interpretation of this Hegelian moment as suggesting a different reading of the relation between indi-vidual and society, whereby both are split (like the Kantian subject, as Žižek has already noted). Lacan therefore rejects the solipsistic hypothesis of the "presupposed self-enclosure of the individual or society" (*TN*, 30). In other words, says Žižek, "I can communicate with the Other ... only insofar as I am already in myself split, branded by 'repression,' ... the Other is originally the decentered Other Place of my own splitting" (*TN*, 31). We know that this structure of recognition is already formulated in Hegel's master–slave dialectic. Žižek here reconfigures this structure (though he does not mention the master–slave dialectic here) in terms borrowed from Lacan (who does indeed discuss it): "I am not simply identical to myself but have an unconscious," and I communicate with others in the hope of receiving from them "the truth about myself, about my own desire." In this light, what allows cultures to communicate, says Žižek, is not shared values but "shared *deadlock*," the fact that they recog-nize different answers in each other (*TN*, 31).

The subject, then, "emerges as the crack in the universal Substance," and comprises what Žižek calls a "vanishing mediator," something that has to be retroactively posited, just like the transcendental ego (*TN*, 37). This idea of subjectivity as a void in capitalism is something that Žižek also finds in the film *Blade Runner*, where everything as subject is an arti-fact (*TN*, 39). What Lacan shows us is that reality is always framed by a fantasy, and that reality is a surplus, a remainder, which resists any kind of modeling or metaphor – which is perhaps why Žižek deliberately uses metaphors that jar. The ultimate lesson of computer-generated reality is the virtualization of true reality. By the mirage of virtual reality, true real-ity is "posited as a semblance of itself, as a pure symbolic edifice" (*TN*, 43–4).

Hence Žižek has used both Kant and Lacan, as well as Marx, to show how, for Hegel, subjectivity is an empty form. This is a valuable insight and building on it, we could argue that what Hegel overlooks is that the interiority of subjectivity is already inscribed, as Freud shows us, from the outside. Much literary theory can be viewed as articulating this re-inscription of content into the empty form of subjectivity. On the other hand, we need to recognize that, for Hegel, subjectivity is a *process* that must engage, in its inherently divided nature, with the other for either to be fully realized.

14.4 Epilogue

In general, Žižek goes to great pains to make Hegel preempt postmod-ernist criticism to render his thought serviceable in a "post-Marxist" cri-tique of capitalism, as a philosopher of "difference." While I have taken issue with the details of his reading of Hegel, his overall project – to demonstrate the open, rather than closed, nature of dialectic – remains of the utmost importance. But we can further this endeavor, I believe, by paying closer attention to the precise ways in which Hegel himself articu-lates the openness of his dialectic. It is clearly a dialectic that never needs to stop. Yes, we can point, like Feuerbach and Marx, to its idealistic and "mystical" affiliations with Neoplatonism, and we can consequently, like Derrida, view the "circular" dialectical progression as ultimately enclosed within a final metaphysical circle. We can also, like Lukács, view the dialectic of capitalism expressed by Hegel as imperialistic, as subjugat-ing not only every aspect of the external world to progressively rational processes of thought but as also assimilating all forms of otherness to itself. But at none of these levels does the Hegelian dialectic leave earlier stages entirely behind, and, since the dialectic operates retroactively and retrospectively – moving backward as well as forward – it always harbors the potential (as shown by Adorno and Benjamin) to revisit earlier stages, to reinvest itself in what has been repressed and forbidden, to recuperate these as part of a new dialectic. Moreover, the points at which the dialec-tic stops in Hegel – at Reason, the state, capitalism – can themselves be treated as mere stages, using the conceptions of dialectic we have found in his own texts.

The process of knowing only comes to an "end" in absolute know-ing, and even then, we have not arrived at a state that is somehow static but is constitutively related to the journey resulting in it. The absolute itself reverberates in relationality. Moreover, it could be argued that, even if this absolute comes to "rest" in self-knowing, from the perspective of human cognition, this absolute is never reached. In a sense, this is Žižek's point: that the agent of the entire process is not the human subject but the system of knowledge itself. But in his reading, this involves the human subject "erasing" herself. I would argue that, on the contrary, the dualism of subject and object is overcome only in the Absolute's self-knowledge – its knowledge of reality as itself. But from the perspective of human cognition, that distinction is never overcome; the object – the infinite variety and richness of the external world – is never fully known, is never fully assimilated to the form of subjectivity. Hence the "remainder" is *not* a product of the subject wholly assimilating the object and then "letting it go." Rather, it is that which forever *remains* to be assimilated and persists in confronting the subject as "other." So, in a sense, Žižek's vision of a dialectic of difference, that is open and non-imperialistic, that is not motivated by desire for mastery, is already contained in the pages of Hegel. And Žižek evinces this version of dialectic by reading Hegel against himself as well as against the grain of most of his commentators.

Overall, what Žižek argues through his misreadings is not only powerfully suggestive but demonstrates the kind of radical reinterpretation that may be needed in order to sustain the richness of Hegel's dialectic, to show how it does indeed address problems that still confront us today. In Žižek's vision – as informed by Marx and Lacan – Absolute Spirit in Hegel becomes a kind of metaphor precisely for the failure to resolve the contradictions of capitalism: contradictions between individual and family, family and civil society, civil society and state, as well as within the individual herself. The positing of Absolute Spirit as the "magical" resolution of all things is, as derided by Marx and Feuerbach, an empty gesture that leaves things as they are. What are these things? According to Žižek, they are alienated labor, the individual reduced to an "empty" or abstract subject of economic processes, and a subject that is also "split," which results in the "shared deadlock" between states and between subjects in civil society, a world of abstract atomistic individuals where the Hegelian project of mutual recognition is abandoned. This vacuum of subjectivity, this Absolute Void (the Lacanian Real that inhabits the absence of Absolute Spirit) is filled by the most abstract subjectivity of all, that of money – itself a metaphor for a new totality, that of the blind and impersonal economic processes which not only reduce our subjectivity to an abstract economic function but govern every aspect of our lives. On the positive side, this kind of totality, which arises by default – always inhabiting an absence, always poised over the departing footsteps of an ethical or spiritual Absolute – leaves the dialectic open to the infinite richness of the world, to other totalities, to alternative visions of humanity and post-humanity.

D.   *Hegel and Gender*

CHAPTER 15

Hegel on Gender: Antigone

15.1   Capitalism and Gender

In the aftermath of Marx's own critiques, many Marxist and non-Marxist thinkers have helped us to see how Hegel's philosophy expressed both the revolutionary impetus of capitalism – assuredly the most transformative revolution in world history, abrogating centuries if not millennia of despotism, absolutism, and feudal hierarchy – as well as the internal contradictions and dilemmas of capitalist society and culture. An important component of Hegel's expression and critique of capitalism was his treatment of the bourgeois family and the role of women in the ethical life of a modern state. In fact, this treatment is integral to Hegel's archetypal expression of capitalism as intrinsically patriarchal as well as Eurocentric. It's well-known, at least among students of Hegel, that much of what he says about "woman" is to modern ears simply outrageous. For example:

> The difference between man and woman is the difference between animal and plant; the animal is closer in character to man, the plant to woman, for the latter is a more peaceful unfolding whose principle is the more indeterminate unity of feeling [*Empfindung*]. (*PR*, §166)

But what is often overlooked, even in the sternest critiques of Hegel, is the overarching feature of his derogation of "woman," namely, that he places her *outside* of history[1] – just as he excludes Africa and various "Asiatic" tendencies from the realm of historical development. Here again is Hegel:

> Women are capable of education, but they are not made for activities which demand a universal faculty such as the more advanced sciences, philosophy and certain forms of artistic production ... Women regulate their

---

[1] This is recognized by a few authors. See, for example, Antoinette M. Stafford, "The Feminist Critique of Hegel on Women and the Family," *Animus*, 2 (1997), 84.

actions not by the demands of universality, but by arbitrary inclinations and opinions.

(*PR*, §166)

Hegel seems to regard these characteristics of women as permanent. Indeed, he states explicitly in the *Philosophy of History* that the family – the sphere in which women find their essential being – "is excluded from that process of development in which History takes its rise" (*PH*, 59).

For Hegel, capitalism – as moderated by the "universal" interests of the state – is the fruition of history, the becoming of the modern world, marching over the ruins of slavery, of despotism, of feudalism and superstition, bearing the banners of Protestant individualism and Enlightenment Reason to raise the promise of subjective freedom in the newly erected coliseum of civil society. But women are simply dragged along in this long historical journey, arrested within the same stage of development they had achieved in ancient Greece – and ancient Greek drama. Woman is created and imprisoned within the timeless mists of myth.

In Hegel's account, man is the bearer of history after the decline of Greek civilization. Hegel does indeed acknowledge a kind of equivalence between men and women in the ancient Greek *polis*. There is a direct conflict between family and state, with no mediation by civil society – which is an institution specific to the modern world. At this stage of history, even the man's identification with the state is largely based on custom and its rational content is not yet developed.[2] Hence, both woman and man exist in a condition of relative immediacy and incompletely realized individuality and subjective freedom. The female principle of duty to family conflicts with the male principle of civic duty, but in this conflict neither can win and each is seen as one-sided; indeed each presupposes the other. This is essentially the picture of woman portrayed in the *Phenomenology*, based not on the actual condition of women in ancient Greece but on Sophocles' drama *Antigone*. But by the time we reach Hegel's later thought, in the *Philosophy of Right*, we find that "man" has indeed progressed: he is viewed as forging his individuality in the newly emerged sphere of civil society, and as creating the institutions – economic, legal, religious, political – of the modern state with which he can rationally identify. Woman, in stark contrast – both with man and

---

[2] Heidi M. Raven sees a symmetry between family and state in ancient Greek culture, both of which involve an ethical identification that is based on custom, "Has Hegel Anything to Say to Feminists?," *Owl of Minerva*, 19.2 (1988), 157.

with some of the enlightened women of Hegel's own era – remains what she was, a drama queen, frozen within the fictional archetype of *Antigone.*

In this chapter, it may be useful for us to work backwards: we'll begin by considering Hegel's later conception of the role of women in the over-all structure of a modern capitalist state, as expressed in the *Philosophy of Right.* We can then trace the roots of this conception in Hegel's earlier views of women in the *Phenomenology,* which themselves are based on his analysis of *Antigone.* The next chapter will offer a close analysis of critiques of Hegel by two of the major theorists of gender, Luce Irigaray and Judith Butler. This entire section of the book will conclude with a glimpse of the extraordinarily diverse range of approaches and themes that characterize feminist readings of Hegel, as well as various feminist endeavors to relate Hegel's views to his own historical context.

15.2   Hegel's *Philosophy of Right:* Woman in Bourgeois Society

Hegel's views of gender and women in the modern state must be under-stood in the context of his analysis of "ethical life." His term *Sittlichkeit,* usually translated as "ethical life," might loosely be said to designate "social morality" as opposed to private morality or *Moralität.* What Hegel means by "ethical life" are the beliefs and actions that pervade three broad spheres. It is expressed through a dialectic which begins with the family, and traverses civil society, to conclude in the State. The family represents the ethical moment in its immediacy and unity. Its main characteristic is love, which is "mind's feeling of its own unity," its self-consciousness of its individuality within the unity of the family, as a member rather than an independent person (*PR,* §157–8). The indi-vidual acquires right *as* an individual only when the family begins to dis-solve. Hence, the family itself undergoes its own dialectic, moving from *marriage,* which embodies the "concept of family in its immediate phase," through *family property and capital,* which is the external embodiment of the concept of family, to the *dissolution* of the family and the education of children (*PR,* §160).

15.3   The Dialectic of Family: Marriage

In a moment, we can look at Hegel's notorious statements about women, which have rightly been impugned. But it's important to contextualize those statements. Hegel repeatedly stresses that in the first phase of fam-ily, i.e. marriage, individuals renounce their individual personality to "make themselves one person." Indeed, the family as a whole is one person and its members are merely "accidents" (*PR*, §§ 162–3). The wedding involves "the complete mutual surrender of the parties to one another." Interestingly, Hegel sees the marriage contract as designed to transcend the point of view of contract, since a contract – so important in the sphere of civil or bourgeois society – views individuals as self-subsistent units (*PR*, §§ 163–4). Moreover, marriage is intrinsically monogamous because it entails "the mutual, whole-hearted, surrender of ... personality." Hegel later calls this a "free surrender by both sexes" (*PR*, §§ 167–8). In his repeated use of the term "mutual," Hegel seems to suggest that marriage *per se* is not a relationship of subordination.

15.4 Division of Ethical Life into Male and Female

However, we now come to the problematic parts of Hegel's account. He states that the difference between the physical characteristics of the two sexes has a "rational basis and consequently acquires an intellectual and ethical significance." In Hegel's terms, the "ethical mind" divides or dirempts itself into the two sexes. He goes on:

> Thus one sex [male] is mind in its self-diremption into explicit personal self-subsistence and the knowledge and volition of free universality, i.e. the self-consciousness of conceptual thought and the volition of the objective final end. The other sex [female] is mind maintaining itself in unity as knowledge and volition ... in the form of concrete individuality and feeling. In relation to externality, the former is powerful and active, the latter passive and subjective. It follows that man has his actual substantive life in the state, in learning, and so forth, as well as in labor and struggle with the external world and with himself so that it is only out of his diremption that he fights his way to self-subsistent unity with himself. In the family he has a tranquil intuition of this unity, and there he lives a subjective ethical life on the plane of feeling. Woman, on the other hand, has her substantive destiny in the family, and to be imbued with family piety is her ethical frame of mind. (*PR*, §166)

It's worth analyzing this passage closely to discern exactly what Hegel is saying. The "ethical mind" which exists still in its immediacy (rather than being fully realized) is the family, and it is this which "internally sunders itself" into the two sexes. That part of ethical mind that is "man" exists *in* its self-diremption or self-division; it is not a unity. It embodies "free universality" or the ability to transcend its own material existence and rise to the level of rational conceptual thinking. Man is "active" and has his "substantive life" in the state, in labor, and is engaged in a struggle with the external world and himself. In other words, man can only achieve his true identity as a social being and in the social sphere, but also, only man, as "free universality," can engage in the dialectic of self-realization through work or labor, a dialectic that obliges him to struggle and to overcome the purely natural dimensions of his existence by means of rational thought and self-discipline. Only man is obliged to do this in order to achieve unity with himself, which is an explicit, conscious, and rational unity.

In contrast, "woman" never emerges from the state of intuitive unity into any kind of self-division (which of course would be a movement to a higher stage). Woman is "mind maintaining itself in unity" and is characterized not by universality and rational thought but by particularity, by "concrete individuality and feeling." In Hegel's vision, woman never gets the opportunity to develop through the dialectic of work. She is already an intuitive unity, who never rises to the plane of self-division or difference. And when man returns home, says Hegel, he too regresses somewhat to a "tranquil intuition" of this unity, and he lives, like woman, "on the plane of feeling." So woman is an immediate unity, whereas man is a mediated unity, a higher-level unity that is not just given but achieved. The family is the woman's "substantive destiny" and woman is forever imprisoned in what Simone de Beauvoir calls "immanence," the mere inhabiting of one's given condition with no opportunity to transcend this.

Yet again, in failing to live up to his own dialectical method, Hegel might be seen as contradicting himself. He has said on several occasions that marriage entails "mutual" surrender. He even explicitly states that "[p]ersonality attains its right of being conscious of itself in another only in so far as the other is in this identical relationship as a person" (*PR*, §167). But how can this surrender be mutual when it occurs between two partners whose personality is achieved on different levels of unity? Hegel's answer might well be that inasmuch as he undertakes this surrender, man draws upon only the intuitive part of himself that exists on the plane of feeling. But still, how could this be a "complete" surrender? Surely the same logic would apply here as in the master–slave dialectic: Just as recognition by the slave is insufficient as an acknowledgment of the master's humanity, so surrender on the part of someone subordinated or by merely one dimension of a person would be equally defective.

Hegel states that the woman's "ethical frame of mind" is to be imbued with family piety. A reader could be forgiven for thinking that Hegel derives his characterization of woman almost wholesale from *Antigone*. And Hegel is not one to thwart our expectations. He immediately informs us that family piety is expounded in Sophocles' *Antigone* ... as principally the law of woman ... the law of the inward life ... as a law opposed to public law, to the law of the land. This is the supreme opposition in ethics and there-fore in tragedy, and it is individualized in the same play in the opposing natures of man and woman. (*PR*, §166)

Hegel's conception of modern woman (but, as we shall see, not modern man) correlates exactly with that portrayed in the ancient Greek drama.[3] So marriage is the ethical idea in its immediacy; this idea is externalized in family property; and the third phase is that the family dissolves as its children are educated and attain independent personalities. These indi-viduals (the children) now enter the stage of "difference," the stage of civil society, which is composed of individuals externally related to one another as atomistic units (*PR*, § 181).

15.5   Divine and Human Law

When we examine Hegel's renowned – perhaps notorious – account in the *Phenomenology* of *Antigone*, we will find that Hegel's analysis of woman is inextricable from his interpretation of this drama.[4] Indeed, it could be argued that Hegel falls headlong into the male convention of which Simone de Beauvoir so eloquently speaks, namely the treating of woman by engaging not with any reality but with a myth. Hegel's account has little connection with what women might be like in actuality – and at best only an accidental connection with the actual condition of women in his era. Rather, his impressions of woman are derived from a fiction, a myth, as it finds archetypal expression in one of the supreme monuments of Western literature. Indeed, the very terms of Hegel's analysis of ethical life derive, as we shall now see, from this ancient Greek dramatization of spiritual life in a Greek city-state.

Hegel tells us that ethical life, or what he calls Spirit, is divided into two broad realms. On the one hand, this ethical Spirit is expressed in its

---

[3] It will be recalled from the play *Oedipus the King* that Oedipus unwittingly fulfilled the prophecy whereby he would kill his father and marry his mother. With Oedipus consequently banished, Creon became king of Thebes. Eventually, a quarrel broke out between Oedipus' two sons Eteocles and Polyneices; Eteocles became king and exiled his brother. Polyneices assembled an army includ-ing foreigners and laid siege to Thebes. The two brothers killed each other in battle, and Creon, resuming power, ordered that Eteocles should be given a proper burial while the body of Polyneices should be left unburied for vultures to maim and devour. The central conflict of the play arises from the defiance of Antigone, who insists on giving her brother the rites of burial. Antigone is often seen as upholding family loyalty and the eternal laws of the gods, while Creon is viewed as a staunch defender of the laws of the state. This view derives partly from Hegel.

[4] As we shall see in Chapter 16, this assertion has been disputed by critics such as Karin de Boer, as has the precise connection of Hegel's views with the status of women in his time.

substance as a nation; as *consciousness*, it is realized in the citizens of a state (*PhM*, 467).[5] Together, these comprise the sphere of human law, which is embodied in both the conventions of a society and in its government. But over against this power of the "ethical secular human order," there is "another power, the Divine Law." This is the "immediate essential being of the ethical order" (*PhM*, 467). So, the divine law is the "immediate" phase in which the ethical order expresses itself in this era. Whereas human law is expressed through the nation's government and the consciousness of its citizens, divine law is embodied in the family, expressed in its relations, rituals, and deities. Hence, both the family and the divine law belong to the first phase, that of "immediate ethical existence," of immediate unity; human law belongs to the realm of the state and public life. It's important to bear in mind, for Hegel's argument, this fact that the human law is *rooted in* divine law.

Why, then, is there a conflict between divine law and human law? To understand this, we need to recall that Hegel is speaking of ethical life in the Greek city-state and the decline of this political order, which makes way for the Roman empire. In the ancient Greek *polis*, there is according to Hegel a harmony between individual and state, whereby the individual finds his fulfillment and his true being in the social and political life of the state. The state thus embodies a universal set of values which stand over and above any purely private interests. However, this is a relatively primitive stage of the development of human consciousness. Eventually it becomes evident to individuals that the purported "universal" embodied in the ethical life of the state is actually limited, expressing merely the values of a particular culture. The individual develops an orientation toward something more truly universal, but this cannot be found in his particular existence, and must be sought beyond this, in death. It is only through death that he can shed his particularity and achieve a kind of universality. This "genuine" universality, suggests Charles Taylor, concerns the individual *as such*, not in his relation to the state. In fact, it pits the individual against the parochial universality of the state, and this truer universality is embodied in the divine law.[6]

What Taylor valuably points to, but does not develop, is the idea that death, "speculatively understood," is the expression of the true

[5] G. W. F. Hegel, *The Phenomenology of Mind*, trans. J.B. Baillie (London and New York: George, Allen & Unwin/Humanities Press, 1977).

[6] In this paragraph, I have to some extent followed the interpretation offered in Charles Taylor, *Hegel* (Cambridge: Cambridge University Press, 1977), pp. 172–3 (hereafter cited as *H*), but I develop this in a further direction.

universality of the human spirit (*H*, 173). We have already come across the idea that death, for Hegel, is a negation or renunciation of mere particularity, of mere material existence and given-ness. It is death in this sense that comprises the profound affinity of human and divine law. Human law aims to raise the orientation of actions toward the universal ends of the state; in this sense, it aims at the "death" of the individual. Divine law, in this context, deigns to preserve in its integrity the universality of the dead individual. Hegel states in the *Phenomenology* that "death … is the *natural* course of the negativity of the individual *qua* existent, in which consciousness does not return to itself and become self-conscious" (*PhM*, 471). In other words, the "negativity" of an individual is his ability to overcome the particularities of his material existence and rise to a universal perspective. The "natural" conclusion of this negativing process is death, the ultimate negation or renunciation of particular existence. If we are able in life to rise to a universal perspective, our consciousness "returns" to itself as *self*-consciousness, as an awareness of what was originally confronted as an external object as, rather, an aspect of itself. In the case of death, of course, there is no such return. And this, as we'll see in a moment, is where the duty of the family comes in.

The crucial point is that, in Hegel's reading, the divine law represents, at this stage of history, a primordial impulsion toward a genuine universality. It is as yet merely intuited by individuals and as such is associated with the family, whose relations rest primarily on intuition and emotion. So, while this aspiration after true universality may conflict with the more contingent universality of a particular political state, this genuine universality embodied in divine law is nonetheless the *ultimate* foundation of the civic universality, just as the family is in a sense the foundation of the state since it educates its members to serve as citizens.

This authentic universality, according to Hegel, is directed toward death. At this historical stage, it is not attainable in life, in the harmony of rational citizens with a rational state. Such a harmony, in Hegel's eyes, comes much later in the historical process, only in the modern state: It requires the mediation of civil society, an arena of struggle and self-realization through which the individual must pass in order to realize himself as a rational ethical being. In the ancient Greek *polis*, that universality is projected into the life beyond, into the nether world, of ghostly shades. Hence the divine law is most deeply embodied in the duty of family members regarding death. Hegel tells us that the act of a family member toward another family member, while directed toward a specific individual, is in its deepest essence directed toward him as a "universal being, divested of his sensuous, or particular reality. The act no longer concerns the living but the dead, one who has passed through the long sequence of his broken and diversified existence and gathered up his being ... into the peace of simple universality." This condition of universality is "mere being, death" (*PhM*, 470). In other words, *within* the family, the individual lived a life of particularity, driven by particular ends, emotion, and capricious bodily demands; only in death does he escape all these contingent aspects of his existence and attain a kind of universality. Indeed, within the family, the individual is "merely unreal insubstantial shadow." It is only as a citizen that he is "real and substantial" (*PhM*, 470).

So the family is locked in a profound affinity with the nether world and with "death" on several levels of significance. In ancient Greek culture – as exemplified in both the *Iliad* and the *Odyssey* – it was considered a dishonor to leave a body unburied; burial was necessary for passage to the underworld. Hegel envisages family duty regarding death not only as fulfilling the profoundest imperative of divine law but also, in doing so, intimating the content of this law, namely the aspiration toward authentic universality. If death is the natural culmination of a negation of physical existence, it acts *upon* an individual; it is very much a process of nature, not the action of a conscious mind. The performance of the rites of burial – the duty of the family – interrupts the work of nature, adding to the natural process the element of consciousness, and rescuing the blood-relation from the condition of mere destruction, reclaiming him – and reclaiming death – for the human community (*PhM*, 471–2). This respect for death, then, is both metaphorically and metonymically a respect for life, for the need to live life in accordance with the universal, even though this universal is only intuited at this stage as an external uncomprehended law, and as conflicting with the version of universality embodied in duty to the state. Death is here a metonym for a universality that will yet take centuries to achieve, and to be truly embodied in the institutions of a rational state.

15.6   The Divine Law in Family Relationships

Hegel's account of woman's role as daughter, mother, and wife also rests upon perspectives in *Antigone*. As a daughter, says Hegel, a woman can attain individual existence only after the passing away of her parents, not in *relation* to them. As mother and wife, however, she is individualized insofar as her relationship to her husband or child is ethical, having a universal reference – not to this or that husband or child but to *a* husband or *a* child. The wife does not know herself as "*this* particular self in and through an other." However, the implication is that in practice, the husband–wife relationship is not ethical and is marked by particular desires and contingency (*PhM*, 477).

The relationship of brother and sister is different. The sister sees in the brother a being "whose nature is unperturbed by desire and is ethically like her own; her recognition in him is pure and unmixed with any sexual relation." This relationship is thus unmarked by ethical contingency and entails the mutual recognition of "individual selfhood." Directly echoing Antigone, Hegel asserts that the "loss of a brother is thus irreparable to the sister, and her duty towards him is the highest" (*PhM*, 477). The brother–sister relationship signifies the "limit" and self-transcendence of the family. Their respective duties devolve upon brother and sister in opposite directions. Whereas the sister is entrusted with preservation of the divine law, the brother turns toward another sphere, leaving the "immediate, rudimentary, and ... negative ethical life of the family, in order to acquire and produce the concrete ethical order" (*PhM*, 477). What is paramount in this entire situation is that the ethical order is essentially a unity but it has divided itself into these two realms, of divine law and human law, family and state, woman and man.

15.7   Family and State

In fact, Hegel is at pains repeatedly to stress that these two realms presuppose each other. And what sets up their contradiction, at its profoundest level, is the internal contradiction within the family and within the state, which rests on the external contradiction *between* them. As with the brother, the husband is sent forth into the life of the community, where he finds his self-conscious reality (*PhM*, 478). Just as the family thereby

> finds in the community its universal substance and subsistence, conversely the community finds in the family the formal element of its own realization, and in the divine law its power and confirmation. Neither of the two alone is self-complete. Human law as a living and active principle proceeds from the divine, the law holding on earth from that of the nether world, the conscious from the unconscious, mediation from immediacy; and returns to whence it came. The power of the nether world, on the other hand, finds its realization upon earth; it comes through consciousness to have existence and efficacy. (*PhM*, 478–9)

Hence family and state presuppose each other. And human law derives its impulse from divine law, while divine law needs ultimately to be realized through human law. Hegel is describing an ancient Greek world where this dialectic has not yet been realized, hence its elements stand separated, in apparent contradiction. This is the external contradiction between family and state.

But this external contradiction rests upon a profounder contradiction, just hinted at, *within* the family and within the state. This internal contradiction rests upon the fact that family and state are internally related; they presuppose each other and internally shape each other. Strikingly, Hegel characterizes the family as the "inner indwelling principle of sociality," which works in an unconscious manner, and "stands opposed to its own actuality when explicitly conscious" (*PhM*, 468). Effectively, the family *is* the unconscious basis of the state. What the family is on an unconscious, immediate level, the state is on a conscious and mediated level. Hegel explicitly states that the family is "the basis of the actuality of a nation," and as such "it stands in contrast to the nation itself" (*PhM*, 468).

As such, membership of a family is intrinsically a divided condition where an individual is torn between obligation to family unity and achieving his individuality through service in the public sphere. Hegel says that though the ethical spirit finds its realization in the state, "the family is the medium in which this realization takes effect." However, this spirit gives family members the feeling that their individuality and their life "only lies in the whole," i.e., in the community (*PhM*, 473). The youth goes forth (Hegel is evidently thinking of Eteocles and Polyneikes here) from the "unconscious life of the family" and becomes the ruler who embodies the individuality of the community but "still shares the natural life from which he has torn himself away" (*PhM*, 493). So a citizen who acts on behalf of the state is conflicted because he is still a member of a family, and a person who acts as a family member is conflicted because he is also a citizen.

Hegel sees the apparent opposition of divine and human law as the "confirmation and substantiation of one through the other" (*PhM*, 481). He states:

> The union of man with woman constitutes the operative mediating agency for the whole, and constitutes the element which, while separated into the extremes of divine and human law, is, at the same time, their immediate union. This union ... unites into one process the twofold movement in opposite directions ... the downward movement of human law ... [and] ... the upward movement of the law of the nether world to the daylight of

conscious existence. Of these movements the former falls to man, the latter to woman. (*PhM*, 482)

What becomes clearer here is the metaphorical nature of upper and lower,
light and dark, life and death. The lower or nether world is the world of the
unconscious (not in a Freudian sense, but in the sense of lacking conscious
awareness), of feeling, of immediacy, and hence of unreality. The upper
world is the realm of rational, conscious action, of mediated existence.
Man and woman, as embodying these realms, are united in their mutual
opposition.

15.8　Hegel on *Antigone*

The foregoing represents Hegel's views of family and state, divine law
and human law, as derived from *Antigone*; they also represent of course
his interpretation of the broad framework underlying the central conflict
in that drama between these realms, as embodied in the characters of
Antigone and Kreon. We can now turn to his analysis of the play itself.
Hegel calls the ethical consciousness "character" and ethical action he calls
"duty." Significantly, he defines an act as "the realized self" (*PhM*, 484–5).
The ethical consciousness is assigned by nature to serving either divine or
human law, in terms of gender. Since the ethical order, as we have seen,
is sundered into these two domains, the ethical consciousness, "taking up
an undivided single attitude towards law, is assigned only to one." It commits itself unreservedly to this, and views its opposition to the other law
as a "collision of duty merely with reality." The proponent of divine law
sees the other side as offering "mere arbitrary fortuitous human violence,"
while the advocate of human law sees its opponent as imbued with the
"disobedience of subjective self-sufficiency" (*PhM*, 485–7).

Interestingly, Hegel sees the opposition of the two laws as "the act of
self-consciousness itself," which creates a division between itself and the
reality over against it. In doing this, the self-consciousness acquires *guilt*
because it fails to "transcend the natural allotment of the two laws to
the two sexes." It merely lays hold of one side of the ethical reality and
adopts a negative attitude toward the other. In other words, in acting
ethically, in defending one kind of law, it necessarily violates the other
(*PhM*, 488–9). This guilt is all the more pure, says Hegel, if it "knows
beforehand the law and the power which it opposes ... and wittingly,
like Antigone, commits the crime" (*PhM*, 491). But against such one-
sidedness, actual reality has "a power of its own; it takes the side of truth
against consciousness" (*PhM*, 487). So, the actual world demonstrates to

the ethical consciousness that its point of view is merely partial. Ethical self-consciousness now learns that the law that has been manifested to it is actually "bound up with its opposite" and that the "essential reality is the unity of both" (*PhM*, 489).

The opposition of these ethical principles leads, then, to mutual destruction since the "victory of one power and its [representative] character" would itself be one-sided and betray the essential unity of those principles (*PhM*, 492). Indeed, the apparent victory of the universal, of the state, over "the family, the rebellious principle of individuation," places it into conflict with the divine law, which is "insulted." But in this "victory," the power of human law has effectively "consumed its own real nature. The spirit which is manifest to the light of day has the roots of its power in the lower world" (*PhM*, 494–5). The true bonds of the nation go back through the bonds of the family whose origins are primordial, lying deep in the "mute unconscious substance of all, in the layers of forgetfulness." Thus the fulfillment of the public or civic spirit learns that "its supreme right is supreme wrong, its victory rather its own defeat" (*PhM*, 495).[7]

We now come to the most infamous of Hegel's comments on women. "Human law," he says, is the "manhood of the community," which has its being by absorbing into itself the "separatist action of the household gods (*Penates*), the individualization into insular independent families which are under the management of womankind" (*PhM*, 496). On the other hand, the family and individual consciousness are the basis of the state, and the state subsists "only by breaking in upon family happiness, and dissolving [individual] self-consciousness into the universal." But, in doing this, the state "creates an enemy for itself within its own gates, creates in it what it suppresses, and what is at the same time essential to it – woman in general" (*PhM*, 496). Again, the very existence of state and family is a condition of simultaneous opposition and unity, a condition of perpetual tension.

"Womankind – the everlasting irony in the life of the community – changes by intrigue the universal purpose of government into a private end" and "perverts" the universal property of the state into a possession of the family. Hegel proceeds to say that women ridicule the wisdom of tradition and encourage youth to defy this wisdom (*PhM*, 496–7). In these statements, Hegel is engaging in generalizations that take us well

---

[7] This mutuality might be viewed as reiterated in Levinas's notion of the face of the other, whereby it is in our very encounter with the other, in relationality itself, that ethics is founded. See Levinas, *Totality and Infinity: An Essay on Exteriority*, pp. 194–226.

beyond *Antigone* but which are rife in the traditions of male thinking: woman as private, cunning, and subversive of conventional values. The community, however, can preserve itself only by suppressing this individualism. But in suppressing it, it also creates and spurs it. It characteristically resorts to war – the "engine of negation and destruction – to preserve the solidity of the community and to thwart excessive individuality" (*PhM*, 497). Individuals "striving after inviolable self-existence" are made to "feel the power of their lord and master, death" (*PhM*, 474). But because the community thus relies on physical strength to preserve its ethical order, this ethical order together with the state which sanctions it dissolves and gives way to the next phase of ethical life, the Roman Empire, where the "universal" consciousness of the ruler, the emperor, relates to particular individuals only abstractly, through force and through recognizing them merely as possessing property rights. In other words, the state no longer embodies the values and aspirations of its people, and a long era of alienation – as expressed in the characteristic Roman philosophies of Stoicism and skepticism – sees its sad inauguration.

15.9   Epilogue

In Hegel's vision, by the time we arrive at the modern era, the ancient equivalence between woman and man gives way to a heavy imbalance and asymmetry. While man embarks upon the increasingly sunlit journey toward self-conscious individuality and freedom, woman remains imprisoned in darkness, in the living tomb of myth, walled off from historical progress. This exclusion of woman from history is integral to Hegel's vision of capitalism: It reverberates profoundly in many registers, shaking the foundations of Hegel's dialectic in its precarious expression of the ethical life of capitalism. Hegel effectively sees capitalism or the sphere of civil society as part of a larger dialectic, mediating between the spheres of family at the beginning and the state as the conclusion. But, just as Marx and Marxists have argued that in Hegel there is no genuinely dialectical relation between civil society and state, so some feminists have pointed to the absence of any dialectical relation between family and civil society. Hegel's notion of the state doesn't genuinely solve the contradictions of civil society or capitalism; nor is his connection of family and civil society free of the contradictions enumerated above. In other words, Hegel's picture of capitalism ends up as marooned between family and state, with its relation to either inadequately articulated and open to reinterpretation.

CHAPTER 16

Feminists on Hegel and Antigone

Irigaray, Butler, (Derrida)

Antigone – as character, as drama, as allegory – embodies the wide range of issues engaged in Hegel's account of the role of women. Much of the encounter between feminism and Hegel has been concentrated into various critiques of Hegel's treatment of this drama. In this chapter, we will look at two such critiques, written by major theorists of gender. The first is by Luce Irigaray, whose work offers one of the most powerful and fascinating feminist engagements with the Hegelian dialectic. The second is by Judith Butler, who equally sheds light on the fissured nature of Hegel's thinking but also shows how it can help us to articulate important dilemmas concerning family and women in our own day.

16.1   Luce Irigaray and Hegel

It's worth looking briefly at Irigaray's use and subversion of the dialectic in order to furnish the broader context of her critique of Hegel on *Antigone*. Indeed, the latter exemplifies the former: Irigaray's critique enlists many of the characteristic techniques she uses to undermine the language of the male philosophical tradition and its reductive conception (or even denial) of female subjectivity. Much of this tradition, moreover, is summarized in Hegel's treatment of *Antigone*. Irigaray advocates undermining patriarchal discourse from within, a strategy she pursues in her readings of several discourses from Plato through Hegel and Marx to Freud and Lacan. She does, however, indicate that a feminine language would be more diffuse, like female sexuality, and less rigidly categorizing than male discourse.

Irigaray's overall project of exploring the possibilities of reconfiguring language and subjectivity grew, like much modern French feminism, out of the widespread unrest and revolutionary milieu of May 1968. Significantly, this historical moment embodied one of the ongoing "crises" of capitalism, in terms of economic discontent and conflict of ideologies, with a general strike by factory workers and activism by leftist students which brought France to a standstill. But these proximate events were the culmination of larger-scale problems, including the collapse of the Bretton-Woods currency agreement between countries, the failure of various imperialistic ventures (as in Vietnam), and the increasing separation of communism in Europe from the communist bloc led by the Soviet Union, not to mention the continued subjugation of women.

In this context, some of Irigaray's central endeavors represent an attempt to unravel the inner structure of Hegel's dialectic in its expression of the promise and perils of capitalism. For example, she rejects the male assignment of gender roles as archetypally expressed by Hegel, which we have seen to be integral to his vision of bourgeois society. Hegel articulately rehearses a conventional male view that imprisons women within the sphere of matter, of nature, of motherhood, while men are at liberty to engage in the world of economics, culture, and politics where they can find and exercise their subjectivity and freedom. Irigaray wants to reconceive the subjectivity of both man and woman, so as to allow for man's rootedness in nature as well as for woman's fitness to participate in the public sphere. She aims also to reconceive the subjectivity of both mother and daughter.

Irigaray's most sustained use and subversion of Hegel dialectic occurs in her book *I love to you* (1990, French version), where she reconfigures the master–slave dialectic to formulate an ethics of intersubjective recognition between male and female. The broad context for this endeavor itself derives from Hegel. Like him, she cites two fundamental options toward human progress that have arisen in the modern world, namely religion and capitalism:

> To say that intense happiness will come from owning goods or that happiness is to be found in the beyond, this earth being just an exile, is to make two illusory promises.[1]

Hegel had termed these options "Faith" and "Insight" (Enlightenment). Like Hegel, Irigaray rejects the transcendent solutions offered by religion and the abstract reason of the Enlightenment. But where Hegel sees both of these as sublated or superseded by a society where reason is realized in both human (male) subjectivity and state institutions, Irigaray attributes a fundamental role to the achievement of an enlightened vision of sexual

---

[1] Luce Irigaray, *i love to you: sketch of a possible felicity in history*, trans. Alison Martin (New York: Routledge, 1996), pp. 14–15. Hereafter cited as *ItY*.

difference which cannot be subordinated either to transcendent authority or the immanent authority of capital:

> Happiness must be built by us here and now on earth, where we live, a happiness comprising a carnal, sensible and spiritual dimension in the love between ... woman and man, which cannot be subordinated to reproduction, to the acquisition or accumulation of property, to a hypothetical human or divine authority. (*ItY*, 15)

Indeed, according to Irigaray, conventional notions of the "citizen," as well as of "human nature," reduce the interaction of man and woman to a false unity, where the male serves as the model: "The natural is at least two: male and female ... Take those two parts of humankind, men and women. It is wrong for them to be brought back to one" (*ItY*, 35–6). These are radical statements which effectively impugn not only Hegel but even Marx and many other thinkers who have seen human nature or citizenship as embodying an essential unity. In a way, however, they are also Hegelian statements since they recognize that identity is never self-identity and is always relational, interacting with its opposite or at least with what is different or other.[2]

For Irigaray, the project of constructing happiness depends on "liberating human subjectivity." Such emancipation requires a reconfiguration of both subjectivity and language, and for Irigaray is effected through a rewriting of Hegel's master–slave dialectic. To begin with, Irigaray asserts that "Man is not, in fact, absolutely free ... He is limited. His natural completion lies in two humans" (*ItY*, 41). But the two humans here are not, as in Hegel's master–slave scenario, both male; rather, in the transposed terms of this dialectic, they are male and female. Moreover, while Irigaray accepts that subjectivity is acquired through recognition, her understanding of such recognition is different from Hegel's in at least two respects. First, it is a recognition that must be enacted in language – not the language advocated by bourgeois philosophy and economics, a language reduced to the purposes of communicating information and material needs – but a language that enables communication between two subjectivities or types of subjectivity. Second, in the kind of recognition of which Irigaray speaks, I recognize an "other" *not* because she is like me but precisely in her difference, her otherness:

---

[2] For an extremely perspicacious analysis of Irigaray's views of sexual difference – and of the possibility of reconciling those views with Judith Butler's notion of gender as performative – see Alison Stone's *Luce Irigaray and the Philosophy of Sexual Difference* (Cambridge: Cambridge University Press, 2006), pp. 42–3, 84–6.

I recognize you, thus you are not the whole or I would have been engulfed by you. Still, I cannot completely identify you, even less identify with you. I recognize you means I cannot know you in thought or in flesh. There is a negative at work between us. We cannot be substituted for one another. I will never be you in body or in thought.

Recognizing you means or implies respecting you as other, accepting that I draw myself to a halt before you as before something insurmountable, a mystery, a freedom that will never be mine, a subjectivity that will never be mine, a mine that will never be mine … I recognize you signifies that you are different from me, that I cannot identify myself (with) nor master your becoming. I will never be your master. And it is this negative that enables me to go toward you.

(*ItY*, 103–4)

Irigaray is reacting here against the Hegelian notion of consciousness as intrinsically imperialistic in its orientation toward others and the world. There is no life-and-death struggle here; there is no attempt to subjugate the other; and there is no attempt to make the other resemble me.

Both of these differences from Hegel – that recognition is effected through a reconfigured language, and that it acknowledges the other as other – are exquisitely illustrated in the very title of Irigaray's book, *i love to you*. Our usual expression "I love you" takes the "you" as a direct object; it grammatically subordinates the "you" as something passive, something to be acted upon, something that falls under the expansive movement of this ego. There is no recognition of another in this statement, no mutuality, no consideration of the interests or independence or indeed the subjectivity of the "you" who is reduced both grammatically and conceptually to an object (*ItY*, 109–11). The insertion of "to" as in "I love to you" introduces indirection, mitigating the burden of objectification, acknowledging a distance to the "you" and allowing the verb "love" to stand ambivalently as intransitive, denoting the circle of the "I" in relation to its own act of loving, a circle of self-relation which can then approach the you, and even this only indirectly. In this formulation, the "you" is granted respect and recognition as a possible subject in the distance that separates it from the "I." At least, this appears to be the kind of transformation of language and recognition that Irigaray has in mind.

In exploring new modifications of language and subjectivity, Irigaray employs a number of characteristic strategies, such as strategic essentialism (for which she has sometimes been criticized) and mimesis. Mimesis refers to a kind of unfaithful rehearsal of a male conception which takes us through it in detail to show its limitations. Irigaray's logic here is that we must confront these negative formulations about women rather than just ignoring them. This confrontation via mimesis might be regarded as a kind of dialectical reversal whereby we revisit the stages of an argument in order to unravel it from within. As we can now see, this is the strategy she uses to effect a powerful critique of Hegel's reading of *Antigone*.

16.2 Irigaray and Hegel's Eternal Irony

In her essay "The Eternal Irony of the Community," Irigaray's strategy is mimesis, whereby she retells Hegel's story of *Antigone* from within the Hegelian text, which she inhabits with her own voice. In other words, she does not offer an explicit critique, but merely summarizes Hegel's narrative in her own words, interspersing this with insights into its own implications. The strategy is a poignant example of "feminine writing," which subverts the male discourse it inhabits through its very style, effectively introducing layers into the Hegelian content.

16.2.1 Antigone's "Manliness"

As an example of the foregoing strategy, Irigaray notes that there are important factors left out in Hegel's account. He entirely ignores the numerous occasions on which Creon expressly states that he will not be bettered by a woman. As Irigaray states, he fears that Antigone "may usurp his manhood." Implicitly questioning Hegel's sharp polarization of family and state, Irigaray describes Creon in the same sentence as both "sovereign" of the city and "the man of the family." She sees Antigone's "manliness" as counterpointed by Ismene, who is indisputably a "woman" in "her weakness, her fear, her submissive obedience, her tears, madness, hysteria" (*SW*, 217–18).[3] The point here seems to be that the lines demarcating masculinity and femininity are far more blurred than Hegel could possibly allow. Again, as we have seen, Hegel attributes to Antigone a single-minded "pathos" or passion in devotion to her ethical principle. But the Sophoclean text, and Irigaray, tell a different story. The Greek drama portrays Antigone as motivated by numerous factors, some of them psychological and personal. Irigaray speculates that her allegiance to the gods below "frees her from the inventions of men. She defies them

---

[3] Luce Irigaray, *Speculum of the Other Woman*, trans. Gillian C. Gill (Ithaca, NY: Cornell University Press, 1985).

by/in her relationship to Hades." And she acts with a perversity that stands aloof from the common corruptions of men revolving around money and greed (*SW*, 218).

Indeed, Irigaray's Antigone is a kind of defiant heroine who "becomes the voice, the accomplice of the people, the slaves, those who only whisper their revolt against their masters secretly" (*SW*, 218). While this is not quite what the drama says – it makes no mention in this context of slaves or masters – Antigone's cognizance that she is expressing a more general discontent (perhaps on the part of both men and women) does not figure in Hegel's argument.[4] Finally, Irigaray points out that, having borne the burden of her entire family's curse and misfortune, Antigone "accepts on her own account the death knell of her jouissance ... by killing herself." She repeats, in effect, the murderous deed of her own mother (*SW*, 219). We might extrapolate Irigaray's insight to say that Antigone is doing for herself on a different level what she is doing for her brother. If, in Hegelian terms, she is transforming through burial rites the contingently natural death of her brother into a spiritual and volitional act, she is surely doing the same thing for herself inasmuch as she is *willing* her own death as a process to be executed (no pun intended) on her own terms, engineering what will be the process of her own "burial" in a cave.

Just as Irigaray's Antigone diverges substantially from Hegel's characterization of woman, so her Creon departs from Hegel's depiction of male subjectivity. Rather than realizing himself and achieving manhood through his service to the state, his "rigid sovereignty" finds itself empty of content, empty of the "substance of blood," the substance of family, in "an omnipotence alien to itself." Not only does his exercise of power self-alienate rather than fulfill his true being, but it also reduces the blood ties between individuals of his family into "abstract universality" (*SW*, 220). The Hegelian interpretative scheme, based on an opposition between family and state, divine law and human law, woman and man, is rapidly crumbling. In a sense, as we have already seen, the Hegelian text already does this, already undoes itself in its claims of both opposition and mutual necessity between each term of these respective dualisms. Irigaray merely brings this self-deconstruction into relief.

---

[4] This line of thought is taken up more explicitly in Tina Chanter's *Whose Antigone: The Tragic Marginalization of Slavery* (New York: State University of New York Press, 2011), pp. 23–4, 29ff. Hereafter cited as *WA*.

16.2.2 Sexual Difference

16.2.2.1 Hegel's Sister, Christiane

As if to illustrate the point that masculine identity can never fully achieve a universality that extricates itself from what Yeats calls "bodily form," Irigaray drags Hegel back into his own text. Not the Hegel whose pristine self-image was speculative philosophy but the Hegel of his own, more messy, biography. Hegel, she notes, expresses an "almost melancholic regret ... and the dream of going back to that attraction to the/his sister ... Hegel reveals his desire for a relationship that is certainly sexuate but does not need to pass through the realization of sexual desire" (*SW*, 220). Irigaray's choice of words here (the/his sister) is compelling. It may be worth remarking, though Irigaray does not pursue the line of thought she so valuably initiates here, that Hegel's relationship to his sister Christiane was both intimate and troubled.

As Terry Pinkard relates in his biography, Hegel and his sister (who was relatively well-educated, like his mother) were very close. After the death of their mother in 1781, Christiane effectively assumed the role of "woman of the house," in place of their mother, toward whom their reverence united them. In 1814, however, when Christiane returned to stay with Hegel and his wife, Marie, the visit was a disaster and shortly thereafter, Christiane, who had suffered mental problems previously, suffered a psychic collapse. She was, with Hegel's endorsement, committed to a sanitarium in 1820, though she was released a year later. Very shortly after Hegel's death she committed suicide by drowning. It's known that she wrote some highly accusatory letters to Hegel, none of which have survived. It's also known that she was highly independent and rebellious. Pinkard suggests that Hegel's view of Antigone, as well as his characterization of the brother–sister relationship in the Greek play, may have been colored by his experience with his sister.[5]

Christiane spoke of some "betrayal" on Hegel's part. While the substance of this may never be known, Irigaray's general point lingers in its relevance. Christiane, notwithstanding her strong-mindedness, fulfilled the domestic role that Hegel thought fitting for women; and she may have served as a substitute for his mother. In his later years he was estranged from her and dealt with her mental illness in a very distant manner. The "nostalgia" of which Irigaray speaks would be for both mother and sister, one lost to death, the other to reason. It may be that

---

[5] Terry Pinkard, *Hegel: A Biography* (Cambridge: Cambridge University Press, 2001), pp. 314–19.

the Antigone Hegel sees and seeks is a mirror of both, but certainly, as sister, she is not necessarily an idealization, as suggested by Derrida, but rather a reminiscence.[6] As Irigaray says, "if the female one can recognize herself in the male one, who has therefore supposedly assimilated her, the reverse is not necessarily true ... male and female will be split further and further apart" (SW, 220). Between male and female there will be an insurmountable alterity, a difference not just of degree but of nature.[7]

16.2.2.2   Wife-Mother and Father-King

Irigaray's reading draws more upon Lacan's view of woman as irreducibly other. She states that the sexual difference, if anything, becomes intensified and more layered:

> The wife-mother will henceforward become more and more associated with nourishing and liquefying *lymph*, almost *white* while she loses her blood in cyclic hemorrhages, *neuter and passive* enough in her matter for various members and organs of society to incorporate her and use her for their own subsistence. The man (father) will persevere in developing his individualization by *assimilating* the external other into and for the self, thus reenforcing his vitality, his irritability, and his activity ... The Father-king will repeat the rupture of (living) exchange between man and woman by sublating it into his discourse. Blood is burned to cinders in the writing of the text of law whereby man produces (himself) at the same time (as) the double – differently in him, in his son, and in his wife – and the color of blood fades as more and more semblances are produced, more atoms of individual egos, all bloodless in different ways. In this process some substance is lost: blood in its constitution of a living, autonomous subjectivity. (SW, 221–2)

This astonishing passage effectively encapsulates the entire substance and style of Irigaray's meditation – and of course requires some explanation.

---

[6] Derrida suggests that Hegel's repressed desire for his sister Christiane lies behind his insistence on "purifying" the male–sister relationship. But this is of course speculative, and I have preferred here to pursue the implications of Irigaray's more oblique suggestion.

[7] In his reflection on Hegel in *Glas*, Derrida suggests that sexual difference is "overcome" when the brother departs to fulfill his function in the state, and the other – indifferently in the form of sister and wife – remain. He states that there is "no more sexual difference as *natural difference*." But this can hardly be an accurate characterization of the matter. Sexual difference is not overcome but *reinforced* by the brother's departure: sexual difference may no longer exist as a natural difference, but it is reestablished at a higher, spiritual, and ethical level. The woman remains at the level of "nature," but the man sublates his natural existence – which means that he both transcends and preserves it. It is in this ability to sublate his lower self that his difference from the woman lies; she is denied that ability and remains in her original state. Nonetheless, the man is, like Creon, like Polyneices, still a family member even while he is a citizen, and in dealing with his family he reverts to action which is not properly ethical but based on emotion and affinity of blood. Tina Chanter offers a nuanced contextualization of Derrida's views, *Whose Antigone*, pp. 24–5.

The male and female, as Irigaray describes them, comprise two polarized movements, inward and outward. The wife-mother is periodically drained of the "blood" which is her substance, and associated with the colorless (neutral) fluid of the "lymph" with its white blood cells, immersed in passive materiality, a source of nourishment and sustenance for the community as needed. As for the Father-King, this is Creon, who sublates the living connection between man and woman into his discourse. In other words, his familial connections with Antigone (as uncle and potential father-in-law) and with Haemon (as father) are abrogated by his relation to them as king, as autocratic ruler, through his "discourse," which is the law. In this way, blood (blood relation) is "burned to cinders" in the "text of the law." The king "produces" himself in this law (he is no longer expressed in his family obligations but in the law) and in the obeisance to it of his son, his wife, and everyone else. All of these egos are a "semblance" of him inasmuch as he is the law, and in having their subjectivity thus redefined in these abstract legal terms, they are rendered "bloodless," or lacking in "living, autonomous subjectivity." So at one end (that of the family) the wife-mother remains, as substance, as blood being depleted; while at the other end (that of the state) the community of individuals is related by the "bloodless" ties of law.

16.2.3   *The Irony of Eternal Irony*

In a final subversion of the Hegelian text from within, Irigaray ends by recapitulating Hegel's remarks on woman as the "eternal irony of the community," as the eternally subversive element always threatening the establishing order by deriding tradition and by harnessing to this end the energies of youth: the son, the brother, the young man. The state responds by diverting these energies toward war so as to impart the lesson of death, the need to overcome particular interests, to vanquish particularity and contingency. But in this way, says Irigaray, the "still living substance of nature will sacrifice her last resources" and "her last drops of *blood*" to a "formal and empty universality" (*SW*, 226). The "eternal irony" is itself ironized by Irigaray inasmuch as the formal and empty universality comprehends not only the physical death of man but also the "death" – to himself – which constitutes his life.

Overall, then, Irigaray's strategy has not been to impugn Hegel's text from the outside. Rather, it is to inhabit the text, to work from within it, just as one must work within the male tradition to unravel it. She retells Hegel's story through a metalanguage – or, rather, a mesalanguage[8] – that infuses the original language, directing it through unauthorized turns and digressions, and destabilizing the sequence of Hegel's interpretative narrative. She infuses that narrative with "blood," with a metaphor of the feminine whereby its very connotation of death is correlated with life and origin, on which are founded and to which must return the "bloodless" categories of masculine universality. Like Marx though in a different direction, Irigaray shows that the basic divisions of Hegel's capitalist state cannot be sustained, and that its entire structure falters on the depth of its own contradictions: sense, matter, intuition, woman, family – none of these can be left behind. Even if we relegate them to subordinate positions, as the male tradition of philosophy has done, they remain at the very least as foundations of further levels of being. To kill femininity would be to kill the Absolute. Perhaps in our world, in the distance we have come from Hegel, the Absolute is itself interned in a kind of living death.

16.2.4   Judith Butler and Kinship Trouble

Judith Butler presents an entirely different approach in her book *Antigone's Claim*, but it nonetheless engages the issue of gender as central to Hegel's vision of capitalist society. Butler is concerned with the legacy of Antigone in an era when one foundational component of the modern state – kinship and family – is in crisis and transformation. She takes issue with the tradition of interpretation, stemming in an inflected form from Hegel, which sees Antigone as a champion of "feminine defiance of statism and an example of anti-authoritarianism."[9] According to Butler, the legacy of Hegel, visible to some extent in Lacan and especially in Irigaray, is to see Antigone "not as a political figure, one whose defiant speech has political implications, but rather as one who articulates a prepolitical opposition to politics ... Antigone comes to represent kinship and its dissolution, and Creon comes to represent an emergent ethical order and state authority" (*AC*, 2–3). Even Lacan situates Antigone at the border of the imaginary and symbolic, seeing her as figuring the "inauguration of the symbolic, the sphere of laws and norms" (*AC*, 3). The Hegelian legacy thus assumes the "separability of kinship and the state, even as it posits as essential relation between them" (*AC*, 5).

---

[8] In Greek, the opposite of "meta" in this context would be "mesa" – denoting inward depth, an operation from within.

[9] Judith Butler, *Antigone's Claim: Kinship between Life and Death* (New York: Columbia University Press, 2000), p. 1. Hereafter cited as *AC*.

16.2.5   Butler's Claim

Butler's central claim is that Antigone's act of defiance is essentially a speech-act, an act whose import lies primarily in its reportage, by herself and others (the sentry). Antigone, she says, "emerges in her criminality to speak in the name of politics and the law: she absorbs the very language of the state against which she rebels" (*AC*, 5). The "act by which she defies Creon's sovereignty, contesting the power of his edict" is a speech act. Butler quotes the Greek text in which Antigone literally says, in answer to Creon who asks her if she is responsible for the offensive deeds reported, not "I did them" but "I say I did them." According to Butler, Antigone's words take "the verbal form of a reassertion of sovereignty," whereby she commits a second criminal act, the "act of publishing one's deed" (*AC*, 8). More importantly, as she "begins to act in language, she also departs from herself."

In other words, Antigone departs from kinship and her embodiment of it, moving into the order of language, into the symbolic, and into the social. She can perform this speech act only through "embodying the norms of the power she opposes" and in fact she "assumes the voice of the law in committing the act against the law." Against Creon, Antigone asserts her own sovereignty. This is Antigone's "claim" (*AC*, 11). As against Slavoj Žižek's view that Antigone's refusal of Creon is an act of negation, Butler sees this negation as positing a "rival autonomy" (*AC*, 68). She inhabits the "language of sovereignty at the very moment in which she opposes sovereign power" (*AC*, 28). The overall point is that, insofar as Antigone opposes Creon, she cannot do this from a somehow "prepolitical" situation. In the very act of opposition she has entered the public sphere, the sphere of state authority, which she can contest only on its own ground. This is why she has departed from kinship and from herself: we might also add here that in the very act of affirming her blood ties, Antigone also leaves them, just as a man would, and so is infused with the same contradiction that besets a man when he leaves the family sphere and ascends to the higher sphere of civil society, the same phase of self-differentiation necessary to a higher level of self-realization.

16.2.6   Antigone and the Modern Crisis of Family

In fact, Butler's approach to the question of Antigone's significance is shaped by her own position as a gender theorist in an era when the notion of family has emerged as a site of intense struggle, pulled between conventional definition and radical transformation. This is a time, she says, in which "the Vatican protests against homosexuality not only as an assault on the family but also on the notion of the human" (*AC*, 22).[10] The stakes could not be higher. This is a time when, owing to migration, exile, global displacements, and changing conceptions of sexuality, the family is being reconfigured in all kinds of ways, where "positions are hardly clear, where the place of the father is dispersed, where the place of the mother is multiply occupied or displaced, where the symbolic in its stasis no longer holds" (*AC*, 23). In the light of these interests, Butler offers "another reading" in which Antigone "exposes the socially contingent character of kinship" (*AC*, 6). Antigone's predicament offers "an allegory for the crisis of kinship: which social arrangements can be recognized as legitimate love, and which human losses can be explicitly grieved as real and consequential loss?" That predicament exposes the "precarious character" of the norms of kinship and gender (*AC*, 24).

As against the arguments of many others in the Hegelian legacy who affiliate Antigone with the claims of kinship, Butler states:

> Antigone represents not kinship in its ideal form but its deformation and displacement, one that puts the reigning regimes of representation into crisis and raises the question of what the conditions of intelligibility could have been that would have made her life possible, indeed, what sustaining web of relations makes our lives possible, those of us who confound kinship in the rearticulation of its terms? (*AC*, 24)

So what Antigone's predicament brings into question is not just kinship or gender but the entire social and ideological structure of representation, the very language in which state power and its relation to individuals – in family settings or otherwise – is embodied. Elsewhere, Butler describes Antigone as "living within death, dying within life" (*AC*, 67). We could add that if we consider all the meanings of "death" that we have encountered in Hegel's analysis of the drama – death as an act of nature, death as the realm of the divine, death as marking the "duty" of woman, death as the leaving of family for "masculine" universality – we can see here how Antigone's "death," occurring as it does on all these levels, undermines any clear distinctions between them, both in Sophocles' time and now.

---

[10] Some have detected a softening of attitudes toward homosexuality in the Vatican of Pope Francis – as, for example, in statements he made on October 12, 2014 – though there has been no change in the church's official stance.

16.2.7 Elements of Butler's Creative Misreading

While Butler's reading is brilliantly creative inasmuch as it takes *Antigone* as an allegory of issues that confront the very substance of social life today, her reading of Hegel is perhaps one-sided. She claims that in the state's "necessary aggression against womankind" and the individualism it fosters, the state "substitutes itself for womankind, and that figure of woman is at once absorbed and jettisoned … Thus Hegel's text trans-mutes Antigone in such a way that her criminality loses the force of the alternative legality that it carries" (*AC*, 37). But this doesn't seem to be true. Hegel makes it very clear that both laws are equally valid and equally one-sided; neither can exist without the other. It's precisely the Greek state's inability to harmonize these sides that leads to its dissolu-tion. There's no mention in Hegel's text of human law or Creon as some-how emerging victorious; we have seen that for Hegel there can be no victory in this situation.[11]

Equally unsubstantiated is Butler's assertion that the state knows enough about divine laws to "oppose them violently" and to view them as "that which must be contained, subordinated, and opposed" (*AC*, 39). This assertion appears to lack a foundation either in Hegel's text or in the play itself. There's no *intrinsic* opposition between divine law and human law; indeed, Hegel states repeatedly the former is the basis and origin of the latter. In Sophocles' text, it can't be said that Creon is unattuned to the demands of divine law. He understands the importance of the rites of burial and states that Eteocles "shall be buried in his grave with every rite/of sanctity" (ll. 215–16). We recall that the divine law for Hegel is not reducible to particularity; in fact, it embodies another form of uni-versality, perhaps more genuine than the parochial universality of the state. Haemon even states that "the natural sense [φρένας, repeating the same word used by Creon] that the gods breed/in men is surely the best of their possessions" (ll. 734–5). When Antigone points out that the god of death demands these rites for both brothers, he replies that "the good

---

[11] In fact, various writers have argued powerfully for the opposite. Allen Speight explains the impor-tance of Hegel's earlier reading of *Antigone* in the *Phenomenology* for his view of agency. Antigone's deed or action prefigures modern notions of conscience and actually carries more, not less, ethical weight than Creon's action, *Hegel, Literature, and the Problem of Agency* (Cambridge and New York: Cambridge University Press, 2001), pp. 48–64. Martha Nussbaum argues that Hegel intends to present both sides as harboring equal claims but could be interpreted as exhibiting a greater nobility in Antigone's action. *The Fragility of Goodness: Luck and Ethics in Greek Tragedy and Philosophy* (Cambridge and New York: Cambridge University Press, 1986), pp. 65–7.

man does not seek an *equal* share only,/with the bad" (ll. 571–2). Indeed, it would be inconsistent for Hegel unreservedly to support Creon, since this is hardly a rational state over which Creon rules. Creon is an autocrat who insists that he "must be obeyed in small things and in just/but also in their opposites" (ll. 718–19). So he insists on being obeyed even when he is wrong, which Hegel would hardly condone.

At the end of the play, Creon acknowledges his fault, acknowledges that it would be "best ... to have kept the old accepted laws" (ll. 1118–81). By the terms of Butler's own argument – that Antigone cannot be correlated unproblematically with kinship – neither can Creon be correlated unproblematically with the state. And Hegel's text acknowledges this fact, in the very sentence that Butler quotes: each must acknowledge the other law "as its own actuality." Creon even remarks how terrible it is for "opposition to destroy my very being" (l. 1159). As for correlating Antigone wholly with death, we might recall that she states:

> Neither among the living nor the dead
> do I have a home in common –
> neither with the living nor the dead.
> ἰὼ δύστανος,
> τοῦτ' ἐν βροτοῖσιν οὔτ' ἐν νεκροῖσιν
> μέτοικος οὐ ξῶσιν, οὐ θανοῦσιν.
> (ll. 898–900; 850–2)

It seems that, ultimately, even the universe of death cannot furnish a home for Antigone: she is to remain placeless, even in human schemes of otherness. But the idea that Hegel's "universal perspective" somehow annihilates the particular, leaving it entirely behind, is completely foreign to Hegel. Without the particular, there can be no universal, without the divine, no human, and without woman, no man.[12]

Overall, however, Irigaray and Butler illustrate two powerful modes of appropriating Hegel for feminist thought. Irigaray's "mimetic" feminist mode of reading Hegel shows that Hegel's treatment of woman effectively destabilizes the entire structure of his political state. For the contradiction between woman and man is also a contradiction between family and civil society; even more importantly, the necessary conflict between

---

[12] Some feminists – rightly, in my opinion – see the feminine as integral to the entire structure of the *Phenomenology*. See for example, the excellent account in Rakefet Efrat-Levkovich, "Reading the Same Twice Over: The Place of the Feminine in the Time of Hegelian Spirit," in *HPF*, pp. 159–70. *Hegel's Philosophy and Feminist Thought: Beyond Antigone?* ed. Kimberly Hutchings and Tuija Pulkkinen (New York: Palgrave MacMillan, 2010).

them reveals the divided or conflicted nature of both man and woman in capitalist society. As Irigaray sees it, the relation between subjects cannot simply be reduced to economic and other types of competition between atomistically conceived abstract individuals as dictated by the requirements of capital where, as Hegel himself acknowledged, property "corresponds ... to being itself." Irigaray acknowledges that Hegel's is "without doubt the most powerful of the Western philosophies," but it can itself be subjected to further dialectic. And sexual difference, the archetype of all real difference, is "the most powerful motor of a dialectic without masters or slaves." In this new dialectic, the natural (embodied in woman) does not have to be abolished in the spiritual (embodied in man). Rather, the spiritual in both men and women cultivates the natural (*ItY*, 49–53). As such, the subjectivity of both woman and man must be reconceived, partly through a transformation in language, in order to enable a process of mutual recognition that is not based on subordination and struggle with the other but rather an acceptance of the other's difference.

Butler also points a way toward harnessing Hegel's dialectic for reconceiving gender relations and the institution of the family in the late capitalist world. She valuably brings Antigone forward through history as a means of interrogating the contemporary scene as regards family, kinship, and sexuality. The same "horror and revulsion" that are compelled by incest, she suggests, are felt toward "lesbian and gay sex" and often toward various kinds of nontraditional parenting arrangements. While Antigone is "not quite a queer heroine," we might ask what is it in her act that is "fatal for heterosexuality in its normative sense" and what other ways of organizing sexuality might be considered. Kinship for us might signify "any number of social arrangements that organize the reproduction of material life" (*AC*, 71–2). Beyond these possibilities, says Butler, certain lines of psychoanalytic theory might take Antigone as a starting point. She is "the one with no place who nevertheless seeks to claim one within speech, the unintelligible as it emerges within the intelligible, a position within kinship that is no position" (*AC*, 76, 78). In other words, Antigone challenges the very terms of much psychoanalysis, based as this is upon normative conceptions of family relations, which she clearly transgresses. Moreover, Antigone becomes for Butler a symbol of all those – not just women – who suffer "social death," who suffer a deprival of rights as living beings, who are entombed in various forms of unfreedom. As such, "Antigone is the occasion for a new field of the human" (*AC*, 82).

CHAPTER 17

Historical Contexts of Hegel's Views on Women

In the last chapter we noted that Hegel was writing during the vast political upheavals of an earlier stage of capitalism. A number of feminists have addressed the need to situate Hegel's views within his own era. Seyla Benhabib argues that to assess Hegel's views in his historical context, we must take account of the "discursive horizon" of his time, including the views of progressive women of his time, of which he must have been aware.[1] She observes that Hegel's lectures on the philosophy of history demonstrate his profound awareness of the socially constructed nature of family and gender relations, which varied, as he himself documents, between cultures. And yet he considers only one model – the European bourgeois nuclear family – as rational and right (*FIH*, 30).[2] She grants that in certain respects Hegel's views were progressive: that he views the family as essential to the modern state and as embodying the "subjective moment" of freedom; that he is opposed to state regulation of family life; that he grants women certain legal rights; that, as an Enlightenment thinker and supporter of the French Revolution, he was in favor of the Civil Code of 1804 which increased women's rights. In these respects, Hegel was ahead of Prussian legal practices (*FIH*, 32–4).

On the negative side, says Benhabib, Hegel's views on love and sexuality were counter-Enlightenment and he was opposed to contemporary currents of female emancipation. She cites Mary Hargrave's remarks on the changes brought about by the Enlightenment and the French Revolution, which included how the minds of female intellectuals were stirred at this time. One of these, Caroline Schlegel, who later married Schelling, advanced more progressive notions of gender relations. Caroline was not only in the Jena circle, of which Hegel was a part,

---

[1] Seyla Benhabib, "On Hegel, Women, and Irony," in *FIH*, pp. 27–8.
[2] *Feminist Interpretations of G. W. F. Hegel*, ed. Patricia Jagentowicz Mills (University Park, PA: Pennsylvania State University Press, 1996).

but actually lived with Schelling and Hegel from 1801–3. She was "a flesh-and-blood example of what modernity, the Enlightenment and the French Revolution could mean for women." But Hegel "did not like what he saw." Hegel was not just falling prey to the prejudices of his time. In such women, he "saw the future and he did not like it" (*FIH*, 36–8).

We might add that Hegel may have had personal misgivings about Caroline, whose emancipated lifestyle was replete with scandal. While married to August Schlegel, she engaged in an affair with Schelling, whom she married in 1803. Amid further scandal, she was even accused of murdering her own daughter Auguste. Schiller referred to her as "Dame Lucifer,"[3] an appellation Hegel almost echoed in a letter after her death in observing how, according to some, "the Devil had fetched her."[4] While these scandals[5] no doubt contributed to the personal animosity between Caroline Schelling and Hegel, it cannot be denied that Hegel's disapproval of her independent spirit was part of a more general pattern in his attitude toward women.

Nonetheless, Hutchings and Pulkkinen contest Benhabib's view (*FIH*, 38) that Hegel's treatment of women was anachronistic. Historical scholarship, they suggest, shows that "Hegel's views fit with the gender ideology emerging at the time of the French Revolution – an ideology in which women were closely connected with 'love' and 'family' and simultaneously excluded from the emerging process of political democratization" (*HPF*, 4). Simone de Beauvoir also notes that the Revolution did very little to change the lot of women; there was a certain amount of feminist agitation which proposed, for example, a "Declaration of the Rights of Woman" in 1789, to match the "Declaration of the Rights of Man" actually adopted by the French National Assembly. The Revolution was essentially a middle-class phenomenon, respectful of middle-class values and institutions, and was accomplished almost exclusively by men. Though some rights were granted to women, the post-revolutionary Napoleonic Code greatly retarded women's emancipation, perpetuating their dependency in marriage; and various middle-class spokesmen, including Auguste Comte and Balzac, reaffirmed the vision of the

---

[3] Pinkard, *Hegel: A Biography*, pp. 111–12. Hereafter cited as *HB*.
[4] Letter to Immanuel Niethammer, October 4, 1809, in *Hegel: The Letters*, p. 205.
[5] It should be remembered that Hegel was hardly in a position to moralize regarding sexual morality; at the very time that he was working out his own ideas about sexual union in 1805–6, he was having an affair with his landlady, Christiana Johanna Burkhardt, who had given birth to their illegitimate son, Ludwig Fischer, in 1807 (*HB*, 192).

antifeminist bourgeoisie, which wished to exclude women from labor and public life (*SS*, 100–2).

As Beauvoir notes, all the European legal codes were based on canon law, Roman law, and Germanic law, all of which were unfavorable to women. In fact, women's legal status remained almost unchanged from the beginning of the fifteenth century until the nineteenth. The essential institutions that demanded such subordination were private property and the family. As the bourgeois class rose to power, it continued the basic patterns of subordination, allowing rights to widows and unmarried girls but not to married women. The rigorous monogamy required of the bourgeois family and woman's continued enslavement to the family gave rise to prostitution throughout Europe. The mechanisms of women's emancipation – including the technological and industrial revolutions, which destroyed landed property – and what Beauvoir called "the grand revolution of the nineteenth century, which transformed the lot of woman and opened for her a new era" (*SS*, 104) – did not occur until after Hegel's death. The first feminist congress, which gave its name to the movement, was not held until 1892, and women did not receive the vote in Germany until 1918 (*SS*, 94–7; 113–16). So it might plausibly be argued that Hegel's treatment of women is entirely in accord with the oppressive thought and practice of his time – which persisted through vast structural and ideological transformations of society effected through the Enlightenment, the French Revolution, and the industrial revolutions.

17.1   Feminist Consciousness in Hegel's Prussia

It's worth bearing in mind the overwhelmingly narrow attitudes toward women that predominated during Hegel's early years. The late eighteenth century in Prussia was rife with propaganda regarding women's domestic "destiny." The ideology of women as mere "supplements" to men drew upon an increasing separation between private and public spheres, confining women rigidly within the domain of household duties.[6] There was indeed a reaction against this ideology on the part of progressive-minded individuals. But any emerging feminist consciousness during this period

---

[6] Some of these developments are astutely traced by Ruth P. Dowson in her essay "'And This Shield Is Called Self-Reliance': Emerging Feminist Consciousness in the Late Eighteenth Century," in *German Women in the Eighteenth and Nineteenth Centuries: A Social and Literary History*, eds. Ruth-Ellen B. Joeres and Mary Jo Maynes (Bloomington: Indiana University Press, 1986), pp. 157–72. Hereafter cited as *GW*.

was desultory and hardly constituted a movement or formulated any coherent stance. Modern feminists have in fact remarked on the "slow and reluctant character" of the German women's movement well into the nineteenth century, way beyond Hegel's era.[7] The few writers espousing feminist views were usually not well-known during their own lifetimes. Theodor Gottlieb von Hippel's feminist manifesto *Über die bürgerliche Verbesserung der Weiber* (On Improving the Status of Women, 1792) was outspoken in its call for improving the lot of women but its author's name remained concealed until after his death. Other "feminist" thinkers such as Marianne Ehrmann and Emilie Berlepsch have remained "almost completely unrecognized" in even the history of feminist thought (*GW*, 157, 169).

Interestingly, Hippel's manifesto was published in the same year as Mary Wollstonecraft's *Vindication of the Rights of Woman* (1792). To some extent, both authors reacted against what Ruth Dowson calls the "ideology of supplementarity," but what is perhaps more pertinent in our context is that both were inspired by the ideals of the Enlightenment and French Revolution and their common program was to extend these ideals – of liberty, equality, civil rights, and the right to education and work – to women. But, again, there is a distinct contrast here to the views of Ehrmann and Berlepsch who, while advocating education and even "self-reliance" for women, proclaimed their acceptance of the doctrine of different "spheres" and even "destinies" for men and women (*GW*, 167–8). So we can certainly lay the charge against Hegel that not only did his commitment to French Revolutionary ideals evanesce somewhat in his later years but that his commitment to the actualization of freedom in world history was incomplete to begin with – leaving out a good half of the human race. On the other hand, our judgment might be tempered by the knowledge that even some of the most progressive women in Hegel's Prussia were starkly ambivalent regarding their own social situation and perhaps failed to perceive the broader implications of work as self-realization. Much of Hegel's philosophy might be based on this premise, but again, it is a realization he opens up only for men.

Hegel was not entirely unacquainted with the progressive women of his time. Not only did he know Caroline Schelling but he also exchanged letters with the novelist Caroline Paulus. Perhaps the most renowned free-thinking woman whose life intersected with Hegel's was Rahel

---

[7] See "Introduction," in *German Women in the Eighteenth and Nineteenth Centuries*, eds. Ruth-Ellen B. Joeres and Mary Jo Maynes, p. xiii.

Varnhagen – the wife of Hegel's friend Karl August Varnhagen von Ense and a leading figure in Berlin's Jewish circles and salon culture – toward whom Hegel appeared to condescend. She complained of Hegel's refusal to discuss ideas with her (*HB*, 482). Hegel must surely have been aware that Rahel was, as Deborah Hertz puts it, "a much-admired, much-discussed phenomenon," who was gifted with "widely-praised intellectual and social talents."[8] Moreover, from 1780 until 1806 (when French troops occupied Berlin), there were at least sixteen thriving salons in the city, and Rahel was the most renowned of the Jewish salonières (*GW*, 275).

There was probably a complex of factors at work in Hegel's attitude here. Rahel was not only a woman but an outspoken woman ("I am as unique as the greatest figure on this earth"), a Jewish woman striving for assimilation into the upper echelons of Berlin society (*GW*, 275, 283). Among other things to Hegel's distaste would have been Rahel's association with Romantic outlooks and Romantic ideologies of free love, which he saw as a threat to the family as an ethical institution. She enjoyed a devoted following of young men who were soon to become some of the founding figures of Romanticism in Germany. These included Wilhelm and Alexander von Humboldt, Johann Fichte, Ludwig Tieck, and Friedrich Schlegel.

17.2   Hegel and Marie

Such was Hegel's opposition to Romanticism that he could not help censuring it in his own fiancée, Marie von Tucher. All of Hegel's attitudes toward women – in their often self-contradictory nature – are well adumbrated in his feelings for her, in the derogation of her entire sex implicit in the very depth of his solicitousness toward her. On the one hand, while courting, he wrote for her a poem containing the following lines, which might be seen as containing some Romantic characteristics:

> I expand myself to you, as you to me.
> May what isolates us go up in fire, cease to be.
> For life is life only as reciprocated,
> By love in love is it alone created.

(*HL*, 237)

---

[8] Deborah Hertz, "Inside Assimilation: Rebeca Friedländer's Rahel Varnhagen," in *German Women in the Eighteenth and Nineteenth Centuries*, eds. Ruth-Ellen B. Joeres and Mary Jo Maynes, pp. 271, 277.

In expressing the need for a larger unity that incorporates individualities, as well as in their emphasis on love, these verses might loosely be termed Romantic.[9] But these qualities characterize many outlooks beyond Romanticism (for example, Neoplatonism and various strands of Christian theology), and we might argue that what they essentially express is a more characteristic Hegelian motif of reciprocity, mutual recognition, and the need for self-transcendence or self-completion in an other. Indeed, around this time, Hegel was anxious that he might have offended or hurt Marie by his "pedantic" censure of her Romantic opinions. Having stayed awake for much of a summer night in 1811, he explained in a letter to her that "marriage is essentially a religious bond" and that romantic love can "only be completed by religion and the sense of duty; for only therein do all particularizations of the temporal self step aside, particularizations which in actuality could cause trouble" (*HL*, 243). Hegel also insists that their respective love for each other cannot be distinguished, and in a subsequent letter to a friend he rejoices in how Marie has completely transformed "my relations with myself and the world through this relation, which alone gives a human being to himself and gives him completion" (*HL*, 245).

What is expressed in these letters of Hegel and his versification are the same notions of equality and reciprocity that he attributes to the marriage relation in both his earlier and later writings. But, as we have seen, this is only half the story and is contradicted by the other half. For Hegel, this reciprocity is an "immediate" one, existing only within the sphere of intuition that governs family relationships. While advocating such intuitive reciprocity and equality, Hegel very emphatically reaffirms the "doctrine of spheres," whereby only the male can seek his fortune in public spheres that extend beyond the family into civil society and political life. But, equally important, we might recall that this separation of spheres, this division of labor, corresponds for Hegel with a difference in innate abilities, whereby the man's mind is attuned to science and rational thought, while the woman is restricted to sensuality and intuition.

---

[9] Hegel's longer poem "Eleusis," written in 1796 to his friend, the poet Holderlin, is much more Romantic in its tone and theme. The poem can be seen in its original German with a good English translation by Alan W. Grose in *The Philosophical Forum*, XXXIII: 3 (2002), 312–17. In fact, this rather beautiful poem bears sustained comparison to Wordsworth's "Lines Composed a Few Miles above Tintern Abbey," not of course in poetic quality but in its appreciation of nature, which develops from a sensual to a more intellectual and spiritual engagement. But by the time Hegel was courting Marie, this youthful Romanticism had subsided and become a target of Hegel's derision.

What is rather astounding – at least from the perspectives of our own era – is that Hegel could voice and apply this distinction to his own fiancée even in his state of solicitude, even when he was anxious over how she might react. In another letter to her written in the summer of 1811, he basically informs her that, unlike him, she is incapable of sustained or connected thought. He states that he does not attribute her Romantic views to her own self. Rather,

> I view them as lying merely within your reflection; that you do not think, know, or gain an overview of them in their [*Ihrer*] logical connection ...
> ... do not forget that if I condemn maxims, I too easily lose consciousness of the way in which they are actual in determinate individuals – in you, for instance. Nor should you forget that such maxims appear before my eyes too earnestly in their universality, in their logical consequences, extended results, and applications ... I know ... that maxims, when they contradict character, are still less important in the case of women than men. (*HL*, 245)

So the prospective husband is so disposed to think in terms of universals that he finds it difficult to acknowledge their operation in particular persons – such as his fiancée! And the prospective wife, according to Hegel, can be excused for her views on the grounds that they are irremediably particular and cannot be unified into any coherent picture in her mind! In a letter of 1811 that Hegel wrote to Caroline Paulus, where Hegel referred to her husband as "lord and master," Marie playfully interjected within the margins the following sentence: "Despite the length at which my lord and master goes on in his epistle, and as humble as the little corner he assigns me may be, I nonetheless know that the good Caroline Paulus will not lose sight of me" (*HL*, 248). No doubt these words are tinged with irony, and they drew an ironic response from Caroline, but one can't help wondering what the real thoughts of both women were.

At any rate, that Hegel could write the foregoing words to his own fiancée shows, perhaps, that his views of women do not spring from any personal misogyny but rather merely replicate the predominant patriarchal conceptions of his era. So overwhelming were these preconceptions that they were in fact repeated and rehearsed by even the progressive and more emancipated women of Hegel's time – perhaps partly through fear of social ostracism. Hegel's comments show also that his philosophical views about marriage and women were deeply embedded in the ethics of his personal life. Having said this, inasmuch as Hegel fails to transcend conventional presuppositions, this surely deviates from the more radical nature of his earlier enterprises in logic, metaphysics, and political thought. Perhaps, most importantly, Hegel's views of women and family cohere with his general advocacy of the institutions of emerging capitalism, whose general revolutionary impetus, operative initially in the economic realm, did not extend to the status of women until well after Hegel's death. The revolutionary nature of capitalism in all its aspects was not realized until at least the twentieth century. Arguably, Hegel's later political views "matured" into greater complicity with the actual. But his views on women and family appear to have stayed more or less the same, to have been imbibed from his surroundings, and to have been stubbornly maintained despite the presence of highly intellectual women who clearly disconfirmed the prevailing stereotypes. As we have seen, his conceptions of woman remained, even in his later writings, enchained to the myth he found in *Antigone*, buried alive within superstitions and stereotypes enduring into modern times.

17.3   Hegel's Legacy for Feminism and Gender

What, then, does Hegel have to offer for contemporary feminist theory and politics? This question was the focus of a discussion among four feminist philosophers – Nancy Bauer, Kimberly Hutchings, Tuija Pulkkinen, and Alison Stone – a highly instructive exchange, on which I would like to comment and elaborate here.[10] There was, naturally, some disagreement among them on various points, and I will focus on those that enjoyed a relative consensus. The general framework of their interchange was an impetus to reconceive gender and gender relations within the larger economic and ideological contexts of capitalism. To begin with, they were agreed that Hegel's concept of recognition, in Beauvoir's appropriation of it, was a "founding insight" of modern feminism. Stone notes a more recent example in Nancy Fraser's view that gay/lesbian/queer politics is primarily a struggle for cultural recognition and that the whole idea of a politics of recognition rests on Hegelian concepts of the subject. Feminism might use these concepts in articulating "the gendered structure of our basic self-understanding" (*HPF*, 234, 241). As Bauer points out, Hegel helps us to see that recognition involves acknowledging a person as both subject and object; as such, it is a concept that should be transposed to the political level (*HPF*, 242).

[10] Nancy Bauer, Kimberly Hutchings, Tuija Pulkkinen, and Alison Stone, "Debating Hegel's Legacy for Contemporary Feminist Politics," in *Hegel's Philosophy and Feminist Thought: Beyond Antigone? Ed.* Kimberly Hutchings, Tuija Pulkkinen (New York: Palgrave MacMillan, 2010), pp. 233–52.

In fact, Hutchings observes an agreement among all these thinkers that Hegel's master–slave dialectic can be used to draw attention to the ways in which human existence is "warped and distorted in a world structured around hierarchical sex/gender difference ... this is about thinking/defining human being in different kinds of ways, drawing on Hegelian/Beauvoirian insights" (*HPF*, 245). Stone suggests that the politics of recognition can never be a politics of radical change as long as what is recognized are preexisting social identities. In Hegel's *Philosophy of Right*, she adroitly observes, "mutual recognition means property-owners respecting one another within a market economy." But we can fully recognize one another "only by transforming our identities, especially our gendered identities," and thereby transforming the kinds of subjects we are (*HPF*, 246). A feminist politics of recognition must then be socialist, but the problem here is that, since the collapse of communism in 1989, it is increasingly hard to "imagine alternative economic arrangements to capitalism." And Hegel shows us that particular forms of recognition rest on given economic and social structures. So we can use the early, more radical, Hegel to acknowledge the historicity of the economic configurations under which we live (*HPF*, 246–7).

A second aspect of this legacy, as agreed by most of these thinkers, is Hegel's dialectical logic which Irigaray, for example, uses to theorize psychical life whereby subjects proceed from a maternal origin, the "immediate unity," and achieve separation, only to "return" through circuitous routes to their source. Hegel was, above all, a critic of binary thinking and in this he "shares a great deal of ground with feminists who argue that binary thinking underpins ... a gendered social order" (*HPF*, 234–5). He was a *contemporary* thinker, aware of the effects of current movements upon thought, hence his dialectic embraces the "incessant, restless motion of thought," which is never arrested and always moves on, as it confronts increasing complexity and the need to confront differing perspectives. The hope, say these theorists, is that Hegel can help us to think differently – and differentially – about the categories of sex and gender, as well as the conditions under which language operates (*HPF*, 236–8). On the contemporariness of feminism, Pulkkinen adds that issues of recognition for sexual minorities, questions of the scarf and veil, and transgender politics were not considered to be feminist issues in Hegel's time, and he might have had interesting insights on these. Indeed, the idea of "transgender" as "going beyond and turning the two sexes into something new" is intrinsically dialectical (*HPF*, 240–1). And Bauer suggests that "what counts as the feminist point of view at any given time ...

is bound to be unstable" (*HPF*, 243). There is, as Hutchings observes, a consensus that "radical political change for feminists is bound up with thinking dialectically about gender" (*HPF*, 245). Hegelian feminists, she remarks, must remember that gender is not equivalent to "women," nor are "women" equivalent to one other (*HPF*, 246).

A third important dimension of Hegel for feminism is that, as "a diagnostician of an emergent modernity," Hegel had important insights into the "structural position of women within the modern state," which still resonate in our era of the "globalization of capitalism." In particular, he shows how the realm of productive labor, property, and exchange depends on the realm of "productive labor and care." The distinction between these two realms, says Hutchings, is essential to both capitalism and the subordination of women (*HPF*, 235). Reinforcing this, Stone acknowledges that, despite his collusion in perpetuating this distinction, "perhaps Hegel can help us to think about how family structure oppresses women" (*HPF*, 241). Given the political contexts of Hegel's writings, says Hutchings, we might be impelled by his inquiries to pose such questions as: "Are feminist goals compatible with liberal, market societies and states?" (*HPF*, 245).

Bauer adds that Hegel can make us see the contradiction between what is heralded as a given truth or ideology and the terms in which these are expressed. Many feminists, she observes, "continue to talk as though Beauvoir had never existed" and thereby fail to make "serious attempts to shift the ways that people construe themselves as gendered beings ... This is why for years I've been calling for a return to Beauvoir – which amounts, of course, to a return to Hegel" (*HPF*, 238–9). If the role of philosophy is to express "the *Zeitgeist* in terms that bring to light its internal contradictions and their intolerableness," the model of feminist philosophy is furnished by Beauvoir, whose *The Second Sex* is "the most influential text ever written in the service of advancing feminist aims" (*HPF*, 248). In contrast with much feminist work which is highly academic and closes off the possibility of impelling any broader change, Beauvoir speaks with "full philosophical depth and rigor to ordinary women ... Here, it goes without saying, Beauvoir did *not* take Hegel as a model" (*HPF*, 248). Pulkkinen is not so happy with Beauvoir as a model. She believes that there is "a deep heterosexuality embedded in her existential project, which builds on the human as a couple" and that Hegel could "inspire feminist thought more toward change and an open future, instead of maintaining the aspiration of revealing the human condition" (*HPF*, 249–50). Hutchings adds the important insight that "a Hegelian feminism" acknowledges that our being is "fundamentally intersubjective" (*HPF*, 252).

In general, these four feminist philosophers give articulate and powerful voice to the various levels and refractions of the feminist encounter with Hegel. I would want to add one more voice to this discussion, that of the political philosopher Seyla Benhabib. We saw earlier that Benhabib outlined three basic ways in which feminists could engage with the male traditions. What is pertinent here is her suggestion that feminists must approach these traditions with a "doubled vision," with one eye viewing what the tradition has trained it to see, while the other looks for what has been hidden or repressed. I would suggest that this itself is a Hegelian strategy, which would find more complete realization when the two "scenes" are placed into dialogue. On one side, what we see is the march of the dialectic and all the social configurations and political relations that have triumphed; on the other side, we see what Benhabib calls the "victims" of the dialectic, all those (people, nations, possible political configurations) that have been left behind, swept under the prayer mat of history. We cannot, says Benhabib, "disentangle the march of dialectic in Hegel's system from the body of the victims on which it treads" (*FIH*, 41). What remains of the dialectic is what Hegel "thought he could dispense with: irony, tragedy, and contingency." Benhabib offers a statement of the "ironic dialectic of modernity" as observed by Hegel:

> [F]reedom that becomes abstract legalism or selfish pursuit of economic satisfaction; wealth that could turn into its opposite and create extremes of poverty; moral choice that would end in a trivial project of self-aggrandizement; and an emancipated subjectivity that could find no fulfillment in its "other." (*FIH*, 41)

The Hegelian system, says Benhabib, repeatedly "expunges" these modes of dialectic; what women can do today is to "restore irony to the dialectic" by giving back to the victims their selfhood (*FIH*, 41). What Benhabib is describing here is the rampant individualism of civil society evoked in Hegel's *Philosophy of Right*.

Building on the insights of these feminist philosophers, we might add that we are living in an era which has all these characteristics of irony, of the second stage of the Hegelian dialectic. The domain of civil society, the domain of capitalism and economic competition, is the domain of males. Hegel is not only the philosopher of capitalism; he is the archetypal theorist of the bourgeois family. Significantly, in both he is Eurocentric as well as patriarchal. Kimberly Hutchings points out that if we are to make use of Hegel, this must be in spite of his ideological position on women, which was both patriarchal and at times misogynist (*Hutchings*, 1). We might say, then, that despite himself, Hegel points toward a dissolution of the concepts of "woman," "gender," and "sexuality" as fixed categories, and toward a recognition of them as economic, ideological, and political constructions. Underlying this is a Hegelian approach to subjectivity itself which sees it defined in a process of social interaction and ever-changing according to its circumstances, both molded by objective institutions but also transforming these in its own evolving image. Crucially, Hegel helps us to see that individuality and subjectivity must be viewed in several contexts at once – family, civil society, state, gender, class, and numerous other settings – which has already proven to be a founding insight for feminist critical race theory. If a person is gay or black or Jewish, this is only one aspect of her overall identity, which is itself in flux, its various facets refracted differentially according to the demands of preoccupation and circumstance.

Many feminists have questioned the concept of reason, viewing it as coercive and embodying male traditions of thought. Hegel – again, despite himself – helps us to see that reason is itself historically conditioned and that it is not possessed of either a definite content or a rigid form. Reason itself and the way we understand it is capable of development in many directions. Not only does Hegel's dialectic impel us to challenge the fixed terms and oppositions of binary thinking, but it also impels us to situate those terms in an ever richer fullness of relation to other forces in the world; for example, we might ask how technology contributes to our visions of gender. Finally, if Hegel is the philosopher of modernity and capitalism, his work impels us to ask how subjectivity and femininity are manufactured in our own time, how women's status as subjects and objects is commodified, and how the nature of their oppression might be understood in both local and global terms. We need a comprehensiveness of vision informed by particulars, by the experiences of actual women in their diversity, in order to continue to end this oppression.

Epilogue: *The Futures of Theory: Towards a Dialectical Humanism*

We have been on a long journey. It has taken us through the structure of Hegel's dialectic and the way that this is shaped internally by Hegel's historical moment, located at the dawn of modern capitalism. We have also traced the foundations of literary theory in the unraveling of this historical moment as its ramifications have spread across the globe. Hegel's encounter with capitalism spans a number of areas that have been addressed by various branches of literary theory: the nature of identity and language, the formation of human subjectivity through the master–slave dialectic of recognition, the dual negating operations of language and labor, the connections between economics and culture, and the status of women, as well as the notions of reason, progress, and history. We have seen in some detail how these Hegelian notions have shaped various seminal branches of literary theory – deconstruction, Marxism, and gender studies – in their orientation toward liberal humanism even as theory reacted against the accommodation of these notions within Hegel's totalizing historical and epistemological scheme.

E.1 Theory's Posthuman Face: The Rise of Particularism

E.1.1 *Historical Context*

As we have seen, Hegel's dialectic is born in the very struggle to accommodate a bourgeois and utilitarian economic outlook – that he saw as characterizing the Enlightenment – within a larger ethical framework, the kind of totality posited by philosophers of Romanticism such as Adam Müller. The German Romantics excoriated Adam Smith, but Hegel's dialectic was intended to preserve Smith's insights within a framework that transcended mere economism. What I have argued throughout this book is that Hegel's dialectic is internally structured by its need to resolve the contradictions of capitalism – contradictions between family and civil society, man and woman, civil society and state, between self-interest and communal interest, ideals of freedom and imperial enslavement of others, between individual identity and self-estrangement, between God and humankind.

I have argued that the underlying perspective of literary theory is necessarily a product of the entire framework of contradictions in capitalism, resulting from the collapse of any totalizing vision. Essentially, this perspective is one that denies universality or teleology in any form; it resists any totalizing or historicizing impulse; and it is skeptical of the powers of rationality and all claims to certainty of knowledge. It derides the notion of an objective world or even of any coherent subjectivity. What it affirms most fundamentally is the value of irreducible particularity, the irreducible importance of the local, the regional, the experiential. Of course, not all modern theory is premised with equal weight upon this assertion, but, as we have seen in considerable detail, it even operates in recent Marxist and feminist criticism. Bourgeois society, for Hegel, embodied the second stage of dialectic, that of unresolved contradiction, externalization, alienation, skepticism; and much literary theory, as Derrida acknowledges, situates itself at this stage, refusing any advance toward a third stage, toward some totalizing integration. Late capitalist theory is the theory of difference and particularism.

Modern theory of course is not new or unique in its critique of totalization. This critique itself has a long history, going back not only to the heterological perspectives of Schopenhauer and Nietzsche but also to the widespread growth of positivism through various fields in the nineteenth century, the analytic philosophies of Bertrand Russell and G. E. Moore, which reacted against the neo-Hegelian absolutism of F. H. Bradley and Bernard Bosanquet, as well as logical positivism, existentialism, and phenomenology. Moreover, just as philosophy unburdened itself of totalizing claims, so political economy, psychology, and other "sciences" eventually saw themselves as preoccupied with merely specific subsystems of society,[1] each defining its field as independent of all others – in a broadly positivistic movement that Marx saw as characterizing the increasingly specialized structure of knowledge in capitalism. In some ways, the modern path into particularism can be traced back to Marx himself, who saw Hegel as affirming a radical humanism but betraying it by situating it

---

[1] For a useful discussion of the transformation of the social sciences, see Jürgen Habermas, *The Theory of Communicative Action: Volume One: Reason and the Rationalization of Society*, trans. Thomas McCarthy (1981; rpt. Boston: Beacon Press, 1984), pp. 2–5. Hereafter cited as *TCA*.

within larger, abstract totalities. This trend eventually overtook even literary criticism, as manifested in various kinds of formalism and the New Criticism. Hegel was the last major philosopher to construct a totalizing system, a system which collapsed into the various strands of thought previously enumerated.

We have already explored the diverse ways in which theory has challenged the totalizing impulse of Hegel's philosophy and has asserted the value of the particular. We will briefly look at the latest modes of this particularist orientation as in the proliferation of posthumanist and digital studies. I will then argue that this emphasis on the particular not only disables theory from addressing the problems – ethical, intellectual, social – that it identifies, but also mires it within their constituting problematics as determined by the forces of the market. Finally, without pretending to assume that Hegel can unproblematically offer solutions in all these areas, I will show how his understanding of dialectic, reason, totality, and language might be useful in formulating a "dialectical humanism" founded on an appropriately complex understanding of human subjectivity.

E.1.2   Posthumanism

The rise of particularism, in both Marxist and non-Marxist theory, has assumed various forms of posthumanism, which has exhibited a number of trends over the last sixty years or so, including the "exorbitation" of language, the rejection of the ideas of history, subjectivity, objectivity, and the very notion of the "human." While its roots lay in the nineteenth century, it received a widespread impetus in the 1960s when thinkers as ideologically far apart as Levi-Strauss, Althusser, Lacan, Foucault, Derrida (and later Barthes and Deleuze) all proclaimed, in their various ways, the "end of man." What they generally shared was a structuralist or poststructuralist outlook that saw the human subject as merely a function of language, whose relational system was itself privileged to serve as the model for all other areas of inquiry and practice: kinship, economics, the unconscious, ideology, popular culture.[2] Many of these thinkers have reacted against the humanism they saw as embodied in Hegel's philosophy.

---

[2] For an insightful account and critique of these tendencies, see Perry Anderson, *In the Tracks of Historical Materialism* (1983; rpt. Chicago and London: University of Chicago Press, 1984), pp. 37–55. He uses the term "exorbitation" to indicate this prioritizing of language as a model.

Various recent theorists have seen the human as sharing existence with both the machine and the animal. They stress that the sphere of our moral concerns has thereby been expanded, extending to machines and computers.[3] N. Katherine Hayles argues that the body is basically translated into information.[4] Frank Furedi suggests that the (Hegelian) narrative of humanity transforming nature has been "recast as a story of environmental destruction."[5] Narratives of cyborgs, robots, computers,[6] and machines all ultimately pose the question of what it means to be human.[7] My connection to the world, and in fact to all relationality, it seems, has fallen under the sovereignty of the machine.[8]

Donna Haraway's prescient vision of the cyborg as a "cybernetic organism, a hybrid of machines and organism"[9] is articulated explicitly against the kind of dialectic advanced by Hegel. In this new mode of particularism, in this latest phase of capitalism, says Haraway, power and imperial domination are exercised primarily through information technology (*SCW*, 164–6, 171).[10] Hence, new methods of resistance must be adopted: the cyborg embodies a commitment to irony, a refusal of dialectical integration and appropriation of the other, a refusal of totalizing theory and a blurring of all boundaries (*SCW*, 170). In stark contrast to any Hegelian vision, reality is now seen as a system of information, created by technology, and is no longer an expression of collective, rational

---

[3] See for example the interesting discussions of subjectivity in Peter Singer, *The Expanding Circle: Ethics, Evolution, and Moral Progress* (Princeton, NJ: Princeton University Press, 1981), pp. 63–9; and in Richard Rorty, *Contingency, Irony, and Solidarity* (Cambridge: Cambridge University Press, 1989), pp. 23–43.

[4] N. Katherine Hayles, *How We became Posthuman: Virtual Bodies in Cybernetics, Literature, and Informatics* (Chicago and London: University of Chicago Press, 1999), pp. 193–4.

[5] Frank Furedi, "The Legacy of Humanism," in *Debating Humanism*, ed. Dolan Cummings (Exeter: Societas, 2006), p. 24. Hereafter cited as *DH*.

[6] Andy Miah, "Posthumanism: A Critical History," in *Medical Enhancements and Posthumanity*, eds. Bert Gordijin and Ruth Chadwick (New York: Routledge, 2007), pp. 8–10.

[7] It might be observed that much of the current anguish about the modern world initially arises from the development of nineteenth-century capitalism – hence Marx's *alienation,* Durkheim's *anomie,* and Weber's view that we live in an *iron cage* created for us by Calvinism and rationality. At root, such alienation might be seen as correlative with the shift from *Gemeinschaft* to *Gesellschaft,* from the personalized interactions of a community to the impersonal networks of a society, as described by the German sociologist Ferdinand Tönnies.

[8] Interestingly, Heidegger sees technology as "a mode ... of rendering beings manifest," "Letter on 'Humanism'," trans. Frank A. Capuzzi, in *Martin Heidegger: Pathmarks*, ed. William McNeill (1967; rpt. Cambridge and New York: Cambridge University Press, 1999), p. 259.

[9] Donna J. Haraway, *Simians, Cyborgs, and Women: The Reinvention of Nature* (New York: Routledge, 1991), p. 149. Hereafter cited as *SCW*. Chapter 8 of this book, cited here and entitled "A Cyborg Manifesto," was originally published in 1985.

[10] Edouard Glissant has observed that merely technological hegemony has allowed the West to sustain its domination of other cultures (*Between the Lines*, p. 70).

human subjectivity created through labor. The capitalist system uses fragmentary and specific performances of human-machine complexes, constructing and deconstructing them according to the needs of the market.

E.1.3   The Capitalist Machine

Deleuze and Guattari's book *Anti-Oedipus* (1972) is one of modern theory's archetypal modern statements of posthumanist anti-Hegelian philosophy. Again, this disavowal embodies a philosophy of irreducible singularity, an attempt to think the part without the whole, difference without identity, the particular in a state of perpetual flux, perpetual nonidentity. The authors take the idea that the "part" need have no relation to the "whole" from Lacan, who urges that the part "performs its role all by itself" (*AO*, 34). "We live today in the age of partial objects," proclaim the authors, and we no longer believe in "a dreary, colorless dialectic" of evolution (AO, 42). In a sense, the very notion of the "machine," as we come across it in Deleuze and Guattari, embodies the vision of a world consisting of fragments, breaks, of "pure" parts. And yet, as the authors acknowledge, there is indeed one overarching totality, the world system of capitalism – the "capitalist machine" – which is inescapable and unable to be transcended. It is this totality against which all parts or fragments ultimately derive their status and their signification (*AO*, 250–9).

Deleuze and Guattari formulate a starkly anti-Hegelian agenda of liberation: what they oppose to the repressive psychoanalysis of bourgeois society is "schizoanalysis." The central figure in this psycho-economic rebellion is the schizophrenic, who has no parents, has his own coordinates for situating himself, and scrambles all codes (*AO*, 20, 23). The figure of the "schizo" is a dissociated ego, cut off from the world, and located as a rupture or intrusion in the very flow of matter (*AO*, 19, 24–5). Like Derridean difference, the schizophrenic is meant to embody a refusal of dialectic, an arresting of it at its second stage of openness, and a resistance to progress to any unifying stage.[11]

---

[11] Theory's posthuman orientation could be read not as a movement toward the machine but toward reenchantment and the divine. Indeed, in the last decade or so, critics and scholars have talked of a "religious turn" in literary theory. Stanley Fish remarked in 2005 that the conventional "triumvirate of race, gender, and class" would be superseded by religion as the focus of literary study. Many recent literary and cultural theorists, notably Derrida, Levinas, Jean-Luc Marion, Richard Kearney, and Žižek, have produced important studies of religion. In 2006 a special issue of *English Language Notes* was devoted to the rising prominence of religion in literary theory. I have treated some of

E.1.4   The Digital Age

If, as Derrida, Deleuze, and Guattari suggest, the machine embodies unassimilable particularity, the emerging field of digital studies enables new modes of particularism. Johanna Drucker has argued that digital humanists have perpetuated the common mythology of "mathesis," which sees human thought processes and even art as proceeding according to rigid logical processes. The most basic precept of the digital humanities is the requirement to "disambiguate knowledge representation so that it operates within the codes of computational processing."[12] For example, for digital purposes, we might have to regard Rousseau's *Confessions* as biography *or* fiction *or* historical document. This subordination to computational protocols is an index of the discipline's alignment with "managerial methods" and, as with any ideological strategy, unexamined assumptions are allowed to be seen as "natural" (*SP*, 4–5).

Of course, digital media can facilitate subversion. Dara N. Byrne has argued that computer-mediated public spheres are important to the cultural identities of various groups.[13] But she acknowledges that these spheres are ultimately dominated by capital and ultimately serve corporate ventures (*RID*, 20–1). Hence, even challenges to the totalizing system are constrained from within – in their very form, their very expression – by the deep methodology of the system itself. As in every sphere, the digital is the latest form in which capital exerts its sovereignty. It is the current mode in which positivist culture rejects dialectic and adapts any Hegelian impulse toward totalization to the narrowly unifying protocols of the capitalist market. What Hegel called civil society uses the digital to infuse and overwhelm all other spheres.

E.2   Hegelian Legacies – for Theory and for Our World

These recent anti-rational, post-human, and even digital inflections of theory – notwithstanding a purported resistance to "factuality" – positivistically take as an unalterable fact the devolution of human subjectivity under contemporary capitalism to fragment, to performance,

---

these developments in another book, *Hegel and Empire: From Postcolonialism to Globalism* (London and New York: Palgrave Macmillan, 2017).

[12] Johanna Drucker, *SpecLab: Digital Aesthetics and Projects in Speculative Computing* (Chicago: University of Chicago Press, 2009), p. 5. Hereafter cited as *SP*.

[13] Dara N. Byrne, "The Future of (the) 'Race': Identity, Discourse, and the Rise of Computer-Mediated Public Spheres," in *Learning Race and Ethnicity: Youth and Digital Media*, ed. Anna Everett (Cambridge, MA: The MIT Press, 2008), p. 33. Hereafter cited as *RID*.

to machine, and reconfigurable object.[14] But I would argue that this debilitating reduction, in order to be both understood and overcome, requires precisely the positing of *broader* contexts and unities, not an even deeper retreat into particularism and "difference." It requires the positing of a human subject as an individual with basic needs and rights, imbued with political and moral agency. What needs to be attacked (and reconfigured) is not humanism *per se* but rather a purported humanism that has in fact *failed* to be human, that has privileged certain groups, certain races, and certain cultures.

In general, liberal humanism is at an impasse, mired in its inability to articulate any connection between particular and universal – on intellectual, political, and ethical levels. And theory's endeavor to work through this stagnancy has largely mimed liberal humanism's impulse to transcend itself only immanently, by turning inward, by delving ever more deeply into its own past configurations and reconstituting them from within, contorting them into subversive or oppositional guises. Even in its antihumanist and posthumanist strains, theory has often merely deepened liberal humanism's impetus to argue ever more intensely and intricately for the irreducibility of the particular, delving further and further into the unconscious, into pre-linguistic drives. But this path, already well-worn, is stale and has led to nothing but dead ends. To follow the Foucauldian and Deleuzian agenda of freeing political action from any kind of totality or unity, to prioritize multiplicity and difference, and to seek abstractly the proliferation of desire – all this seems to be ineffectual without recourse to specific political interventions whose rationale is capable of inviting consensus.[15]

As we have argued throughout this book, Hegel can point us in directions beyond this impasse. Needless to say, Hegel's influence spans numerous vast fields and no single book could do justice to the depth and range of this impact. But we can at least indicate here some of the major ways in which Hegel might point a way forward for the fields that comprise literary theory regarding issues that remain of vital importance

---

[14] As Timothy Brennan observes, the discourses of posthumanism base themselves on a "homology with the latest theories of the metropolis's industries of science and technology," *The Oxford Handbook of Postcolonial Studies,* ed. Graham Huggan (Oxford: Oxford University Press, 2013), pp. 158–9.

[15] Michael C. Behrent issues a powerful challenge to many conventional readings of Foucault: "How is it that the man who is arguably the most discussed thinker of our era seems simultaneously essential and woefully inadequate to conceptualizing what is perhaps the critical issue of our age – the hegemony of globalized liberalism?" *Foucault and Neoliberalism,* eds. Daniel C. Zamora and Michael C. Behrent (Cambridge, UK and Malden, MA: Polity Press, 2016), p. 183.

to our world. I will focus here on what I believe to be five areas in which we can still benefit from engaging with Hegel's thought: (1) dialectical thinking, (2) our understanding of identity and subjectivity, (3) our need to rehabilitate the notion of reason, (4) our reconfiguring the notion of "totality" in the light of Hegel's idea of the "concrete universal," and (5) considering how Hegel's legacy in these areas might point in the direction of a "dialectical humanism."[16]

E.2.1 Dialectical Thinking

If Hegel's legacy can be summed up in one word, it is surely "dialectic." As we have seen in detail through many chapters, the dialectic is a mode of thinking that is dynamic. It views not only the world of phenomena as fluid, as moments in a process, but the very process of thought as always developing, always self-correcting. It is a mode of thought that is both relational and historical, always insisting that any entity must be understood in its relations with other entities and in its developing contexts. We have found that many recent theorists reject the notion of dialectic as the product of a closed metaphysical system. Žižek and Jameson, for example, regard it as "open." And Kristeva sees the possibility of dialectic moving to a fourth stage. Indeed, Hegel himself characterizes the ending of one dialectic as furnishing the ground for a further dialectic, in a potentially endless progression. At the root of dialectical progression lies the notion of negativity, of refusing the world as it is merely given to us. In other words, it is incumbent upon us to transform that world – through the two modes of negation, language and labor – so that it truly expresses who we are, our deepest desires and dreams. And through transforming the world, we transform ourselves, overcoming what is merely "given" in our selves and rising to our highest potential.

Hence, dialectic is far more than a mode of thought. It is the means whereby we create ourselves and the world. Yet in Hegel's hands, the dialectic is specific to the movements of capitalism, on many levels. To begin

---

[16] This is a term used by John Edward Toews in his superb study *Hegelianism: The Path toward Dialectical Humanism, 1805–1841* (Cambridge: Cambridge University Press, 1980). But the emphasis of his book is on the humanist "inversion" of Hegel's philosophy by members of the left-Hegelian school up until 1841. Moreover, he understands "dialectical" humanism as essentially focused on a structure of human essence and existence which is dialectical inasmuch as it mediates between individual and communal being, consciousness and existence, theory and practice (pp. 356–68). My use of the term, as suggesting a humanism informed by what we have described in some detail as dialectical principles, is rather different.

with, the very process of thought is imperialistic inasmuch as it must negate or overcome the other. Thought must find in any object it confronts its own operations. Hegel goes so far as to say that, in the object, reason "seeks and finds only itself" (*Enc.* §467 Zus). He describes thought as "taking possession" of the object as "its own property" (*Enc.* § 468).

In its character as intrinsically dominating and possessive, thought – and hence subjectivity itself – is defined by this "negative" orientation toward both the world and itself, as well as toward others. For Hegel, language is the very mode of this negation. Language is an act of subjugation, which destroys the independent existence of things and recreates them in the mind's image. We might recall here that Hegel defined consciousness itself as "the sign in general." Hence, as against his many detractors, the operation of thought for Hegel is hardly abstract; it is the corollary of labor in an active overcoming of the world. Of course, the world that needs to be negated in Hegel's eyes – on many levels, religious, economic, social, and political – is the world bequeathed by feudalism, hence Hegel's dialectic in its very conception is revolutionary. Once the feudal order is overcome, it is arguable that Hegel sees the dialectic as stabilized, and reposing in absolute knowledge; but, like many others, I have argued against such an interpretation, urging that Hegel's Prussia hardly embodied his vision of the ideal State. In fact, we have seen that the bourgeois state, in Hegel's eyes, is not stable. It is intrinsically restless. As Hegel characterizes it, the capitalist market itself exhibits an outward, expansive, dialectical movement. Not only is capitalism intrinsically imperialistic in terms of necessary economic expansion, but it is sustained by an adventurous mentality that always seeks to encounter and overcome the other. So, the process of subjectivity, of language, of the world, and specifically of capitalism all display the same dialectical movement. And this movement is intended to situate the world of individuality or singularity – which is conflicted at many levels – within a larger, harmonizing context.

The dialectic, then, is a powerful way of engaging with the world and with ourselves. It is intrinsically revolutionary, suggesting that whatever is merely given is incomplete and needs to be developed in the light of its own potential and of more universal interests. Throughout this book, we have tried to show that various branches of theory have treated Hegel's dialectic in numerous and often conflicting ways, because that dialectic is itself polysemic, dynamic, self-criticizing, and ultimately *open*.[17] Despite

---

[17] While Levinas, Derrida, Lyotard, and Deleuze view Hegel as a totalizing thinker, we have seen that other theorists such as Žižek (*HI*, 4–6), Negri (*HI*, 38–44), and Jameson (*VD*, 4–5, 10) regard the

Hegel's own views, which are patriarchal and Eurocentric, his dialectic points toward a dissolution of *all* concepts – including "woman," "man," "gender," "race," and even "God" – as fixed categories, and to a supersession of binary thinking (characteristic of the Understanding) by more inclusive modes of thought (characteristic of Speculative Reason). In Hegel's hands, the very notions of Understanding and Reason are historical evolutions, and, as we can now see, the potential of dialectic reaches into the depths of our rethinking of issues such as identity, subjectivity, and gender, as well as the fraught notions of reason and totality, with the implication that all of these may have for our endeavors to reconceive the very notion of the "human."

E.2.2   *Understanding Identity and Subjectivity*

It emerged earlier that Hegel's conception of identity arose within his attempt to integrate the insights of bourgeois economics into an ethical framework. In general, Hegel shows us in his analysis of capitalism that human subjectivity and personality are deeply embedded within deeply intersecting contexts which problematize the connection of universal and particular – of property, class relations, family, gender, the individualistic and imperialistic nature of a market economy, and broader ethical norms. If Hegel is the philosopher of identity-in-difference, he is also the philosopher of intersectionality. Much literary theory – as in the entire field of Critical Race theory – is premised on this deeply Hegelian notion. I am never just a black woman; indeed, I am never just black or just woman; my identity is always a shifting focus of various points of intersection between class, ethnicity, nationality, age, gender, economic status, religion, and so many other factors. And, if I call myself a "white" man, I am "burdened" under layers of fiction and metaphor, under figures of speech and thought embedded in imperial history which have fictionalized my very being: we inevitably know ourselves – and others – not only through

---

dialectic as open rather than closed. Mark C. Taylor also sees an intrinsic openness or "restlessness" in Hegel's absolute. Effecting a "double" reading of Hegel and Derrida each through the other, and influenced by Jean Luc Nancy's conception of "infinite restlessness," Taylor argues that Hegel's absolute is characterized by a restless passage between infinite and finite: "Might this infinite restlessness be Hegel's Absolute, which, contrary to his own intentions can be itself only by not being itself?" Indeed, Taylor sees freedom itself as "inwardly divided" and as characterizing creative imagination. In this way, Hegel provides guidance in how we might preserve freedom that is under assault in the era of late capitalism, as well as how we might transcend sectarian difference (*HI*, 91–4, 109–11). In like manner, Furedi argues that humanism itself should be regarded as open and resisting dogma or fixity of ideas (*DH*, 22–3).

fictions but *as* fictions. Again, such an understanding of intersectionality as fictive is embedded in Hegel's conception of language.

Moreover, Hegel demonstrates that capitalism structures the very ways in which we are able to think about human identity. He anticipates, at a profounder level than is usually acknowledged, Marx's notion of alienation. But, more than Marx, he understands that the human subject is internally configured by its commercial orientation. Perhaps inspired by Locke and by Smith who viewed the human as essentially a "trading animal," Hegel defines the human self in terms of its capacity to *possess*. The self at this stage of history is in its very conception a bourgeois self. Hegel even states that a person achieves rationality initially only in his property, and that we have an "absolute right of appropriation" over all things (PR, §41, Add, 44). We have seen that, in its endless quest to integrate all otherness into its own ever expansively mediated identity, Hegelian subjectivity is a microcosm of the outward movement of capital. Hegel shows, further, that there is an internal connection between property relations and reason, between economic existence and intellectual-ethical life.

Again anticipating Marx, Hegel saw also a profound connection between subjectivity and what Žižek characterizes as the new "universal" that is money. Hegel's views on capitalism have a particular resonance today when health, education, and leisure are all organized around economic imperatives. And, while Hegel saw that machines could have an emancipative function, he thought the increasing reliance on machines could lead to a mechanistic human subjectivity, reduced even in its own eyes to thinghood. As we have seen throughout this book, this insight has been taken up by many literary theorists, including Horkheimer, Adorno, Benjamin, Deleuze, and Guattari, who have analyzed capitalism's manufacturing of machinic dissolutions of subjectivity. Hegel shows that the human subject in civil society is always inwardly divided between personal and general aims, always in a restless struggle. As such, he furnishes the groundwork for reconfiguring the human subject in many branches of theory beyond Marxism, as in Kristeva's view of the human subject as intrinsically pathological under capitalism, or Deleuze and Guattari's conception of the "schizo" as a kind of anti-subject.

Indeed, as we saw in Chapter 17, Hegel's notion of identity opens up new paths for feminism and gender theory. His exclusion of women from the historical process and his assessment of women's role in bourgeois society is germane to our own endeavors to understand gender today. Following Judith Butler, we might ask, as against Hegel, if the family is capable of development. Can there be models or patterns other than the standard bourgeois model described by Hegel? If family must remain the sphere of feeling, as Hegel says, how can its members have a truly ethical relationship that is congruent with their status as rational and free citizens? Indeed, how can women and men legitimately engage in a process of mutual recognition?

The master–slave dialectic shows us that the process of recognition is central to Hegel's picture of subjectivity – and humanity. Yet thinkers such as Luce Irigaray and Žižek have argued that recognition need not be conceived as a power struggle between master and slave that ends up affirming our common, pre-given and fixed identities. As Irigaray argues, recognition could be granted to an other precisely in her difference, her otherness, in the very changeability of her composition. Hence, notwithstanding his own views, Hegel shows that gender cannot be conceived independently of its economic and political situation. More fundamentally, as Seyla Benhabib and other feminists have recognized, he himself gives us the tools and strategies to rethink both gender and its relation to capitalism.

The implications of Hegel's conceptions of subjectivity are by no means restricted to Marxist and feminist theory. It is the Hegelian notion of identity that enables the founding principle of the various movements of posthumanism: The "human" is not simply given, but must work itself out in relation to other forms of existence, as well as to various forms of otherness within itself. We can see that in posthumanist critiques of humanism, the already existing relational potential of Hegelian subjectivity is actually realized – instead of being confined, as in Hegel, to specific forms of negation. In other words, subjectivity must encounter not just *its* other (as in Hegel) but *any* other. Subjectivity must undergo the differentiation not only of Hegelian "difference" but also of what Hegel would call "diversity" – the difference potentially offered by any kind of otherness. This is the diversity endemic to capitalism, where any entity can be related to any other in virtue of its status as a commodity and the universal system of disassembly, reassembly, and exchange. Hence, Hegelian subjectivity – and objectivity – already contain the seeds of their post-modernization, their own devolution into the registers of relationality and performance.[18]

---

[18] Indeed, as Jameson sees it, Hegel's concept of "diversity" as opposed to "difference" indicates an opposition that "passes over into an inert multiplicity of various things, all different from each other but entertaining no particular relationship ... the two phenomena thus contrasted may simply drift away from each other into the teeming variety of inert multiples. Here, then, powerful reasons must be invoked for positing any kind of relationship between the incommensurables" (VD, 25).

Hegel himself, then, anticipates the fragmentation of subjectivity into machines, into what F. H. Bradley long ago called "finite centers" of experience, into the performance of multiple selves which resist integration into any overarching unity. Similarly, Hegel foreshadows what Halberstam and Livingstone describe as posthumanist challenges to the "body" as a coherent organism.[19] Hegel even prefigures the thesis that our "bodies" have effectively been translated into language. We recall that, in Hegel's eyes, the world comes to our cognitive faculties as sense, as materiality, and it leaves as language. For Hegel, the body itself – as something merely given, merely presented to our minds, is itself sublated, translated into concepts, whereby we can situate it within a relational and historical context. Even if we admit that the human is continuous with the animal, the machine, and the digital, the Hegelian notion of subjectivity can accommodate these expansions of itself. It's evident here that, even when we are dealing with contemporary theory, it is very difficult to pass entirely beyond Hegel's vision.

E.2.3 Rehabilitating Reason

If the increasingly complex capitalist machine and digital technology have reshaped and deepened posthumanism, its fundamental rejection of the "human" is grounded in its recalcitrance not only from any totalizing narrative but also from the very notion of reason itself. Nikolas Kompridis is hardly exaggerating when he says that the entire culture of modernity is paralyzed by a profound skepticism regarding reason. "Posttruth," we learn, has just been announced as the OED's word of the year.[20] We might add that literary theory not only exhibits this paralysis but is to some extent responsible for it. The revolt against reason has a long history, most of which we don't need to engage here. In our modern context, it's worth recalling briefly that, in general, Romanticism reacted against the primacy of reason as a human faculty. Adam Müller, the foremost political philosopher of Romanticism in Hegel's time, viewed reason as calculative, utilitarian, and divisive, both as a tool of industrial capitalism and as an index of its abstract individualism. The Romantics sought to constrain reason within a comprehensive group of faculties

---

[19] *Posthuman Bodies*, eds. Judith Halberstam and Ira Livingston (Bloomington and Indianapolis: Indiana University Press, 1995), pp. 2–3.

[20] The OED defines the term as denoting circumstances where emotion and personal belief, rather than facts, influence public opinion.

at whose apex was the unifying power of the imagination, which could posit totalities that might harmonize the various fragments of bourgeois society.

Over the last century or so, reason – often called "Western" reason – has been challenged from numerous directions, and has been variously identified with a closed metaphysical system, unremitting totalization, authoritarianism, sexism, racism, and imperialism. In fact, the entire heterological tradition – from Nietzsche and Schopenhauer through Bergson, Freud, and Heidegger to Derrida, Foucault, and Rorty – has issued these various challenges, denying that reason is somehow a neutral instrument or faculty and affirming instead that it is intrinsically related to survival instincts, ideological perspectives, and the exercise of power and domination. We have already seen that Hegel's dialectic is intrinsic to his expression of capitalism and Eurocentrism.

One of the most pronounced critiques of rationality has come from Richard Rorty, who sees reason as an "overarching structure," which embodies an appeal to already institutionalized norms and criteria and presupposes an unchanging reality. According to Rorty, it is metaphor, not reason, which has the power to open up new modes of thought and action. Ironically, as Stuart Barnett observes, Rorty's project is continuous with Hegel's inasmuch as Rorty sees change as a dialectical transition from old to new vocabularies. Indeed, Rorty acknowledges that Hegel exhibited the intrinsic instability of given vocabularies and paradigms of knowledge, each progressing toward self-contradiction and then supersession by a new vocabulary.[21]

Other recent theorists have attempted to reconceive the notion of reason in terms of its various functions. We could cite Habermas's well-known division of it into cognitive-instrumental reason, moral-practical reason, and aesthetic reason.[22] Instrumental reason, which Habermas sees as deeply marking the self-understanding of the modern era, is used in pursuit of specific practical ends in fields such as economics, technology, or politics (*TCA*, 10–11). In contrast to this, Habermas urges a broader notion of "communicative reason," which is grounded in dialogue, in human interaction (which Habermas sees as inhering in the necessarily intersubjective structure of language), and is largely exercised in the spheres of ethics and morality. This kind of reason is based on the

---

[21] Richard Rorty, *Consequences of Pragmatism* (Minneapolis: University of Minnesota Press, 1982), p. 148.
[22] Habermas, *The Theory of Communicative Action: Volume One*, pp. 10–11.

consensual force of argumentation, the overcoming of merely subjective views, and the viewing of the objective world as unified in its intersubjectivity (*TCA*, 10–11). Habermas sees rationality not only as capable of being grounded but as necessitating a learning process and self-reflection (*TCA*, 18–20). We have seen that every one of these features is contained in Hegel's dialectic. Other thinkers, for example Foucault, have reiterated Kant's distinction between private reason, geared toward individual interests, and public reason, which is more orientated toward a public discourse. Nikolas Kompridis has urged a wider notion of reason that encompasses, for example, ethical imperatives.[23]

However, through all the often heated debates in the last few decades about reason and rationality, there has been almost no systematic endeavor to define or redefine reason beyond its usual designations as given in the history of logic and philosophy. These designations have centered on the various kinds of operations that, according to Plato and Aristotle, reason can perform, such as deduction, induction, analogy, associating and categorizing ideas, discovering relations of identity, difference, and causality or relations between means and ends or general and particular. The pre-Socratic philosophers and the Neoplatonists – and a great part of the Judaeo-Christian tradition – saw reason as not just restricted to the human mind but as operating objectively throughout the cosmos, imbuing it with order and direction. In modern times, Descartes located the seat of reason within the human self, and the Enlightenment philosophers variously saw it as a calculative faculty or as associating ideas. Kant limited the operations of reason to the phenomenal realm, but saw reason as predominating in this sphere and human morality as necessarily grounded on rational principles. Hegel, as we have seen, viewed reason as progressively unfolding through history, from less developed to more mature manifestations, each stage overcoming the one-sided or self-contradictory nature of previous stages.[24]

My point here is that none of the recent attempts to overturn or undermine or redefine reason adds anything in definitional terms to what is already yielded by this history. Heidegger, Levinas, and Derrida variously claim to offer broader models of reason, which are participatory or ethical

---

[23] Nikolas Kompridis, "So We Need Something Else for Reason to Mean," *International Journal of Philosophical Studies*, 8:3 (2010), 293.

[24] For a collection of brilliant essays on the intrinsically historical character of Hegel's philosophy, see *Hegel on Philosophy in History*, eds. Rachel Zuckert and James Kreines (Cambridge: Cambridge University Press, 2017), especially pp. 1–12 and 15–58.

or posthumanist.[25] But none of these thinkers offers a viable definition, and merely presupposes the definition of reason as conventionally understood, which they want to direct toward communal or ethical ends. Even Habermas does not define reason; he merely cites various uses of it. Even the staunchest opponents of reason have had recourse to reason as conventionally defined to formulate their opposition, and indeed to articulate their entire worldview. In other words, it simply does not make sense to talk of "Western" reason, or calculative reason or postcolonial reason or any other kind of reason. If what we understand by "reason" is the basic set of operations enumerated above – for no one to my knowledge has shown reason to be anything else[26] – then what we are talking about is not different *types* of reason but different *uses or applications* of reason, according to various ideological and intellectual orientations. This is not to say that Habermas's division is not helpful or that reason has not in fact been used – as many theorists have argued – for purposes of domination and control. But it *is* to say that reason in itself can be neither coercive nor emancipatory. Nor, on the other hand, is it ever neutral. It is always used in the service of some perspective, good, bad, selfish, or benevolent.

And this, I believe, is precisely why we can still learn from Hegel's notion of reason. For one thing, Hegel's distinction between understanding and reason anticipates Habermas's distinction between instrumental and communicative uses of reason. The understanding is used toward specific ends, as in mathematics, technology, and economics. It is reason

---

[25] Heidegger claims that "there is a thinking more rigorous than conceptual thinking" which "exceeds all contemplation." Such thinking has "no result" and "no effect" and "builds upon the house of being" ("Letter on 'Humanism'," pp. 271–4). I am not aware that anyone has explained in what such thinking consists.

[26] This is not to say that countless valuable attempts have not been made. Mario Bunger, for example, suggests seven desiderata or concepts of rationality. These include "conceptual," geared toward clarity, "logical," striving for consistence, and "methodological," which is concerned with questioning, doubting, and justifying. While Bunge acknowledges that these form a "system," the problem is that these distinctions hardly command consensus and these several forms could overlap indefinitely; M. Bunge, "Seven Desiderata for Rationality," in *Rationality: The Critical View*, eds. Joseph Agassi and Ian Charles Jarvie (Dordrecht, Boston, and Lancaster: Martinus Nijhoff, 1987), pp. 5–6. Max Black's schematization of rational actions is also subject to such qualifications. The same holds for all the attempts to define reason in terms of evolutionary function or practical/moral goal orientation or decision-making or belief or utility. None of these theories actually offers a definition of reason; they merely (though valuably) examine various applications of it or its formal conditions. A classic overview of this subject is offered in *Rationality*, ed. Bryan R. Wilson (1970; rpt. Oxford: Blackwell, 1974), which contains important essays by Steven Lukes and Martin Hollis. For more recent works, see Robert Nozick, *The Nature of Rationality* (Princeton, NJ: Princeton University Press, 1993) and John Broome, *Rationality through Reasoning* (Oxford: Wiley Blackwell, 2013). Max Weber also distinguished four kinds of rationality: practical, theoretical, substantive, and formal – but again, these denote various applications of reason.

reduced to use as an instrument, a reduction Hegel (and Habermas) sees as characterizing capitalism. Indeed, Hegel attributes this type of thinking to the business class, which he sees as focused on the particular rather than the universal. Reason proper, for Hegel, is a higher faculty that is able to discern the larger context of things, a context that is ultimately ethical. So we already have in Hegel a distinction between a purely instrumental use of our intellect and a more comprehensive use that is both ethical and unifying. To this we might add a number of other features, which anticipate much modern theory. For Hegel, as we have seen, when used dialectically, reason is always a process, a self-correcting process, which develops into higher forms as it progresses through history. It can be manifested in perspectives that often appear to conflict with one another, as in empiricism and rationalism. Moreover, reason is not only subjective and intersubjective, not only a function of the way our minds operate and of the way in which we relate to others, but is also objectively embodied in the institutions and laws that we create.

It is true, as we have seen in earlier chapters, that Hegel's vision of reason is employed in the service of a Eurocentric and even racist view of history. But the foregoing features of that vision can surely be dissociated from the *use* to which they were put. The idea that somehow we can abandon reason is neither fruitful nor realistic. In fact, this idea has proven in recent history to have disastrous consequences on a large scale for humankind.[27] It has surfaced in numerous forms of irrationalism, notably in fascism, and more recently in various brands of so-called Islamic fundamentalism. As Terry Eagleton, Jens Zimmermann, and Christopher Norris have pointed out, the recalcitrance toward reason on the part of modern theorists – which also embodies a rejection of humanism, since the greater part of Western thought (including Hegel) has identified the human with the rational – has somewhat disabled them from saying anything substantive about human nature, ethics, justice, or many of the global dilemmas that confront us today.[28] Zimmermann valuably points

---

[27] A much-neglected and sometimes vilified but valuable and comprehensive study of the very real dangers of irrationalism in all its modern manifestations from Schelling and Schopenhauer, Kierkegaard, and Dilthey through Heidegger and Jaspers to Fascist and Racial theory is George Lukács, *The Destruction of Reason*, trans. Peter Palmer (1962; rpt. London and Atlantic Highlands, NJ: Merlin Press/Humanities Press, 1981).

[28] Terry Eagleton, *After Theory* (London and New York: Allen Lane/Basic Books, 2003), p. 102. Jens Zimmermann, *Incarnational Humanism* (Downers Grove, IL: InterVarsity Press, 2012), pp. 44–5. Mohanty too observes that postmodernism's critique of knowledge is limited because it ignores "reasonable" alternatives (*Between the Lines*, p. 245). See also Christopher Norris 's powerfully argued *Uncritical Theory: Postmodernism, Intellectuals, and the Gulf War* (Amherst: University of

out that, as a result of these onslaughts and the general skepticism they represent, Western culture suffers from a loss of identity and cannot define or defend its values, nor can it – as Baudrillard explains – furnish clear goals for education.[29] This is not to say that the theorists have not sometimes contributed vitally to public discourse. Žižek, Jameson, Eagleton, Derrida, Martha Nussbaum, and Elaine Scarry are among the figures who have intervened insightfully in political and social issues. But they have done this precisely by utilizing, not jettisoning, what we might call "communal" reason. Our historical moment requires that we retain reason at every level – intellectual, political, ethical, and even religious – as part of a broadly reconceived humanism so that it is not imprisoned within its merely calculative potential as harnessed by technological capitalism.

Hegel encourages us to see that reason is not simply something that we are born with. Rather, it is something that we must achieve; it is not static and given but is a dialectical *process* which must be undergone by both the human self and the objective world. As Stuart Barnett observes, it was Hegel who "introjected cultural and historical difference into the very idea of reason" (*HAD*, 5). Finally, following Kant and espousing a principle of bourgeois democracy, Hegel sees reason as absolutely integral to human freedom and self-determination. It's vital for us to understand and learn from Hegel's insight that reason is not something that inheres in any one individual. Just as freedom can arise only in a reciprocal manner, through mutual recognition, so reason is born in an intersubjective model of consciousness, through the very process of achieving social consensus (*PM*, 176).

Most fundamentally, Hegel's achievement was to situate the development of reason within history, to see its culmination within capitalism, and to see its potential and its limitations as tied to the very nature of capitalist society, its economic structure, and its cultural, political, and ethical frameworks. It is this achievement that enables us to see that when we talk of the deficiencies of reason or of its coercive or imperialistic force, we are really talking of reason as shaped within and by the development of capitalism. In Hegel's scheme, the inner dialectic of capitalism turns out to be the very structure of reason itself. The pinnacle of reason, reason in its highest development, is the transcendence

---

Massachusetts Press, 1992), which explains how the skepticism and relativism of much theory disables its engagement with real-world issues.

[29] Jean Baudrillard, *Simulacra and Simulation*, trans. Sheila Faria Glaser (Ann Arbor: University of Michigan Press, 2004), p. 149.

of whatever is contingent and irrational in capitalism, in the transition to the State. Yet, we can surely reconceive reason as extricated from these shaping forces and as serving larger, ethical, and humanitarian purposes.

E.2.4 *Grasping Totality as a Concrete Universal*

Notwithstanding the overwhelming impetus of modern theory to reject so-called grand narratives, and Hegel's totalizing scheme in particular, I would argue that it is precisely his endeavor to unify that allows us to see the deep internal connections between various domains such as family and gender, economics and ethics, free markets and imperialism, history and Eurocentrism. All of these are related – not in some abstract "Absolute" but as part of the very real totalizing impetus of capitalism. When we say that they are related, we are talking of two levels of internal relation: the first is the ontological and epistemological level where the "being" of any entity is already implicated in its relations with other entities and with more developed versions of itself. The second level is that which is imposed by the capitalist market, whereby entities are related as commodities, as products of both consumption and labor. Of course, the two levels are mutually implicated since the ontological internality of relation is integral to the creation of an objective world through human labor – and language.

If we simply reject the notion of totality, we are effectively colluding with the most fundamental principles of bourgeois ideology which have positivistically reduced the world to its calculable surface. And, more importantly, we preclude ourselves from understanding both these levels of internal relation: we need, for example, to be able to situate gender within both economic and ideological frames. And this requires the positing of a totality that includes all three registers: gender, economics, and ideology. If we refuse to posit a totality, we will implicitly be accepting the default totality of capitalism where all relations are reduced to an economic plane. Capitalism has its own modes of totalization – which can be resisted only by alternative modes.

Hence the answer to our immersion in the coercive and totality and uniformity of capitalism lies surely not in merely wrenching ourselves into increasing depths of irreducible particularity and immediacy, into "experience" and unconscious drives, and the radically incoherent notions of "parts" without wholes or "difference" without identity. This merely sinks us into a regressive positivism, whereby we assert the reality or authenticity of immediate experience, or of the sensuous materiality of the external world before it is worked upon by thought, or the intrinsic value of pure "difference," of uniqueness that is resistant to all categorization. The problem with all these forms of "thisness" or haecceity, as Hegel famously argues early in the *Phenomenology*, is not only that they effectively espouse an undifferentiated obeisance to things as they are – a managerially guided positivism – but also that they are incoherent, in both their conception and their use of language. They presuppose that terms such as "difference" and "particular" can have meaning independently of any notion of identity or universality.

Surely, what we need is not such desperately positivistic gestures but rather the creation of alternative modes and models of mediation. An example of this might be a recapitulation of socialist and feminist principles which refract the totalizing gaze of capitalism, whereby private property, gender, class, and the ownership of wealth, as well as the relation between human beings and the means of production are radically reconfigured. Undoubtedly, many of Marx's predictions have been proven wrong and in most cases the model he envisaged has proven to be disastrous in its practical implementation, its spirit sabotaged by "Communist" regimes in the Soviet Union and elsewhere. But this does not vitiate all aspects of the model itself, which retains the potential to offer an internal critique of capitalism that can result in transformation from within. Some of Marx's central predictions – such as the widening gap between rich and poor,[30] the recurrent economic crises of capitalism, its need to expand over the entire globe, its failure to live up to its democratic ideals, and the psychoses suffered by its citizens as integral to their very identity – have proven to be realized with even more glaring intensity than either Marx or Hegel might have imagined.

In its commitment to the particular, theory effectively arrests the dialectic at its second phase. Theory within capitalism, as Hegel predicted, is necessarily constrained within the reflective modes of the Understanding, unable to proceed to the perspectives of Speculative thought. We cannot positively transcend the binary oppositions that have structured the history of our thinking, in whatever sphere – whether between woman and man, slave and master, black and white, East and West, the owners of capital and the dispossessed, truth and falsehood, mind and body – without positing a broader perspective that can accommodate or situate the depthless and unbounded relativism entailed in coercing each side of

[30] See Thomas Piketty's interesting analysis of this discrepancy between rich and poor as a global phenomenon in *Capital in the Twenty-First Century*, pp. 430–70.

these oppositions into mutual relation. We can transcend these binarisms only negatively. For example, we can impugn the opposition of "male" and "female." We might acknowledge that these notions are historical and cultural constructions that are sustained by ever-renewed performance. We can point out that there is no fixed distinction between them, that they are in many respects mutually continuous, that they pass into each other in varying degrees according to context and perspective. And we can claim that "transgender" embodies a dialectical synthesis. But, without some consensus as to the nature of this resulting "synthesis" or the parameters of a more synthetic perspective, we are effectively frozen at the stage of criticism, of skepticism, of deconstruction.

Hence, we are obliged to impugn traditional notions of gender in the absence of any new, more comprehensive model of gender – we are still, historically, at the second dialectical stage where we view gender as open, as differential, as relational, as constructed, and as performed – but we cannot articulate this openness in any specific direction. We are fearful that any definition will be constrained by its regionalism of perspective and circumstance; that any gesture toward universalism will risk imposition and imperialism, overriding the realities of local difference. The most we can do is to posit, albeit provisionally, a commitment to some larger ethical framework.

Regarding this very fundamental quandary of modern theory – how we can move beyond the second, destructive, deconstructive stage of the dialectic without positing a more comprehensive totality – Fredric Jameson offers a crucial insight as to how we might proceed. Talking of how "the" dialectic is thought to imply totality, he observes that "totality is not something one ends with, but something one begins with ... it is capitalism as a new global system which is the totality and the unifying force (so that we can also say that the dialectic itself does not become visible historically until capitalism's emergence)" (*VD*, 15). This profound statement, as I read it, means that, if our historical reality is the world system of capitalism – which is the only "totality" that exists on a global scale – whatever local dialectics we identify as operating in the world or in our thinking will ultimately be driven by development toward proximate totalities that are unavoidably refracted through that world system.

In other words, whatever totality we posit – at the beginning, as the projected end of our thought or activity – will already be shaped from within by its ultimate positioning within a global dynamic of power and economics. These proximate "totalities" necessarily comprise local interventions in political and legal practice. So, for example, we can with much labor educate ourselves about other cultures, and we can struggle to oppose certain atrocious customs such as female genital mutilation. But it is an even harder and more complicated task to alter the conceptions of "woman" that underlie such practices. Hence, the "totality" toward which we move must be posited as something ever deferred, ever projected into a transformed future, and the thinking that drives our dialectic (here, toward a reconception of gender) must terminate in local practical exigency; theory is constrained, and perhaps even moderated, by praxis – of which it must be an interactive component. In some countries, reformists have succeeded in imposing certain limitations upon this terrible practice, but those reforms are underlain by what must inevitably be merely an incipient educational endeavor that can barely begin to modify the habits of thinking behind it.

Hence, the notion of totality cannot simply be jettisoned, even if it is acknowledged to have a merely strategic function. Our thinking here can be guided by Hegel's notion of the "concrete universal," whereby the universal subsists *only* in and through its particular manifestations. For Hegel, there is no God outside of his development through human history. There is no Absolute Spirit that somehow transcends the very human institutions of the state. There is no human personality above and beyond – or underlying – its expression in particular forms of behavior. The "mystical" Hegel is simply a myth.

E.2.5   *Toward a Dialectical Humanism*

As this book has persistently argued, theory's retreat into particularism dangerously rehearses and extends the positivistic principles of bourgeois ideology, which are themselves recapitulated in milder forms in liberal humanism. We have seen that much literary theory has valuably analyzed the fragmentations and distortions of bourgeois subjectivity into the one-dimensionality of mechanism, sense-impressions, economic unit, linguistic signifier, and ultimately machine. Yet, in its noble endeavor to show how so many areas of life – including education – have been dehumanized, theory itself has, through its unwitting collusion with the founding principles of bourgeois thought – decentered empiricism, positivism, and worship of difference – reached a point of self-exhaustion, where the paths of both liberal humanism and its posthumanist variants have led merely to intellectual, political, and ethical stagnation. The recent reawakening of religious fundamentalism reminds us that the world today is divided into insulated communities, each with its own set of values. How do we move beyond the vast cultural conflict embodied in the controversy over cartoons of the prophet Muhammad? How, in a world where we espouse depthless relativism and jettison the notion of truth, can anyone argue against Creationists who see evolution as just another theory? This problematic dialectic between universal and particular haunts our pursuit of human rights, of international law, and the numerous conflictual eruptions within indigenous traditions generated by a global market economy.

We sometimes seem to forget that humanism in its various guises through history has always had a radical impetus. Instead of being a mere predicate of the Divine or of some Neoplatonic Primal "One," the "human" becomes the *subject* of a historical process, the prime agency of its own development. In his critique of Hegel's dialectic, Marx's objection to Hegel's philosophy was that it moved in this subversive direction, only to foreclose it by viewing the human as finding its realization in totalities that lay beyond itself, as in Absolute Spirit and the state. Much literary theory, even as it claims to supersede Hegel, is subject to the very same criticism: It supersedes the dilemmas and contradictions of capitalism *only* in the realm of thought, leaving everything – even the realm of thought – just as it was. Symptomatically, whereas Hegel saw both labor and language as modes of transforming the world, Bataille and Derrida characterize labor as a form of language. Modern theory tends to abrogate the "human" – seeing it not as an emanation of the One or the Divine but as an emanation of Language, of Difference, of the Machine – all invested with transcendent status, all posited as primordial, as irreducible, as inescapable, as simply "there." To displace the human subject with fragments of particularity – whether unconscious, linguistic, machinic, or informational – is effectively to rob the "human" of its self-creative, subversive potential and to make it once again the predicate of a new subject, namely, the impersonal economic process, which ultimately governs language, difference, and the machine. In adopting such a gesture, what theory is expressing is human subjectivity as *reduced* to its economic facet under capitalism, not subjectivity in its actual potential. Hegel already supersedes this vision – descended from the bourgeois economists – in his conceptions of both labor and language.

The arguments over humanism have raged across many disciplines from the Pre-Socratics through the Renaissance and Enlightenment thinkers and Victorians into postmodernism, and they cannot be settled here. As Dolan Cummings states, the "debate is wide open" (*DH*, 11). But we can conclude by indicating that the core components of Hegel's legacy as analyzed in the previous section point toward a "dialectical humanism" which would include a number of core components: (1) its conception of the "human" might be underlain by a Hegelian notion of identity as already fluid and relational, as intrinsically requiring mutual recognition, and as finding fulfilment in larger spheres beyond its own immediate being; (2) a dialectical, historical, self-correcting notion of reason; (3) an acknowledgment of the notion of totality as a concrete universal, as susceptible of degrees, and as sustaining a balance between the particular or regional and the general; and (4) a vision of humanity that integrates its material, psychological, aesthetic, intellectual, and spiritual dimensions.

It's important to grasp that these components are mutually inseparable. Our conception of the "human" requires the notion of reason, which in turn presupposes the notion of totality – all of which arise only in an intersubjective consensus. As we have seen, Hegel views reason as a necessarily intersubjective and dialogic phenomenon; one human being in isolation cannot possibly be rational. Moreover, reason – in all its imperfections and all its failure to be utilized in any purity – is intrinsic to our humanity. We cannot possibly become human by isolating ourselves within a fragmented particularity. We become rational by interacting with others, by internalizing some aspects of them, by interacting with the world – through all of which operations we realize what we truly "are." Hegel also shows the necessity for self-transcendence, for the need to realize oneself by participating in a larger, collective, good. He shows that we derive our identity from values and principles that are embodied in institutions beyond ourselves.[31] Hence, we _can_ speak of a common humanity, founded not on some static conception but on our actual common experiences, needs, and aspirations.

Perhaps the central dilemma of humanism – or its lack – today is one that Hegel identified, and that has been noted by Haraway and many others: The market economy has expanded well beyond what Hegel would see as the limits of civil society – not only into the deepest recesses of our private lives, but also controlling the very mechanisms of public

---

[31] It is worth remembering that even Heidegger – who is commonly viewed as an antihumanist – espouses what he sees as an extreme form of humanism, one that rejects the conventional humanist vision of the human as merely an _animal rationale_. Heidegger urges a more elevated conception of the _humanitas_ of a human being, whose essence must be located as ἦθος or "dwelling" within the unfolding of Being in language. As such, like Hegel, Heidegger urges that the essence of "human" entails being more than merely human ("Letter on Humanism," pp. 239, 247–8, 259–61, 274).

and political life. These are areas which should be structured by emotional affinities and the ties of kinship on the one hand, or by general ethical principles on the other. So, in structural terms, Hegel's insight is still pertinent today: The powers of the market should be constrained, should not be allowed to intrude into areas which are underlain by ethical imperatives, such as our spiritual and emotional lives, education, and health care.[32] In brief, commercial life should be acknowledged as having a limited role in defining the human.

When we say that Hegel is the philosopher of capitalism, we are saying that he is the philosopher of our world, of our own present and foreseeable future. If this book has helped to show one thing, I hope it is this: whether we like it or not, Hegel is our legacy. He is the face of our racism, our ethnocentrism, our patriarchalism, our rationality as coercively deployed, our complacency with poverty, our complicity in colonialism. He is also in many ways the foundation of our moral and social conscience, our liberal humanism and posthumanism, our awareness of the deficiencies and contradictions of modernity, our alienation from ourselves and our world. As such, he can also serve as the foundation whereby theory and the humanities might play their part on the global stage in transcending the economic reductionism of our era and of reconfiguring the concepts of reason and totality that are needed in creating a viable definition of – and a viable future for – humanity. He is the face of capitalism, its discontents, and our ability to supersede them.

---

[32] Fredric Jameson notes the "ever more systematic servility of all governments today in the face of business orthodoxies" such as balancing budgets or IMF policies (*VD*, 376).

Index

www.ingramcontent.com/pod-product-compliance
Ingram Content Group UK Ltd.
Pitfield, Milton Keynes, MK11 3LW, UK
UKHW020451010325
455719UK00015B/521